Lauritz Gerlach

Anonymization and Identifiability

Global and Comparative Data Law

Edited by

Moritz Hennemann
Lea Katharina Kumkar
Linda Kuschel
Björn Steinrötter

Volume 8

Lauritz Gerlach

Anonymization and Identifiability

Enhancing Data Protection Through
Differential Privacy and Artificial Intelligence

DE GRUYTER

ISBN 978-3-11-914260-1
e-ISBN (PDF) 978-3-11-222216-4
e-ISBN (EPUB) 978-3-11-222256-0
ISSN 2751-0174

Library of Congress Cataloging-in-Publication Data
A CIP catalog record for this book has been applied for at the Library of Congress.

Bibliographic information published by the Deutsche Nationalbibliothek
The Deutsche Nationalbibliothek lists this publication in the Deutsche Nationalbibliografie; detailed bibliographic data are available on the Internet at http://dnb.dnb.de.

Cover image: peshkov / iStock / Getty Images
Printing and binding: CPI books GmbH, Leck

www.degruyterbrill.com
Questions about General Product Safety Regulation:
productsafety@degruyterbrill.com

MIX
Papier | Fördert gute Waldnutzung
FSC® C083411
FSC www.fsc.org

To my parents

Preface

This dissertation was accepted by Bucerius Law School in the spring trimester of 2025. It was completed in July 2024; the defense took place on June 12, 2025. Literature and other developments have been considered through March 2025.

I am grateful to my doctoral supervisor, Prof. Dr. Linda Kuschel, LL.M. (Harvard), for her excellent guidance and extraordinarily swift review of this work. I also thank the series editors for including this volume in the series. I am indebted to the second examiner, Prof. Dr. Dirk Heckmann, for his prompt review and valuable suggestions. The research originated within the HILANO project on distributed automatic anonymization of documents at the Bucerius Center for Legal Technology and Data Science, funded by the Federal Ministry of Education and Research.[1] I am especially thankful to Prof. Dirk Hartung for his support during my time as Assistant Director at the Center.

My special thanks go to my parents, Solveig and Philipp Gerlach, to whom this thesis is dedicated. Finally, I am grateful to Ronja May for her steadfast encouragement.

Comments and errata are welcome at mail@lauritzgerlach.com.

Hamburg, Spring 2025

1 The project was funded under the initiative “kmu-innovativ”, funding code 01IS18085.

https://doi.org/10.1515/9783112222164-202

Contents

Glossary

AI	Artificial Intelligence
AO	Authorship Obfuscation
API	Application Programming Interface
Art. 29 Working Party	Article 29 Data Protection Working Party
B2B	business-to-business
B2C	business-to-consumer
BDSG	German Data Protection Law, "Bundesdatenschutzgesetz"
BDSG a.F.	Bundesdatenschutzgesetz as superseded by GDPR on 2018-05-25
BfDI	German Federal Commissioner for Data Protection and Freedom of Information
BGH	German Federal Court of Justice
BVerfG	German Constitutional Court
C.E.	Common Era
CFR	Charter of Fundamental Rights of the European Union
CJEU	Court of Justice of the European Union
Convention 108	Convention for the Protection of Individuals with regard to Automatic Processing of Personal Data 1981
COVID-19 Pandemic	Coronavirus Disease 2019 Pandemic
CS	computer science
Data Protection Directive	Directive 95/46/EC
DNS	Domain Name System
DP	differential privacy
DP-SGD	Differentially Private Stochastic Gradient Descent
DPO	Data Protection Officer
EC	European Commission
ECJ	European Court of Justice
EDPB	European Data Protection Board
EDPS	European Data Protection Supervisor
EGC	European General Court
EU	European Union
Eur. Conv. Human Rights	European Convention on Human Rights
FL	federated learning
GAN	generative adversarial network
GDPR	Regulation (EU) 2016/679, "General Data Protection Regulation"
GDR	German Democratic Republic
GPT	Generative Pre-Trained Transformer
HE	homomorphic encryption
HiL	Human-in-the-Loop
HILANO	Human-in-the-Loop Anonymization Research Project
HIPAA	Health Insurance Portability and Accountability Act
HTTP	Hypertext Transfer Protocol

https://doi.org/10.1515/9783112222164-204

IAA	inter-annotator agreement
IBAN	International Bank Account Number
ID	identifier
IP	Internet Protocol
ISP	Internet Service Provider
LLM	large language machine learning model
MAC address	media access control address
ML	machine learning
NAT	Network Address Translation
NLP	natural language processing
PATE	Private Aggregation of Teacher Ensembles
PET	Privacy Enhancing Technologies
PRNG	pseudo-random number generator
RAM	Random-Access Memory
RDBMS	Relational Database Management System
Regex	regular expressions
RFID	Radio Frequency Identification
ROI	Return on Investment
SSN	Social Security Number
StPO	German Code of Criminal Procedure—“Strafprozessordnung”
TFEU	Treaty on the Functioning of the European Union
U.S.	United States of America
UI	User Interface
UK	United Kingdom
ULD	Independent Center for Data Protection Schleswig-Holstein
UUID	Universally Unique Identifier
VIN	Vehicle Identification Number
VPN	Virtual Private Network
w.f.r.	with further references

Introduction

It is a trivial observation that data analysis and data protection seem irreconcilable. Especially with regard to the stringently regulated European Union (EU), it is a pervasive narrative that the Regulation (EU) 2016/679, "General Data Protection Regulation" (GDPR) is fundamentally at odds with the economic viability of businesses that rely on personal data. I disagree with this pessimistic assessment. Instead, I believe that through the use of privacy-enhancing technologies and through measured oversight, both data analysis and data protection can thrive. In other words: Through technology and shrewd regulation, we can square the incompatible. This dissertation aims to play a tiny part in this process, by laying out the technology (differential privacy, machine learning) and the regulation (a better understanding of identification and identifiability) needed for anonymization.

In doing so, this dissertation tells two stories that are intertwined: On the one hand, it talks about methods of anonymization—from the trivial to the complex. The word "anonymization" is used here in the context of anonymizing *data*. The discussion surrounding shielding one's identity from others, using technologies such as Tor[1], is an adjacent field, but wholly beyond the scope of this inquiry. On the other hand, it talks about different types of data: From the simple (dates, numeric values, names) to intermediate problems (images, texts, video, sound) to the forefront of the discourse (model weights and parameters).

Many legal treatises on anonymization are focused on the question of absolute or relative identifiability.[2] In my opinion, this age-old question has been resolved in many aspects by the European Court of Justice (ECJ)'s landmark *Breyer* case and later decisions. What I found more interesting and less resolved in my research was the question of what identification actually means under the GDPR. As anonymization hinges on identifiability, this question is especially salient.

Most technical treatises on anonymization take a technology-centric view: They evaluate technologies and criteria, such as k-Anonymity[3] or differential privacy[4] and explain them with their benefits and shortcomings. While I will certainly also do this, in this dissertation, I will mainly adopt a *data*-centric view: Substantial dif-

1 "The Onion Router", a software that routes internet connections through other computers and then through a so-called exit node, thereby obfuscating the true user's IP address.

2 See p. 102.

3 See p. 138.

4 See p. 156.

https://doi.org/10.1515/9783112222164-001

ferences exist between anonymizing structured and unstructured data.[5] In practice, these data types expose different privacy risks. Therefore, these types of data need to be treated (*i.e.*, anonymized) differently. Finally, we will touch upon data that is not even readable to humans—the weights and parameters of a deep neural network.[6]

We must also face the tough reality that anonymization is not the "silver bullet"[7] it is often made out to be: As has been demonstrated through decades of research in re-identification science, anonymization and data usefulness exist along a continuum of trade-offs. Perfect anonymization may come with a significant penalty to the utility of the data, *i.e.*, make it unusable.[8] Nonetheless, all is not lost: As we will show, the GDPR does not require perfect anonymity. Even armed with a good understanding of the legal standards, how anonymization should work in practice remains an open question: How do we publicly share data from school records without compromising any student's privacy? How might we de-identify census data? How should we train Artificial Intelligence (AI) models without feeding them personal data?

To answer all of these questions, we will require increasingly sophisticated technology: While simple types of anonymization such as suppression or generalization for *k*-anonymity can be done using pen and paper, more advanced methods such as differential privacy (DP) require more mathematical precision. As far as non-structured data, such as text, is concerned, we will go from simple search algorithms to using machine learning (ML) to find personal data within it. As ML only works when given large amounts of training data, federated learning (FL) is required to help with distributing the workload between human anonymizers who train an anonymization model. However, it has been shown that FL cannot by itself protect from model inversion attacks, so we come full circle: DP can be used to anonymize model weights. All of this technology will be explained throughout this dissertation.

It is important to note that—while some technical approaches have stood up better to the test of time than others—this is a dynamic field with lots of scholarly and enterprise activity. What is state-of-the-art today can be catastrophically destroyed tomorrow.[9] It is therefore important to remain technologically open. This

5 This distinction is chiefly inspired by *Winter*, *Battis*, and *Halvani*, "Herausforderungen für die Anonymisierung von Daten" (2019).

6 See p. 214.

7 See: *Narayanan* and *Felten*, "No silver bullet: De-identification still doesn't work" (July 9, 2014).

8 Formulated in the extreme as "Data can be either useful or perfectly anonymous but never both." (*Ohm*, "Broken Promises of Privacy" (2009–2010)). For a criticism of this—pessimistic—characterization, see p. 96.

9 Similar: *Rachut*, "Grundrechtsverwirklichung in digitalen Kontexten" (2025), p. 344.

dissertation tries to always show avenues of possible technologies, but will stay on the aforementioned path: We will first take a look at anonymizing structured data using "old" (k-anonymity) and "new" (DP) technologies. Then, we will shift our focus to non-structured documents, a field of study that has traditionally been neglected, and point out "old" (manual) ways of anonymizing this data, as well as "new" avenues for performing this task. The latter will be enabled by AI models that can suggest which text to anonymize. In order to train these models while minimizing the risk of exposing their potentially sensitive training data later, a combination of DP and FL can be used.

Privacy-preserving data mining has been explored from the vantage points of multiple research communities, such as the database, statistical disclosure control, and cryptography communities.[10] However, most of the research activity in this increasingly important area has been focused in the computer science disciplines, whereas legal scholarship has mostly refrained from partaking in this discussion. Even though this work will be interdisciplinary in nature—we will be discussing computer science (CS) approaches to a legal problem—it is, at its core, a *legal* question: How do we anonymize just enough so that the legal requirements are fulfilled and at the same time retain the maximum utility of the data? I subscribe to the view most succinctly put forth by *Altman, Cohen, Nissim*, et al.:

> Legal and technical approaches to data protection have developed in parallel, and their conceptual underpinnings are growing increasingly divergent. When lawmakers rely on purely legal concepts to engage areas that are affected by rapid scientific and technological change, the resulting laws, when applied in practice, frequently create substantial uncertainty for implementation, provide contradictory recommendations in important cases, disagree with current scientific technical understanding, and fail to scale to the rapid pace of technological development.[11]

As a result, my aim is to continue some of the excellent work started by *Altman, Cohen, Nissim*, et al. and contribute to bridging this legal–technical divide.[12]

Other legal questions surrounding anonymization, for example the question of whether it is processing, how it should be justified, its impact on rectification, deletion, *etc.*, are beyond the scope of this dissertation.[13]

10 *Aggarwal* and *Yu*, "An Introduction to Privacy-Preserving Data Mining" (2008), p. 1.

11 *Altman, Cohen, Nissim*, et al., "What a Hybrid Legal-Technical Analysis Teaches Us about Privacy Regulation" (2021), p. 4.

12 For more on the differences in terminology and mindset between the technical and legal discourse, see in depth: *Hölzel*, "Anonymisierungstechniken und das Datenschutzrecht" (Aug. 2018), pp. 506 sqq.

13 For an introduction, see: *Storms*, "Datenschutz in der Unternehmenstransaktion" (Feb. 15, 2022), pp. 199 sqq.

Part I: **Personal Data and Anonymization**

1 Data and Data Protection

Modern civilizations cannot function without data. Long before the invention of the written word, humans used systems for recording and storing information. The first and most notable example of such a system are so-called *tally sticks*. Tally sticks are thought to have recorded debts and other records of legal and financial transactions. These sticks were made from different materials—wood, bone, or similar—that were carved with markings to represent information. A notable example is the *Ishango Bone*, commonly dated to 20,000 BCE.

With the advent of large amounts of data came a desire to protect citizens from its potential impact. Given *Moore*'s Law[1] and Kryder's Law[2], the potential for high-performance data collection and analytics has grown to a point where detailed analyses of people's habits, predilections, and actions are possible.[3] Emblematic of these developments is the rise of LLMs such as OpenAI's GPT-4 at the basis of its ChatGPT product,[4] which have proven the mass-market end user potential of AI. These developments have also been noticed within the European Union.[5]

Large troves of data tend to create information asymmetry. With limited exceptions (for example, in the form of the open data community), data is "proprietary information". Asymmetries like this one, especially where natural persons are concerned, are a prime target for regulation.

1 Simply stated: The density of transistors on a microprocessor will double every 18 months. This is not a law in the pure sense, but rather an observation about the silicon industry (*Moore*, "Cramming more components onto integrated circuits" [Apr. 19, 1965]).

2 A corollary of Moore's Law named after Mark Kryder of Seagate Technology (a hard drive manufacturer). Kryder's Law states that the pace of hard disk capacity increases at an even greater pace than transistor density (*Walter*, "Kryder's Law" [Aug. 1, 2005]), even though this prediction has recently not held true anymore.

3 *Bellovin*, *Dutta*, and *Reitinger*, "Privacy and Synthetic Datasets" (2019), p. 11.

4 *OpenAI*, "ChatGPT" (Nov. 30, 2022).

5 *European Commission*, "Towards a Thriving Data-Driven Economy" (July 2, 2014).

https://doi.org/10.1515/9783112222164-002

1.1 Protection Purposes of Data Protection Legislation

Data protection legislation and the GDPR especially serve to protect the fundamental rights of natural persons.[6] The protection of personal data is mandatory in EU legislation, cf. Art. 8 Charter of Fundamental Rights of the European Union (CFR).[7]

Early understandings of privacy in other jurisdictions give multiple functions, such as self-autonomy, emotional release, self-evaluation, and limited and protected communication.[8]

The most straightforward explanation of the term "data protection" would be to understand it as rules that protect the data itself.[9] This sounds trivial and unnecessary—after all, data is not a legal subject and does, on the face of things, not need legal protection. However, protecting the *integrity* of data is also worthy of consideration: For example, a public registry must not be corrupted (for example, the land registry), and data loss would also oftentimes be disastrous. Nonetheless, protecting the integrity and veracity of data is an integral part of data protection. Data protection is a principle that goes beyond the commonly associated privacy aspect. Imagine a database of pension information: Here, it is in the data subject's interest that the data itself be protected.

A second, and more important explanation is protecting individuals from the harm that could befall them if someone misused their data. As *Solove* and *Citron* note for a U.S. context, harm in data-breach cases is typically classifiable in three overarching categories: First, a data breach creates "a risk of future injury",[10] second, it creates the need to "take preventative measures to reduce the risk of injury",[11] and third, it induces anxiety and emotional distress.[12] Overall, they conclude that data breaches cause *risk and anxiety*.[13] In "Privacy Harms," *Citron* and *Solove* extend this into a systematic topology that includes economic harms,[14], reputational

6 *Klabunde* and *Horváth*, "DS-GVO Art. 4 Begriffsbestimmungen" (2024), margin no. 7.

7 *Gola*, "DS-GVO Art. 4 Begriffsbestimmungen" (2022), margin no. 5; for Art. 8 CFR in detail, see *Marsch*, "Das europäische Datenschutzgrundrecht" (2018), pp. 127 sqq.

8 *Westin*, "Privacy and Freedom" (1967), pp. 32 sqq.

9 *Hornung* and *Spiecker genannt Döhmann*, "Einleitung" (2025), margin nos. 2 sqq.

10 *Solove* and *Citron*, "Risk and Anxiety" (2017–2018), p. 750.

11 Ibid., p. 752.

12 Ibid., p. 753.

13 Ibid., p. 756.

14 *Citron* and *Solove*, "Privacy Harms" (2022), pp. 834 sqq.

harms,[15] psychological harms,[16] autonomy harms,[17] discrimination harms,[18], and relationship harms[19]. These harms can hail from two different sources: state and private actors.

At its core, privacy legislation used to be fundamentally about shielding individuals from a state's potential omniscience. State actors have vast potential for collecting data: They "own" the population register, the land register, all tax information, *etc.* They can also use their nearly infinite resources towards surveilling their people, either through manpower (police and others) or through technology.

A more recent understanding is that of privacy legislation to protect individuals from private actors. One catalyst was the increasing privatization of previously state-owned enterprises such as telecommunications providers. Especially with the advent of social networks in the early 2000s, more and more people became concerned about the amount of data collected and its potential uses. As a result, more stringent regulation was enacted to ensure data protection.

In the international discourse, the term "data protection" is uncommon. Rather than "data protection", which is a European term, the term "privacy" is more commonly used. Even though some parts of the GDPR are colloquially referred to using the "privacy" umbrella,[20] the Regulation itself uses "data protection" throughout.[21]

Some define privacy as concerning the "personal sphere", while data protection applies independently of the sphere.[22] Another approach would be to see "data protection" as a quasi-trademark of the distinctly European approach epitomized by the GDPR, and "privacy" as the umbrella term or to mean the American understanding of *Warren* and *Brandeis*[23]. However, this understanding is just one definition of privacy: In the technical literature, especially when viewing differential privacy, its meaning is closer to that just sketched of data protection, as it obfuscates any singular person's contribution to an output—regardless of the sensitivity of this output.[24]

---

15 Ibid., pp. 837 sqq.

16 Ibid., pp. 841 sqq.

17 Ibid., pp. 845 sqq.

18 Ibid., pp. 855 sqq.

19 Ibid., pp. 859 sqq.

20 *e.g.*, "privacy by design", "privacy by default", "privacy impact assessment".

21 "data protection by design and data protection by default" (Recital (78), (108), Artt. 25, 47); "data protection impact assessment", (Recital (84), (89), (90) sqq., Artt. 35 sq., 39, 57, 64).

22 *Oostveen*, "Warum Privacy != Datenschutz ist (und wie sie sich überschneiden)" (May 4, 2016).

23 *Warren* and *Brandeis*, "The Right to Privacy" (1890).

24 For more on DP, see p. 156.

Another approach is to refrain from a definition and see data protection and privacy as "essentially contested concepts".[25]

As a result, the dogmatic difference between data protection and privacy really depends on the discussion and is of little consequence to our scope. To avoid confusion, this dissertation will primarily use the term "data protection", while "privacy" is taken to have the same meaning. Where specific differences exist, I will make note of them.

1.2 Practical Impact of Data Protection Legislation

Data protection is now a core consideration for entire business models. Nearly all large enterprises need to evaluate and mine data to inform their decision making ("business intelligence"). Online advertising alone is a billion-dollar industry. In light of these developments, data is now a commercial good and thus the role of data protection itself has changed: In the past, data protection was purely a compliance pursuit. Nowadays, however, a world-class data protection team can enable and drive business models that would not be possible otherwise, by continually keeping the (legal) use of data in mind.

Anonymization is therefore highly relevant in practice: Data Analytics enable new kinds of business models. In many cases, the data cannot—legally—be processed directly, but needs to be anonymized first.[26] Many players in the ecosystem have accepted this importance and started to cater to this new market of anonymization solution providers: For example, the German "Stiftung Datenschutz"[27] recently held a conference on anonymization[28] and asserted its importance. Debates about identifiability and whether model weights of neural networks can constitute personal data are still raging.[29] The viability of an anonymization solution can frequently determine the (compliant) viability of a business model. Of course, a frequent answer to more stringent regulation is non-compliance. In data protection

---

25 *Pohle*, "Datenschutz: Rechtsstaatsmodell oder neoliberale Responsibilisierung? Warum Datentreuhänder kein Mittel zum Schutz der Grundrechte sind" (Feb. 2022), pp. 7 sqq.

26 This step is, in itself, processing (differing opinion: *Thüsing* et al., "Anonymisierung an sich ist keine rechtfertigungsbedürftige Datenverarbeitung" (2021)). The debate surrounding this issue, the question of the lawfulness of anonymization and the impact on the rights of the data subject (Artt. 12 sqq. GDPR) is beyond the scope of this inquiry.

27 A government-sponsored thinktank for privacy in Germany: https://stiftungdatenschutz.org/.

28 *Stiftung Datenschutz*, "DatenTag: Anonymisieren von Daten" (Dec. 7, 2022).

29 See p. 214.

especially, this regulation can be difficult to enforce, as noticing non-compliance in the first place requires some transparency on the part of the processor.

I. Data as Economic Goods

In the Information Age, data is a new category of economic value.[30] Especially personal data is of great importance for many business models, chiefly in the advertising and business-to-consumer (B2C) space.[31]

One of the most popular and earliest examples of consumer data monetization in Germany is the customer loyalty program Payback, in which consumers can earn points for purchases with various partner stores. These points can be paid out at a value of EUR 0.01 per point. This value is the floor of possible cash-back, as consumers can increase their points earnings using coupons and co-branded credit cards. In return, the consumer allows Payback to analyze their spending behavior. To me, the long history and large customer base of this program drives two points home: First, consumers are perfectly willing to sell their spending data to a third party. Second, this bargain has reached an apparent equilibrium at somewhere vaguely north of one percent of transaction volume for B2C shopping data.[32]

Another example is Google Analytics. For years, Google Analytics[33] was the *de facto* standard of web analytics. The product provided website administrators detailed information about their visitors and their use of the site. Recently, a slew of decisions by supervisory authorities in the EU have rendered the use of Google Analytics problematic. It cannot be used in accordance with the GDPR, even if the controller takes additional measures such as requiring explicit consent (Art. 49 § 1 lit.(a) GDPR).[34] Most notable is here a decision by the Austrian supervisory authority,[35] in which the authority has outlined that privacy measures in Google Analytics are not sufficient to fill the gaps outlined in the ECJ's *Schrems II* decision.[36] In 2023, the Swedish Data Protection Authority implored companies to stop using Google

30 For an economic perspective and with especial regard to the effects I am outlining here, see *Acquisti, Taylor*, and *Wagman*, "The Economics of Privacy" (June 2016), pp. 454 sqq.

31 For reasons that will become apparent in the section about personal data and its relation to natural persons (see p. 87), the business-to-business (B2B) sector is not of great consequence here.

32 As this is the typical cash-back one can achieve using Payback.

33 *Google, Inc.*, "Analysetools und -lösungen für Ihr Unternehmen – Google Analytics" (2024).

34 *Deiwick*, "Droht das Aus für Google Analytics in der EU?" (2022), Heading 6.

35 *Austrian Data Protection Authority*, "Datenübermittlung durch Implementierung von Google Analytics" (2022).

36 *European Parliament*, "Schrems II" (July 16, 2021).

Analytics.[37] According to Google's own help page, the company does not see IP addresses and other pseudonymous data as personal data. It acknowledges that this is a different assessment from that of the GDPR and ECJ, but provides the user with no alternative.[38] The saga surrounding Google Analytics illustrates an overarching development: In the early years of the internet economy, there was little to no regulation on tracking and advertising.[39] As a result, many business models emerged that relied heavily on tracking to provide advertising. In the EU, this has recently been met with regulatory pushback.

II. Data Protection as Driver of the Business Model

Especially in the advertising business, GDPR has served as a catalyst for innovation. Additionally, users have become more savvy in using methods to circumvent tracking through ad blockers, cookie blockers, or VPNs. With "traditional" ways of collecting information about users for targeted advertising thereby becoming less viable, new approaches are needed. This regulatory and practical pressure on advertisers has led to remarkable innovations, some examples of which shall be shown in this section.

1. Example: Telekom/Vodafone, TrustPid, and iCloud Private Relay

A good example for the rising importance of customer data are telecommunications providers. Going from a position purely as providers of a utility, these providers are coming of age as brokers of advertising. From a business perspective, this is sensible: As the market for telecommunications services—*e.g.*, cell phone service or DSL/Fiber home service—nears saturation, these businesses need to expand into other areas to fuel further growth.

A straightforward way of doing this is to monetize the trove of user data these businesses collect as utility providers. As telecommunications providers, they necessarily have access to their users' browsing behavior. This is valuable information, as it can give detailed information about a certain user's proclivities and be used

37 *Swedish Authority for Privacy Protection*, "Companies must stop using Google Analytics" (July 3, 2023).

38 *Google, Inc.*, "Personenidentifizierbare Informationen in Verträgen und Richtlinien von Google - Google Analytics-Hilfe" (2023).

39 The CAN-SPAM Act of 2003 (!) being a notable counterexample, *U.S. Congress*, "16 CFR Part 316 - CAN-SPAM RULE" (2004).

to sell advertising. This can be circumvented using a Virtual Private Network (VPN) service[40] or using a third-party DNS provider.

When Apple, Inc.[41] introduced their iCloud Private Relay[42] feature, which functions similar to a VPN service, a number of ISPs voiced opposition and called on the European Commission (EC) to outlaw the service.[43] As of the writing of this thesis, this was not successful.

However, the ISPs are now working on different ways of monetizing user data and providing the advertising industry with a replacement for third-party cookies: A new service spearheaded by Vodafone, but supported by Deutsche Telekom AG, that is currently in the testing states, "TrustPid"[44], wants to use the data available to the ISPs to centrally identify users via a persistent identifier ID. Advertisers can then obtain temporary tokens from TrustPid to target their advertising. This solution is controversial.[45] Notwithstanding the legality or desirability of such a construct, this shows the remarkable amount of energy that is used not just to innovate in the space of user tracking but also to lobby regulators and supervising authorities.

2. Example: Cookie Banners and Ad Blocking

Additionally, recent examples have shown that lobbying both for privacy legislation and for supervisory approval is becoming more and more important. In online marketing, so-called A/B testing[46] allows testing measures such as cookie banners[47] on a large scale. Finding a version that is *barely* in compliance with GDPR and still leads to a high amount of user consent into targeted advertising as well as high user en-

---

40 VPNs work by routing all internet traffic through a different computer over an encrypted connection. The assumption here is that the VPN provider (the operator of the "different" computer) provides a higher privacy level than the user's Internet Service Provider (ISP). Using this method, the user can prevent their ISP from seeing their traffic. This is commonly done for higher privacy in unknown networks or sometimes to hide illicit activity, such as file sharing.

41 https://apple.com/.

42 *Apple, Inc.*, "About iCloud Private Relay" (Dec. 20, 2022).

43 *Woods* and *Titcomb*, "Apple under fire over iPhone encryption tech" (Jan. 9, 2022).

44 Meanwhile renamed to "Utiq", see *Die Bundesbeauftragte für den Datenschuz und die Informationsfreiheit*, "FAQ zu Utiq."

45 *Penfrat* and *Masse*, "TrustPid" (Feb. 10, 2023); *Kleinz*, "TrustPid" (May 28, 2022).

46 Here, multiple versions of a User Interface (UI) are created and served at random to users. These different versions are then evaluated on how they affect user behavior. For example, experimenting with the placement and color of a "Sign Up" button on a page can have drastic effects on how often users click on it.

47 A wide-ranging topic in its own right, see: Cookie-Einwilligung II (May 28, 2020); Cookie-Einwilligung (Oct. 5, 2017); Cookies (Oct. 1, 2019); *Kühling*, "'Cookie-Banner', 'Cookie-Walls' und das 'PUR'-Modell" (2022).

gagement has become a competitive exercise. Advertisers are therefore subjected to a high amount of *regulatory* pressure.

Another force reducing the efficacy of online advertising is user adoption of *ad blockers*.[48] This has required advertisers to innovate: Some ad blockers have featured a so-called “Acceptable Ads”[49] program that selectively blocks certain advertisements. “Large advertisers” need to pay to be included in the program, which funds the ad blocker’s development.[50] This business model has been the subject of litigation, but was held to not be in violation of competition laws.[51]

III. Anonymization as a Potential Driver of Business Models

Having outlined that data protection can be a driver of business models, it follows that a prudent use of anonymization can enable processing that would not be possible without it. On the flip side, anonymization is non-trivial and therefore always associated with a cost. As a result, anonymization is performed only where it makes business sense to do so.[52]

1. Motivation

As we have seen, the cost of compliance with the GDPR is high, especially in data-driven business models. Efficient anonymization can be a good mitigation strategy: Controllers may use anonymization to perform additional analyses on their data once it has been anonymized. This is especially interesting where this data is used to train AI models, which benefit from accumulating training data. Anonymization could be seen as an upfront cost which enables a long lifetime of data afterwards that justifies this expense. Of course, anonymizing this data only remains a viable strategy where the benefits outweigh the costs. Therefore, the value of the “remaining”, anonymized data needs to be higher than the cost of anonymization plus the expected cost of maintaining GDPR compliance surrounding the anonymized data. This is a classic Return on Investment (ROI) relationship. When evaluating whether an investment into anonymizing a dataset is worth the cost of anonymization and

48 Programs that remove advertising from webpages and disable tracking, such as *uBlock Origin*: https://ublockorigin.com/. See also the current state of ongoing litigation surrounding the ad blocker *AdBlock Plus*: Adblocker (Jan. 14, 2022).

49 https://acceptableads.com.

50 *eyeo GmbH*, “About Adblock Plus” (2023).

51 OLG Hamburg: Werbeblocker (Mar. 15, 2018).

52 For a detailed look from an economic angle, see *Acquisti*, *Taylor*, and *Wagman*, “The Economics of Privacy” (June 2016), especially pp. 481 sqq.

the cost of ongoing compliance, the lifetime value of this anonymized data needs to be considered. Of course, all of these variables contain some uncertainty. For example, it is unclear how much effort (which translates to cost) is needed to anonymize. Depending on the effort invested in the anonymization, compliance costs over the lifetime of the data may also be lower: If data has been anonymized "well", it may not need to be re-anonymized as technology advances.

The cost of compliance depends heavily on the trajectory of de-anonymization technology. As technology advances and the availability of large amounts of data increases, it will become possible to de-anonymize data that was previously thought to be "perfectly" anonymized.[53] The European legislator has foreseen this challenge and acknowledges it in Recital (26) s. 4 GDPR.[54] Unforeseen leaps in technology move this goalpost in irregular increments, such as the discovery of the transformer model in 2017[55], which, combined with ample training, enabled OpenAI's Generative Pre-Trained Transformer (GPT) models to pass the U.S. Uniform Bar Exam[56] just five years later—a barely thinkable feat just months before.[57]

Another example for the pace of technology is how hashing algorithms have advanced from the 1990s to the present day.[58] As computing power increases and research in cryptanalysis[59] advances, the "recommended" hash function has been replaced time and again: The formerly safe MD5 algorithm invented in 1995[60] was con-

53 *Bruegger*, "Towards a Better Understanding of Identification, Pseudonymization, and Anonymization (v 1.0)" (June 11, 2021), p. 101.

54 See p. 101.

55 *Vaswani* et al., "Attention is All you Need" (2017).

56 D. M. *Katz, Bommarito*, et al., "GPT-4 Passes the Bar Exam" (2023).

57 "Despite thousands of hours on related tasks over the last two decades between the authors, we did not expect GPT-3.5 to demonstrate such proficiency in a zero-shot setting with minimal modeling and optimization effort.", *Bommarito* and D. M. *Katz*, "GPT Takes the Bar Exam" (2022), p. 6. To make this feat even more remarkable, GPT models are not even specifically trained on legal data—the general assumption here is that models perform better when they are specifically trained for the target domain (*e.g.*, for the medical or legal domain, see also D. M. *Katz, Hartung*, et al., "Natural Language Processing in the Legal Domain" (2023), p. 2)—but rather for domain-independent question answering (*Bommarito* and D. M. *Katz*, "GPT Takes the Bar Exam" (2022), p. 2).

58 Hashing is a cryptographic operation in which an input of any size is transformed to a fixed-length output. Knowing the output, one can (ideally) not guess the input, but using the same input always yields the same output. This is very useful in practice, *e.g.*, to validate passwords: A user chooses a password. A hash is generated from the password. This hash is saved. The password is discarded and not saved in plain text. When the user wants to log in, their password is run through the hash function again. If the hash matches the hash in the database, the password is correct.

59 The field concerned with breaking ciphers.

60 *Rivest*, "The MD5 Message-Digest Algorithm" (Apr. 1, 1992).

sidered broken less than ten years later.[61]. Its replacements, SHA-1 and, to a lesser extent, SHA-2,[62] befell the same fate. Today, SHA-2, SHA-3, and bcrypt are used. This dynamic is emblematic of cybersecurity research.

As anonymization is a field adjacent to cryptography, there are parallels to be drawn here: As technology and research advance, what used to be considered "safe" or "anonymous" may not remain that way. This may affect just one row of a dataset, the anonymization of an entire dataset, or an entire type of anonymization technique.

2. Risk

There are risks associated with anonymization: As per Recital (26) s. 4 GDPR, the controller needs to continuously evaluate if their anonymization efforts are still sufficient, especially when technology and other factors have moved on. The cost of risk can be assessed easily[63] by multiplying the probability of re-identification with the potential economic cost of such an event.

Both components are difficult to quantify: The risk of de-anonymization depends on a multitude of factors, as does the potential cost. The risk of de-anonymization depends on how diligently anonymization was performed, the motivation of third parties to de-anonymize,[64] and the general trajectory of technology and data availability. Significant advances in technology (such as the Transformer architecture[65]) are hard to foresee. However, incremental gains are to be expected. The motivation of third parties to de-anonymize is generally not known, but can be estimated as a function of the amount of data and the perceived value of the de-anonymized data.[66] Finally, the diligence exercised in anonymization is a factor the data processor can influence. This is the most important piece of the risk assessment: As I will

---

61 *Black, Cochran*, and *Highland*, "A Study of the MD5 Attacks" (2006).

62 "Secure Hash Algorithm" 1 and 2. SHA-1 was introduced in the 1990s using the same mechanism as MD5 and was considered broken by the early 2000s. SHA-2 was published in 2001, with collision attacks becoming practical as of the early 2010s.

63 A corollary thought for a slightly different context (assessing the harm for data breaches in general) can be found in *Solove* and *Citron*, "Risk and Anxiety" (2017–2018), p. 774.

64 *Sweeney*, "Guaranteeing anonymity when sharing medical data, the Datafly System" (1997), p. 53.

65 First defined in *Vaswani* et al., "Attention is All you Need" (2017).

66 Or, how *Solove* and *Citron* put it in their theory of harm, the "sensitivity of data", *Solove* and *Citron*, "Risk and Anxiety" (2017–2018), p. 774. However, here we are trying to assess the motivation of third parties, not the harm to the data subject. As a result, data sensitivity and the perceived value of this data are often correlated, but not the same. Information may be very sensitive, but not very valuable, or very valuable, but not very sensitive.

show in the balance of this thesis, if sufficient caution is exercised, anonymization can be performed well.

The potential cost of de-anonymization can be divided into legal costs and loss of goodwill. Legal costs are fines, the right to compensation, and cost for litigation. First off, fines are imposed by supervisory authorities for mishandling data. These fines can be substantial under the GDPR: Art. 83 § 5 GDPR allows for penalties of up to 4% of worldwide annual revenue or up to EUR 20M in certain cases. Second, member states can impose additional penalties pursuant to Art. 84 GDPR. In Germany, certain violations of GDPR even carry criminal sanctions (§ 42 German Data Protection Law, "Bundesdatenschutzgesetz" (BDSG)).[67] Also, data subjects can claim compensation pursuant to Art. 82 GDPR. Third, these fines, compensations, and criminal sanctions are often the subject of litigation, which can add substantial legal expenses to the equation. Another, more subtle cost of subpar anonymization is goodwill. As has been shown in various data breaches over the years,[68] users do not respond kindly to companies "losing" their data. This can damage a brand's reputation for years and lead to users leaving for competitors.

IV. Open Data and Anonymization for the Greater Good

Another important area in which anonymization is of great importance is for the open data movement.[69] For example, the German state of Hesse is in the process of creating an "Open Data Law".[70] Easy access to data can enable better policy and better allocation of resources at non-governmental organizations and charities. This is most important with official documents. The GDPR acknowledges this interest in Recital (154), where it states that "[GDPR] allows the principle of public access to official documents to be taken into account ...". However, the regulation states a clear priority on the protection of personal data. As a result, potent anonymization tools can enable legal access to public data, which makes institutions more account-

67 Both § 42 para. 1 and para. 2 BDSG are a possibility when anonymization is carried out insufficiently. However, this risk of prosecution occurs mostly for the party that de-anonymizes, not the processor who anonymizes.
68 See most recently the case of LastPass: "The most recent breach should have LastPass subscribers seriously considering dropping the service and seeking an alternative.", *Tomaschek*, "LastPass Issues Update on Data Breach, But Users Should Still Change Passwords" (Mar. 1, 2023).
69 See also for a constitutional perspective: *Rachut*, "Grundrechtsverwirklichung in digitalen Kontexten" (2025), p. 295.
70 "Hessisches Gesetz über offene Daten der Träger der öffentlichen Verwaltung (Hessisches Open Data-Gesetz – HODaG), Entwurf vom 17.01.2023" (Jan. 17, 2023).

able and can benefit access to justice. It is also an area where the conflict between individual privacy and the collective interest in an open judiciary are juxtaposed.[71]

V. Research

The GDPR is also a large factor in designing research around data, for example in evaluation tasks.[72] When researchers want to use sensitive data, they need to jump through a large number of regulatory hoops to gain access. Despite Art. 89 GDPR, which promises less regulation for research purposes, "owners" of data are often slow to give access to their treasures.

A special impact is felt by the very community that inspired a large amount of this dissertation: Re-identification researchers—who try to break anonymization in the spirit of improving it—are frequently in danger of doing something illegal under the GDPR and other statutes. Like 'white hat' hackers in more traditional cybersecurity disciplines, they would benefit from a larger legal recognition of so-called responsible disclosure practices.[73]

1.3 Conclusion

In summary, as the industry moves towards a data-centric economy, accumulating data and especially personal data has become a prime objective for many enterprises. In this endeavor, adhering to ever more stringent regulation and pushback from users leads to difficulty and high compliance costs.[74] The use of anonymization techniques is only useful where they stay economically relevant. In the following chapters, we will take a look at different approaches and evaluate them on their

71 For a good example of this, see the ongoing dispute over an (allegedly) insufficiently anonymized court decision that was published on the free web portal openJur, *Bremert*, "Keine Zukunft für frei dokumentierte Rechtsprechung? - openJur wird verklagt" (Jan. 22, 2024).

72 *Rangel* and *Rosso*, "On the Implications of the General Data Protection Regulation on the Organisation of Evaluation Tasks" (2018).

73 See p. 230.

74 Or, as the Hamburg Data Protection Officer (DPO) puts it: "A society oriented towards data collection, data sharing, and data use cannot be minimizing their use of data. On the contrary … This will present new challenges for data protection.", (translation by the author), *Fuchs*, "31. Tätigkeitsbericht Datenschutz 2022 Datenschutz des Hamburgischen Beauftragten für Datenschutz und Informationsfreiheit" (2023), p. 12. For more detail on this conflict between data use and data protection, see in depth: *Rachut*, "Grundrechtsverwirklichung in digitalen Kontexten" (2025), pp. 303 sqq.

privacy and data usability merits. By performing a "return on investment" calculation, one can assess them through the lens of economic viability.

The cost of compliance is—in some instances—higher than it would need to be: Where data protection laws are unclear, authorities often cooperate with controllers to determine a way forward. This may prevent a larger amount of jurisdiction on the subject, which could feed into over-compliance.[75]

Anonymization can be one way to mitigate these difficulties, yet it requires a careful selection of methods and additional efforts to make sure that data *stays* anonymous.

75 Similar, but without the conclusion: *Kühling* and *Klar*, "Unsicherheitsfaktor Datenschutzrecht – Das Beispiel des Personenbezugs und der Anonymität" (2013), pp. 3615 sq.

2 Personal Data

The business models shown above rely on personal data, *i.e.*, information that relates to an identifiable natural person.[1] As a result, they all need to operate in accordance with data protection laws. As shown, compliance with these laws can be arduous. Removing the relation to identifiable natural persons—*i.e.*, anonymizing—means going outside of the scope of these data protection laws. As a result, anonymization is often regarded as a solution for enabling processing that would have been more difficult with personal data. To find out if this confidence is well-placed from a legal perspective, we must first define personal data.[2] Understanding the concept of personal data is paramount to finding ways to anonymize.

Thankfully, the GDPR defines personal data and there is rich literature and jurisdiction on the subject. To better understand anonymization and anonymous data, we need to go into detail on the definition of personal data under the GDPR. The GDPR presupposes that it only regulates personal data. This is obvious from the term "personal data", used throughout the regulation.[3] "Personal data" is defined in Art. 4 § 1 GDPR as "any information relating to an identified or identifiable natural person ('data subject'); ...".

This is also echoed in Recital (26) to the GDPR, which outlines that the "principles of data protection should apply to any information concerning an identified or identifiable natural person.", Recital (16) of Regulation (EU) 2018/1725[4], and Recital (21) of Directive (EU) 2016/680[5]. All of these reference the same definition.[6]

1 See Art. 4 § 1 GDPR for the full definition.

2 "... the anonymisation of data is a process that operates upon personal data, it does not, of itself, assist in the definition of personal data.", *Booth* et al., "What are 'Personal Data'? – A study conducted for the UK Information Commissioner" (2004), p. 3.

3 *e.g.*, in the regulation's title, which contains "the processing of personal data" and Art. 2 § 1, Art. 4 § 1 *etc.* GDPR.

4 Concerning the protection of natural persons with regard to the processing of personal data by the Union institutions, bodies, offices, and agencies and the free movement of such data.

5 Concerning the protection of natural persons with regard to the processing of personal data by competent authorities for the purposes of the prevention, investigation, detection, or prosecution of criminal offences or the execution of criminal penalties, and the free movement of such data.

6 O.C. (Mar. 7, 2024), para. 43. Curiously, Regulation 2016/680, the "sister directive" to the GDPR, defines "personal data" in its Art. 3 § 1 (in the same way as defined in the GDPR). In Regulation 2018/1725, this is done more cleanly in Recital (5), which clarifies that it should be interpreted "homogeneously" with the GDPR.

https://doi.org/10.1515/9783112222164-003

The Article 29 Data Protection Working Party (Art. 29 Working Party), a body devised to help interpret the Directive 95/46/EC (Data Protection Directive),[7] divides the definition up into four elements: "any information", "relating to", "identified or identifiable", and "natural person" in a paper published in 2007, entitled "Opinion on the concept of personal data".[8] Even though the Art. 29 Working Party's Opinion[9] hails from 2007 and is partially outdated, it has continued to prove very influential.[10] Although the GDPR has completely replaced the Data Protection Directive, its definition is largely identical, and both Data Protection Directive-era scholarship and jurisdiction continue to be relevant under the GDPR.

To better understand the definition of personal data, we must now go into detail on each criterion.

2.1 Information

The first criterion is that personal data needs to be some kind of "information". "Information" is difficult to define.[11] Notwithstanding this difficulty, it is a universally useful and pragmatically usable concept.[12] As one observer notes, using "armchair

7 The Working Party was set up by the eponymous Art. 29 Data Protection Directive, where it was given "advisory status". From its first meeting on January 17, 1996, to its eventual replacement with the European Data Protection Board (EDPB) on May 25, 2018, the Art. 29 Working Party created guidelines, held public consultations, and published opinions. The Art. 29 Working Party contained representatives of the national independent authorities on data protection. For more on the Art. 29 Working Party's founding, see *Article 29 Data Protection Working Party*, "First Annual Report" (June 25, 1997), pp. 5 sq.

8 *Article 29 Data Protection Working Party*, "01248/07/EN WP 136" (2007).

9 From here on, the capital-O Opinion refers to the Art. 29 Working Party's papers, such as "01248/07/EN WP 136," "00569/13/EN," and "0829/14/DE WP216."

10 With more explanation: *Purtova*, "The law of everything. Broad concept of personal data and future of EU data protection law" (Jan. 2, 2018), pp. 59 sq.; *Altman, Cohen, Falzon*, et al., "A Principled Approach to Defining Anonymization As Applied to EU Data Protection Law" (May 9, 2022), p. 2.

11 As evidenced by an extensive philosophical discussion on the subject, see *Adriaans*, "Information" (2020). See also *Karg*, "DSGVO Art. 4 Nr. 1 Begriffsbestimmung „Personenbezogenes Datum“" (2025), margin no. 26; *Hallinan* and *Gellert*, "The Concept of 'Information'. An Invisible Problem in the GDPR" (Aug. 2020), pp. 279 sqq.

12 Pragmatically usable here in the sense that a concept need not be exhaustively defined to be useful.

etymology", we can arrive at the sense that something that is *in formation* is non-random.[13] This means that the antonym of information is *noise*, *i.e.*, randomness[14].[15]

The Art. 29 Working Party's Opinion refrains from defining information directly, but rather uses the term in the context of personal data: The Opinion states that any sort of statements about a person are covered (the "nature" of the information),[16] not limited to "personal" data but rather anything that is *about* an individual,[17] and in any format.[18] In the Art. 29 Working Party's example, even drug prescription information can be personal data about the physician who prescribed the medication.[19]

Even before the Art. 29 Working Party wrote their Opinion on personal data, the ECJ ruled that "information" needs to be seen in a wide scope.[20] This interpretation should include "all kinds of information, not only objective but also subjective, in the form of opinions and assessments, provided that it 'relates' to the data subject."[21] This interpretation is also supported by the Art. 29 Working Party, who noted in 2007 that "the term 'any information' … clearly signals the willingness of the legislator to design a broad concept of personal data [which] calls for a wide interpretation."[22] There are no requirements as to the format of the data—textual and tabular data are as much covered as are acoustic, photographic, or video data.[23] Using the Art. 29 Working Party's examples: Information covers both "objective" data ("Titius was born on July 15, 353 Common Era (C.E.) in Rome") as well as "subjective" data ("Titius is a good worker and merits promotion").[24] Generally, the courts, the supervisory authorities (represented by the Art. 29 Working Party and later the EDPB), and legal

13 *Sequoiah-Grayson* and *Floridi*, "Semantic Conceptions of Information" (2022).
14 Ibid.
15 A duality that will become clear when speaking about randomization for anonymization, see p. 143.
16 *Article 29 Data Protection Working Party*, "01248/07/EN WP 136" (2007), p. 6.
17 Ibid., pp. 6 sq.
18 Ibid., pp. 7 sq.
19 Example 1 ibid., p. 7.
20 Lindqvist (Nov. 6, 2003), paras. 24, 50; recently upheld in: FF v. ÖDSB and CRIF (May 4, 2023), para. 23; most recently: O.C. (Mar. 7, 2024), para. 45.
21 Nowak (Dec. 20, 2017), para. 34.
22 *Article 29 Data Protection Working Party*, "01248/07/EN WP 136" (2007), p. 6.
23 *Article 29 Data Protection Working Party*, "01248/07/EN WP 136" (2007), p. 7; Ryneš (Dec. 11, 2014), paras. 21 sq.; *Klabunde* and *Horváth*, "DS-GVO Art. 4 Begriffsbestimmungen" (2024), margin no. 9.
24 *Article 29 Data Protection Working Party*, "01248/07/EN WP 136" (2007), p. 6.

scholarship seem in broad agreement that the term "information" in Art. 4 § 1 GDPR needs to be understood with a very wide scope of application.[25]

Nonetheless, even where there is agreement about the scope of the term, the term "information" itself requires some clarification.[26] This is apparent where information or knowledge exists, but is not represented corporeally—for example, where Betty *knows* James's birthday, but has not written it down. One could argue that—as the GDPR remarks in Art. 2—the law only makes sense when it applies to data that is processed automatically or committed to a filing system of some sort and that the European legislator cannot legislate what goes on in someone's head. However, when viewing Art. 2 § 1 GDPR, it becomes clear that the GDPR only regulates automated processing and non-automated processing where personal data has been committed to a filing system. From this we can gather that there must exist personal data outside of filing systems and automated processing. It does not fall upon Art. 4 § 1 GDPR to distinguish between personal data that falls within the material scope of the GDPR and that which does not, but rather to Art. 2 § 1 GDPR. Therefore, "information" under the GDPR is broader than data and also means data that is not corporeal, like knowledge.[27] [28] It also includes knowledge held by a person.[29]

25 Most recently: Single Resolution Board v. EDPS (Apr. 26, 2023), margin no. 68; *Farinho*, "GDPR Art. 4 § 1: Personal Data" (2023), margin no. 8; *Karg*, "DSGVO Art. 4 Nr. 1 Begriffsbestimmung „Personenbezogenes Datum"" (2025), margin no. 25; *Ernst*, "DS-GVO Art. 4 Begriffsbestimmungen" (2021), margin no. 3; implicit in: *Gola*, "DS-GVO Art. 4 Begriffsbestimmungen" (2022), margin no. 5; *Klabunde* and *Horváth*, "DS-GVO Art. 4 Begriffsbestimmungen" (2024), margin no. 9.

26 One of these questions is whether DNA qualifies as "information" under the GDPR. For a detailed argument on why it is, see *Hallinan* and *Gellert*, "The Concept of 'Information'. An Invisible Problem in the GDPR" (Aug. 2020), pp. 286 sqq.

27 *Ziebarth*, "DS GVO Art. 4 Begriffsbestimmungen" (2022), margin no. 8; in this direction: *Bruegger*, "Towards a Better Understanding of Identification, Pseudonymization, and Anonymization (v 1.0)" (June 11, 2021), p. 24; similar: *Karg*, "DSGVO Art. 4 Nr. 1 Begriffsbestimmung „Personenbezogenes Datum"" (2025), margin nos. 25 sq.; similar: *Mühlenbeck*, "Anonyme und pseudonyme Daten" (2023), p. 79; differing opinion, making a distinction between "data" that is necessarily corporeal and information as "interpreted" data: *Specht*, "Ausschließlichkeitsrechte an Daten – Notwendigkeit, Schutzumfang, Alternativen" (2016), p. 290.

28 While one could be quick to dismiss this part of the definition as academic, it will play a significant role later on in our discussion of identification, where oftentimes, identification requires linking knowledge with other information, see p. 70.

29 *Bruegger*, "Towards a Better Understanding of Identification, Pseudonymization, and Anonymization (v 1.0)" (June 11, 2021), p. 8.

2.2 Relating to a Natural Person

According to Art. 4 § 1 GDPR, this information must be "relating to" an identified or identifiable natural person. We will first cover the "relation" to a person. Distinguishing this requirement from the next element—whether a person is identifiable/identified or not—should be done as follows: "Relating to a natural person" is meant to distinguish data about a person from data that is not about a person (non-personal data).[30] The next requirement ("identified or identifiable") is to find out whether we can find out the person's identity.

It is not immediately clear what "relating" to a natural person means. Using a grammatical approach,[31] "relating" commonly means to establish a connection between two things—the data on one hand, the person on the other hand[32] or that something relating to something else concerns it[33]. As far as systematic arguments[34] go, the GDPR provides examples of data "relating to natural persons" in a couple of places. For example, in Recital (30) s. 1 GDPR, it states that "Natural persons may be associated with online identifiers provided by their devices, applications, tools and protocols, such as internet protocol addresses, cookie identifiers or other identifiers such as radio frequency identification tags". From this, we can see that the GDPR considers "online identifiers" that regularly concern a *device*, not a human, as "associated" with that person. Indeed, as we will see later in the case of IP addresses[35], European data protection law does indeed consider identifiers that relate to devices as relating to their users.[36] It is stated in Recital (71) s. 2 GDPR that profiling consists of "... automated processing of personal data evaluating the personal aspects relating to a natural person, in particular ... aspects concerning the data subject's performance at work, economic situation, health, personal preferences or interests, reliability or behaviour, location or movements, where it produces legal effects concerning him or her or similarly significantly affects him or her." Even though profiling is irrelevant to our current discussion, the EU legislator also uses "relation to a person" here, and it appears that the concerns outlined "relate to" the data subject in much the same way as in the definition of personal data.

30 *Karg*, "DSGVO Art. 4 Nr. 1 Begriffsbestimmung „Personenbezogenes Datum“" (2025), margin no. 34; *Mühlenbeck*, "Anonyme und pseudonyme Daten" (2023), p. 80.

31 *Lenaerts* and *Gutierrez-Fons*, "To Say What the Law of the EU Is" (2013–2014), pp. 8 sqq.

32 "relate" (2024), Meaning 2.

33 Ibid., Meaning 1.

34 *Lenaerts* and *Gutierrez-Fons*, "To Say What the Law of the EU Is" (2013–2014), pp. 16 sq.

35 See p. 105.

36 *Zuiderveen Borgesius*, "Singling out people without knowing their names – Behavioural targeting, pseudonymous data, and the new Data Protection Regulation" (Apr. 2016), p. 11.

Looking through a historical lens, the requirement of "relation" is old. It first appeared in the European arena in 1981 through Art. 2 lit. a of Convention for the Protection of Individuals with regard to Automatic Processing of Personal Data 1981 (Convention 108).[37] Later, it became part of EU law through the Data Protection Directive. In the German version of the text, the wording changed: Under the Data Protection Directive, it used to be information "about" an identified or identifiable person,[38] whereas now the information must "relate to" that person. Nonetheless, this change does not signify a difference in meaning, as the English version stayed the same.[39] Here, the Art. 29 Working Party laid down a three-pronged definition[40] that is still widely used and cited under the GDPR today.[41]

I. The Art. 29 Working Party's and the ECJ's Definition

The ECJ later indirectly confirmed the criteria laid down by the Art. 29 Working Party:[42] According to the ECJ, information is "relating to" a person where the information "by reason of its content, purpose or effect, is linked to a particular person".[43] These three criteria are known as the "content", "purpose", and "result" elements, respectively.[44]

37 " 'personal data' means any information relating to an identified or identifiable individual ('data subject')", *Council of Europe*, "Convention for the Protection of Individuals with regard to Automatic Processing of Personal Data" (1981).

38 *Rat*, "RL 95/46/EG vom 24.10.1995 zum Schutz natürlicher Personen bei der Verarbeitung personenbezogener Daten und zum freien Datenverkehr" (Dec. 13, 1995) Recital (26).

39 *Krügel*, "Das personenbezogene Datum nach der DS-GVO" (2017), p. 456.

40 *Article 29 Data Protection Working Party*, "01248/07/EN WP 136" (2007), p. 10.

41 *e.g.*, *Klabunde* and *Horváth*, "DS-GVO Art. 4 Begriffsbestimmungen" (2024), margin no. 10.

42 With more detail on how the ECJ does not cite the Art. 29 Working Party's Opinions, see: *Purtova*, "The law of everything. Broad concept of personal data and future of EU data protection law" (Jan. 2, 2018), p. 59.

43 Nowak (Dec. 20, 2017), para. 35; FF v. ÖDSB and CRIF (May 4, 2023), para. 23; O.C. (Mar. 7, 2024), para. 45; agreeing: BGH: Umfang und Gegenstand des datenschutzrechtlichen Auskunftsanspruchs (June 15, 2021), margin no. 22; *Farinho*, "GDPR Art. 4 § 1: Personal Data" (2023), margin no. 9; *Karg*, "DSGVO Art. 4 Nr. 1 Begriffsbestimmung „Personenbezogenes Datum“" (2025), margin no. 33; *Gola*, "DS-GVO Art. 4 Begriffsbestimmungen" (2022), margin no. 6; *Klabunde* and *Horváth*, "DS-GVO Art. 4 Begriffsbestimmungen" (2024), margin nos. 10 sq.

44 Nowak (Dec. 20, 2017), para. 35; *Article 29 Data Protection Working Party*, "01248/07/EN WP 136" (2007), pp. 10 sq.; referring to the first element as the "about" element: *Rupp* and *Von Grafenstein*, "Clarifying "personal data" and the role of anonymisation in data protection law" (Apr. 2024), p. 2.

1. Content Element

The content element is the most straightforward case. It is given where the information is “about” a particular person.[45] This corresponds to the intuitive meaning of the word “relate”.[46] In the Art. 29 Working Party’s examples, a medical diagnosis relates to the patient, and a company’s customer database contains information that relates to these customers.[47] In a similar vein, the fingerprints of a natural person “objectively contain unique information about individuals”.[48]

To form a definition, the content element is present where the information directly corresponds to a person.

2. Purpose Element

A second element introduced by the Art. 29 Working Party is the purpose element: Where data is “used or [likely to be used], taking into account all the circumstances surrounding the precise case, with the purpose to evaluate, treat in a certain way or influence the status or behaviour of an individual.”[49]

The example the Art. 29 Working Party provides, a call log in a business, however, is a non sequitur—they fail to communicate why this call log is an example of a purpose element (and, to my eye, it is not). For example, the call log contains information in the sense of a content element (1.) that someone made a call to someone else. The phone log can, of course, be used in the way of a purpose element—*e.g.*, to evaluate if an employee or the cleaning staff are making personal phone calls over the business line—yet the example concentrates on “data … insofar as all of them contain information concerning people’s private life, social relationships and communications.”[50] A better example can be found in the ECJ’s *Nowak* decision, as “the purpose of collecting [answers] is to evaluate the candidate’s professional abilities and his suitability to practice the profession concerned.”[51] Other examples are the use of online data to create profiles of users,[52] the processing of data related to

---

45 *Article 29 Data Protection Working Party*, “01248/07/EN WP 136” (2007), p. 10.

46 Ibid., p. 10.

47 Ibid., p. 10.

48 Schwarz v. Bochum (Oct. 17, 2013), para. 27.

49 *Article 29 Data Protection Working Party*, “01248/07/EN WP 136” (2007), p. 10, underlining from the original.

50 Ibid., p. 11.

51 Nowak (Dec. 20, 2017), para. 38.

52 *Klabunde* and *Horváth*, “DS-GVO Art. 4 Begriffsbestimmungen” (2024), margin no. 10; *Mühlenbeck*, “Anonyme und pseudonyme Daten” (2023), p. 85; *Arning* and *Rothkegel*, “DS-GVO Art. 4 Begriffsbestimmungen” (2022), margin no. 13; *Karg*, “DSGVO Art. 4 Nr. 1 Begriffsbestimmung „Personenbezogenes Datum“” (2025), margin no. 36.

the use of a vehicle to assess the user's driving style[53], or personalizing the price of groceries.[54]

The salient aspect of the purpose element is that the information can be *used* or is *intended to be used* in a certain way.[55]

3. Result Element

Finally, the Art. 29 Working Party introduces a result element, where data "can be considered to 'relate' to an individual because [its] use is likely to have an impact on a certain person's rights and interests, taking into account all the circumstances surrounding the precise case."[56] In the Art. 29 Working Party's example, a system to assign cabs to riders—set up to optimize the routing and save fuel—is not set up to monitor drivers (*i.e.*, as its purpose element), but can be used to monitor drivers, *e.g.*, if they abide by traffic laws, and thus can have a "considerable impact" on them.[57] In the *Nowak* case, the exam data that was at the center of the case had an impact on Mr. Nowak's chances of becoming a tax professional in Ireland.[58]

Of the three elements, the result element is most often criticized, as it provides the least distinction and is thereby not found to be helpful.[59]

4. Discussion

This "three-element definition" has found considerable usage, with judiciary and legal literature agreeing on it. The ECJ still uses the definition, as do member state courts such as the German Federal Court of Justice (BGH).[60] It also remains largely undisputed in legal literature.[61]

Some authors in the literature introduce an additional distinction between indirect and direct relation to a person:[62] When data corresponds to a person, that

53 *Weichert*, "Weichert" (2017), p. 510.

54 *Freiling*, "Hofmann/Freiling" (2020), p. 334.

55 *Haase*, "Datenschutzrechtliche Fragen des Personenbezugs" (2015), p. 256.

56 *Article 29 Data Protection Working Party*, "01248/07/EN WP 136" (2007), p. 11, underlining from the original.

57 Ibid., p. 11.

58 Nowak (Dec. 20, 2017), para. 39.

59 *Haase*, "Datenschutzrechtliche Fragen des Personenbezugs" (2015), p. 256.

60 BGH: Umfang und Gegenstand des datenschutzrechtlichen Auskunftsanspruchs (June 15, 2021), margin no. 23.

61 *Gola*, "DS-GVO Art. 4 Begriffsbestimmungen" (2022), p. 6; *Weichert*, "Geodaten — datenschutzrechtliche Erfahrungen, Erwartungen und Empfehlungen" (June 1, 2009), p. 350.

62 Quoting the Art. 29 Working Party: *Haase*, "Datenschutzrechtliche Fragen des Personenbezugs" (2015), pp. 241 sqq.

would be a direct relationship of content and natural person. In their view, where the data formally corresponds to something else, it can indirectly still satisfy the content element.[63] The example they give is that a statement about the value of a house formally only relates to the house, but indirectly also relates to the owners of the house.[64] Others state that information "indirectly" relates where it does not contain direct information about a person, but allows for deriving such information.[65] For similar reasons as given in detail below in a corollary case[66], however, this distinction is merely academic, does not provide any additional legal clarity, and is even less granular or useful than the broad three-element definition.

Others have criticized the Art. 29 Working Party's explanation of the "purpose" element in particular, as it may lead to uncertainty in practice if the possible *future* use of data can determine its status.[67] Nonetheless, as the Art. 29 Working Party argues, the purpose element requires current use of the data in that way or a likelihood that the data will be used in that way.[68] I will agree that this can lead to uncertainty in practice, yet it puts a bound on the future uses of the data, by requiring a prognosis at the time of processing.

Some authors have criticized the three-element definition for adding little clarity.[69] Another criticism has been that the criteria are difficult to distinguish, with many types of (personal) data satisfying multiple elements at the same time.[70] Finding a clear boundary between the purpose and result elements in particular is difficult. As the Art. 29 Working Party's taxi driver example shows, the system may very well also have been set up to find out about drivers' performance, which would have meant that the purpose element applied instead of the result element. However, finding a clear distinction is seldom necessary. The Art. 29 Working Party itself notes that information can "relate" to persons using multiple "elements" at the same time, and even to different persons using different elements.[71] Despite this, distinguishing these criteria would never be relevant in practice, as they are cumulative.

---

63 *Klabunde* and *Horváth*, "DS-GVO Art. 4 Begriffsbestimmungen" (2024), margin no. 10.

64 Ibid., margin no. 10.

65 *Spindler* and *Dalby*, "DS-GVO Art. 4 Begriffsbestimmungen" (2019), margin no. 6.

66 See p. 83.

67 *Altman, Cohen, Falzon*, et al., "A Principled Approach to Defining Anonymization As Applied to EU Data Protection Law" (May 9, 2022), p. 13.

68 *Article 29 Data Protection Working Party*, "01248/07/EN WP 136" (2007), p. 10.

69 *Pahlen-Brandt*, "Datenschutz braucht scharfe Instrumente Beitrag zur Diskussion um „personenbezogene Daten“" (Jan. 2008), pp. 35 sq.

70 *Haase*, "Datenschutzrechtliche Fragen des Personenbezugs" (2015), p. 256.

71 "The same information may relate to individual Titius because of the 'content' element (the data is clearly <u>about</u> Titius), AND to Gaius because of the 'purpose' element (it will be used <u>in order to</u> treat Gaius in a certain way) AND to Sempronius because of the 'result' element (it is likely to have

On the whole, I do not know of a case in which this—very broad—definition leads to concrete issues.

In summary, to preserve the rights of natural persons with regard to the processing of their personal data under the CFR, a broad definition of "relation" should be favored. The current "three-element" definition by the Art. 29 Working Party and the ECJ is a viable solution that achieves this goal.

II. Non-Personal Data

With this very broad interpretation of "relation", one could be forgiven for thinking there is no such thing as a non-personal piece of information. After all, as humans inhabit the earth, they have shaped every aspect of it—and thus are related to it, either through content, purpose, or result. With the advent of so-called big data applications, some have argued that anonymous data can no longer exist.[72] They argue that all data may be connected and cross-referenced in such a way that it can be traced back to a natural person.

It can, however, be shown that this boundless interpretation is not intended by the EU legislator and, indeed, would be counterproductive. Object-related Data[73] is free of relation to natural persons. For aggregate data, things are not quite as clear-cut.

1. Object-Related Data

The salient point to determine whether something "relates to" a person is whether the data is about a person and not about an object. Some use the criterion "information"[74] to demarcate non-personal data, *i.e.*, data about things and other "processes of the exterior"[75].[76] However, this is not convincing. In reality, this data is very well "information", it just lacks "relation" to a natural person. The question of whether

---

an impact on the rights and interests of Sempronius)", *Article 29 Data Protection Working Party*, "01248/07/EN WP 136" (2007), pp. 11 sq. (underlining from the original).

72 *Boehme-Neßler*, "Das Ende der Anonymität" (July 2016), p. 422; *Sarunski*, "Big Data – Ende der Anonymität?" (July 1, 2016), p. 427; seemingly agreeing: *Kneuper*, "Anonymisierte Daten brauchen keinen Datenschutz – wirklich nicht?" (2022), p. 163; similar: *Jäger* et al., "Jäger/Meier/Möhring/Ferroli/Nida-Rümelin/Peters" (2024), p. 491; *Hüger*, "Hüger" (2024), p. 270.

73 In the German terminology: "Sachdaten".

74 See p. 21.

75 *Dammann*, "BDSG 2003 § 3 Weitere Begriffsbestimmungen: Personenbezogene Daten" (2014), margin no. 57.

76 *Krügel*, "Das personenbezogene Datum nach der DS-GVO" (2017), p. 457.

data contains information about persons *at all* is a criterion of personal data. Data that does not contain information about persons is "in no way relevant to data protection"[77].[78]

Some have held the view that the latter category does not exist and all data is—or will eventually be—personal data. To support this view that "all data is personal data", *Boehme-Neßler* cites the German constitutional court case on the census[79]: "Due to automated data processing, 'insignificant' data does no longer exist."[80] However, in this decision, the German Constitutional Court (BVerfG) rather sought to contrast with the widely-held belief at the time that some ("insignificant") data *about persons* was not worthy of protection.[81] This view is convenient, as it foregoes the difficult task of demarcating personal and non-personal data. Yet, it is at odds with the existence of non-personal data. For example, the information that Mount Everest is 8,848 m high does not relate to a person. Even data about humans can be non-personal data, insofar as it relates to all humans equally, *e.g.*, "humans are mortal" is not personal data.[82]

Klar and *Kühling* appear to postulate that identifiability can be given even where data does not relate to a person.[83] However, this is doubtful: In the example they give ("Mount Everest is the highest mountain on earth."—with the background knowledge that a certain person scaled Mount Everest), the information about Mount Everest does not relate to any natural person. It could be argued that this information about Mount Everest can be used in conjunction with the knowledge that a certain person scaled it to treat this person differently. Or, to give a different example: The information that a certain neighborhood is a crime hotspot does not relate to a person.[84] Given the information that a person resides in that neighborhood, however, we can infer something about that person given both data in conjunction.[85] As a result, the case of data that does not relate to a person, but where a person is identifiable, is a logical impossibility.

77 (translation by the author) *Roßnagel* and *Scholz*, "Datenschutz durch Anonymität und Pseudonymität – Rechtsfolgen der Verwendung anonymer und pseudonymer Daten" (2000), p. 723.

78 Distinguish, however, information that is anonymous—it contains information relating to a person, but that person cannot be identified, ibid., p. 723.

79 Volkszählungsurteil (Dec. 15, 1983).

80 Ibid., 422 (translation by the author).

81 Similar: *Haase*, "Datenschutzrechtliche Fragen des Personenbezugs" (2015), p. 136.

82 Ibid., p. 136.

83 *Klar* and *Kühling*, "DS-GVO Art. 4 Nr. 1 personenbezogene Daten (inkl. betroffene Person)" (2024), margin no. 12.

84 It may be aggregate data, see p. 31.

85 See also an Austrian case in which a processor had access to data concerning social milieus: ÖVwGH, Ra 2023/04/0005 (May 17, 2024), p. 145.

Even though information may be "about" an object, it can nonetheless be "related" to a person. Some authors introduce the term "object-related personal data"[86] for this phenomenon.[87] In effect, however, this is a non-category: Even though data that is "about" an object may not satisfy the content element of the Art. 29 Working Party's definition, it is still personal data under the other elements of the definition. The distinction between personal data and object-related personal data is of no legal consequence and thus does not provide any additional legal clarity.

2. Aggregate Data

In the past, the German version of the Data Protection Directive, the Bundesdatenschutzgesetz as superseded by GDPR on 2018-05-25 (BDSG a.F.), used the wording "Einzelangabe" ("piece of information"[88]). As a result, the German discussion concentrated on single pieces of information as opposed to aggregate information.[89] With the GDPR, this distinction became obsolete.

Aggregation plays a crucial role in anonymization.[90] From a legal perspective, the GDPR expressly mentions aggregate data in Recital (162) s. 5, where it is stated that "… the result of processing for statistical purposes is not personal data, but aggregate data …". From this, one could argue that "aggregate" data is a distinct category for the EU legislator. However, even aggregate data can leak personal information. For example, even the sum of two person's data is, technically, an aggregate, but would not preserve privacy very well. Additionally, if, for example, a dataset of 32 patients contains information on their HIV status and the aggregate count of patients tested positive is 32, then we can infer easily that every single one of the patients in the dataset is HIV-positive. These intuitions can be formalized, and the principles of l-diversity and t-closeness[91] will better illustrate that aggregate data is not necessarily devoid of personal data.

As a result, aggregate data is not a separate category; and while aggregation *can* alleviate some privacy concerns, a lot of aggregate data is still personal data.

3. Other Types of Data

As a recurring theme in this dissertation is the heterogeneity of data structures, it is only fitting to apply the "element definition" to some less conventional types of data.

---

86 German: "Personenbezogenes Sachdatum" (translation by the author).

87 *Karg*, "Anonymität, Pseudonyme und Personenbezug revisited?" (Aug. 2015), p. 522.

88 (translation by the author).

89 See in detail *Haase*, "Datenschutzrechtliche Fragen des Personenbezugs" (2015), pp. 177 sqq.

90 See p. 134.

91 See p. 142.

Fig. 2.1: Schematic illustration of different types of data and their *perceived* "amount of anonymity".

For example, a recurring question is if pictures of someone's private living quarters constitute personal data. This is a regular point of contention in the context of video conferencing, especially during the COVID-19 Pandemic.[92] They contain information about how the person decorates their living space (even a plain white wall will say something about the person), so they satisfy the "content" element. As a result, even these photographs "relate" to a natural person.

III. Relevance in the Age of 'Big Data'

Some commentators have called for a new definition of personal data,[93] as "big data" enables the production of "data where someone is—without access to their personal data in the earlier sense of the term—categorized using predictive analytics into a group of persons the members of which are ascribed certain properties that could have adverse impacts for the natural person."[94]

I would argue that this is neither necessary nor useful. As a rebuttal, I would like to offer the following line of argumentation: Predictive Analytics means extrapolating something that happens in the future from something that happened in the past, often using AI.[95] Like any computation, these predictions require an input and produce an output. *Hoffmann-Riem*'s position appears to be that currently, the output of these computations are not "personal data" under GDPR, and that this situation needs to be rectified by changing the definition. Going by the definition of "relating to a natural person"[96] first put forward by the Art. 29 Working Party under the Data Protection Directive, classifying a person into a group of, say, non-creditworthy in-

92 See *e.g.*, *Heider*, "Videotelefonie im Homeoffice" (2021), p. 1154.

93 *Hoffmann-Riem*, "Verhaltenssteuerung durch Algorithmen – Eine Herausforderung für das Recht" (2017), p. 38.

94 (translation by the author) ibid., pp. 38 sq.

95 Alternatively, extrapolating something unknown from something known. In any case, it makes predictions using large amounts of data.

96 See p. 24.

dividuals would be a clear example of data that has an impact on a person's rights and interests. This would be a "result" element[97] in the Art. 29 Working Party's definition. Therefore, classifying a person into a certain group is certainly data that relates to this person. This person would also be identifiable, as we need identifiability to express their membership in the group in the first place.[98]

Additionally, I would like to challenge the assumption that predictive analytics can somehow classify a person without access to personal data. If the input of a predictive analytics method is empty, there is simply nothing to predict.[99] Any data *about the person* that could be used as an input for the method is, however, by definition, personal data.[100]

To conclude, the term personal data and its definition hold up well even in the face of "big data" applications.[101]

IV. Conclusion

In summary, a broad interpretation of "relating to" in the definition is sensible. The "three-element" definition first put forward by the Art. 29 Working Party and later endorsed by the ECJ is far from perfect, but adequately distinguishes non-personal data from information that relates to a natural person. As a result, it remains convincing.

---

97 *Article 29 Data Protection Working Party*, "01248/07/EN WP 136" (2007), p. 11.

98 It must be noted that *Hoffmann-Riem*'s hypothetical contains no information on this.

99 To restate: A person cannot be classified into a group on the basis of *nothing*.

100 Though *Schantz* agrees with *Hoffmann-Riem*, they note a similar result in *Schantz*, "C. Die unterschiedlichen Kodifikationen des Datenschutzrechts" (2017), margin no. 296—without a need for changing the definition.

101 As an aside, I would also argue that "big data" or "predictive analytics" do not yield categorically different results than earlier methods. Big data (see *Tigani*, "MotherDuck" (Feb. 7, 2023)), predictive analytics, ML, AI, and other terms usually mean nothing else but using data to reach insights—something that has been done for millennia: Actuaries have calculated life expectancies for centuries. Car insurers have charged higher premiums for young, male drivers than for middle-aged drivers with a long history of safe driving. Loan officers have used creditors' past behavior to calculate interest rates. The fundamental principle has stayed the same—only the accuracy of the results has improved with better methods, better data, and better technology. Thus, it is not surprising that law created for these "old" methods works well for "new" methods, too.

2.3 Identified or Identifiable

The naturally most contentious part of the definition of "personal data" is that of the "identified or identifiable" person. As the preceding criteria are broad[102] and vague[103], this part of the definition is typically the distinguishing criterion. It frequently determines whether a certain piece of information is personal data. Despite or perhaps even because of this importance, nearly everything about this criterion is contentious. It is also essential in understanding anonymization: As we will see, anonymization is nothing more than the removal of identifiability[104]. For this reason, it is a main focus of my analysis. Surprisingly, the pivotal term when defining "identified or identifiable"—the verb "(to) identify"—is not explained in the GDPR. Instead, the GDPR uses a circular definition for what is meant by "identifiable", noting in Art. 4 § 1:

> an identifiable natural person is one who can be identified, directly or indirectly, in particular by reference to an identifier such as a name, an identification number, location data, an online identifier or to one or more factors specific to the physical, physiological, genetic, mental, economic, cultural or social identity of that natural person;

As we can readily analyze, the definition of "identifiable natural person" under the GDPR is a person that can be (…) identified through an identifier. Yet, this tautology tells us nothing about the nature of this process.[105]

More clues can be found in Recital (26):

> To determine whether a natural person is identifiable, account should be taken of all the means reasonably likely to be used, such as singling out, either by the controller or by another person to identify the natural person directly or indirectly. To ascertain whether means are reasonably likely to be used to identify the natural person, account should be taken of all objective factors, such as the costs of and the amount of time required for identification, taking into consideration the available technology at the time of the processing and technological developments.

---

102 See p. 24.
103 See p. 21.
104 See p. 111.
105 *Conrad* and *Treeger*, "§ 34 Recht des Datenschutzes" (2019), margin no. 89; for a corollary case in the "Video Privacy Protection Act", see *Schwartz* and *Solove*, "The PII Problem" (2011), p. 1829.

While Recital (26) clarifies what to factor in when determining identifiability, it does not help in finding out what "identified", "identifiable", or "identification" actually means.[106]

I. Traditional Methods of Interpretation

However, taking these two pieces of text together, we can make a couple of high-level observations. The question of what "identified or identifiable" or even "identification" on its own *actually* means is surprisingly difficult to answer. Similarly surprising is the fact that the topic has stayed relatively obscure in legal literature.[107] This question is not answered in the GDPR, but rather, an "I know it when I see it" approach seems to be used.[108]

To aid with this difficulty, we can use the traditional canones of legal interpretation. It should be noted that EU law is interpreted in an autonomous manner and thus requires the use of canones that are specific to EU law.

To complicate things further, the GDPR is in effect in all 27 member states and translated into all 24 official languages. The Court of Justice of the European Union (CJEU) has held that all of these languages are "equally authentic" in EU law and that therefore any "interpretation of a provision of Community law ... involves a comparison of the different language versions".[109] Because EU law needs to be applied in a uniform and consistent manner, it should be interpreted on the basis of the real intentions of its authors and the aim pursued by them. These can be inferred in the light of the versions in the EU's official languages.[110] It is thus impermissible to view just one version in isolation.[111] However, terms akin to "identified or identifiable" can be found in the vast majority of the 24 languages.[112] As a result,

106 I will later cover the latter part of Recital (26) GDPR, namely the "means reasonably likely to be used" and the factors enumerated, in the section on anonymization, see p. 101.

107 *Purtova*, "From knowing by name to targeting" (Sept. 5, 2022), p. 163; *Davis*, "Facial Detection and Smart Billboards" (2020), p. 375; for an early attempt at a definition, see *Leenes*, "Do They Know Me? Deconstructing Identifiability" (2007), pp. 138 sqq.

108 For the origin of the phrase, see Jacobellis v. Ohio (Mar. 26, 1963).

109 CILFIT (Oct. 6, 1982), para. 18; *Rafał Mańko*, "Briefing: Legal Aspects of EU Multilingualism" (Jan. 2017), p. 7.

110 Conféderation Paysanne (Oct. 3, 2013), para. 21; Internetportal und Marketing (June 3, 2010), para. 35.

111 Alter Channel (June 9, 2011), para. 23.

112 16 languages (including English) involve some word that is obviously derived from the same root—presumably the Latin "identificare": "identificada o identificable" in Spanish, "identifikované nebo identifikovatelné" in Czech, "identificeret eller identificerbar" in Danish, "identifizierte oder

there is little cause to be concerned that a plain-language evaluation of these (English) terms could yield results that are different from those in other member states. Of course, there may be nuance in the interpretation of these words in each of the enumerated 24 languages, and there could be subtle differences that only native speakers of these languages can appreciate. However, with the overwhelming majority of languages being etymologically close to "identified or identifiable", I feel that it is adequate to base my examination around the English version of the text interspersed with references to the German version.[113]

1. Grammatical Interpretation of "identified or identifiable"

First, we can take a grammatical view and interpret the plain language of the GDPR.[114] The words used in the GDPR, "identified or identifiable", stem from the

---

identifizierbare" in German, "identifiée ou identifiable" in French, "identificata o identificabile" in Italian, "identificētu vai identificējamu" in Latvian, "identifikata jew identifikabbli" in Maltese, "geïdentificeerde of identificeerbare" in Dutch, "zidentyfikowanych lub możliwych do zidentyfikowania" in Polish, "identificada ou identificável" in Portugese, "identificată sau identificabilă" in Romanian, "identifikovanej alebo identifikovateľnej" in Slovak, and "identifierad eller identifierbar" in Swedish. The romanization of the Bulgarian text "identifitsirano ili mozhe da bŭde identifitsirano" (romanization performed by Google Translate) also stems from the same root.

On the other hand, in six languages, namely Estonian "tuvastatud või tuvastatavat", the romanization of the Greek text "taftopoiiméno í taftopoiísimo", Gaelic "sainaitheanta nó in-sainaitheanta", Hungarian "azonosított vagy azonosítható", Finnish "tunnistettua tai tunnistettavissa", and Slovenian "določenim ali določljivim", the words hail from a different etymological root, but can be translated to have a very similar meaning to "identified or identifiable" (all translation and romanization by Google Translate).

The Croatian text "čiji je identitet utvrđen ili se može utvrditi" is interesting as it can be literally translated to "whose identity is determined or can be determined" (translation by Google Translate)—introducing the concept of "identity" into consideration. The same can be found in the Lithuanian text "kurio asmens tapatybė yra nustatyta arba gali būti nustatyta", which can be translated to "whose identity is or can be determined" (translations by Google Translate).

Note also that *Davis* performs a similar analysis (in which he also consulted with native speakers) but comes to a different conclusion, citing Slovenian as the sole "odd one out", without considering Bulgarian, Estonian, Greek, Irish, Latvian, Lithuanian, Hungarian, or Polish (and having similar qualms regarding the Croatian version), see Note 100: *Davis*, "Facial Detection and Smart Billboards" (2020), p. 375.

113 Not entirely coincidentally, these are also the only two of these languages of which I have enough of a command to examine them in detail. Nonetheless, I will assume that a similar result would be reached by examining either of the other 15 language versions that trace their lineage back to the Latin "identificare", see p. 35 fn. 112.

114 The basis of any interpretation of a legal text, especially in the EU: *Riesenhuber*, "§ 7: Die Auslegung und Fortbildung des Primärrechts" (May 25, 2021), p. 190.

verb "(to) identify", the corresponding noun is "identification".[115] The verb "(to) identify" is commonly used in everyday language. It can take on multiple meanings.

I can distinguish five grammatical contexts salient for our discussion[116] in which the verb "(to) identify" can be used: First, in the sense of a person (the subject) identifying someone or something. Second, in the sense of something identifying someone or something else. Third, in the sense of someone identifying *as* something. Fourth, in the sense that you (the subject) identify *yourself* to someone. Fifth, in the sense that you (the subject) identify something *with* someone or something.

The first sense is surely the most useful for our analysis, as it appears to be the best fit with an intuitive understanding of "identification" in the GDPR sense of the term. However, it should be noted that in the GDPR, "identified" is a participle and "identifiable" is an adjective, which thus can be interpreted more openly than just in this one sense. Moreover, looking at all senses of the word can help us better contour the term.

To simplify, I will focus only on the senses where a *person* is being identified, even though the meaning of the word "identification" frequently also extends to things. Consequently, I will only be referring to "identifying … someone", not "identifying … something"—even though that is oftentimes a part of the definition. As our discussion in the GDPR necessarily only involves data subjects and thus natural persons,[117] this simplification seems justified.

a) Identifying Someone

In the first context, a person (the grammatical subject) identifies another person (the grammatical object).

---

115 I will from here on use these terms interchangeably.

116 I will also briefly address those contexts and meanings which are irrelevant to our examination of "identification" in the GDPR sense.

117 For the natural–legal person difference in this context, see p. 88.

Identification is binary.[118] In other words: Either a person is identifiable or not.[119] The explanation of "identification" the Art. 29 Working Party delivers (being 'distinguished' from others in a group[120]) does not allow for a "half"-identification.

When we think of identification, it is as an activity: Someone identifies someone else.[121] This activity requires[122], at a minimum,[123] two people: For one, a subject—the person who identifies—for lack of a better term: the "identificator"[124],[125] as well as an object—the person who is identified—the "identifyee"[126].[127]

As *Bruegger* rightly notes, under the conception of the GDPR, data can be in the hands of a controller, processor, recipient, or third parties (Art. 4 §§ 7–10 GDPR), and all of these could perform identification.[128] Thus, the identificator is not necessar-

---

118 As is the entire concept of data relating to persons: Either information is personal data or it is not, see *Karg*, "DSGVO Art. 4 Nr. 1 Begriffsbestimmung „Personenbezogenes Datum“" (2025), margin no. 14.

119 An approach that seeks to make identification itself part of a proportionality has remained unconvincing, see for a full reasoning: *Mühlenbeck*, "Anonyme und pseudonyme Daten" (2023), pp. 69 sqq. There are, however, worthy points to be made for such a non-binary approach. As *Hintze* notes, this binary conception may incentivize controllers to not anonymize (*Hintze*, "Viewing the GDPR through a de-identification lens" (Feb. 1, 2018), p. 5), even though I will add that the far-reaching positive effects of pseudonymization mandated within the GDPR make this point less important.

120 *Article 29 Data Protection Working Party*, "01248/07/EN WP 136" (2007), p. 12.

121 *Bruegger*, "Towards a Better Understanding of Identification, Pseudonymization, and Anonymization (v 1.0)" (June 11, 2021), p. 23.

122 *Karg*, "Anonymität, Pseudonyme und Personenbezug revisited?" (Aug. 2015), p. 520.

123 For three-person constellations, see p. 102.

124 *Bruegger* uses "actor", *Bruegger*, "Towards a Better Understanding of Identification, Pseudonymization, and Anonymization (v 1.0)" (June 11, 2021), p. 23. As a matter of personal preference, I consider "actor" to be lacking the specificity that the grammatically more dubious "identificator" can provide.

125 It is an interesting, yet mostly philosophical, question if only natural persons can perform identification. I would argue that in the majority of cases, identification will be performed not by humans, but rather through a computer. However, making this distinction is of little *legal* consequence: Ultimately, there will always be a (natural or legal) person that has set up the computer to perform this task, *e.g.*, in an automated immigration gate at an international airport, this "identificator" would be the respective government.

126 Borrowing from Pfitzmann/Hansen's setting in *Pfitzmann* and M. *Hansen*, "A terminology for talking about privacy by data minimization: Anonymity, Unlinkability, Undetectability, Unobservability, Pseudonymity, and Identity Management" (Aug. 10, 2010), pp. 6 sq.; "Wiktionary: "identifyee"" (May 4, 2023).

127 We will revisit this thought in the discussion about relative and absolute theories of identifiability, see p. 102.

128 *Bruegger*, "Towards a Better Understanding of Identification, Pseudonymization, and Anonymization (v 1.0)" (June 11, 2021), p. 23.

ily the controller. The identifyee is usually the "data subject" that Art. 4 § 1 GDPR references. However, this is not always the case: For example, an identificator can wrongly identify a person that is not even within the dataset.[129] They could also identify an aliud, such as a legal person.[130] As a result, the identifyee is not necessarily always the "data subject" as in Art. 4 § 1 GDPR.[131] For this first context, a number of definitions for "identification" are given in different sources.

The first meaning is given as "if you can identify someone or something, you are able to recognize them or distinguish them from others."[132] [133] The definition of "(to) recognize" is given in the same dictionary as "if you recognize someone or something, you know what that person is or what that thing is".[134] Therefore, "recognizing something or someone" implies connecting something that is currently being experienced with past experience. Recognition requires prior knowledge of something that is recognized. Consequently, if you recognize a person, you already know them. By recognizing them, you can also determine that a certain person you are observing is in fact the same person you already know. Thus, recognition consists of two parts: Prior knowledge of a person to which to compare, and the capability of comparing (and equating) persons. I will call this sense of "identification" the *recognition* dimension of identification.[135]

129 To my mind, this is equally as or even more problematic as if they identified the "correct" person and thus should still fall under personal data and identification. As I see it, it is wholly unproblematic if the identificator "identifies" a non-existent person (and thus not a case of identification or personal data) Similar: Nacionalinis (Dec. 5, 2023), para. 59. For other contexts, there should be differentiation: For example, if a human name is generated randomly through an AI system that just so happens to be a name of a real person, I believe this should not fall under our definition of identification; while a (mistaken) identification of someone who is in the dataset or could conceivably be in the dataset should be a case of identification. This question is a promising avenue for further research.

130 Note that "identification" under the GDPR does not pre-suppose that only living natural persons can be identified—otherwise, the reference to "natural persons" and in other places, such as in Recital (14) GDPR, would be superfluous.

131 Apparently with a different opinion, see Figure 5 *Bruegger*, "Towards a Better Understanding of Identification, Pseudonymization, and Anonymization (v 1.0)" (June 11, 2021), p. 24.

132 "Collins: "Identify"" (2024), Meaning 1.

133 The examples given are: "There are a number of distinguishing characteristics by which you can identify a Hollywood epic", "I tried to identify her perfume", and "a uniformed chauffeur identified me among the crowd", ibid., Meaning 1.

134 "Recognize" (2024), Meaning 1, first alternative.

135 Amalgamating this dimension with the definition dimension (see below) to form part of a definition: *Haase, Martin*, "Rechtmäßigkeit der Benutzung personenbezogener Daten zum Trainieren künstlicher Intelligenz nach den Vorschriften der Datenschutz-Grundverordnung" (2023), p. 68; *Haase*, "Datenschutzrechtliche Fragen des Personenbezugs" (2015), p. 276.

The second meaning given—"distinguishing someone or something from others"—implies that an individual thing or person can be separated from someone or something else.[136] It means that the actor is able to tell (at least) two things or persons apart from each other.[137] There is some level of cognitive dissonance when discussing distinguishing natural persons—after all, humans are *individuals* and thus necessarily distinct and easily distinguished from one another in a face-to-face setting. Nonetheless, if we take a look at, say, a dataset of patient data, it becomes more difficult to distinguish records of blood samples by person. Nonetheless, even in face-to-face settings, persons can be distinguished in the sense of the definition. This will most commonly happen *within* a group of persons or objects, *e.g.*, in an example given in the dictionary: "a uniformed chauffeur identified me among the crowd".[138] Here, the chauffeur tells apart the group of people who they are not supposed to pick up from the person they *are* supposed to pick up. It also seems possible to use "distinguish" in the "recognition" sense of the word, *i.e.*, to distinguish a current experience from past experience. An example would be distinguishing a new visitor at a café from regulars. Saying that the new-comer had been "identified as a first-time visitor" necessarily means that they have been distinguished from every other "familiar face" in the eyes of the identifying party, *i.e.*, they are *not* recognized. This in itself is a piece of "identifying" information: If you can distinguish the "new" person from a group of people you already know, you have identified them *without* having recognized them. The act of distinguishing someone from someone else requires being able to point out their differences. A person may be distinguished from another, *e.g.*, by their outward appearance. This is the *distinction* dimension of identification.

A third meaning is given as "if you identify someone or something, you name them …".[139] Naming something or someone means attaching a name to a person. This is the classic semiotic relationship between a sign and the thing or person it represents.[140] Names are assigned, in the case of natural persons usually at birth. To be of significance, a name also needs to be communicated and known to the outside world—so it can address the person using the name. In essence, the name, the per-

136 "Recognize" (2024), Meaning 1, second alternative.

137 The same dictionary defines "(to) distinguish" as "if you can distinguish one thing from another or distinguish between two things, you can see or understand how they are different", "Distinguish" (Mar. 3, 2024), Meaning 1.

138 "Collins: "Identify"" (2024), Meaning 1.

139 Ibid., Meaning 2.

140 For more on the semiotic foundations of personal data, see also: *Augsberg* and *Buchheim*, "Von der Verarbeitung personenbezogener Daten zur personenbezogenen Datenverarbeitung" (Apr. 29, 2024), p. 369.

son, and the relationship tying the name and the person together need to be known to the identifying person in order for them to identify someone by name. For example, the name “Julius Caesar” represents a Roman emperor. This representation is contextual: Nearly any person in a European country would be able to associate the words “Julius Caesar” with Julius Caesar of Rome, whereas people in other parts of the world may not have the same association. The name itself is arbitrary, but the context in which it exists is meaningful: “Julius Caesar” identifies Julius Caesar because it was his given name (assignment)—and because his historical significance and notoriety has led to the name still being tied to the person today (knowledge). The knowledge that a Roman emperor existed by this name is learned in school or through cultural references. Naming a person—like recognition—requires prior knowledge of the name *and* the relationship between a person’s name and that person. In this aspect, naming is similar to recognition. I will call this aspect the *naming* dimension of identification.

A fourth meaning is defined as “if you identify someone or something, you … say who or what they are.”[141] This meaning is important, because in some instances, it is given as the *only* definition of “identification”.[142] It is also the most difficult to grasp. Stating “who someone is” can be as simple as naming them (see directly above) or can be a way of talking about a person’s qualities and personality. A person can be referenced not only through their name but also defined through their differentiating features. The colloquial “this is just who they are as a person” is a great example of this sense: It means that a person is defined by something, be it a mannerism, an intense enjoyment or hatred of a certain thing, or a personality trait. A definition in a different dictionary is given as “perceiving or stating the identity of someone”.[143] Composing this definition with that of “identity” in the same dictionary,[144] we can define the plain-language sense as “perceiving or stating the distinguishing character or personality of an individual”. Put simply, we can “identify” someone by finding their distinguishing characteristics—what makes them “unique”. I will call this aspect of the definition the *definition* dimension of identification.

Stating “what someone is” can mean classifying them into a certain group of people. For example, the examples given in the dictionary include “Police have already identified around 10 murder suspects”.[145] In this case, the police has appar-

141 “Collins: “Identify”” (2024), Meaning 2, second alternative.

142 *e.g.*, in “Britannica: “Identify”” (Feb. 22, 2024), Meanings 1–2; “Cambridge: “Identify”” (Feb. 21, 2024).

143 “Merriam-Webster: “Identifying”” (Apr. 11, 2023).

144 “the distinguishing character or personality of an individual”, “Definition of “Identity”” (May 4, 2023).

145 “Collins: “Identify”” (2024), Meaning 2, examples 1–3.

ently followed a number of leads and classified 10 of these potential suspects as possible perpetrators of the murder. I will call this aspect of the definition the *classification* dimension of identification.

Another definition is "to recognize someone or something and say or prove who or what that person or thing is".[146] Looking closely, we can see that this definition is merely a composition of the *recognition* and *naming* dimensions of identification.

Another common interpretation of "identification" would be to find out someone's name or using their ID card or passport to find out "who they are".[147] This is a composition of multiple dimensions, as a name allows for naming, distinction, and sometimes classification (in the case of family names).

In summary, in the first context, we can distinguish the recognition, distinction, naming, definition, and classification meanings of "identification".

b) Something Identifies Someone

A second context in which the verb "identify" can be used is where something identifies someone.[148] This is defined as "if a particular thing identifies someone or something, it makes them easy to recognize, by making them different in some way".[149] One example given is "his boots and purple beret identify him as commanding the Scottish Paratroops".[150] This example is a kind of classification as outlined above—the uniform tells the observer "what" the wearer is. Another example would be a name tag that allows anyone to observe the wearer's name. In essence, through the name tag, an observer is enabled to name the wearer, thus performing the naming dimension of identification.

Going from these two examples, it appears that this context is but a different lens through which we can view the first context and the meanings contained in it. It introduces no additional meaning that is relevant to our understanding of identification. Bear in mind that the act of identification in each dimension is still performed by a human. The thing itself—in our example, the boots and beret—do not perform identification, but they are instrumental to performing it. In other words, a certain piece of clothing or other indicator—a *thing*—enables identification by a human that would not be possible otherwise.

---

146 "Cambridge: "Identify"" (Feb. 21, 2024).

147 Similar, with reference to § 127 German Code of Criminal Procedure—"Strafprozessordnung" (StPO): *Karg*, "DSGVO Art. 4 Nr. 1 Begriffsbestimmung „Personenbezogenes Datum"" (2025), margin no. 49.

148 "Collins: "Identify"" (2024), Meaning 3.

149 Ibid., Meaning 4.

150 Ibid., Meaning 3, example 2.

c) Identifying *as* Someone or Something

A third context is identifying *as* someone or something. One of the examples is given as "You don't need to identify as LGBT in order to join us".[151] This example shows that "identifying as" is another facet of the "classification" dimension of identification. By saying that they identify as something, people want to express their belonging—the meaning is given as "if you identify as someone or something, you say that you are that kind of person or belong to that group".[152]

d) Identifying Oneself to Someone

A fourth context is where a person identifies themselves to someone else. This can be defined as "saying who you are".[153] An example would be to tell one's name to a police officer when asked.[154] In this example, the person offers up the information needed to tie a name to them. Commonly, using "identify" in this context also involves other types of "ID", such as a government ID card, a passport, or a driver's license. These forms of "ID" or identification are standardized, governmentally-sanctioned ways of offering information about oneself that allows for uniquely naming or defining a person. In summary, this context is a different lens on the *naming* or *definition* dimensions of identification.

e) Identifying Someone With Someone or Something

A fifth context is where someone is identified with something, which is defined as "to think of (someone) as being very closely associated with (something)".[155] Examples given include "She hates playing the types of women that audiences identify her with",[156] "she has always been identified with the civil rights movement",[157] and "the candidates all want to identify themselves with reform".[158] This is another example of the *classification* dimension of identification.

---

151 Ibid., Meaning 6, example 2.

152 Ibid., Meaning 6.

153 "Britannica: "Identify"" (Feb. 22, 2024), Meaning 3.

154 Ibid., Meaning 3, example.

155 "Britannica: "Identify"" (Feb. 22, 2024), Meaning 2, sub-meaning 2; Similar: "closely associated or involved in some way": "Collins: "Identify"" (2024), Meaning 7; Similar: "to believe that someone or something is closely connected or involved with something": "identify with someone" (Mar. 6, 2024), Meaning 2.

156 "Collins: "Identify"" (2024), Meaning 7, example 1.

157 "Britannica: "Identify"" (Feb. 22, 2024), Meaning 2, sub-meaning 2, example 1.

158 "Collins: "Identify"" (2024), Meaning 7, example 2.

f) Other Contexts

Another context is "identifying with someone", which is defined as "understanding them or their feelings and ideas".[159] A similar phenomenon is the concept of "identifying oneself with something", *e.g.*, an employer or a soccer club. These are different phenomena altogether and irrelevant to our analysis.[160]

Another meaning is that "if you identify something, you discover or notice its existence", giving as an example scientists that "claim to have identified natural substances with cancer-combating properties".[161] This meaning is also not related to "identifying" natural persons in the sense of the GDPR.

g) Summary

In summary, we can distinguish five dimensions in the grammatical interpretation of "identifiability": The *recognition* dimension, the *distinction* dimension, the *naming* dimension, the *definition* dimension, and the *classification* dimension.

Using these dimensions to interpret the GDPR, we can theorize that a person is identifiable once they can be recognized, distinguished, named, defined, or classified. Recognition is an easy criterion to apply: If a person can be reliably recognized in a dataset, they can be labeled as identifiable. Distinction is more difficult: It is questionable if it is sufficient to distinguish a person within a dataset for them to be identifiable. What if the dataset consisted of three records—two female, one male? In this case, the male person is "distinct" from all others within the dataset. At the same time, on the basis of being male, he would not be distinct within the general population (or any group of a larger size).[162] Using naming as a criterion means that a person is identifiable once their name is known. This is a certainly common understanding of identifiability, even though names are frequently impractical as unique handles[163] for humans—oftentimes, names are not unique and can change over a lifetime. Nonetheless, they are the most "natural" way of addressing humans and thus play an outsized role in theory and practice. Additionally, it stands to reason that a person is "identifiable" once they have been "defined" in the definition sense. Finally, a classification—like a distinction—requires a certain significance to be relevant for identification.

---

159 "Collins: "Identify"" (2024), Meaning 5.

160 *Haase*, "Datenschutzrechtliche Fragen des Personenbezugs" (2015), p. 277.

161 "Collins: "Identify"" (2024), Meaning 3.

162 I will further address this question in my examination of singling out, see p. 58.

163 A term advanced in *Bruegger*, "Towards a Better Understanding of Identification, Pseudonymization, and Anonymization (v 1.0)" (June 11, 2021).

2. Systematic Interpretation

Next, we can take a hybrid systematic and grammatical view, interpreting Art. 4 § 1 and Recital (26) GDPR themselves and other provisions in the GDPR. Systematically, it needs to be noted that "relating to a person"[164] is a necessary precursor to identification or identifiability.[165] If data does not relate to a person, this person cannot be identifiable.[166]

It is also notable that the GDPR distinguishes between scenarios in which a person is "identified" and those in which they are "identifiable".[167] [168] Additionally, a person can be identified directly or indirectly.[169] [170] However, neither of these distinctions result in any *legal* difference to the outcome, as there is no provision that mandates different treatment of direct or indirect identifiedness or identifiability. The verb used in Art. 4 § 1 GDPR is "(to) identify", and the noun "identification" is also used, as well as throughout the GDPR.[171]

We can also note that identification can happen, *i.a.*, by reference to an identifier or an identity-specific factor[172]. Apparently, however, identification can also occur in other ways.[173] Examples of identifiers are given in Art. 4 § 1 GDPR and include "a name, an identification number, location data, [or] an online identifier". The list is non-exhaustive[174] and also includes factors "specific to the … identity"

---

164 See p. 24.

165 *Urgessa*, "The Protective Capacity of the Criterion of Identifiability under EU Data Protection Law" (2016), p. 521 fn. 1 with further references (w.f.r.)

166 differing opinion: *Klar* and *Kühling*, "DS-GVO Art. 4 Nr. 1 personenbezogene Daten (inkl. betroffene Person)" (2024), see p. 30.

167 Art. 4 § 1 GDPR: "an identified or identifiable person"; Recital (26) s. 1, 5 GDPR: "identified or identifiable". The single other reference to this distinction can be found in Art. 4 § 5 GDPR on pseudonymization.

168 For a detailed critique of this distinction, see p. 83.

169 Art. 4 § 1 GDPR: "who can be identified, directly or indirectly,"; Recital (26) s. 3 GDPR: "to identify the natural person directly or indirectly." This distinction is only made in these provisions and nowhere else in the GDPR.

170 For a detailed critique of this distinction, see p. 83.

171 Namely in Recitals (26) s. 3, (51), (57), and (156), as well as in Artt. 4 § 1, 4 § 14, 5 § 1 (e), 11, 87, and 89 GDPR. Other references to "identification" exist, but here, they are used in a different sense of the word that is irrelevant to our discussion (*e.g.*, "identification of risk", Recital (77) s. 1 GDPR).

172 A term coined in *Bruegger*, "Towards a Better Understanding of Identification, Pseudonymization, and Anonymization (v 1.0)" (June 11, 2021), p. 9.

173 Note that it is unclear whether the GDPR gives additional examples of ways in which identification can be performed. There are good reasons to assume that "means to identify" is nothing other than "ways in which identification can be performed" and that thus singling out is a second example of "identification" in the sense of the GDPR, see p. 46.

174 "… such as, …"

of a person. This standard has broadly remained the same that was introduced in Art. 2 lit. (a) Data Protection Directive, where the list of examples was shorter.[175]

At the same time, the identity-specific factors are just characterized by category: Physical, physiological, genetic, mental, economic, cultural, or social identities (plural![176]) have factors that are specific to them and can lead to identification. While the physical, physiological, and genetic identities clearly require some kind of physical relation to the person, the mental, economic, cultural, and social identities are less clear. It would be reasonable to assume that an author's mental identity can be gleaned from a long text, such as a novel: The writing style and themes would be so idiosyncratic as to allow matching it to the author.[177] The terms "economic, cultural, and social" identities remain more hazy: An economic identity may be determined by a person's assets and liabilities, by their spending power or the nature of their asset composition. A cultural identity is more difficult to define, as cultures by and large require groups of people to be their members, thus creating an individual identity from it is difficult. Finally, a social identity is more easily defined, as stems from a persons relationships with other persons. Some of these identities—chiefly, the genetic identity—are immutable, while most of the others are more transient. Someone's cultural or social identity can change. As a result, to complicate things further, an identification needs to match a piece of data to a person's identity *at a given point in time.*

When identifying, one can use "means" to identify. These means are neither identifiers nor identity-specific factors, but rather a third category. Apparently, "means" are more procedural in nature. This can be seen by the only example given: One means is singling out.[178] Singling out is one means, but just an example ("such as"). The relationship between "means" and "singling out" is weaker than the relationship between "identification" and "reference to an identifier or identity-specific factor": The former is a "such as"-relationship, the latter is a "in particular by"-relationship. From this we can gather that singling out is just one

175 Notably, the GDPR introduced the following: "(is one who can be identified … by reference to) *an identifier* such as a *name, location data, an online identifier*, or to … factors specific to the … *genetic*, … identity *of that natural person. Emphasis* denotes additions in the GDPR.

176 Going from the text, it appears that a person can all categories of identity, but only one per category. Namely: I can have both a physical and a cultural identity, yet I can, apparently, only have one of these—as it is "the … identity" and not "*an* … identity of that natural person". However, this is grammatical hair-splitting and, when going beyond face value, it seems highly dubitable: Mental, cultural, and social identities especially change over time, and people may have multiple "distinct" identities at once. If we're being more correct, I would argue that it should be "an identity" in the legal text to reflect (and emphasize) the transience of the enumerated "identities".

177 See also authorship analysis and obfuscation, see p. 203.

178 See p. 58.

among many means, while "reference to an identifier or identity-specific factor" is the primary kind of identification. Going from this, it seems logical that "reference to an identifier or an identity-specific factor" is also a means to identification, just like singling out.

Some systematic doubts surrounding "identifiability" are cast on first glance by Art. 11 GDPR. This provision mandates that a controller need not maintain additional information that enables the identification of a data subject for the sole purpose of complying with the GDPR. If the controller is "not in a position to identify the data subject", Artt. 15–20 GDPR shall not apply, unless the data subject provides said data itself.[179] If read by the letter, this is paradoxical: If the controller is not able to identify the data subject (*i.e.*, the data subject is not *identifiable* (by the controller)), wouldn't that mean that it is not personal data in the first place? Art. 11 GDPR is commonly interpreted in a different way: A controller does not need to keep data around for the sole purpose of complying with the GDPR's provisions. Some even go as far as seeing a third category of data in that which concerns Art. 11 GDPR.[180] The thrust of Art. 11 GDPR is indeed a different one: It is concerned with the *authentication* of data subjects in case they want to exercise their GDPR rights. The word "identification" in Art. 11 § 2 GDPR is really an "authentication" (as the corollary Recital (57) s. 3 GDPR indirectly reveals when it speaks of "authentication mechanisms") and thus a red herring for our investigation. Art. 11 GDPR does not concern fully anonymized data, as this is beyond the scope of the GDPR.[181] Thus, the data it talks about is always personal data, where data subjects are "identifiable".

Additional information can be found in Recital (30) s. 2 GDPR, where it is noted that "[traces from online identifiers] … may be used to create profiles of the natural persons and identify them". From this we can gather that profiling is adjacent, but separate from identification. Additionally, it shows that online identifiers, an addition not present in the Data Protection Directive, are of special significance.[182]

179 Art. 11 § 2 s. 1 GDPR.

180 *Hu* et al., "Bridging policy, regulation and practice? A techno-legal analysis of three types of data in the GDPR" (2020), p. 4; *Hintze*, "Viewing the GDPR through a de-identification lens" (Feb. 1, 2018), p. 10.

181 M. *Hansen*, "DS-GVO Art. 11" (2025), margin no. 21.

182 For the IP address as the standard example of an online identifier see p. 105.

3. Historical Interpretation

Tracing the lineage of the requirement of "identifiability" in data privacy legislation, we find that under the Convention 108, the wording "identified or identifiable" was already part of the definition in 1981.[183]

The current implementation of Recital (26) and the definition of personal data can trace its direct lineage to the Data Protection Directive, where a very similar wording was used. Even though the language was similar, under the Data Protection Directive, the concept of identifiability was ambiguous, which translated into differing interpretations in member states.[184] Even for the text of the Data Protection Directive, *Poullet* and *Dinant* remarked: "[The Data Protection Directive's] concept of identity remains ambiguous and this ambiguity also remains tangible with regard to the way it was interpreted by various European countries …"[185]. The GDPR was created in part as a reaction to the "fragmentation in the implementation of data protection across the Union".[186] This difference in interpretation is an example of such fragmentation.

At this point, we can also trace the idea of a broad interpretation of identifiability. As *Poullet* and *Dinant* note:

> Without even enquiring about the "identity" of the individual—ie, his or her name and address—it is possible to categorise this person on the basis of socio-economic, psychological, philosophical or other criteria and attribute certain decisions to him or her since the individual's contact point (a computer) no longer necessarily requires the disclosure of his or her identity in the narrow sense. In other words, the possibility of identifying an individual no longer necessarily means the ability to find out his or her identity. The definition of personal data should reflect this fact.[187]

I would disagree on the issue: Even though the use of internet-enabled computers has certainly brought this issue to the forefront of the debate, it is dubitable that a different interpretation of personal data would have been warranted without them.[188] It seems that anonymous business processes—*e.g.*, using telephones, fax, or mail—were commonplace and required the same kind of safeguards. Nonetheless, this idea of a broad understanding of identifiability took hold.

---

183 *Council of Europe*, "Convention for the Protection of Individuals with regard to Automatic Processing of Personal Data" (1981), Art. 2 lit. a.

184 *Poullet* and *Dinant*, "Thoughts on Convention No. 108 for the purposes of the future work of the Consultative Committee (T-PD)" (Dec. 13, 2024), p. 32.

185 Ibid., p. 32.

186 Recital (9) s. 1 GDPR.

187 *Poullet* and *Dinant*, "Thoughts on Convention No. 108 for the purposes of the future work of the Consultative Committee (T-PD)" (Dec. 13, 2024), p. 33.

188 For a similar argument, see p. 33 fn. 101.

Between the Data Protection Directive and GDPR, the exact wording "identified or identifiable natural person"[189] has remained the same in the English version of the text, with differences in the German version[190] being purely down to differences in translation and not signifying any *legal* change.[191] Therefore, case law, scholarship, and positions taken under the Data Protection Directive, by and large, continue to be relevant under the GDPR.[192]

A comprehensive source of information about identifiability under the Data Protection Directive were two papers by the Art. 29 Working Party, namely the aforementioned WP 136 on the concept of personal data[193] and WP 216 on anonymization techniques[194]. As the successor to the Art. 29 Working Party, the EDPB, has not issued replacement guidance on the concept of personal data or anonymization techniques.[195] As the Data Protection Directive and the GDPR have large amounts of textual and legal overlap, the Art. 29 Working Party's papers continue to be persuasive for the GDPR. At the same time it should be noted that while the EDPB has officially endorsed a number of working papers by the Art. 29 Working Party, WP 136 on personal data is not among them.[196] The paper on anonymization techniques (WP 216) has suffered the same fate.[197]

4. Teleological Interpretation

As the GDPR states in Recital (75), we must evaluate the risks to the "rights and freedoms of natural persons, of varying likelihood and severity",[198] even when assessing whether data is identifiable and therefore "personal data" under the GDPR.[199]

---

189 Art. 4 § 1 GDPR and Art. 2 lit. (a) Data Protection Directive.

190 Where it used to say "bestimmt oder bestimmbar" under the Data Protection Directive and now says "identifiziert oder identifizierbar" under the GDPR.

191 *Ernst*, "DS-GVO Art. 4 Begriffsbestimmungen" (2021), margin no. 3; *Karg*, "DSGVO Art. 4 Nr. 1 Begriffsbestimmung „Personenbezogenes Datum“" (2025), margin no. 6; *Franzen*, "VO (EU) 2016/679 Art. 4 Begriffsbestimmungen" (2024), margin no. 2.

192 "the relevant provisions of [the GDPR] have essentially the same scope as that of the relevant provisions of [the Data Protection Directive], the Court's case-law on that directive is also applicable, in principle, to [the GDPR]", M.I.C.M. (June 17, 2021), para. 107; see also: *Karg*, "Anonymität, Pseudonyme und Personenbezug revisited?" (Aug. 2015), p. 521.

193 *Article 29 Data Protection Working Party*, "01248/07/EN WP 136" (2007).

194 *Article 29 Data Protection Working Party*, "0829/14/DE WP216" (2014).

195 Though the latter is, apparently, scheduled see p. 91 fn. 20.

196 *Purtova*, "From knowing by name to targeting" (Sept. 5, 2022), p. 137.

197 *European Data Protection Board*, "Endorsement 1/2018" (2018).

198 Recital (75) s. 1 GDPR.

199 Note that Recital (75) GDPR expressly only applies to "personal data processing".

From a teleological perspective, we can ask why the concept of "identification" is of such paramount importance in the GDPR. For this question, it is helpful to look at the potential harms that the GDPR wants to protect citizens from.[200] The basic right to the protection of personal data laid down in Art. 8 CFR is the focal point of these protections. As *Marsch* notes, the term "personal data" can be interpreted in such a way as to maximize the protection afforded by this basic right.[201] As we have lined out in the section on grammatical interpretation, we can distinguish the recognition, distinction, definition, naming, and classification dimensions of identification. Building on these dimensions, there are specific privacy harms that can be inflicted through violations.[202] The question concerning identifiability is which specific harms are enabled by identification in the senses outlined above?

The recognition dimension allows the person who identifies to extract patterns from recurring behavior, such as when a supermarket uses facial recognition software to track regular customers and their preferred shopping times. Understanding identification as distinction allows for different treatment of singular persons (literally: singling someone out for special treatment).

The naming dimension gives more food for thought: A common interpretation of "identification" is to find out someone's *civil identity*, *i.e.*, their name and other details that are typically printed on their ID cards.[203] Given this intuitive understanding, we must ask why the civil identity is of such importance and if there is a teleological reason for this significance. Especially names are commonly understood to be among the most sensitive types of data, even though they fail to be very good at distinguishing people[204] and are—in and of themselves—not suitable to create harm.[205] Explaining this fixation on names and the civil identity is a post-hoc rationalization. Nonetheless, I will submit as a theory that the missing piece of the puzzle is *persistence*. Persistence in this context means to retain certain information beyond the scope of one's memory. The GDPR especially is focused on persis-

---

200 See p. 8.

201 *Marsch*, "Das europäische Datenschutzgrundrecht" (2018), p. 146.

202 For a detailed typology, see p. 8 and see *Citron* and *Solove*, "Privacy Harms" (2022).

203 These details vary by country. For example, in Germany, there are a couple of "numbers" meant to uniquely identify a person, such as the passport number, ID card number ("Personalausweisnummer"), or the tax ID number ("Steuer-ID"). At the same time, in the United States of America (U.S.), the Social Security Number (SSN) plays an outsized role in practice and needs to be kept completely secure and private.The national identification number gains special prominence within the GDPR in Art. 87 GDPR.

204 With many first and last names being "common".

205 For example, if one knows a person's address, one can visit this address. If one knows a person's phone number, one can call them. Knowing the name alone without any further information affords none of these possibilities.

tence: Its scope according to Art. 2 § 1 GDPR contains automated processing and (some) non-automated processing of personal data. Automated processing necessitates some sort of storage, and thereby some sort of persistence.[206] Non-automated processing is only covered by the GDPR where it is "[(intended to be)] part of a filing system" (Art. 2 § 1 GDPR). This filing system is defined in Art. 4 § 6 GDPR as "any structured set of personal data which are accessible according to specific criteria …".[207] In other words, the GDPR assigns significance to data being committed to storage as opposed to memory. This is sensible, as most of the harms that can occur due to breaches of data protection rely on this storage. Put simply: Data protection law becomes relevant where people can "write things down", and it is typically not relevant where they can simply observe the world.[208] Civil identities are a great example of something that can be "written down".[209] Someone's name is a stand-in for that person. However, there are more ways to write a reference to a person down in a way that could harm them other than noting someone's name. Exactly these should be covered by a definition of "identification" under GDPR.

"Definitions" of people are much more fuzzy, but can serve the same purpose. For example, defining someone as "chancellor of Germany between 2005–2021" can uniquely identify Angela Merkel. Like civil identities, they can be written down and enable nearly all of the same harms that civil identities do.

The classification dimension, on the other hand, goes in a different direction: It allows to categorize people. This is an area adjacent to the GDPR's handling of profiling. Here, additional harms, such as a wrongful categorization, can negatively impact data subjects' lives. These impacts are most commonly economical in nature.

---

206 This can be derived as follows: All types of automated processing require working memory. In the case of computers, this function is typically performed by Random-Access Memory (RAM). RAM is typically volatile, *i.e.*, the data is "deleted" once the module loses power. Nonetheless, "persistence" as I use it here is not at odds with the volatility of RAM. Rather, it is a question of perspective. Additionally, most typically, the inputs and outputs of automated processing are committed to a more persistent type of memory, such as non-volatile storage.

207 We can further look at Recital (15) GDPR, which states that these provisions are meant to prevent "creating a serious risk of circumvention". Interestingly, according to Recital(15) s. 3 GDPR, "Files … which are not structured according to specific criteria should not fall within the scope of this Regulation". In practice, however, this exception is of little significance, *Roßnagel*, "DSGVO Art. 2 Sachlicher Anwendungsbereich" (2025), margin no. 16.

208 This is also a result of the limitation to "data", which by definition involves "writing things down". The latter is relevant for secrecy, which is a separate category beyond the scope of this dissertation.

209 Or, more broadly: Committed to some kind of more or less persistent storage.

II. Evaluating Definitions of Identifiability: Standard

Having outlined the need for a definition of identifiability and some foundational interpretation of the relevant legal text, we need to establish how we can evaluate definitions. When we think about the "correct" definition of "identification" under EU law, we can evaluate the contenders on different criteria. Of course, a definition of "identifiable" should conform to traditional methods of interpretation—grammatical, systematic, historical, and teleological. These have been illuminated above.

However, there are additional concerns that are of importance here. To me, there exist three primary concerns that a definition needs to satisfy. First, we need to pay attention to the autonomous methods used to interpret EU law and thus pay special attention to the EU principle of *effet utile*. Second, I believe that a definition needs to be practically usable—either through simplicity or through operationalization. Third and finally, I want to find a definition that is logically stringent and consistent with the real-world process of identification. As I will show, some of the approaches put forward fail this test.

1. *Effet Utile*

As for the first concern, a recurring theme in the ECJ's interpretation of European laws is the notion of *effet utile*. *Effet utile* has two meanings. In the first sense of the term, it prohibits the functional negation of provisions of EU law.[210] Functional negation means that EU law must not be interpreted in such a way as to render it useless.[211] On the contrary, *effet utile* means that any provision needs to still have a baseline amount of efficacy. In the second sense of the term, *effet utile* means that provisions of EU law should also gain "full effect"[212], meaning that provisions shall be interpreted in such a way that their purpose can be reached.[213] This is a more specific version of the commonplace teleological method of interpretation.[214]

In other words, a provision needs to be interpreted in such a way that it delineates all cases that "should" be covered by it from those cases that "should not" be covered by it. It should create a good fit between that which we want to regulate and

210 *Tomasic*, "Effet utile" (2013), p. 14.
211 Ibid., p. 14.
212 Commission v. Grand Duchy of Luxembourg (July 2, 1996), para. 48; *Tomasic*, "Effet utile" (2013), pp. 16 sqq.
213 Most recently: "according to settled case-law, the interpretation of a provision of EU law requires that account be taken not only of its wording, but also of its context and the objectives and purpose pursued by the act of which it forms part", Pankki S (June 22, 2023), para. 38.
214 *Tomasic*, "Effet utile" (2013), p. 20.

that which falls under the definition.[215] What it is that should be regulated needs to be "interpreted on the basis of both the real intention of [the GDPR's authors] and the aim [they sought] to achieve"[216].

Luckily, these aims are available in EU law through Recitals and supplementary materials.[217] In the case of the GDPR, Recital (1) refers to the fundamental right to data protection and specifies that Art. 8 CFR and Art. 16 § 1 Treaty on the Functioning of the European Union (TFEU) provide that everyone has a right to the protection of data concerning them. Even though Art. 8 CFR provides for a right to data protection on the level of EU primary law, it is helpful to note that the Data Protection Directive predates the CFR and that the right to data protection was created "from" the Data Protection Directive, not the other way around.[218] As a result, trying to use Art. 8 CFR to illuminate the GDPR is largely circular, as the Data Protection Directive is the GDPR's direct predecessor and shares large portions of text with it. Using the lineage traced above—through the Data Protection Directive and the Convention 108—is closer to the actual genesis of most provisions in the GDPR.

If a definition is too narrow, it does not cover enough cases. In our case, this would mean that the GDPR is not applicable in cases where it "should" be in order to adequately protect EU citizens' basic rights. If a definition is too wide, it covers too many cases. In the case of "identifiability", this would mean that the GDPR could experience a boundless expansion of its applicability. One could argue that this is a good thing: The GDPR regulates data protection, and in the more circumstances citizens can benefit from its protections, the better. However, over-inclusivity means, for example, that the resources of authorities policing violations of the GDPR are spread even thinner. As a result, large violations of the GDPR can be drowned out in the noise of too many small violations that all demand the authorities' collective attentions.

More importantly, impeding and restricting nearly all flows of data goes against the concept of the GDPR and other EU legislation. The GDPR acknowledges the positive role that technology has had on everyday life, noting how it has transformed "the economy and social life" (Recital (6) s. 4 GDPR), also noting the importance of a "consistent and high level of protection of natural persons", while at the same time "[removing] the obstacles to flows of personal data within the Union" (Recital (10) s. 1 GDPR). Moreover, it is oft-forgotten that the GDPR does not want to curtail, but

215 Poetically, this is in many ways analogous to the design and training goal at the heart of many machine learning algorithms: Maximizing precision and recall (see p. 208).

216 Junk (Jan. 27, 2005), para. 33; *Riesenhuber*, *Pechstein*, and *Drechsler*, "§ 10: Die Auslegung" (May 25, 2021), pp. 291 sq.

217 *Riesenhuber*, *Pechstein*, and *Drechsler*, "§ 10: Die Auslegung" (May 25, 2021), p. 292.

218 *Kühling*, "GRC Art. 8 Schutz personenbezogener Daten" (2023), margin no. 2 sq.

"ensure the free flow of personal data between Member States" (Recital (3) GDPR), and notes that the "right to the protection of personal data is not an absolute right", but rather should be considered in relation to its function in society and be balanced against other fundamental rights" (Recital (4) s. 2 GDPR). In the eyes of the EU legislators, there exist vast swathes of non-personal data—hailing from, *i.a.*, the "expanding Internet of Things, artificial intelligence and machine learning" (Recital (9) s. 1 Regulation 2018/1807), with specific examples including "aggregate and anonymised datasets used for big data analytics".[219] In summary, the GDPR and other EU legislation acknowledge the existence of non-personal data, and the importance of the distinction, which means it is in accordance with *effet utile* to find definitions of "identifiability" that contour the term.

Thus, a definition needs to thread the needle between being under-inclusive, thus failing to protect citizens' rights from the CFR and the European Convention on Human Rights (Eur. Conv. Human Rights), and being over-inclusive, making enforcement nigh impossible and overly restricting the use and free flow of data within the Union.

2. Practicability

The second requirement by which I want to evaluate definitions of identifiability is by their practicability. In a highly technical field such as data protection, practicability can be achieved either through simplicity or through operationalization. Ideally, a standard laid down by a piece of legislation is simple enough that it can be applied by anyone. Where that is not possible, it can also be operationalized in such a way that anyone can use the process to arrive at a conclusion.

Simplicity means that a definition requires some kind of ease of use to be widely used and adhered to. Any definition contains an (implicit) model of the real world to which it will be applied. All models are—by definition—wrong[220]. They are a necessary simplification of the world. The degree to which this simplification is done is nothing more than a judgment call. A more complicated model may cover more of the desired use cases, while a simpler model may cover less of them. At the same time, when we think about how to apply the GDPR, it is necessary to consider the subject of a piece of legislation. The simpler a model is, the easier it is to use for citizens. Yet, a legal design that is more complicated does not necessarily mean that it is

219 "Regulation (EU) 2018/1807 of the European Parliament and of the Council of 14 November 2018 on a framework for the free flow of non-personal data in the European Union (Text with EEA relevance.)" (Nov. 14, 2018), Recital (9).

220 … though some are useful, *Box*, "Science and Statistics" (Dec. 1, 1976), p. 792.

more effective at reaching a certain policy goal.[221] Nonetheless, the relationship between complicatedness and achieving policy goals or "just" outcomes is oftentimes a continuous tradeoff. Trading off clarity for achieving policy goals could lead to greater compliance. Making understandable laws that are easy to apply can lead to greater acceptance in the population, which in turn leads to compliance even where enforcement is not possible. Simplicity is therefore an important consideration when defining parts of the GDPR.

Even where laws and definitions are not "simple" in the way laid out above, they can nonetheless be operationalized to enable compliance. In this context, I use "operationalization" to mean that the law provides for a set of operations that allows its "users" to interpret it despite its complexity.[222] This is especially salient in the case of the GDPR, as it often concerns data stored in computer systems.[223] Computer systems lend themselves to quickly performing complicated operations. Therefore—similar to the idea of Computational Law[224]—a law that allows for its application through a set of instructions that resemble a computer program is more "practical" in these applications than a heuristic standard that is designed to be used by a human, not as part of a computer program. An extreme example of a theoretical, highly complicated[225] definition would be to provide a neural network that determines whether or not a certain piece of data is "identifiable" or not. Theoretically, providing such a neural network could enable a better "fit" of regulation to policy goals than a set of rule-based questions. At the same time, it would be impossible to understand for any human.

In summary, a prospective solution needs to thread the needle between being overcomplicated and too simplistic.

3. Logical Stringency

Finally, I am looking for a solution that is logically stringent and is in accordance with the real-world process of identification. As I have outlined in the section on interpretation using traditional methods, identification is a multi-faceted phenomenon that deserves a coherent model in the legal realm. This model should also

221 *Ruhl* and D. M. *Katz*, "Measuring, Monitoring, and Managing Legal Complexity" (Feb. 17, 2015), p. 198.

222 In this regard, I am using the term "operational" in a broadly similar, but distinct way to Purtova in: *Purtova*, "From knowing by name to targeting" (Sept. 5, 2022), p. 167.

223 Or, to use Genesereth's formulation, it deals in "digitally mediated activity" *Genesereth*, "Computational Law: The Cop in the Backseat" (2015), p. 6.

224 Ibid., pp. 3 sqq.

225 Not "complex" as in the systems context that *Ruhl* and D. M. *Katz* describe, cf. *Ruhl* and D. M. *Katz*, "Measuring, Monitoring, and Managing Legal Complexity" (Feb. 17, 2015), p. 201.

simplify where needed and lend itself to easy and robust application. For lack of a better term, a solution should be stood on a dogmatically sound foundation and correspond with reality. As the threshold criterion determining the applicability of the GDPR, the definition of "identifiability" is of high significance. It is thus only fitting that we give this criterion the scientific attention it deserves.

III. Current Approaches, Evaluated

A number of approaches have been put forth over the years, the most important of which I will now explain and evaluate on the criteria set forth above.

1. The "Tautology" Approach

The first approach is to embrace the tautology put forth by the wording of Art. 4 § 1 and Recital (26) GDPR and accept that identification just means identifying natural persons through an identifier. The ECJ seems to take this approach.[226] Instead of going into detail on identification, the Court has ruled that certain types of information constitute personal data, without specifying the route to identifiability through this information.[227]

Other voices in the literature also refrain from defining "identification" further, which means they apparently see it as sufficiently defined.[228] However, refraining

226 Breyer (Oct. 19, 2016), paras. 42 sq.; Lindqvist (Nov. 6, 2003), para. 24; Scarlet Extended (Nov. 24, 2011), para. 51.

227 The Internet Protocol (IP) address and the ISP's information (M.I.C.M. (June 17, 2021), p. 110; Breyer (Oct. 19, 2016), paras. 45 sqq.); a "TC string" combined with "an identifier, such as, inter alia, the IP address … may make it possible to … actually identify the person" (IAB Europe (Mar. 7, 2024), paras. 44 sq.); names (see p. 57 fn. 232); worker time-tracking (Worten (May 30, 2013), para. 22); the image of a person "inasmuch as it makes it possible to identify the person"—without specifying this further (Buivids (Feb. 14, 2019), para. 31, first held in: Ryneš (Dec. 11, 2014), para. 22); "penalty points" per driver in a country, stored with reference to a national identification number (Penalty Points (June 22, 2021), paras. 59 sq.); VINs and other information relating to motor vehicles (Valsts ieņēmumu dienests (Feb. 24, 2022), paras. 33 sq.; and most recently, with more information on the route to identifiability: Gesamtverband Autoteile-Handel (Nov. 9, 2023), paras. 48 sqq.); name and address (Rijkeboer (May 7, 2009), para. 42); "the data relating to the applicant … such as the applicant's name, date of birth, nationality, gender, ethnicity, religion and language, are information relating to that natural person, who is identified in that minute *in particular* by his name, and must consequently be considered to be 'personal data' " (*highlighting* by the author)—*i.e.*, the other types of information may also contribute to identifiability (YS and others (July 17, 2014), para. 38); detailed personal information from a government register (Huber (Dec. 16, 2008), paras. 31, 43).

228 *Schild*, "DS-GVO Art. 4 Begriffsbestimmungen" (Feb. 1, 2025), margin nos. 14 sq.; *Spindler* and *Dalby*, "DS-GVO Art. 4 Begriffsbestimmungen" (2019), margin no. 7.

from defining identification is not a solution. As I have outlined above, identifiability contains multiple meanings, all of which also have some teleological bearing on the outcome. The "tautology" solution falls down in all aspects lined out above. Neither can it help realize *effet utile*, nor can it provide a simple or operationalizable definition, nor provide a logically stringent model of identification under the GDPR.

2. Finding Out Someone's Name

Finding out a name for a person in a dataset is not only a common layperson's definition of "identification",[229] The most straightforward way of "identifying" someone is by linking data to a real person, *e.g.*, through their name.[230] Most people would agree that a person can be identified through their name (it is even the prime example of an "identifier" in the GDPR[231]),[232] insofar as it is sufficiently unique[233]. Some call this establishing the "unique civil identity" of a person.[234]

However, it is vital to understand that the GDPR and the Data Protection Directive use a much broader interpretation of "identifiability". Under the Data Protection Directive, the ECJ established that "personal data" involved not only people's names or other identifiers, but also "information regarding their working conditions and hobbies".[235] Correspondingly, the Art. 29 Working Party established that "… identifying an individual no longer necessarily means the ability to find out his or her name."[236] This is commonly accepted nowadays.[237]

229 *Arning* and *Rothkegel*, "DS-GVO Art. 4 Begriffsbestimmungen" (2022), margin no. 24; *Klabunde* and *Horváth*, "DS-GVO Art. 4 Begriffsbestimmungen" (2024), margin no. 15; with additional requirements: *Schantz*, "C. Die unterschiedlichen Kodifikationen des Datenschutzrechts" (2017), margin no. 291; *Schild*, "DS-GVO Art. 4 Begriffsbestimmungen" (Feb. 1, 2025), margin no. 16.

230 *Schantz*, "C. Die unterschiedlichen Kodifikationen des Datenschutzrechts" (2017), margin no. 291; *Karg*, "DSGVO Art. 4 Nr. 1 Begriffsbestimmung „Personenbezogenes Datum"" (2025), margin no. 49.

231 "an identifiable natural person is one who can be identified … in particular by reference to an identifier such as a name …", Art. 4 § 1 GDPR.

232 See *e.g.*, Manni (Mar. 9, 2017), para. 34: "particulars concerning the identity of the persons referred to in Article 2(1)(d) and (j) of Directive 68/151" (in the text of the Directive, literally "particulars" surrounding officers and liquidators of a company)— *Pitruzella* takes this to mean that first and last name "constitute … 'personal data' [under the Data Protection Directive]."; *Pitruzella*, "Opinion on Case C-487/21 ("Österreichische Datenschutzbehörde and CRIF")" (Dec. 15, 2022), margin no. 36.

233 We will disregard for a second the implications of a name that is not unique.

234 *Davis*, "Facial Detection and Smart Billboards" (2020), p. 374.

235 Lindqvist (Nov. 6, 2003), para. 27.

236 *Article 29 Data Protection Working Party*, "01248/07/EN WP 136" (2007), p. 12.

237 *e.g.*, in: *Karg*, "DSGVO Art. 4 Nr. 1 Begriffsbestimmung „Personenbezogenes Datum"" (2025), margin no. 50; *Schild*, "DS-GVO Art. 4 Begriffsbestimmungen" (Feb. 1, 2025), margin no. 17; *Oostveen*,

This broadens the scope of "personal data" considerably. Neither the ECJ nor the Art. 29 Working Party provide a concise definition of identifiability.

3. Singling Out

In their 2007 opinion, the Art. 29 Working Party appears to consider singling out as the only way of identifying someone.[238] In any case, they appear to be very focused on the concept of singling out, as it appears as a recurring theme throughout the Opinion.[239] Some have also called for allowing for "singling out" as an *alternative* criterion to "identifiability".[240]

For example, the Art. 29 Working Party begins their examination of "identifiedness" by defining: "In general terms, a natural person can be considered as 'identified' when, within a group of persons, he or she is 'distinguished' from all other members of the group".[241] Conveniently, wording this in the passive voice makes it possible to forego specifying *who* distinguishes, as well as when and how this happens.[242] Subsequently, the Art. 29 Working Party keeps equating identification with singling someone out in an arbitrarily sized group.[243] Other voices in the literature have implicitly endorsed this approach, typically by using a wording that involves "sufficient individualization of a person".[244] Singling out can also be formulated as isolating data from a dataset that allows for the identification of a natural person.[245]

"Identifiability and the applicability of data protection to big data" (Nov. 2016), p. 305; *Conrad* and *Treeger*, "§ 34 Recht des Datenschutzes" (2019), margin no. 90.

238 As evidenced by the use of "*i.e.*" in "… to identify someone—*i.e.* to single someone out—…", *Article 29 Data Protection Working Party*, "01248/07/EN WP 136" (2007), p. 13.

239 Ibid., pp. 13–15.

240 *Haase*, "Datenschutzrechtliche Fragen des Personenbezugs" (2015), p. 267.

241 *Article 29 Data Protection Working Party*, "01248/07/EN WP 136" (2007), p. 12; similar regarding an early draft of the GDPR: *Costa* and *Poullet*, "Privacy and the regulation of 2012" (June 1, 2012), pp. 255 sq.

242 As I will argue later, this is precisely why the category of "identified" natural persons does not exist, see p. 83.

243 "… will be sufficient to identify someone—i.e. to single someone out—…" *Article 29 Data Protection Working Party*, "01248/07/EN WP 136" (2007), p. 13.

244 *Mühlenbeck*, "Anonyme und pseudonyme Daten" (2023), pp. 93 sq.; *Karg*, "DSGVO Art. 4 Nr. 1 Begriffsbestimmung „Personenbezogenes Datum"" (2025), p. 50; *European Union Agency for Fundamental Rights., Council of Europe (Strasbourg).*, and *European Court of Human Rights.*, "Handbook on European data protection law" (2014), p. 39; *Farinho*, "GDPR Art. 4 § 1: Personal Data" (2023), margin no. 19.

245 M. *Hansen*, "DSGVO Art. 4 Nr. 5 Begriffsbestimmung „Pseudonymisierung"" (2025), margin no. 51.

Oftentimes, there is a group of people *within which* a person can be isolated. This is called the *anonymity set* or identity set.[246]

Historically, including singling out in the definition of identifiability—especially as prominently as it is currently featured in Recital (26)—was the subject of controversy. This reference was included in the GDPR at the request of the Art. 29 Working Party, who lobbied for this inclusion by contending that "a natural person can be considered identifiable when, within a group of persons, they can be distinguished from others and consequently be treated differently".[247] *Stevens* argued that the inclusion of "singling out" in the GDPR is a different sense of the word than used previously and that this effectively broadens the scope of data protection law substantially.[248] *Zwenne* argued that adding singling out to the definition of personal data would disincentivize the use of privacy-enhancing technologies and the "privacy by design" principle.[249] Through the "extensive interpretation", as he calls it,[250] these technologies would no longer help with compliance cost, which is their justification in the first place.[251] *Zuiderveen Borgesius* gives five reasons for including singling out in the definition of identifiability and compares it to "name-only" identification[252]: First, teleologically—the harm and risks that stem from collecting large amounts of data that relates to natural persons can result even where it is unlikely that the data subject's name can be tied to the data.[253] For one, he argues with the potential harm that can come from data processing even where a person's name is unlikely to be matched to the data, especially noting chilling effects—people adapting their behavior when they know they are being tracked.[254] Second, names are only one among many identifiers and at the same time, not a

---

246 *Pfitzmann* and M. *Hansen*, "A terminology for talking about privacy by data minimization: Anonymity, Unlinkability, Undetectability, Unobservability, Pseudonymity, and Identity Management" (Aug. 10, 2010), p. 9.

247 *Article 29 Data Protection Working Party*, "Appendix: Core topics in the view of trilogue" (June 17, 2017), p. 5.

248 *Stevens*, "The Proposed Data Protection Regulation and Its Potential Impact on Social Sciences Research in the UK" (2015), p. 104.

249 *Zwenne*, "Over IP-adressen en persoonsgegevens, en het verschil tussen individualiseren en identificeren" (2011), p. 336.

250 (machine translated through Google Translate) ibid., p. 336.

251 Ibid., p. 336.

252 See p. 57.

253 *Zuiderveen Borgesius*, "Singling out people without knowing their names – Behavioural targeting, pseudonymous data, and the new Data Protection Regulation" (Apr. 2016), p. 31; similar: *Urgessa*, "The Protective Capacity of the Criterion of Identifiability under EU Data Protection Law" (2016), p. 522.

254 *Zuiderveen Borgesius*, "Singling out people without knowing their names – Behavioural targeting, pseudonymous data, and the new Data Protection Regulation" (Apr. 2016), p. 31.

very good identifier—as names may not be unique or don't work in the specific constraints of the application.[255] Additionally, he points out that—especially with behavioral targeting, the subject of his inquiry—data subjects lack control over the data collected about them,[256] even when this is exactly one of the purposes of the GDPR. He also points to the possibility of a data breach or inquiries by law enforcement agencies into the data.[257] Third, he points out that it should not matter *how* a person is identified, but rather *if*. The purpose of targeting advertising is to track individuals, be it through their name or through other means. The GDPR aims to protect individuals, thus it makes sense to apply it where individuals are concerned.[258] For the purposes of tracking, it is meaningless if the name is used or a different kind of identifier. As privacy legislation wants to protect fundamental rights, it makes sense to have it apply where information about natural persons is processed.[259] And fourth, he remarks that GDPR aims at a high level of protection, and using a broad definition of identifiability such as singling out is helpful to achieve that goal.[260] Fifth, *Zuiderveen Borgesius* remarks that re-identification is typically easy.[261]

Today, it seems that the notion of singling out has been universally accepted in legal scholarship, even though it is seldom employed or explained in-depth. Yet, it is not intuitive. For example, one could easily fall under the impression that a person is singled out just by virtue of their data differing from others, in other words, when their data is unique. Given a small number of datapoints, is isolating some datapoints that differ from other datapoints sufficient? It is not, because it always needs to come back to isolating a *person* in the data. This is done by finding criteria that *distinguish* one person's data from that of other persons. At the same time, this shows the *identity* (in the "sameness" meaning of the term)[262] of the person by pointing out a unifying combination of properties that all datapoints by a certain person share.

However, oftentimes, the task of monitoring if persons can be singled out in data often requires information that goes beyond the dataset itself. For example, in the example provided by the Art. 29 Working Party, it was shown for a pseudonymized

255 *Zuiderveen Borgesius*, "Singling out people without knowing their names – Behavioural targeting, pseudonymous data, and the new Data Protection Regulation" (Apr. 2016), pp. 33 sq.
256 Ibid., p. 32.
257 Ibid., p. 32.
258 Ibid., p. 34.
259 Ibid., p. 34.
260 Ibid., p. 35.
261 Ibid., p. 35.
262 See p. 75.

dataset of location data of 1.5 million people that 95% of the population could be singled out through just four location points.[263] To verify this assumption, the original data is needed.

Francis, Probst-Eide, Obrok, et al. formalized singling out as: "...when an analyst correctly makes a statement of the form 'There is exactly one [person in the dataset] that has these attributes.' "[264] In their example, the analyst may make a claim that only one person in the dataset is male, 48 years old with the last name "Ng". If this claim is correct, the analyst has singled out this person.[265] They also remark that these attributes do not need to be strictly personal: If the analyst should claim correctly that only a single individual had a certain geolocation at a certain time, this also results in singling out this person.[266] *Altman, Cohen, Nissim,* et al. even argue that not just simple statements should be considered when singling persons out (*e.g.*, age ≤ 50), but also more complicated statements can be used (*e.g.*, income $\leq \$5,000 \times$ age).[267]

To determine whether someone has *actually* been singled out requires access to the source dataset, *i.e.*, the non-anonymized data. This can be reasoned as follows: Looking at the anonymized data, it may seem possible to single a person out. This might be treacherous, as anonymization may use techniques such as randomization[268] that change values and thus "create" new possibilities for singling persons out. Actual singling out can only occur on the *source data, i.e.*, if an attacker correctly singles out a person from the non-anonymized data using *only* the anonymized data.[269]

Building on the mathematical definition first published by *Cohen* and *Nissim*, *Altman, Cohen, Nissim,* et al. defined the concept of *predicate singling out*, which is a subset of singling out. A *predicate* (by convention: *p*) is, simply put, a statement about information on natural persons.[270] An example of a predicate would be, for example, that a person's age is larger than 50. Given a predicate, records in a dataset can be said to *satisfy* the predicate if they match the conditions in the predicate (in the example above, all records in which a person is older than 50). If only the

---

263 *Article 29 Data Protection Working Party*, "0829/14/DE WP216" (2014), p. 23, referring to *de Montjoye* et al., "Unique in the Crowd" (Mar. 25, 2013).

264 *Francis, Probst-Eide, Obrok*, et al., "Diffix-Birch" (Aug. 21, 2019), p. 3.

265 Ibid., p. 3.

266 Ibid., p. 3.

267 *Altman, Cohen, Nissim*, et al., "What a Hybrid Legal-Technical Analysis Teaches Us about Privacy Regulation" (2021), p. 26.

268 See p. 143.

269 *Altman, Cohen, Nissim*, et al., "What a Hybrid Legal-Technical Analysis Teaches Us about Privacy Regulation" (2021), p. 30.

270 Ibid., p. 28.

records corresponding to one person in the dataset satisfy the predicate, that person is singled out. For example, in a student database, if the predicate is "the student's birthday is on February 14" and only one student was born on that day, that student is singled out.

However, *Altman, Cohen, Nissim*, et al. point out that singling out a person through this predicate is too easy to be a meaningful measure of anonymized datasets. Predicate singling out can be defined as any situation where an attacker can make a *predicate* that is sufficiently rare.

A dataset is susceptible to predicate singling out if an attacker can make a sufficiently rare predicate that isolates a natural person in the source data *by using his access to the anonymized data*. This last requirement is crucial: A privacy breach can only be regarded as a privacy breach if it occurred due to an actual release of data.[271] To find out whether this access to data can meaningfully affect an attacker's opportunity to de-anonymize, *Altman, Cohen, Nissim*, et al. use a hypothetical attacker that does not have access to the data as a comparison. As they note, "future regulatory guidance should incorporate these ideas—baseline, rarity, and probability—which are absent from the Working Party opinions ...".[272]

I take issue with using singling out as a full definition of identification, as it is both too broad and also inadequate to capture the true meaning of identification (as I see it). If we were to accept this definition as it is, it would depend on the arbitrary selection of the anonymity domain whether a person can be singled out.[273] Even when adding the sensible improvements by *Altman, Cohen, Nissim*, et al., this definition cannot fully capture identifiability under the GDPR.[274] Uniqueness of information on its own does not necessarily lead to identifiability.[275] There exist cases where even though no one has been singled out, knowledge can be inferred about people,[276] which can lead to naming and categorization. Thus, limiting our definition to singling out does not ensure *effet utile*, as it does not create a good fit be-

271 *Altman, Cohen, Nissim*, et al., "What a Hybrid Legal-Technical Analysis Teaches Us about Privacy Regulation" (2021), p. 32.

272 Ibid., p. 54.

273 As put by *Altman, Cohen, Falzon*, et al.: ... [we] have argued [in the past] that the [Art. 29 Working Party's] guidance understands singling out as the ability to 'isolate': to identify a set of attributes that distinguishes an individual from all other individuals in the data ... But singling out as isolation is an unworkable theory. It ignores a high inherent risk of isolation present in all data releases—even those that are unquestionably anonymous.", *Altman, Cohen, Falzon*, et al., "A Principled Approach to Defining Anonymization As Applied to EU Data Protection Law" (May 9, 2022), p. 5.

274 As *Altman, Cohen, Nissim*, et al. note, this is not their goal—they just want to define singling out.

275 *Haase*, "Datenschutzrechtliche Fragen des Personenbezugs" (2015), pp. 319 sq.

276 See p. 141.

tween the traditional interpretation of identification and the definition. Moreover, singling out as a concept is complex enough to warrant scientific articles on modeling it mathematically, which can be taken as enough of a sign that the definition is not practicable enough. Finally, it fails to capture linking, which is a large part of the common interpretation of identification.[277] As a result, singling out is insufficient as a definition of identification.

4. Singling Out, Linking, and Inference

This historical focus on singling out has remained,[278] however, in their 2014 Opinion[279], the Art. 29 Working Party contended that identification "not only means the possibility of retrieving a person's name and/or address, but also includes potential identifiability by singling out, linkability and inference."[280] They further note that eliminating singling out, linkability, and inference would be "robust against re-identification performed by the most likely and reasonable means the data controller and any third party may employ".[281]

To sum up, the Art. 29 Working Party asks that anonymization mechanisms provide three guarantees against harm from individuals: Singling out, linking, and inference.[282] As anonymization is nothing more than the removal of identifiability[283], it is warranted to examine how they relate to identification. Singling out has already been discussed above.[284] Linking refers to the notion of finding other data that corresponds with the source data. Inference allows for drawing conclusions from the data. Note that only the Art. 29 Working Party has outlined these three means for "potential identifiability". Viewing only the text of the GDPR, singling out is given as an example of a "means" in Recital (26), while the others are not mentioned. This leaves potential, *e.g.*, for the EDPB, to define other means for identifiability in the

277 For one example, see *Ohm*, "Broken Promises of Privacy" (2009–2010), p. 1725.

278 Singling out remains an oft-studied and -referenced way of identification, where detailed studies from the legal and technical arenas abound, see *e.g.*, *Nissim*, "Privacy" (June 20, 2021), *Altman, Cohen, Nissim*, et al., "What a Hybrid Legal-Technical Analysis Teaches Us about Privacy Regulation" (2021), *Zuiderveen Borgesius*, "Singling out people without knowing their names – Behavioural targeting, pseudonymous data, and the new Data Protection Regulation" (Apr. 2016), and *Cohen* and *Nissim*, "Towards formalizing the GDPR's notion of singling out" (Apr. 14, 2020).

279 *Article 29 Data Protection Working Party*, "0829/14/DE WP216" (2014).

280 Ibid., p. 10.

281 Ibid., p. 12.

282 Ibid., p. 14.

283 See p. 90.

284 See p. 58.

future.[285] Below, we will take a look at the remaining two and evaluate the literature.

a) Linkability

The second technique for identifiability named by the Art. 29 Working Party in their 2014 opinion is *linkability*,[286] defined there as "the ability to link, at least, two records concerning the same data subject or a group of data subjects (either in the same database or in two different databases)."[287]

Linking is the oldest and most straightforward approach to de-anonymization in a dataset: In a dataset that has been scrubbed[288] of immediately identifying information like names, other attributes will remain. These attributes can often be combined to form "unique combinations",[289] where individuals can be re-identified through a combination of properties. For example, using just a postal code and a date of birth, 97% of people in a sample database were uniquely identifiable.[290] As a result, if one has access to a second database that contains these same identifying properties, one can link the two to re-identify persons from the first database.

Most prominently, this was demonstrated by *Sweeney*'s re-identification attack on Massachusetts governor William Weld's medical data. Weld had authorized a state insurance provider to publish "anonymized" medical data. At the same time, Weld was publicly known to have been hospitalized, so he would certainly be contained in the data. This data did no longer include names or addresses, but other pieces of identifying information such as postal codes and birthdays allowed for a perfect match.[291] There exists an overlap between singling out and linkability, yet the concepts are distinct.[292] Other authors define that a person is identifiable where

---

285 This could happen in the upcoming guidelines for anonymization, see p. 91 fn. 20.

286 Both terms, "linkability" and "linking", exist and can be taken to mean different phenomena. In the context of this thesis, however, they are used interchangeably and are taken to mean the same phenomenon.

287 *Article 29 Data Protection Working Party*, "0829/14/DE WP216" (2014), p. 11.

288 *Ohm* proposes this terminology for "privacy-motivated data manipulation that connotes only effort, not success", *Ohm*, "Broken Promises of Privacy" (2009–2010), p. 1744.

289 So called in *Article 29 Data Protection Working Party*, "01248/07/EN WP 136" (2007), p. 13.

290 Note this is a study from 1997: *Sweeney*, "Weaving Technology and Policy Together to Maintain Confidentiality" (1997), p. 100.

291 The story of William Weld's re-identification is told in detail in the section on *k*-anonymity, see p. 138.

292 As the Art. 29 Working Party also notes: "If an attacker can establish … that two records are assigned to a same group of individuals but cannot single out individuals in this group, the technique provides resistance against 'singling out' but not against linkability", *Article 29 Data Protection Working Party*, "0829/14/DE WP216" (2014), p. 11.

"the information itself is not sufficient to match it with a person, but where this is possible by combining the information with other data."[293]

Linking is an example of an area where technological progress may enable new kinds of de-anonymization attacks. Especially in the case of LLMs, they may have learned about information that can be linked to de-anonymize natural persons.[294]

b) Inference

The third "risk" outlined in the Art. 29 Working Party's 2014 opinion is *inference*, which is defined as "the possibility to deduce, with significant probability, the value of an attribute from the values of a set of other attributes."[295] Like linkability, this risk is often seen as a means to re-identify under GDPR.[296] This criterion has been criticized as overly broad.[297] To be strict, a definition of inference should only include such instances where the inference is only possible due to the data subject's inclusion in the data.[298] Even making this—necessary—restriction, however, inference not only fails to capture the nature of identification but is wholly unrelated to it. It is a question worth asking if "inference" is a risk the GDPR seeks to protect from. While inference itself is a risk to *privacy*, it does not aid in recognizing, distinguishing, naming or defining a natural person.[299] [300]

The inclusion of inference is out of place, because being able to deduce relationships within data is a principal reason for analyzing data in the first place,

293 *Klar* and *Kühling*, "DS-GVO Art. 4 Nr. 1 personenbezogene Daten (inkl. betroffene Person)" (2024), margin no. 19 (translation by the author).

294 For example, as the technical report for GPT-4 notes: "The model can complete multiple basic tasks that may relate to personal and geographic information…For example, the model can associate a Rutgers University email address to a phone number with a New Jersey area code with high recall, and explain its reasoning as being through that route. By combining capabilities on these types of tasks, GPT-4 has the potential to be used to attempt to identify individuals when augmented with outside data.", *OpenAI*, "GPT-4 Technical Report" (Mar. 16, 2023), p. 13.

295 *Article 29 Data Protection Working Party*, "0829/14/DE WP216" (2014), p. 12.

296 *Mühlenbeck*, "Anonyme und pseudonyme Daten" (2023), p. 242.

297 "Taken at the extreme, the Working Party's definition of inference could be read to include inferences such as 'people who are over 50 years old are also over 40 years old' …", *Altman*, *Cohen*, *Falzon*, et al., "A Principled Approach to Defining Anonymization As Applied to EU Data Protection Law" (May 9, 2022), p. 21.

298 This is precisely the guarantee that differential privacy can provide, see p. 146.

299 See p. 39.

300 Even though a (weak) argument can be made that it may somewhat capture the "classification" dimension of identification.

but does not necessarily play a part in identification.[301] It is understandable in the context that *k*-Anonymity[302], a syntactic anonymization method explained in the Art. 29 Working Party's Opinion,[303] is prone to so-called homogeneity attacks[304], which are, in essence, attacks after which a person can deduce something about a person contained in a dataset. Nonetheless, *k*-anonymity can prevent identification.[305] Using this explanation, we can reframe "inference": The reason why inference as described by the Art. 29 Working Party is an issue in the example they give,[306] is because it is not really inference that is the problem here, but rather linking. This can be derived as follows: In the example given by the Art. 29 Working Party, harm is brought on a person because we can find out their postal code,[307] but only after we have matched prior knowledge about the person's medical condition, gender, and birth year to two records in the table. This is nothing else than linking outside knowledge with the table, the only difference being that linking does not result in a one-to-one match, but rather a match corresponding to two records. It should also be noted that neither this nor other examples of "inference" given by the Art. 29 Working Party satisfy their definition of inference given above.[308] Only in the section on swapping[309], an example of inference in the sense mentioned above is given—where they note that swapping may still allow for the extraction of values based on other values.[310] In conclusion, the element of "inference" introduced by the Art. 29 Working Party is misleading, as it does not serve to distinguish methods that allow identification and those that do not.

This notwithstanding, *once a person has been identified*, using the information to infer information about them may be undesirable from a data protection view-

301 I am of the opinion that some observers have it backwards when they note: "profiling and data analysis are less and less hindered by organizational or cryptographic measures, such as anonymization or pseudonymization" (*Reimer* and *Wegener*, "Pseudonym ... anonym ... privat?" (July 2016), p. 468). Data Protection serves to *enable* data analysis while preserving individual privacy, not prevent it. The GDPR's objective is to enable the free flow of data within the Union by providing a legal framework to make sure that individual rights are preserved.

302 See p. 138.

303 *Article 29 Data Protection Working Party*, "0829/14/DE WP216" (2014), p. 16.

304 See p. 141.

305 *Aggarwal* and *Yu*, "Privacy-Preserving Data Mining" (2008), p. 26.

306 A *k*-anonymized table contains multiple values for males born in 1964 that had heart attacks and their generalized ZIP codes all begin in "750", which means we can deduce that each individual resides in Paris, *Article 29 Data Protection Working Party*, "0829/14/DE WP216" (2014), p. 17.

307 Ibid., p. 17.

308 Ibid., pp. 12, 21.

309 Called "permutation" in the text, see p. 144.

310 *Article 29 Data Protection Working Party*, "0829/14/DE WP216" (2014), p. 14.

point. Inference is gaining information *about* a person, but not on the identity of the person. It is logically only possible *after* a person has been identified. While it is understandable that data protection scholars and policymakers want to protect from this harm, it is directly in conflict with the clear wording of the GDPR, which does not provide for making something personal data because it allows for inference.

It can be argued that inference allows to deduce more information which can then enable linking. For example, if a dataset does not include information about the sex of a patient, but contains that a patient had a disease such as prostate cancer, one can deduce the former with sufficient probability based on the latter.[311]

c) Summary

In summary, two of the three elements put forth by the Art. 29 Working Party can capture identification, but even these are complicated to apply and their relationship is unclear. All three criteria together provide for a very wide scope of identifiability and thus application for the GDPR, thus maximizing *effet utile*. The definition of singling out given by the Art. 29 Working Party[312] is difficult to understand or operationalize. The inclusion of inference in these three elements is out of place, as it does not relate to identification.[313] As a result, the typology put forward by the Art. 29 Working Party is, while hugely influential in practice, flawed with regard to its simplicity and the logical stringency provided (which is lessened by the inclusion of inference).

5. R-, L-, C-, S-, (and T-)Identification

Leenes created an early typology of identification, which was later expanded by *Purtova*.

The first of the types he defines is L-identifiability. In short, L-identifiability means *look-up identifiability* and describes any situation where data can be used to look up someone's civil identity[314] using a secondary source of data, such as a list of static IP addresses, a driver's license number registry, or a phone book.[315] He contrasts this with R-identifiability, which is about *recognition*: Here, the individual is identified through its actions, by presenting an "identifier, token or feature set

311 With more examples: *Bruegger*, "Towards a Better Understanding of Identification, Pseudonymization, and Anonymization (v 1.0)" (June 11, 2021), p. 21.

312 See p. 58.

313 See p. 65.

314 This being the line that *Leenes* draws: We need to end up with a *named* individual, *Leenes*, "Do They Know Me? Deconstructing Identifiability" (2007), p. 148.

315 Ibid., p. 148.

(*e.g.*description of physical appearance) [recognizable] by the recipient …"[316] For example, given a cloak room token, the individual will be *recognized* as the owner or authorized user of a said coat.[317] This rather contrived example pales in comparison to the target of the definition: the (internet) cookie.[318] A parallel can be drawn to *authentication* methods online: Users are typically authenticated through a username/password combination, a passkey,[319] or a bearer token.[320] All of these methods rely on "R-identifiability". A third category, C-identifiability, relies on *classification*. Persons are classified as belonging to one or more pre-existing categories, based on their interaction with a website.[321] [322] *Purtova* later expanded this typology with t-identifiability, which relates to the phenomenon of targeting.[323]

The typology developed by *Leenes* was far ahead of its time and added the valuable insight that identification is not a single activity but rather a multitude of distinct processes. Nonetheless, it is ultimately too specifically focused on on-line identifiers and the context of website transactions, which makes it unsuitable for wider application. This means it is neither a good fit for *effet utile* nor is its level of complexity acceptable in the context of the GDPR.

6. Handshake Identification

A separate phenomenon is where *Haase* references the concept of "handshake identification", in which a person can be identified through being physically in the same place as someone else.[324] This concept originated in a study written in 2004 for the United Kingdom (UK) Information Commissioner.[325] Handshake identification is not (thought to be) a distinct theory of identification, but rather a specific context in

316 *Leenes*, "Do They Know Me? Deconstructing Identifiability" (2007), p. 149.

317 Ibid., p. 149.

318 Ibid., p. 150.

319 For this new type of authentication, see *FIDO Alliance*, "Passkeys (Passkey Authentication)" (2024).

320 This is often used for Application Programming Interface (API) access. For more information, see *Jones* and *Hardt*, "The OAuth 2.0 Authorization Framework" (Oct. 2012).

321 *Leenes*, "Do They Know Me? Deconstructing Identifiability" (2007), p. 151.

322 *Leenes* also introduces a fourth category called *S-identifiability*, "session" identifiability. It relates to the technical instrument of Hypertext Transfer Protocol (HTTP) sessions, see ibid., pp. 152 sq. This category, however, is irrelevant to our enquiry.

323 *Purtova*, "From knowing by name to targeting" (Sept. 5, 2022), pp. 170 sqq.

324 *Haase*, "Datenschutzrechtliche Fragen des Personenbezugs" (2015), pp. 278 sq.

325 *Marsch*, "Das europäische Datenschutzgrundrecht" (2018), p. 127; introduced in Germany by *Dammann*, "BDSG 2003 § 3 Weitere Begriffsbestimmungen: Personenbezogene Daten" (2014), margin no. 22.

which a person can be said to be identified.[326] However, it is just a different way of looking at recognition—where a person can be recognized as long as they are within the field of view of the observer. It is thus not necessary to compare handshake identification with the other, full-fledged theories of identification.

7. *Bruegger*'s Definition

In a 2021 whitepaper on identification, anonymization, and pseudonymization authored at the Independent Center for Data Protection Schleswig-Holstein (ULD), *Bruegger* proposes a different terminology and model of identification under the GDPR.[327]

Bruegger's central insight is to re-define identification as an operation solely based on linking.[328] In his explanation, he uses the parallel terminology "unique handles" instead of "identifier" or "identity-specific factor" in order not to conflict with the terms in the GDPR. His definitions do not intend to completely capture them, but rather are optimized to be more clearly definable.[329]

He defines "unique handles" as "… an information element … with the purpose of referring to a single entity within a pre-defined set of possible entities. Every entity in the set has exactly one handle; the handles of two distinct entities of the set are always different".[330] This understanding relies on an idea that can be traced back to *Pfitzmann* and M. *Hansen*'s terminology, which is that of identifiability sets. The identifiability set is the "set of possible subjects",[331] within which an "attacker can sufficiently identify the subject".[332] Identity domains as defined by *Bruegger* are a related phenomenon,[333] defined as "… a context consisting of a group of eligibly entities … and an actor (called *domain owner*) who is responsible

326 The scenario of "smart billboards" discussed by *Davis* is very similar to "handshake identification", see in depth: *Davis*, "Facial Detection and Smart Billboards" (2020), pp. 371 sqq.

327 *Bruegger*, "Towards a Better Understanding of Identification, Pseudonymization, and Anonymization (v 1.0)" (June 11, 2021).

328 For an illustration, see Figure 5: *Bruegger*, "Towards a Better Understanding of Identification, Pseudonymization, and Anonymization (v 1.0)" (June 11, 2021), p. 24; a similar observation is also made in: *Hölzel*, "Differential Privacy and the GDPR" (2019), p. 9.

329 *Bruegger*, "Towards a Better Understanding of Identification, Pseudonymization, and Anonymization (v 1.0)" (June 11, 2021), p. 11.

330 Ibid., p. 11.

331 With regard to the converse concept of anonymity sets *Pfitzmann* and M. *Hansen*, "A terminology for talking about privacy by data minimization: Anonymity, Unlinkability, Undetectability, Unobservability, Pseudonymity, and Identity Management" (Aug. 10, 2010), p. 9.

332 Ibid., p. 30.

333 Note 49: *Bruegger*, "Towards a Better Understanding of Identification, Pseudonymization, and Anonymization (v 1.0)" (June 11, 2021), p. 27.

for issuing *unique handels* (*sic!*), and a procedure to determine the handle of a given entity … ".[334] Note that in *Bruegger*'s conception, the uniqueness of these handles is guaranteed as long as the handle is used within its identity domain. As soon as a handle is used outside of this domain, it becomes a "non-unique handle".[335] Meta-Information about datasets is important,[336] because it helps define the scope of the identifiability set.[337] For example, knowing the context that an identifiability set is set in rural India means that having blonde hair in this setting is highly identifying.[338]

Using this terminology, he defines "identified" as where a "data subject described by a *data* record is considered to be *identified* when a whole data record, a subset thereof, or data elements that are derived from it can be *linked* to a *unique handle* for persons used [a)] in a model of the world (i.e., knowledge) by a human actor, [b)] in a virtual model of the world (i.e., data) available to the actor, [c)] as address in some real-world interaction system accessible to the actor … ".[339] He then defines "identifiable" as follows: "A data subject described by a *data record* is considered to be *identifiable* if any actor exists at present or in the future who is able to identify (i.e., render identified) the data subject by using any realistically available additional information and linking methodology".[340]

He also highlights the important distinction between different kinds of linking: while some values can be linked deterministically, *i.e.*, where discrete[341] values are

334 *Bruegger*, "Towards a Better Understanding of Identification, Pseudonymization, and Anonymization (v 1.0)" (June 11, 2021), p. 12.

335 Defined as "… an originally unique handle that is used outside of its identity domain and is therefore no longer guaranteed to be unique" (ibid., p. 12). They can often act as quasi-identifiers, (ibid., p. 12) which he defines as "… composed of one or a combination of information elements that are unique for at least a significant number of persons contained in a data set" (ibid., p. 13).

336 Ibid., p. 8.

337 *Bruegger*, "Towards a Better Understanding of Identification, Pseudonymization, and Anonymization (v 1.0)" (June 11, 2021), p. 27; referencing *Pfitzmann* and M. *Hansen*, "A terminology for talking about privacy by data minimization: Anonymity, Unlinkability, Undetectability, Unobservability, Pseudonymity, and Identity Management" (Aug. 10, 2010), p. 30.

338 *Bruegger*, "Towards a Better Understanding of Identification, Pseudonymization, and Anonymization (v 1.0)" (June 11, 2021), p. 8.

339 (Alphabetical numbering inserted by the author), ibid., p. 25.

340 Ibid., p. 26.

341 A term borrowed from CS. Think of discrete values like integers, which are "stepped", in contrast to their antonym, continuous values, which range on a spectrum, like floating point numbers. See for a full definition ibid., p. 17.

compared for equality,[342] others can only be linked probabilistically, *i.e.*, through comparison for "similarity, proximity, or correlation"[343].

While I agree in large part with *Bruegger*'s assessment that identification is, at its core, just linking,[344] I find this definition too complicated for widespread use. Its strength, which lies in defining terms that are outside of the GDPR's terminology—such as "unique handle"—at the same time bounds its utility for defining terms from the GDPR.[345] Despite this, I would argue that basing our understanding of identification around *Bruegger*'s whitepaper indeed leads to the "better understanding" its title heralds. As such, the paper has had positive impact on the *effet utile* of the GDPR. It should also be said that what the concept lacks in simplicity, it makes up for in operationalization: It is very much focused on a technical understanding of identification and proposes concrete technical countermeasures to identification in the balance of the paper. To my personal preference, it also does not incorporate the phenomenon of singling out enough in its definition—a concept that has had significant influence in the GDPR arena.[346] Finally, I would argue that it also does not fully capture all elements of linking, namely heuristic linking, which is commonly done by humans.[347]

IV. Proposal for a Different Definition

I propose a simpler, more general approach, building on *Bruegger*'s definition. We can dissect and better define identification by breaking it down into its most elemental parts, consisting of just one atomic operation (comparison) that enables two more advanced operations (linking and singling out). This definition can later be used to find out how to make identification more difficult (and thereby anonymize).

1. Breaking Down Identification Into Its Elemental Part: Comparison

If we break down identification, it is based on just one fundamental atomic operation: Comparing two pieces of information and finding out if they relate to the

342 Ibid., p. 18.
343 Ibid., p. 18.
344 See p. 71.
345 *Bruegger* defines identifiers as "composed of one or several pieces of information that are suitable to identify a person" (ibid., p. 10). He then defines identity-specific factors as "potentially unique [combinations] of information elements that can indirectly identify a person" (ibid., p. 11).
346 See p. 58.
347 See p. 72.

same person.[348] [349] In other words, finding out, given two pieces of information: Is the person this information relates to identical? For example, given the information "Patient 24601 has a blood pressure of 121/76" and the information "Patient 24601's blood group is AB positive" from the same healthcare provider, we can determine that these two pieces of information relate to the same person: Patient 24601. In this instance, the patient number is a unique identifier[350] that allows us to determine that both pieces of information refer to the same patient.

This operation can be performed both deterministically and probabilistically.[351] Nonetheless, I would argue that defining comparison as being either deterministic or probabilistic lacks a human dimension. Humans can perform deterministic comparison (by comparing two values), but it is more typical of them to perform *heuristic* linking, which is a separate category. I would argue that humans cannot (easily) perform probabilistic comparison, as probabilities and mathematical measures of "similarity, proximity, or correlation"[352] do not lend themselves well to the ways humans compare information.

Heuristic comparison is the human feat of determining that two pieces of information relate to the same person. This can be done for the same reasons as with probabilistic comparison, yet it is a different process—usually without a sound, mathematical reasoning to back up a comparison, but rather a "feeling" that this information relates to the same person. For example, a visual comparison between two photos of a person made by a human *works* differently than having a computer compare these pictures. In this example, a computer vision algorithm may extract certain biometric features from each picture and match them using a probabilistic

---

348 As this is a definition of identification that is—for once—designed not to be tautological, it is neither required nor useful for the person in question to be "identified or identifiable".

349 *Bruegger* also notes that comparison is the basis for linking, see *Bruegger*, "Towards a Better Understanding of Identification, Pseudonymization, and Anonymization (v 1.0)" (June 11, 2021), pp. 16 sqq. See also a similar observation in: *Hölzel*, "Anonymisierungstechniken und das Datenschutzrecht" (Aug. 2018), p. 507 and *Hölzel*, "Differential Privacy and the GDPR" (2019), p. 9. *Hölzel*'s observation is similar to redefining the operation at the basis of linking and singling out as comparison (without using the latter term), by noting the "logical status of identity as relation", see ibid., pp. 9 sq. However, he does not go into detail on how to "terminate" this chain (see p. 79), simply noting that identification is complete when the "sameness of entities represented in *two* distinct sets of observations" is established (ibid., p. 9).

350 See p. 76.

351 As will be explained momentarily, this operation lies at the basis of linking. *Bruegger* therefore explains probabilistic and deterministic *linking* instead of the more general comparison posited here. The distinction holds nonetheless, see p. 70 or compare *Bruegger*, "Towards a Better Understanding of Identification, Pseudonymization, and Anonymization (v 1.0)" (June 11, 2021), pp. 16 sqq.

352 Ibid., p. 18.

approach, resulting in a confidence score. If the confidence score exceeds a certain threshold, the two pictures relate to the same person.[353] If a human were given the same task, they would solve the problem in an entirely different way. Just by looking at the picture—and usually even without comparing singular features, such as the nose, eyebrows, *etc.*—a human can arrive at the same conclusion as a computer vision algorithm.

While probabilistic and heuristic comparison are functionally similar, it is important to distinguish between them, as they have different failure modes. Staying with the example of comparing faces, persons who are viewed as "lookalikes" of other persons may be erroneously matched by humans, whereas a probabilistic biometric matching may be more exact and label them as distinct from one another. Conversely, a matching algorithm may be thrown off by other things, such as reflections or shadows in the source photograph. Depending on whether the comparison happens heuristically or probabilistically, these potentials for failure can compound over time, for example if the probabilistic model used for comparison exhibits bias, *e.g.*, on the basis of skin color.[354]

Comparison—be it deterministic, probabilistic, or heuristic—can trivially be found to lie at the basis of linking, yet it is distinct from it: Comparison happens on an information-to-information basis, while linking happens on entire datasets. In other words, linking is nothing more than a mass-comparison exercise. Given two datasets, we can iteratively compare the records of one with the other and find matching information.

Using this operation, we can also explain a second phenomenon in the realm of identification: Singling out can be explained as comparing all members of a group with one another and finding that one is unique in a certain regard.[355] This is a version of the distinction dimension of identification named above.[356] Other variations of our grammatical interpretation outlined above can also be viewed in this framework. The recognition dimension is the result of a successful comparison of current experience and memory of a person.[357]

Using these basic operations we can find all items that are identical and all that are unique in a dataset. Declaring two items to be identical remains true irrespec-

---

353 For a similar, biometric example, see: ibid., 19 sq. and Fig. 4.

354 For that matter, neither bias in general nor this specific kind of bias is limited to software performing probabilistic comparison, but can also befall humans performing heuristic comparison—depending on the application.

355 Noting the same phenomenon: *Hölzel*, "Differential Privacy and the GDPR" (2019), pp. 8 sq.

356 See p. 39.

357 See p. 39.

tive of how many things we look at.[358] Declaring one item to be unique, however, is always dependent on a reference set *within which* the thing is unique. We can only declare something unique within a set of other things that we have examined, but we cannot declare something to be unique unequivocally—as we cannot view the totality of things.[359] As a result, to qualify statements about uniqueness, we must always consider the reference set of things within which our subject is unique. For the claim that two things are the same, the reference set is irrelevant.

Oftentimes, identifiability is not black-and-white: Data may concern an identifiable person, but the (potential) identification cannot be performed without uncertainty. Especially in cases of linking, the data that is used for linking may be incomplete or contain errors. For example, the infamous linking attack on Governor Weld's data by Latanya Sweeney[360] may not have been possible without the additional publicity of his collapse on television in 1996, which led to an easier de-identification of the data.[361] At face value, the oft-repeated claim that 97% of humans can be re-identified using just the population register banks on the population register being accurate. This, however, is oftentimes not the case.[362] *Barth-Jones* calls this the "Myth of the Perfect Population Register".[363]

To give another example, in speaker identification using speech (sound) data, recognition is based on probabilistic models that operate on a confidence level rather than positively identifying natural persons.[364] In these cases, this data is personal data nonetheless.[365] The confidence level required is a question that needs to be determined in each case separately, as it depends on the consequences of the matching and thus on how critical the processing is to individual rights. This is a *legal* question, but at the same time one beyond the scope of this dissertation. In the following chapters, I will assume that the confidence level in linking is sufficient for the application, and not question it any further unless warranted.

---

358 Apparently holding a differing opinion, noting that it is "of central importance to define the candidate set… while assessing the identity of two elements", *Hölzel*, "Differential Privacy and the GDPR" (2019), p. 9.

359 A corollary of which can be stated as: "Absence of evidence does not mean evidence of absence".

360 See p. 138.

361 *Barth-Jones*, "The 'Re-Identification' of Governor William Weld's Medical Information" (2012), p. 3.

362 Ibid.

363 Ibid., p. 9.

364 *International Speech Communication Association (ISCA)*, "Comments: EDPB Guidelines 02/2021 on Virtual Voice Assistants" (2021), p. 2.

365 *Gola*, "DS-GVO Art. 4 Begriffsbestimmungen" (2022), p. 11.

2. Identifiers and Identity-Specific Factors

Having reframed the elements of identification as operations based on comparison, the question remains *on what* this comparison can occur. The information which is compared—for example, the face of a person in a heuristic comparison, "Patient 24601" or the Vehicle Identification Number (VIN) of a vehicle[366] in a deterministic comparison, or a fingerprint in a probabilistic comparison—is of great importance.

Looking at these examples, we can identify two themes: On the one hand, the use of unique identifiers (such as "Patient 24601" or, to a lesser extent, the VIN), and on the other, the use of facets of the identity of persons (such as their outward appearance). This understanding is clearly shared by the GDPR, as it specifies that identification can be performed "... by reference to an identifier ... or to ... factors specific to the ... identity" of a natural person (Art. 4 § 1 GDPR).

a) Identity-Specific Factors

Some have defined "identification" as "[perceiving or stating] the identity of someone" or "[ascertaining] the identity of (someone or something that is unfamiliar or unknown)".[367] This definition shifts attention towards the term "identity". Identity itself is a contested term. To better understand "identity", it is helpful to look at its etymology. The English word "identity" traces its roots to the Latin "identitas", which in turn can be traced back to the Latin "idem"—"the same". In other words, "identity" and "sameness" have the same meaning.[368] This is counterintuitive. After all, a first step at defining "identity" would be to state that it is its identity that makes something *unique*. However, this only seems like a contradiction. In reality, these are two sides of the same coin: Identity enables us to distinguish things that are *identical* (that share the same identity) and things that are different. To find that which is different, we must be able to tell that which is the same. What makes things (and persons) "different" are their *properties*.[369] The "identity" of something, then, is a set of its properties.[370] This way of defining "identity" is in line with the GDPR: In Art. 4 § 1 GDPR, it refers to "factors specific to the physical, physiological, genetic,

---

366 Gesamtverband Autoteile-Handel (Nov. 9, 2023), margin nos. 44 sqq.

367 "Merriam-Webster: "Identifying"" (Apr. 11, 2023).

368 *Noonan* and *Curtis*, "Identity" (2022).

369 "Either a thing has properties which no other has, and then one can distinguish it straight away from the others by a description and refer to it; or, on the other hand, there are several things which have the totality of their properties in common, and then it is quite impossible to point to any one of them.", *Wittgenstein*, "Tractatus Logico-Philosophicus" (1922), numbered item 2.02331.

370 Note that multiple things can share a common identity if their properties are identical. They can be equal ("das Gleiche" in German), while not being the same ("dasselbe" in German).

mental, economic, cultural or social identity of that natural person".[371] These factors are nothing more than properties of a natural person. For some of them, it is straightforward to compare and match on them, most notably, the genetic, physical, and physiological identity. There exist robust mechanisms for matching faces, fingerprints, and DNA that are commonly deployed everywhere, for example at an immigration desk when entering a country or when boarding a ski lift.

Comparing two mental, economic, cultural, or social identities is much less straightforward. Nonetheless, one can conjure up a situation in which this would be possible, for example, an online social network could be an (imperfect) representation of a person's social identity, and the social graph of two people could be compared. Similarly, the aforementioned methods for authorship attribution could enable us to compare two texts and find out if they were written by the same person, thus giving us a way to utilize the mental identity to match information. While it is important not to read too much into the tea leaves that are the wording of the GDPR, the enumeration of "identities" in Art. 4 § 1 GDPR is exhaustive (as seen by the lack of "such as", which clearly only relates to the identifiers), even though "reference to an identifier … or … factors specific to the … identity" is just one way of identifying a person. Nonetheless, the terms enumerated are themselves so broad that it is hard to imagine an aspect of a person's identity that would not fall under the enumerated categories.

Coming back to "identification", this means that to "identify" something using the identity-specific factors means perceiving or stating some of a person's properties from information in a way that allows for comparing them with and distinguishing them from a set of other information or finding them to be identical with other properties. These matches can be exact or probabilistic (as is usually the case with biometric matches[372]).

b) Identifiers

The second category of data on which matching can be performed are identifiers. In the technical discourse, a distinction is usually made between identifiers and quasi-identifiers.[373] Identifiers, in the sense in which the word is typically used, are either

---

371 For more on each category, see p. 46.

372 See in detail: *Bruegger*, "Towards a Better Understanding of Identification, Pseudonymization, and Anonymization (v 1.0)" (June 11, 2021), pp. 19 sq.

373 The latter term was first introduced in 1986: *Dalenius*, "Finding a Needle in a Haystack or Identifying Anonymous Census Records" (1986), p. 330.

"formal" identifiers such as names or addresses,[374] or "unique" identifiers such as a tax identification number[375].

Unique identifiers are only unique within a certain "identity domain"[376].[377] For tax identification numbers, this is typically within the entity that is collecting the tax, for national ID card numbers or social security numbers, this is typically within the country, and for some other identifiers, such as the researcher ID ORCID[378], they can be global. This uniqueness typically needs to be enforced by a "domain owner".[379] Cleverly, the technological standard for a so-called Universally Unique Identifier (UUID) enables the creation of 128-bit identifiers that can, for certain implementations, practically guarantee "uniqueness across space and time"[380] without the need of a domain owner or other centralized entity who would enforce uniqueness.[381] These UUIDs are, as a result, in widespread use in software applications today and thus should be mentioned here—both due to their ingenious design features and their ubiquity.

Formal identifiers as first defined by *Dalenius* are probably closer to an intuitive understanding of "identifier". Names, which are the most important identifiers in practice, are frequently not unique. While uncommon combinations of names can be globally unique, most typically, even a combination of name and surname will not be.[382] Addresses are also not unique, as multiple households can live at one address and multiple people can live in each household. It should be noted that names can be unique identifiers within a certain identity domain, yet they are almost never guaranteed to be unique.[383] As formal identifiers are not guaranteed to be unique (but often will be), their usefulness for comparison is dependent on the piece of information in question.

---

374 Ibid., p. 329.

375 This meaning is in line with the "unique handle" defined in: *Bruegger*, "Towards a Better Understanding of Identification, Pseudonymization, and Anonymization (v 1.0)" (June 11, 2021), p. 11.

376 See p. 69.

377 *Bruegger*, "Towards a Better Understanding of Identification, Pseudonymization, and Anonymization (v 1.0)" (June 11, 2021), p. 12.

378 https://orcid.org.

379 *Bruegger*, "Towards a Better Understanding of Identification, Pseudonymization, and Anonymization (v 1.0)" (June 11, 2021), p. 12.

380 *Leach*, *Salz*, and *Mealling*, "A Universally Unique IDentifier (UUID) URN Namespace" (July 2005), p. 1.

381 Ibid., p. 3.

382 *Bruegger*, "Towards a Better Understanding of Identification, Pseudonymization, and Anonymization (v 1.0)" (June 11, 2021), pp. 12 sq.

383 In the example given by *Bruegger*, even within a core family, sometimes names are shared and monikers such as "junior" must be used to distinguish, ibid., p. 11.

In the absence of unique identifiers, matching can oftentimes also be done on "unique combinations" of data. This operation requires two pieces of information and–in most cases–some knowledge about the outside world.[384] For example, a combination of gender, date of birth, and ZIP code was shown to be globally unique within the U.S. in 2000.[385] This is the phenomenon of "quasi-identifiers", in which a "set of data elements … in combination associates uniquely or almost uniquely to an entity and therefore can serve as a means of … recognizing … the subject of the data."[386] Some have argued that the ECJ itself endorsed considering combinations of identifiers in the definition of personal data in *Lindqvist*[387].[388] The Art. 29 Working Party also refers to quasi-identifiers, without using the term, when they regard someone as "'indirectly' identified or identifiable" when unique combinations allow for the information to be combined with other information which will "allow the individual to be distinguished from others"[389].[390]

It should be noted that the distinction between unique identifiers, formal identifiers, and quasi-identifiers does not result in a different legal outcome. Nonetheless, these three phenomena are different in practice, and they should all be considered when designing an anonymization mechanism. It can also be gathered from the definition in Art. 4 § 1 GDPR that the European legislator envisioned all three when drafting the GDPR: The first example given, the name, is a formal identifier. It can also be a unique identifier under the circumstances given above, but often will not be.[391] The second example, an "identification number", is a unique identifier. The third is "location data", which is possibly a reference to work by *de Montjoye* et al. and an example of quasi-identifiers.[392] The final example is an "online identifier". "Online identifiers" are more diverse in nature than just IP addresses, as Recital (30)

384 Bruegger calls this "meta-knowledge", *Bruegger*, "Towards a Better Understanding of Identification, Pseudonymization, and Anonymization (v 1.0)" (June 11, 2021), p. 8.

385 *Sweeney*, "Simple Demographics Often Identify People Uniquely" (2000), p. 16.

386 Informal definition, given in: ibid., p. 7.

387 Lindqvist (Nov. 6, 2003), para. 27.

388 Note 57: *Oostveen*, "Identifiability and the applicability of data protection to big data" (Nov. 2016), p. 305.

389 *Article 29 Data Protection Working Party*, "01248/07/EN WP 136" (2007), p. 13.

390 Here, again, the Art. 29 Working Party words things confusingly. If these "unique combinations" are actually unique, they should allow for distinguishing the individual from others—without the need for additional information.

391 See p. 77.

392 They found that in a dataset of cell phone carrier data, four datapoints of location data (with temporal information) are sufficient to identify 95% of persons uniquely (*de Montjoye* et al., "Unique in the Crowd" (Mar. 25, 2013)). Here, the four datapoints are in themselves a "unique combination" of places and times, which serve to distinguish a person uniquely and thus are a quasi-identifier.

s. 1 GDPR enumerates.[393] An earlier version of the Recital[394] included additional language that "… online identifiers … as such should not be considered as personal data if they do not identify an individual or make an individual identifiable."[395] We can note that the IP address in itself is not sufficient to identification, but rather enables identification.[396] Technically speaking, IP addresses can be unique identifiers, as they are enforced to be unique, but IPv4 addresses usually are not, as multiple people share an IP address using Network Address Translation (NAT).[397] In practice, they will therefore more often take the role of quasi-identifiers. This diversity in the nature of identifiers is also echoed in the ECJ's jurisdiction on identifiability.[398]

c) Distinction

As noted, the distinction between different types of identifiers enumerated above is difficult, but also not necessary in practice. Oftentimes, the distinction between identifiers and identity-specific factors will be equally blurry. It should be noted here that what is termed "identity-specific factors" above can be translated into identifiers and quasi-identifiers by capturing it in a structured manner (such as sequencing someone's DNA and comparing these values to one another, thereby creating a unique identifier in most cases). The distinction is therefore not required in order to differentiate legally between the two. At the same time, it adds value in practice, as it clarifies the types of identifiers the European legislator found most important and it also clarifies that identification in the sense of the GDPR is not just about "firm" identifiers such as identification numbers, but also more soft criteria such as the "mental identity", which can be compared using a written text.

3. Constructing the Linking Chain

Having established that linking and singling out are based on comparison, and that comparison happens on the basis of formal identifiers, unique identifiers, quasi-

---

This work was both high-profile and published in 2013, so it is possible and likely that it played into the inclusion of "location data" in Art. 4 § 1 GDPR.

393 Again, Recital (30) s. 1 uses a non-exhaustive list ("such as"), with the other examples being cookie identifiers and Radio Frequency Identification (RFID) tags.

394 Back then as Recital (24).

395 "Proposal for a Regulation of the European Parliament and of the Council on the protection of individuals with regard to the processing of personal data and on the free movement of such data (General Data Protection Regulation) - Preparation for Trilogue" (Nov. 27, 2015), p. 11; *Urgessa*, "The Protective Capacity of the Criterion of Identifiability under EU Data Protection Law" (2016), p. 526.

396 See also Recital (30) s. 2 GDPR.

397 For a detailed look at IP addresses, see p. 105.

398 See p. 56 fn. 227.

identifiers, and identity-specific factors, we now have all utensils required to define identification proper. Identification through linking and singling out is frequently a multi-step process. Using additional steps, we can at some point trace a piece of information back to a separate piece of information and agree that identification is complete. The glaring question in identification, then, is not how to construct a chain of linking and singling out (and which information held by whom can be used[399]), but rather where the chain *ends*. At which point has someone positively been identified?

To answer this question, consider a recent case in which the ECJ constructed such a chain. In this case, the question was answered whether a VIN can become personal data.[400] Reframing part of the question posed by the referring court,[401] it needs to be determined whether the VIN can be said to relate to an identifiable natural person. Nonetheless, it argues that identification means linking a real person to a piece of information.[402] This means the VIN needs to be "associated with a specific person".[403] Here, however, the ECJ holds, it is for the referring court to determine whether the identificators[404] are reasonably likely to have means to "link a VIN to an identified or identifiable natural person".[405] Nonetheless, as the ECJ argues, "the VIN must appear on the registration certificate for a vehicle, as must the name and address of the holder of that certificate … in addition, … a natural person may be designated in that certificate as [owner or person in possession of] the vehicle".[406] Ultimately, then, the ECJ apparently considers a combination of name and address as sufficient, as it does not go any further "down the chain".[407]

A common understanding of identification is that someone has been "identified" as soon as one can tie a name to some data. The dogmatic foundation for this type of identification is shaky, however. For example, in a set of medical records, a record would be "identified" in this understanding as soon as a name appears next to it. To my eyes, this is a conflation of names and persons—assuming that a person is "identified" through their name, when in a semiotic sense, a name is a sign that

399 See p. 102.
400 Gesamtverband Autoteile-Handel (Nov. 9, 2023).
401 Which also contained other questions on the GDPR not related to the definition of personal data: ibid., para. 24.
402 This meaning is implicit in: "the VIN … becomes personal as regards someone who reasonably has means enabling that datum to be associated with a specific person.", ibid., para. 46.
403 Ibid., para. 46.
404 See p. 38.
405 Gesamtverband Autoteile-Handel (Nov. 9, 2023), para. 49.
406 Ibid., para. 47.
407 Ibid., para. 47.

references an object (the person). Knowing a name does not, by itself, enable us to link a person and their name. From there on, it is still a multi-step process to *actually* linking a human to this name. We need additional information—namely, that a certain human goes by a certain name. One such link between a flesh-and-blood person and their name is a photo ID. Photo IDs would allow us to make a *visual comparison* between the person on the ID card and the physical person before us. Given the information "Titius[408] is the registered holder of the vehicle with the VIN ...", given that we are in the same room as Titius, given that he is showing us his photo ID, and given that we can link his photo to his person, we have—indubitably—identified Titius. To my eyes, this is a clear-cut case of identification (via an identity-specific factor—his outward appearance and thus physical identity). In the case where we can visually confirm that the human before us is the person to which the VIN relates, there can be little debate that this is sufficient for identification. However, it is also very unrealistic, because it requires a number of hypotheticals (that we are actually in a room with Titius, that he has a photo ID with him, that he produces it voluntarily, and that we can visually match his picture and his current appearance).

A person is therefore "identifiable" when an unbroken chain of links can be constructed that link the information available to us to the visual comparison. Other ways to link a person and their name would be if they volunteered their name, if they wore a name tag, or if we overheard someone else address them using their name. Even this identification via visual comparison may lead to a fallacious identification in the case of a lookalike or identical twins. Leaving these difficulties aside for a minute, the question is if it is *necessary* to trace every identifier to a flesh-and-blood person.

In *Breyer*, the ECJ held that an ISP holds enough additional information to identify the natural person "behind" an IP address.[409] This explicitly reins in the previous line of the Court in *Scarlet Extended*, where it was held that IP addresses allow for the identification of natural persons—however, in the case of an ISP, who holds all necessary information.[410] Again, the information needed to "end the chain" is not described. The judgment only concerns itself with assembling the "frontmost" parts of the chain. An ISP in Germany will typically have a name, address, email address, and phone number for an account holder.[411] These datapoints, however, do not identify a natural person, but rather only serve as an additional link in identi-

408 Borrowing the generic name placeholder used by the Art. 29 Working Party in: *Article 29 Data Protection Working Party*, "01248/07/EN WP 136" (2007), pp. 6 sqq.

409 Breyer (Oct. 19, 2016), para. 47.

410 Scarlet Extended (Nov. 24, 2011), para. 51.

411 None of this is mentioned in the decision, and when we take a closer look, even this seems doubtful. For example, as Zwenne notes, in a communal setting such as in his example, the air-

fication. In *Breyer*, the ECJ does not make this distinction.[412] While I agree that the ISP's data is *sufficient* to perform identification in most cases, this still *needs to be done.*

To me, the only sensible point at which to terminate the chain is where there exists a conceivable path to affecting the natural person or their assets in the real world, thereby treating them differently.[413] Conceivability, in this context, is to be understood in the same way as the "reasonably likely" standard under Recital (26) GDPR. For example, given a name and an address, one can visit this address and conceivably meet the natural person living there under that name. In a different example, given a International Bank Account Number (IBAN), one can issue a direct debit from that account, which directly impacts the real-world assets of this person.[414] On the other hand, knowing an IP address or a VIN by themselves offers no conceivable path to affecting a natural person in the real world. Knowing an online pseudonym for a person, in the absence of other identifying information, similarly offers no conceivable path to affecting a natural person in the real world. As seen above, this model is in accordance with the ECJ's jurisdiction on the matter. This model also conforms to a logically stringent view of identification (as I have hopefully laid out over the preceding pages). It is straightforward to understand and put into practice, but can also be operationalized: For example, certain kinds of combinations of information, such as a name and an address, always present a conceivable path to "just going there" to meet the natural person in question and thus affect them in the real world. It also helps with *effet utile* by giving the GDPR a considerably large scope of application without making it overly broad. And finally, it is also useful in the broader teleological framework of the GDPR: While the digital realm can certainly cause enough harm in itself, it makes sense to define identifiability and thus a resulting privacy harm in terms of an "offline" effect: If we can theoretically affect this person in the analog world, they have been identified.

---

port lounge, the account holder and the user are entirely different (*Zwenne*, "Over IP-adressen en persoonsgegevens, en het verschil tussen individualiseren en identificeren" (2011), p. 4).

412 Breyer (Oct. 19, 2016), para. 48.

413 *Bruegger* also wants to, *i.a.*, "terminate the chain" in real-world interaction, yet this is only one option for "identifying" natural persons in his model, while I argue it is the *only* option, *cf. Bruegger*, "Towards a Better Understanding of Identification, Pseudonymization, and Anonymization (v 1.0)" (June 11, 2021), p. 25. See also *Clarke*, "The Id-Anonymity Spectrum" (Apr. 30, 1999), Numbered item 3.1, who defines: "Identification is a process whereby a real-world entity is recognised, and its 'identity' established".

414 An entire separate discussion could be held on where "anonymous" assets, such as blockchain-based currencies, fall into this discussion. However, this issue is beyond the scope of this dissertation.

V. Direct and Indirect, Identifiedness and Identifiability

Having defined identification, we must now turn our attention to the distinctions repeatedly made in the text of the GDPR between the "directly or indirectly" "identified or identifiable". As I see it, these common dichotomies of identifiedness and identifiability as well as that of direct and indirect identification are superfluous and misleading.

Where a lot of the literature on the subject assigns meaning to the differences between these kinds of identification,[415] I argue that they serve no legal or practical purpose and do not aid in our understanding of identification but rather lead to additional confusion. Under the Data Protection Directive, the ECJ ruled that a natural person is "identified" where the person's information "directly [reveals its] identity". This was not the case for an IP address.[416] Others agree that, to be "identified", the person's identity needs to be immediately obvious from the information itself.[417] This is most commonly the case through a reference to a person's name.[418] However, sometimes the name itself is not sufficient for identification but needs to be combined with other pieces of information to relate to an identified person[419]—for example, when the person has a very common name. Some even go as far as saying that a combination of user names and IP addresses are sufficient for an "identified" dataset, referencing the AOL case[420].[421]

Some do not even make the distinction between identified and identifiable, only defining identifiability.[422] As the Art. 29 Working Party notes, identifiability is the practical "threshold condition".[423]

I will freely admit that both of these distinctions are clearly made in the text of the GDPR,[424] and that the ECJ has also referred to and defined the difference

---

415 See for instance: *Hintze*, "Viewing the GDPR through a de-identification lens" (Feb. 1, 2018), pp. 6 sq.; *Mühlenbeck*, "Anonyme und pseudonyme Daten" (2023), pp. 94 sqq.; *Davis*, "Facial Detection and Smart Billboards" (2020), pp. 374 sqq.

416 Breyer (Oct. 19, 2016), para. 38.

417 *Klar* and *Kühling*, "DS-GVO Art. 4 Nr. 1 personenbezogene Daten (inkl. betroffene Person)" (2024), margin no. 18, (translation by the author).

418 *Article 29 Data Protection Working Party*, "01248/07/EN WP 136" (2007), p. 13.

419 Ibid., p. 13.

420 See p. 195.

421 *Hintze*, "Viewing the GDPR through a de-identification lens" (Feb. 1, 2018), pp. 6 sq.

422 *Schild*, "DS-GVO Art. 4 Begriffsbestimmungen" (Feb. 1, 2025), margin nos. 14 sqq.; *Klabunde* and *Horváth*, "DS-GVO Art. 4 Begriffsbestimmungen" (2024), margin nos. 15 sqq.; *Weichert*, "DSGVO Art. 4 Begriffsbestimmungen" (2020), margin nos. 17 sqq.

423 *Article 29 Data Protection Working Party*, "01248/07/EN WP 136" (2007), p. 12.

424 Art. 4 § 1 GDPR: "identified or identifiable natural person ('data subject'); an identifiable natural person is one who can be identified, directly or indirectly".

between identifiedness and identifiability[425] as well as taken a stab at "indirect" identification[426]. Nonetheless, in striving to make "identifiability" more understandable, we should endeavor to find out the spirit of the provision without staying too close to its wording. I can support my aversion to identifiedness threefold: First, the distinction is of no legal or practical relevance. Second, identifiability logically includes identifiedness, *i.e.*, everything that is identified is also necessarily identifiable. Third, identifiedness is a mental state, which makes it wholly unsuitable as a legal test.

The first reason is simple enough: The GDPR does not tie a *legal* difference to this distinction.[427] The term also does not help in understanding the practical process of identification better.[428] The word "identified" occurs five times in the GDPR.[429] In all of these cases, "identified" occurs in tandem with "identifiable", and in none of these cases does the distinction matter for the legal outcome. It applies in the same way if someone is "identified" as when they are merely "identifiable".

Second, identifiability (by that I mean cases of an "identifiable" natural person) is wider than identifiedness (by which I mean cases of an "identified" natural person). When taking the expression at face value, we must conclude that someone is "identified" once identification has been performed successfully.[430] Likewise, someone is "identifiable" if identification has not been performed, but it is possible to do so. We can therefore define identifiability as the possibility of identification—this is also what the GDPR does when it says "an identifiable natural person is one that can be identified, ...". Someone being identified logically presupposes them also being identifiable: There is no case in which someone is identified, yet it is impossible

425 The Court has said that a dynamic person does not make a person "identified", as it "does not directly reveal the identity of the natural person ...": Breyer (Oct. 19, 2016), para. 38; Nacionalinis (Dec. 5, 2023), para. 58; Penalty Points (June 22, 2021), para. 60.

426 Breyer (Oct. 19, 2016), para. 41.

427 For the Data Protection Directive: *Haase*, "Datenschutzrechtliche Fragen des Personenbezugs" (2015), p. 260.

428 As I have hopefully demonstrated by not using the distinction in the preceding pages, see p. 71. Presenting a differing opinion: *Davis*, who finds practical use in "identified" in the context of smart billboards, (*Davis*, "Facial Detection and Smart Billboards" [2020], pp. 374 sqq.).

429 By which I mean five times in the sense of "identifying a person", namely in Recital (26) (twice), Art. 4 § 1 on personal data (twice), Art. 4 § 5 on pseudonymization (once). Art. 36 § 2 GDPR contains "identified the risk", which is a different meaning.

430 With a graphic showing as much, see *Stummer*, "Issues of Verifying Anonymity" (2022), p. 185; "the distinction between 'identified' and 'identifiable' ... does not primarily refer to the substantive but merely to the temporal dimension because every factually performed identification presumes its possibility": *Hölzel*, "Differential Privacy and the GDPR" (2019), p. 9.

to identify them (they are not identifiable).[431] Thus, the narrower term "identifiedness" is wholly contained in the wider "identifiability", making it superfluous. One symptom of this is the fact that the Art. 29 Working Party remarks "[identifiablity] is therefore the threshold condition determining whether information is within the scope of [identified or identifiable]."[432] Another symptom is that the criterion "identified" is largely irrelevant in practice.[433]

Third, identification is a mental process. Taking the view espoused above, identification is nothing more than linking a piece of information to something else up to a point where the person can be affected in the real world. Whether someone does the mental effort to identify someone and if they are successful are two highly subjective questions. The question whether all the requisite information is available (to them), on the other hand, is more objective. This holds true independently of the—admittedly—idiosyncratic way in which identification is defined above. Take, for instance, the Art. 29 Working Party's view of identifiedness, in which a person is "identified" where they are "distinguished" from all other members of a group.[434] [435] Nonetheless, even this distinction still needs to happen in the mind of an observer. Finding out whether they can see this distinction would require knowing something about their state of mind. It stands to reason that attempting to regulate on the basis of mental states is futile.

One faces similar conundra when examining the language of Art. 4 § 1 GDPR and Recital (26) s. 2 GDPR, which clearly indicate that there is "direct" and "indirect" identification.[436] I find this equally unconvincing, based on two reasons: First, someone being directly or indirectly identifiable, again, makes no legal difference. Second, the explanations of direct versus indirect identifiability typically make contradictory definitions.

First, let us take a look at direct and indirect identifiability as defined by the GDPR in Art. 4 § 1[437] and Recital (26) s. 3[438]. Under the Data Protection Directive, Art. 2 lit. (a) provided the same distinction.[439] If we probe beneath the surface, it turns out

---

431 Similar: *Hölzel*, "Differential Privacy and the GDPR" (2019), p. 9.

432 *Article 29 Data Protection Working Party*, "01248/07/EN WP 136" (2007), p. 12.

433 *Davis*, "Facial Detection and Smart Billboards" (2020), p. 371.

434 *Article 29 Data Protection Working Party*, "01248/07/EN WP 136" (2007), p. 12.

435 For criticism of this definition see p. 58.

436 Going further, the Art. 29 Working Party appears to believe in all four combinations of these distinctions, even though they fail to distinguish them: "concerning 'directly' identified or identifiable persons ... As regards 'indirectly' identified or identifiable persons ...", *Article 29 Data Protection Working Party*, "01248/07/EN WP 136" (2007), p. 13.

437 "... can be identified, *directly or indirectly*, ..." (*emphasis* added).

438 "... to identify the natural person *directly or indirectly*" (*emphasis* added).

439 "... can be identified, *directly or indirectly*, ..." (*emphasis* added).

that this distinction has little meaning. Even worse: Like the "identified/identifiable" distinction,[440] it creates unnecessary confusion.

Some authors conclude that "direct" identifiability means that the identity of the person can be directly inferred from the information itself.[441] In the *Breyer* decision, the ECJ briefly touches on the subject, where it remarks that it would be "common ground" that IP addresses do not make an "identified" natural person, because they "[do] not directly reveal the identity of the natural person who owns [or uses] the computer."[442] In other words, the ECJ assumes that for a person to be identified, their identity needs to be directly revealed in the data.[443] Some state that singling out[444] is an example of indirect identification.[445] Some authors draw the line between direct and indirect identification at the use of names. In any case, there is a significant overlap in definition between what is considered "identified" by some authors and "directly identifiable" by others—and sometimes even the same voices. If a name is available, a person shall sometimes be *directly* identifiable through it.[446] They find social security numbers or tax identification numbers[447] to be equivalently sufficient for direct identification.[448] At the same time, these same authors contend that persons can be identified *indirectly* through car number plates, a passport number, *etc.*[449]—all data that allows for "recognizing" a person in data.[450] *Leenes* calls this type of identification "L-identification", because it allows for individuals to be *looked up* in a second dataset, such as a registry.[451] As both the tax ID and a passport number are strings that can uniquely identify a person, it is unclear why the former allows for direct, the latter only for indirect identification. As a result, this distinction is not convincing.

440 See p. 83.
441 *Mühlenbeck*, "Anonyme und pseudonyme Daten" (2023), p. 102.
442 Breyer (Oct. 19, 2016), para. 38; most recently quoted in: O.C. (Mar. 7, 2024), para. 47.
443 Similar: *Mühlenbeck*, "Anonyme und pseudonyme Daten" (2023), p. 95.
444 See p. 58.
445 *Albrecht* and *Jotzo*, "Teil 3: Allgemeine Bestimmungen" (2017), margin no. 3.
446 *Schild*, "DS-GVO Art. 4 Begriffsbestimmungen" (Feb. 1, 2025), margin nos. 16 sqq.
447 Especially where they have been elevated to national identification numbers and Art. 87 GDPR applies, for Germany, see *Ehmann*, "Ehmann" (2021), pp. 511 sqq.
448 *Schild*, "DS-GVO Art. 4 Begriffsbestimmungen" (Feb. 1, 2025), margin no. 16; in this direction also: *European Data Protection Board*, "Guidelines 01/2025 on Pseudonymisation (Version for Public Consultation)" (Jan. 16, 2025), para. 83.
449 *Schild*, "DS-GVO Art. 4 Begriffsbestimmungen" (Feb. 1, 2025), margin no. 17.
450 Ibid., margin no. 17.
451 *Leenes*, "Do They Know Me? Deconstructing Identifiability" (2007), p. 148.

VI. Summary

In summary, "identified or identifiable" can be reduced to "identifiable". Identifiability means being able to create an unbroken chain of links that ends in a piece of data that conceivably enables affecting the data subject or its assets in the real world. From this building block, one can compose the recognition, distinction, naming, definition, and classification dimensions of identification.

2.4 Natural Person

The fourth point—that only data concerning *natural persons, i.e.*, humans[452] shall fall under the definition—seems trivial at first. Looking at edge cases, it becomes more subtle: There need to be provisions made for cases where life begins or ends as well as for legal persons.

Unborn children "generate" a sea of data: For example, ultrasound images and other medical procedures yield information about the soon-to-be natural person. "Their" data is not personal data as they are not yet a natural person in the legal sense, yet they are typically at the same time personal data relating to the bearer of the child.[453]

Additionally, dead persons, especially in recent years,[454] inevitably leave behind a trove of personal information. However, it is clear from the GDPR in Recital (27) s. 1 that the regulation does not apply to deceased persons.[455] Nonetheless, as becomes clear from the wording in Recital (27) s. 1, 2 GDPR, data relating to identifiable deceased persons is *personal data*, yet it is personal data to which the GDPR does not apply.[456]

It should also be clarified in this context that the notion of personal data is not limited to "private" activity, but also contains natural persons' professional activ-

452 *Article 29 Data Protection Working Party*, "01248/07/EN WP 136" (2007), p. 21.
453 differing opinion: *Karg*, "DSGVO Art. 4 Nr. 1 Begriffsbestimmung „Personenbezogenes Datum"" (2025), margin no. 42; left open by: *Ziebarth*, "DS GVO Art. 4 Begriffsbestimmungen" (2022), margin no. 12.
454 As the collection and storage of personal information has increased significantly over the last few decades.
455 *Karg*, "DSGVO Art. 4 Nr. 1 Begriffsbestimmung „Personenbezogenes Datum"" (2025), margin no. 40.
456 differing opinion: *Klabunde* and *Horváth*, "DS-GVO Art. 4 Begriffsbestimmungen" (2024), margin no. 13; *Schild*, "DS-GVO Art. 4 Begriffsbestimmungen" (Feb. 1, 2025), margin nos. 11 sq.

ities. The ECJ has repeatedly held that personal data includes data that relates to humans in their professional capacity.[457]

In contrast, legal persons such as corporations[458] are not covered by the definition of "personal data" under GDPR.[459] This is clear from the grammatical interpretation ("natural person" in Art. 4) and Recital (14) s. 2 GDPR. It is also a result of basing the GDPR on the competency in Art. 16 § 2 s. 1 TFEU, which specifically mentions "natural persons".[460] Nonetheless, the ECJ has stated that where a legal person's official title "identifies" one or more natural persons, they are subject to the protection of Artt. 7 and 8 CFR and thus the regulations on data protection apply.[461]

2.5 Conclusion

In conclusion, the four-element definition as traced in Art. 4 § 1 GDPR and outlined in the Art. 29 Working Party's 2007 Opinion is composed of three very broad elements that require little attention and one important condition doing the "heavy lifting": the test of "identified or identifiable". This test can be reduced to "identifiability", which is the possibility of identification.

Identification is a multi-faceted term that has multiple dimensions, such as the recognition, distinction, naming, definition and classification dimensions. Identification can be re-defined as an operation that is elementally based on comparison. Comparison can be done either deterministically, probabilistically, or heuristically. These comparisons enable two more complex operations: Linking and singling out. Using these two operations, we can assemble a chain of information that links the piece of information in question to a natural person. This chain ends, *i.e.*, identification has been performed once this information allows for affecting the natural person or their assets in the real world. Additional distinctions, such as one between indirect and direct identification, fail to provide any clarification or additional value.

---

457 Client Earth v. EFSA (July 16, 2015), para. 30; Worten (May 30, 2013), para. 19; first held in a case where names and pensions of Austrian public servants were shared: Österreichischer Rundfunk and Others (May 20, 2003), para. 64.

458 In Germany, the GmbH, UG (haftungsbeschränkt), and the AG come to mind.

459 *Albrecht* and *Jotzo*, "Teil 3: Allgemeine Bestimmungen" (2017), margin no. 23.

460 Ibid., margin no. 23.

461 Volker und Markus Schecke (Nov. 9, 2010), para. 52.

3 Anonymous and Anonymized Data

3.1 Foundations

Having defined personal data, we can now turn our attention to anonymous data and anonymization. Like the question of identification, this area requires scholarly and regulatory attention.[1]

Anonymization can be defined as the task of turning personal data into anonymous data.[2] Anonymous data is all information that does not relate to an identifiable person.[3] There are different kinds of anonymous data: First, there is data that never contained any relation to a person in the first place—this is non-personal data.[4] In this first case, the "relation to" element of the definition of personal data is missing. Second, some data relates to a person, yet that person is not identifiable. In this second case, the "identifiability" element is missing. This is always the case with anonymized data, *i.e.*, data that used to be personal data but has been (successfully) anonymized. Not all of this second kind of data has necessarily been anonymized: Sometimes, the data is captured in such a way that there never was an identifiable

---

1 Or, as *Altman, Cohen, Falzon*, et al. put it: "… despite the significance of the concept, it is undertheorized and poorly articulated in regulatory guidance", *Altman, Cohen, Falzon*, et al., "A Principled Approach to Defining Anonymization As Applied to EU Data Protection Law" (May 9, 2022), p. 1.

2 Note that this definition is only apt for the anonymization of data (the subject of this text), but not for the "anonymization" of internet users via Tor or similar services. This sense of anonymization is covered in depth elsewhere, *e.g.*, in the setting described in *Pfitzmann* and M. *Hansen*, "A terminology for talking about privacy by data minimization: Anonymity, Unlinkability, Undetectability, Unobservability, Pseudonymity, and Identity Management" (Aug. 10, 2010), p. 6.

3 *Mühlenbeck*, "Anonyme und pseudonyme Daten" (2023), pp. 296 sq. As *Mühlenbeck* notes, the GDPR speaks of "anonymous information" in Recital (26) s. 5 (ibid., pp. 295 sq., referencing *Wójtowicz* and *Cebulla*, "Anonymisierung nach der DSGVO" (Aug. 29, 2017), p. 187). His explanation is that "information" itself is part of the definition and thus, if something is not "information relating to an identifiable person", it is not "data" either. I disagree: The GDPR is very consistent in using "personal data" as a fixed term and does not use "data" on its own. Nonetheless, it does not follow that this distinction allows for a definition of "data" itself. While I do agree that there exists a distinction between anonymous data that does not relate to a person and anonymous data that relates to a person who is not identifiable, I do not think this distinction is contained in Recital (26) s. 5 GDPR. The distinction exists between non-personal data (data that does not relate to a person) and anonymous data (data that does relates to a person who is not identifiable). Anonymous data can be divided into data that has always been anonymous and anonymized data. As *Hölzel* notes, the technical literature distinguishes "identity disclosure" and "attribute disclosure", with only the former being of interest here, see: *Hölzel*, "Anonymisierungstechniken und das Datenschutzrecht" (Aug. 2018), p. 503.

4 For example, data about the height of Mount Everest. For a detailed evaluation see p. 29.

https://doi.org/10.1515/9783112222164-004

person tied to it, and thus it was originally anonymous.[5] *Acquisti*, *Taylor*, and *Wagman* note that anonymity is "a form of privacy for identity information: it removes the link between a person and data items relating to that person".[6]

In practice, the determining factor in anonymization is necessarily identifiability.[7] This follows, for in the definition of personal data laid out above[8], identifiability is the threshold criterion.[9] For information that does *not* relate to a natural person, there can logically be no identifiability.[10] Thus, there are essentially three ways in which information can *not* be personal data under the GDPR: First, if it does not relate to a person, *i.e.*, is non-personal data. Second, it relates to a person, yet they are not identifiable (anonymized and non-identifiable data). Third, it relates to an identifiable person, yet they are deceased.[11] Personal data cannot be made into non-personal, *i.e.*, object-related data, but identifiability can be removed. This is called anonymization.

The reverse is also true: Due to the progress in technology and data availability, data that used to be anonymous or anonymized may become personal data later if the natural person to which the data relates becomes identifiable. This is called "re-identification".[12] For instance, before the invention of dactyloscopic methods to match humans with their fingerprint and the understanding that fingerprints are unique, a picture of a fingerprint may well have been anonymous data. As the relevant standard relies on a *possibility* of identification,[13] as soon as this re-identification becomes technically possible, the data becomes personal again. It became personal data as soon as it could reasonably likely be used to identify a natural person. This is presciently regulated in the GDPR, as Recital (26) s. 4 states that "account should be taken of all objective factors, … taking into consideration the available technology at the time of the processing and technological developments."

It could be argued that the wording of the Recital only requires that account should be taken of factors that could be foreseen at the time of processing. However, the term "technological developments" alone incorporates a field that moves forward in irregular leaps. These developments can frequently enable new kinds of re-identification, without their being foreseeable at the time of processing. As a result,

5 Similar: *Mühlenbeck*, "Anonyme und pseudonyme Daten" (2023), p. 296.
6 *Acquisti*, *Taylor*, and *Wagman*, "The Economics of Privacy" (June 2016), p. 449.
7 *Mühlenbeck*, "Anonyme und pseudonyme Daten" (2023), p. 296, for identifiability see p. 83.
8 See p. 20.
9 Similar: *Hölzel*, "Differential Privacy and the GDPR" (2019), p. 7.
10 See p. 30.
11 Technically, this is still personal data according to the GDPR, yet it is outside of its scope, see p. 87.
12 *Ohm*, "Broken Promises of Privacy" (2009–2010), p. 1707.
13 See p. 83.

the wording of the GDPR *does* only call for a prognosis as to the re-identification, yet this prognosis incorporates such volatile and unforeseeable factors that in practice, the viewpoint that needs to be taken is closer to *ex post* than to *ex ante*.

Anonymization itself is mentioned only in Recital (26) GDPR.[14] This is not dissimilar to its predecessor, the Data Protection Directive, where anonymization was mentioned in its Recital (26).[15] It is also (implicitly) mentioned in Art. 89 § 1 s. 4 GDPR.[16] Some member states, *i.a.* Germany, added their own definition into their derivations of the Data Protection Directive. In Germany, this definition could be found in § 3 para. 6 BDSG a.F.[17]

Its legislative obscurity notwithstanding, anonymization in the context of the GDPR has been acknowledged and even endorsed by various players in the regulatory and business arenas. In 2014, under the Data Protection Directive, the Art. 29 Working Party released a set of guidelines on anonymization techniques,[18] which have been widely influential and continue to be of high relevance under the GDPR.[19] To update these guidelines and reflect on the near-decade that has passed since then, the EDPB has promised to create new "guidelines on [anonymization] and [pseudonymization]".[20] In the meantime, the EDPB continues to endorse anonymization as a means to securing personal data, making reference to the sin-

---

14 S. 5: "… or to personal data rendered anonymous in such a manner that the data subject is not or no longer identifiable".

15 S. 1: "to data rendered anonymous in such a way that the data subject is no longer identifiable".

16 "Where those purposes can be fulfilled by further processing which does not permit or no longer permits the identification of data subjects, those purposes shall be fulfilled in that manner."

17 "Anonymization is the modification of personal data in such a manner that information of a personal or factual nature can no longer or only with a disproportionate effort in terms of time, cost, and labor be associated with a identified or identifiable natural person.", (translation by the author).

18 *Article 29 Data Protection Working Party*, "0829/14/DE WP216" (2014).

19 *Valkanova*, "8.1 Trainieren von KI-Modellen" (2020), p. 343 margin no. 22.

20 This action item was present in both the 2021–2022 (*European Data Protection Board*, "EDPB Work Programme 2021/2022" (Mar. 16, 2021), p. 4) and 2023–2024 (*European Data Protection Board*, "EDPB Work Programme 2023/2024" (Feb. 14, 2023), p. 4) "work programmes". Public records show that the guidelines were first put on the agenda in December 2020 (*European Data Protection Board*, "Agenda: 43rd EDPB Meeting 2020-12-15" (Dec. 15, 2020), p. 2), where it was agreed that a guideline should be composed (*European Data Protection Board*, "Minutes – 43rd Plenary Meeting on 2020-12-15" (Jan. 14, 2021), p. 6). However, judging solely from the public record of meeting minutes on the EDPB's website (see *European Data Protection Board*, "Plenary Minutes Archive" (2024)), the action item has not been discussed in meetings since. It was again cited as a future avenue for the EDPB's work in the 2022 Annual Activity Report as endorsed by "stakeholders" (*European Data Protection Board*, "EDPB Annual Activity Report 2022" (Apr. 17, 2023), p. 39). These guidelines will likely replace the Art. 29 Working Party's 2014 opinion on anonymization techniques (see *Article 29 Data Protection Working Party*, "0829/14/DE WP216" (2014)) and "address recent developments in

gling out/linking/inference formula put forth by the Art. 29 Working Party.[21] The European Data Protection Supervisor (EDPS) has also endorsed anonymization, publishing a booklet with the Spanish data protection agency on "10 Misunderstandings Related to Anonymisation", *i.a.*, contending that "a proper anonymisation process keeps the data functional for a given purpose".[22] At the same time, the EDPS and the Spanish agency have taken care to emphasize that some data cannot be anonymized while retaining useful data[23], and that previously anonymized data may be de-anonymized with new technical advances.[24] Even the ECJ has acknowledged anonymization.[25]

Some have also proposed that a new provision in the GDPR should be created to give legal certainty.[26] This provision should enable anonymization, especially in the cases of special categories of data pursuant to Art. 9 GDPR.[27] Personally, I think it is fitting that the GDPR does not speak about that which it does not directly regulate, and thus I believe that an additional provision would not yield the clarity that we might hope for (as indeed the GDPR did not, for example, clarify in its text the raging discussion of relative or absolute views of identifiability under the Data Protection Directive[28]).

privacy engineering and anonymisation technology", *European Data Protection Board*, "Minutes – 43rd Plenary Meeting on 2020-12-15" (Jan. 14, 2021), p. 6.

21 *European Data Protection Board*, "Secure personal data" (Apr. 27, 2023).

22 *Agencia Española Protección Datos* and *European Data Protection Supervisor*, "10 Misunderstandings Related to Anonymisation" (Apr. 27, 2021), Misunderstanding 8.

23 *Agencia Española Protección Datos* and *European Data Protection Supervisor*, "10 Misunderstandings Related to Anonymisation" (Apr. 27, 2021), Misunderstanding 3; see also *Ohm*, "Broken Promises of Privacy" (2009–2010), as in:

24 *Agencia Española Protección Datos* and *European Data Protection Supervisor*, "10 Misunderstandings Related to Anonymisation" (Apr. 27, 2021), Misunderstanding 4.

25 Even though the question which was asked of the Court results in a strange framing, leading to the impression that anonymized data is still personal data, yet its use shall not be "processing" under the GDPR, see in detail: Nacionalinis (Dec. 5, 2023), para. 59. This, however, is not the ECJ's intent, as can be seen from ibid., para. 57, where anonymous data is defined as distinguished from personal data.

26 *Schweinoch* and *Peintinger*, "Anonymisierung im Datenschutz – terra incognita?" (Oct. 1, 2020), margin no. 76.

27 Ibid., margin no. 76.

28 See p. 102.

3.2 Distinguishing Anonymization...

Anonymization is similar to two other similar, yet distinct activities: pseudonymization and de-identification. Some authors introduce a third term, "de-personalized" data, to mean 'data that once was personal data but has been manipulated with the goal of turning it into anonymous data.[29] This, however, is nothing other than "anonymized" data, despite the confusing terminology.

I. ... From Pseudonymization

Unlike anonymization, pseudonymization is defined explicitly in the GDPR, namely in Art. 4 § 5 GDPR[30].[31] Pseudonymization is also mentioned a couple of other times in the GDPR: It can serve as an "appropriate safeguard" when using data for other purposes (Art. 6 no. 4 lit. (e) alt. 2 GDPR), is an example of privacy by design and privacy by default (Art. 25 no. 1 GDPR), an appropriate technical measure to ensure security of processing (Art. 32 no. 1 lit. (a) GDPR), and a safeguard for the processing of archiving/scientific/historical/statistical data (Art. 89 no. 1 GDPR). The GDPR also recognizes that pseudonymization may need to be specified further and could be the subject of a code of conduct (Art. 40 no. 2 lit. (d) GDPR). Additionally, pseudonymization is mentioned in Recitals (26), (27), (29), (75), (78), (85), and (156) to the GDPR. This is in stark contrast to anonymization, which is only mentioned once in passing. Nonetheless, there is a good reason for this distinction: As pseudonymized data is still personal data under the GDPR, it makes sense to regulate it within the GDPR. Anonymous data is—by definition—outside of the GDPR, which means it is sensible that it is scarcely mentioned within.

Pseudonymization means that identifying information is removed from the dataset and externalized into an attribution method or dataset.[32] Without the

29 *Finck* and *Pallas*, "They who must not be identified—distinguishing personal from non-personal data under the GDPR" (2020), p. 11.

30 "pseudonymisation' means the processing of personal data in such a manner that the personal data can no longer be attributed to a specific data subject without the use of additional information, provided that such additional information is kept separately and is subject to technical and organisational measures to ensure that the personal data are not attributed to an identified or identifiable natural person".

31 For a detailed introduction to pseudonymization, see *Mühlenbeck*, "Anonyme und pseudonyme Daten" (2023), pp. 145 sqq.; see also most recently: *European Data Protection Board*, "Guidelines 01/2025 on Pseudonymisation (Version for Public Consultation)" (Jan. 16, 2025).

32 M. *Hansen*, "DSGVO Art. 4 Nr. 5 Begriffsbestimmung „Pseudonymisierung“" (2025), margin no. 31.

means for attribution, no person in the dataset is identifiable.[33] Using the means for attribution, the pseudonymized data can be re-identified. The means for attribution need to be kept separate and secured through technical and organizational measures.[34]

Pseudonymized data serves a similar function to anonymous data, yet it presents two straightforward paths to re-identification:[35] First, the list of pseudonyms can be linked to re-identify the pseudonymized dataset.[36] This can happen willingly, *e.g.*, as part of a legal dispute, or unwillingly, if it can be accessed by third parties as a result of lacking IT security practices. The second path is more subtle: Through linking multiple pieces of information that have the same pseudonym, re-identification can be successful.[37] Sometimes, this record linkage through the use of the identical pseudonym is intended: This way, insights can be generated across pseudonymized datasets, if the same pseudonym is used.[38]

Anonymization can be distinguished easily from pseudonymization, as in anonymization, there is no additional data kept for attribution. Nonetheless, some state that one cannot necessarily transform pseudonymous data into anonymous data by deleting the additional information used for attribution, but rather, a separate anonymization procedure may need to be followed.[39] Turning anonymous data into pseudonymous data, on the other hand, is easily possible by all accounts.[40] Depending on the definition of pseudonymization used, this is dubitable: If pseudonymous data is defined such that identification without the attribution data is not possible or at least not possible without resorting to means that are not "reasonably likely to be used" under Recital (26) s. 3 GDPR,[41] then it stands to reason that

---

33 w.f.r.: *Mühlenbeck*, "Anonyme und pseudonyme Daten" (2023), pp. 160 sq.

34 M. *Hansen*, "DSGVO Art. 4 Nr. 5 Begriffsbestimmung „Pseudonymisierung“" (2025), margin no. 31.

35 *Roßnagel* and *Scholz*, "Datenschutz durch Anonymität und Pseudonymität – Rechtsfolgen der Verwendung anonymer und pseudonymer Daten" (2000), p. 728.

36 Ibid., p. 729.

37 Ibid., p. 729.

38 *Schwartmann* and *Weiß*, "Anforderungen an den datenschutzkonformen Einsatz von Pseudonymisierungslösungen" (2018), p. 26; *Mühlenbeck*, "Anonyme und pseudonyme Daten" (2023), p. 211.

39 *Schwartmann* and *Weiß*, "Anforderungen an den datenschutzkonformen Einsatz von Pseudonymisierungslösungen" (2018), p. 25; agreeing: M. *Hansen* and B. *Walczak*, "Pseudonymisierung à la DS-GVO und verwandte Methoden" (2019), p. 56.

40 See only: *Schwartmann, Jaspers*, et al., "Praxisleitfaden Anonymisierung" (Dec. 2022), p. 19.

41 As done in: M. *Hansen*, "DSGVO Art. 4 Nr. 5 Begriffsbestimmung „Pseudonymisierung“" (2025), margin no. 45.

throwing away this attribution data should theoretically render the remaining data anonymous.[42]

II. ... From De-Identification

Another important distinction is that between anonymization and de-identification. These terms are often used interchangeably.[43] For the purposes of this dissertation, however, "anonymization" is the subject of our enquiry and used in the GDPR's meaning of the term, while "de-identification" is a term from the U.S. discussion on the subject—where "anonymization" typically means compliance with laws such as Health Insurance Portability and Accountability Act (HIPAA). These laws are more statically concerned with the removal of specific identifiers. As a result, de-identification is often taken to mean that all explicit identifiers, such as names, ID numbers, etc. are removed.[44] *Ohm* traces this term back to *Sweeney*'s research, which was hugely influential on HIPAA.[45]

In the United States, anonymization is mostly a topic concerning medical data, as—typically—plaintiffs and defendants in court cases are not anonymized.[46] For medical data, the HIPAA[47] requires that certain kinds of data are removed. For example, HIPAA states in § 164.514 (b) (2) (i) a method for removing identifiers relating to name, address and geographical information as well as identifying numbers such as social security numbers. HIPAA terms this "de-identification". Especially remarkable is the procedure that is used to anonymize geographical information: All identifiers are removed, except the ZIP code which is truncated to the initial three digits, unless the "geographic unit" formed by the ZIP code contains less than 20,000 people.[48] Due to the simplistic nature of this list of identifiers, automatic de-identification is possible, with many tools and approaches in use.[49] In so doing, the U.S. congress has "embraced a wholly data-centric approach", which as-

42 However, as pseudonymization is not the focus of this dissertation and this point hinges on its definition, this question is left open here.

43 *Meystre* et al., "Automatic de-identification of textual documents in the electronic health record" (Dec. 2010), p. 2.

44 Ibid., p. 2.

45 *Ohm*, "Broken Promises of Privacy" (2009–2010), p. 1744.

46 Except in cases where the identity of parties must not be disclosed, such as *Roe v. Wade*, where the plaintiff appeared under the pseudonym "Jane Roe".

47 45 CFR § 160 and 164, available at *U.S. Congress*, "45 CFR Part 164 – Security and Privacy."

48 45 CFR § 164.514 (b)(2)(i)(B).

49 A 2010 overview is provided by *Meystre* et al., "Automatic de-identification of textual documents in the electronic health record" (Dec. 2010).

sumes that some data categories have an innate "riskiness" to privacy and that confers lawmakers with the power to regulate which categories are suitable to create re-identification risk and which are not.[50] Nonetheless, further-ranging proposals than HIPAA have recently been enacted, namely in the state of Washington in the form of the "My Health My Data Act"[51], which defines "deidentified data" as "data that cannot reasonably be used to infer information about, or otherwise be linked to, an identified or identifiable consumer, or a device linked to such consumer, ... ".[52] De-Identification in the sense of HIPAA is a necessary, yet not sufficient element of anonymization as the GDPR sees it. While the removal of explicit identifiers is required,[53] additional data remains in the dataset that enables identification, such as quasi-identifiers[54]. When I henceforth use the term "de-identification", I am talking about the U.S. understanding of the term, which is much narrower than a European understanding of "anonymization".

3.3 The Privacy–Utility Tradeoff

One recurring theme of anonymization research is that there exists a tradeoff between privacy and utility.[55] Generally speaking, data usefulness and the degree of anonymization form a continuous tradeoff.[56] The more anonymized data is, the less useful it becomes.[57]

Some have taken a pessimistic view on this tradeoff, and take it to mean that anonymization is useless at best and impossible at worst. A prominent critic of anonymization, *Ohm*, maintains that "data can be either useful or perfectly anony-

50 *Ohm*, "Broken Promises of Privacy" (2009–2010), p. 1734.

51 "Engrossed Substitute House Bill 1155 as passed by the House of Representatives and the Senate on the dates hereon set forth." (Apr. 17, 2023).

52 Ibid., (10).

53 See p. 125.

54 See p. 77.

55 For a contemporary approach to finding the sweet spot between privacy and utility in a medical application of DP and ML, see: *Appenzeller*, *Leitner*, et al., "Privacy and Utility of Private Synthetic Data for Medical Data Analyses" (Jan. 2022), pp. 14 sq.

56 *Dwork* and *Roth*, "The Algorithmic Foundations of Differential Privacy" (2013), p. 6; *Sweeney*, "Computational disclosure control" (2001), p. 33; for an overview of this relationship in LLMs, see: *Feretzakis* et al., "GDPR and Large Language Models" (Mar. 28, 2025), p. 18.

57 See for an experimental verification of this general correlation: *Brickell* and *Shmatikov*, "The cost of privacy" (Aug. 24, 2008), pp. 5 sqq.

mous but never both."[58] Indeed, *Ohm* contends that the utility of a dataset and its privacy are "intrinsically connected".[59] *Ohm* not only criticizes HIPAA and its American corollaries, but also the then-current Data Protection Directive: In his view, the advances in re-identification science render the definition of personal data overly broad and thus make the application of the Data Protection Directive overly broad, expanding it "like an ideal gas to fit the shape of its container."[60] All instances of "release-and-forget anonymization", as he terms it,[61] have failed to protect privacy.

Viewing *Ohm*'s critique, many years later, it must be conceded that he raised valuable points at a time in which public perception of anonymization was still in its infancy. Some of his more grand statements, such as the sweeping generalization "so long as data is useful, even in the slightest, then it is also potentially reidentifiable"[62] have aged less well.[63] [64] I would make two points against his argument: First, we now have nearly fifteen more years of research that we can draw upon. This technical advantage enables better insights into anonymization than when the article was written. For example, we now have a robust understanding and research community surrounding differential privacy[65] and other techniques that have shown that they can protect privacy while preserving data utility.[66] At the same time, the privacy–utility tradeoff that *Ohm* mentions is very much real. However, the nature of the tradeoff is still not certain and depends on the method used: It is not necessarily the case that, "as the utility of data increases even a little, the privacy plummets"[67].[68] The nature of the tradeoff can be visualized as in Figure 3.1.[69] Second, the question *Ohm* brings up is ultimately a *legal* one. Even where some release-and-

58 *Ohm*, "Broken Promises of Privacy" (2009–2010), p. 1704; this is a corollary statement to the one echoed later in the "No Free Lunch in Data Privacy" paper: *Kifer* and *Machanavajjhala*, "No free lunch in data privacy" (June 12, 2011).

59 *Ohm*, "Broken Promises of Privacy" (2009–2010), p. 1705.

60 Ibid., p. 1741.

61 Ibid.

62 Ibid., p. 1751.

63 F. T. *Wu*, "Defining Privacy and Utility in Data Sets" (2013), p. 1129.

64 *Ohm* nonetheless continues to stand by these critiques as recently as 2017, *AXA ResearchFundLive*, "Internet of Things & Data Protection Conference (Paul Ohm)" (Nov. 20, 2017), 16:37 min.

65 Which is mentioned in the article, see *Ohm*, "Broken Promises of Privacy" (2009–2010), pp. 1756 sq., but Ohm's statements about it are refuted aptly in F. T. *Wu*, "Defining Privacy and Utility in Data Sets" (2013), pp. 1137 sqq.

66 See p. 164.

67 *Ohm*, "Broken Promises of Privacy" (2009–2010), p. 1751.

68 Similar: F. T. *Wu*, "Defining Privacy and Utility in Data Sets" (2013), pp. 1127 sqq.

69 It is difficult to trace the origin of this visualization. I first saw it in a presentation by *Ohm*, who admitted he did not create the visualization, but rather saw it presented once and "just annotated it" (*AXA ResearchFundLive*, "Internet of Things & Data Protection Conference (Paul Ohm)" (Nov. 20,

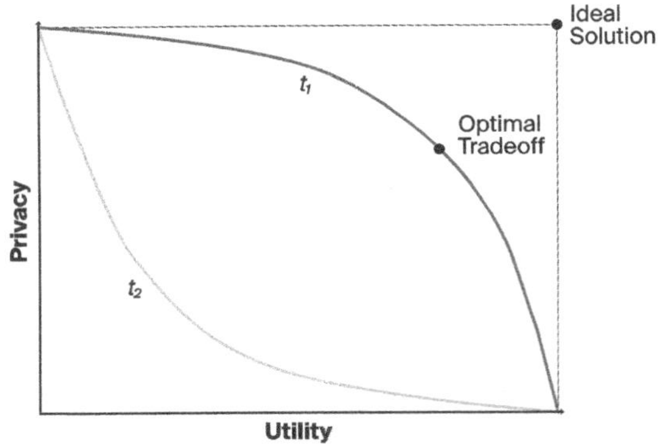

Fig. 3.1: Visualization of the privacy–utility tradeoff.

forget methods of anonymization have failed, the evaluation of their failure falls on legislators and supervisory authorities.[70] Personally, I am optimistic about the capabilities of current anonymization technology, while at the same time, I am aware that it cannot achieve perfect anonymity.

Nonetheless, as we will discuss next, the GDPR does not call for perfect anonymity. More realistically, anonymization exists along a continuum. Conversely, under the GDPR, there is a lot of reason to believe that anonymization exists and can successfully be performed.[71] At the very least, this view can be ascribed to the legislator, who implicitly endorsed anonymization in Recital (26) and its corollary, pseudonymization in Art. 4 § 5 GDPR. It can also be seen in the ECJ's views on the subject, *e.g.*, in the *Breyer* case.[72] And finally, it can also be seen in the supervisory authorities' approaches to anonymization and the ecosystem surrounding it, with the EDPS,[73] the German Federal Commissioner for Data Protection and Freedom of

2017), 15:40 min.). It can be found elsewhere, too, for example in: *Carvalho* et al., "Survey on Privacy-Preserving Techniques for Microdata Publication" (Mar. 28, 2023), p. 4 and in: *tss*, "Blog-Artikel" (May 11, 2023). Neither of these sources attribute the graphic, yet it has become pervasive in the discussion surrounding privacy and utility. It is up for debate whether the curve of the tradeoff is better represented by the optimistic t_1 (where there exists an acceptable tradeoff between privacy and utility) or by the pessimistic t_2 (where there does not).

70 See also below see p. 99.

71 As a result of this duality, *Altman, Cohen, Nissim*, et al. decided to use small-capitals ANONYMIZATION to denote GDPR's notion of it as defined in *Article 29 Data Protection Working Party*, "0829/14/DE WP216" (2014) and surrounding literature, see *Altman, Cohen, Nissim*, et al., "What a Hybrid Legal-Technical Analysis Teaches Us about Privacy Regulation" (2021), p. 9.

72 Breyer (Oct. 19, 2016), para. 46.

73 *Agencia Española Protección Datos* and *European Data Protection Supervisor*, "10 Misunderstandings Related to Anonymisation" (Apr. 27, 2021).

Information (BfDI),[74] the German foundation on data protection ("Stiftung Datenschutz"),[75] as well as the EDPB[76] explicitly or implicitly endorsing anonymization. In summary, while *Ohm* brought up valuable points that were sorely needed in the debate at the time of publication, it can be said that the state of the art has moved on, both legally and technologically.

3.4 Legal Standards in Anonymization

As outlined above, it is important to find out which definition of anonymity is sufficient for "anonymization" under the GDPR. Here, there are multiple positions that can be taken. Broadly, these positions fall between two poles, neither of which are (still) actively held today, but remain illustrative of the spectrum of opinions:

The first is an absolute and unequivocal view of anonymization. Any possibility of identification, no matter how minute, by piecing together data from all thinkable sources with no regard to practical feasibility, would mean that data still remains personal data under this view.[77] Due to the aforementioned tradeoff between privacy and utility, this is highly impractical—anonymizing a dataset to this standard would frequently render it unusable. Regarding any kind of possible current method of re-identification, as well as any dataset that could be used to re-identify the data, is unrealistic. Adding the requirement that an anonymized dataset should also be robust against all future methods and datasets is downright impossible. Perfect anonymity is therefore not a suitable model for anonymization.

The second position would be the other extreme: As long as one person practically does not identify a data subject, the data is anonymous. This view also does not accurately reflect the realities of processing. As the GDPR states, its provisions should be in effect even when no one has been identified, but a natural person is merely *identifiable*.[78]

---

74 *Der Bundesbeauftragte für den Datenschutz und die Informationsfreiheit*, "Öffentliches Konsultationsverfahren des Bundesbeauftragten für den Datenschutz und die Informationsfreiheit zum Thema Anonymisierung unter der DSGVO unter besonderer Berücksichtigung der TK-Branche" (Feb. 10, 2020).

75 *Schwartmann, Jaspers*, et al., "Anonymisierung und Pseudonymisierung von Daten" (Jan. 2023).

76 See p. 91 fn. 20.

77 For a summary of this viewpoint held under the Data Protection Directive, see w.f.r.: *Roßnagel* and *Scholz*, "Datenschutz durch Anonymität und Pseudonymität – Rechtsfolgen der Verwendung anonymer und pseudonymer Daten" (2000), p. 726.

78 See p. 83.

A third view would be placed somewhere in the middle between these two extremes: Anonymization is achieved when, *de facto*, no re-identification can be achieved. This is plainly the intended option in the GDPR and even more so under the Data Protection Directive. In contrast to the GDPR, the BDSG a.F. contained a provision on anonymization in § 3 para. 6 BDSG a.F., defining it as:

> Anonymization is the modification of personal data in such a way that individual data about personal or factual relationships can no longer or not without disproportionate investments of time, cost, and work be matched to an identified or identifiable natural person. [79]

The Art. 29 Working Party stated about Recital (26) of the Data Protection Directive (which was similar to the equivalent in the GDPR):

> An undesirable result would be that of ending up applying data protection rules to situations which were not intended to be covered by those rules and for which they were not designed by the legislator. The material exemptions under Article 3 mentioned above and the clarifications in recitals 26 and 27 of the Directive show how the legislator wanted to see data protection applied.[80]

Even though the GDPR uses different terminology, the basic sentiment is echoed in Recital (26) GDPR:

> To ascertain whether means are reasonably likely to be used to identify the natural person, account should be taken of all objective factors, such as the costs of and the amount of time required for identification, taking into consideration the available technology at the time of the processing and technological developments.

Despite this relative clarity, there still remains some legal uncertainty surrounding this definition. Even though the objective factors to be taken into account are enumerated in Recital (26) s. 4 GDPR, there are practical implications that still need to be clarified.

First, what are the "means" used, and second, whose knowledge matters when determining whether a person is de facto identifiable.

---

79 German original: "Anonymisieren ist das Verändern personenbezogener Daten derart, dass die Einzelangaben über persönliche oder sachliche Verhältnisse nicht mehr oder nur mit einem unverhältnismäßig großen Aufwand an Zeit, Kosten und Arbeitskraft einer bestimmten oder bestimmbaren natürlichen Person zugeordnet werden können.", translation by the author.
80 *Article 29 Data Protection Working Party*, "01248/07/EN WP 136" (2007), p. 5.

I. All Means Reasonably Likely to be Used

As noted above, means are just a different word for the atomic operation of linking that is contorted into different shapes, such as singling out.[81] Both of these are always "reasonably likely to be used". This can be derived as follows: Linking is implied in Art. 4 § 1 GDPR ("by reference to"), and singling out is named in Recital (26) s. 3 GDPR. As singling out and all other operations are merely derived from the atomic operation of comparison at the basis of both linking and singling out, these two are in any case "reasonably likely to be used". Nonetheless, probabilistic linking and other techniques become more powerful as time goes on and data grows.

The Art. 29 Working Party summarizes anonymization techniques as preventing three essential risks: Singling out, linking, and inference.[82] Singling out and linking have been covered in depth above, and they are the basis of identification.[83] Inference, however, is not.[84]

As a result, all operations that lead to identification can be traced back to comparison as the atomic operation behind singling out and linking.[85] Nonetheless, this operation contains multitudes: For example, probabilistic linking is a means in which a record can be matched to another even when they are not identical.[86] Here, new technologies such as AI models can permit better comparison and thereby linking. As Recital (26) s. 4 GDPR states, the technology "at the time of the processing" and technological developments should be taken into account. Here, it is uncertain to what "at the time of the processing" should refer. Most authors concur that data can "become" personal data over time, *e.g.*, when additional data to which it can be linked becomes available or when technology advances so far as to make new kinds of analyses possible that allow for singling out natural persons.[87] The alternative would be so-called "release-and-forget" anonymization:[88] Someone removes identifiability from data, releases it, and then "forgets about it", *i.e.*, ignores the ongoing implications.

These enumeration of objective factors in Recital (26) s. 4 GDPR and the "reasonably likely to be used" standard leave out factors such as the sensitivity of the

---

81 See p. 71.
82 *Article 29 Data Protection Working Party*, "0829/14/DE WP216" (2014), pp. 11 sq.
83 See p. 71.
84 See p. 65.
85 See p. 71.
86 For a general, mathematical introduction, see the seminal *Fellegi* and *Sunter*, "A Theory for Record Linkage" (Dec. 1, 1969).
87 We shall explore this idea in more detail in the technical chapters of this dissertations and find that some methods, such as DP, offer guarantees even for the future, see p. 160.
88 Coined in *Ohm*, "Broken Promises of Privacy" (2009–2010), p. 1711.

data[89] or the motivation of potential adversaries[90]. It is worthy of consideration to include these aspects. Sometimes, data is costly and time-intensive to re-identify, yet there are actors motivated to do so. Some data is very sensitive, other data loses its sensitivity over time.[91] For example, the ECJ has shown time[92] and again[93] that it considers state-sponsored surveillance a substantial threat to the GDPR privacy protections. As soon as state actors enter the arena of potential adversaries, however, what is in the realm of "reasonably likely" changes significantly: States typically have access to large amounts of computing power,[94] large amounts of human capital, and large amounts of data.[95]

Nonetheless, the GDPR makes a clear decision in Recital (26) s. 4: Only objective factors should be taken into account. At first sight, this sounds like it would preclude these additional factors, as they could be a subjective view. However, it is unclear what "objective" means in this context, and as the list of factors is exemplary and not exhaustive[96], I contend that one should include factors such as a risk for state-sponsored re-identification.

II. Relative vs. Absolute Identification: Who Identifies?

1. Problem Statement

Even more prominently, legal scholarship has focused on s. 4 of Recital (26) GDPR, which states:

> To determine whether a natural person is identifiable, account should be taken of all the means reasonably likely to be used, such as singling out, either by the controller or by another person to identify the natural person directly or indirectly.

While this provision clearly names both the controller and other persons as those who can potentially perform identification, it does not make a clear determination

89 Which can, of course, factor in through Art. 9 GDPR.

90 Arguing for the inclusion of this criterion: *Hubert*, "Daten und Sicherheit" (2025), p. 78.

91 M. H. *Hansen*, "Insuring confidentiality of individual records in data storage and retrieval for statistical purposes" (1971), p. 580.

92 Schrems I (Oct. 6, 2015).

93 *European Parliament*, "Schrems II" (July 16, 2021).

94 For a list of civilian "supercomputers", see *TOP500.org*, "November 2022 | TOP500" (Nov. 2022). Note that participation in the list is voluntary and that it is thus possible, if not likely, that military or intelligence facilities exist beyond the scope of the list.

95 Especially, state actors may have access to large amounts of census, financial, and other data about its own citizens or even those of foreign countries.

96 As denoted by the words "such as ...".

as to whose knowledge, means, and additional data need to be examined to determine identifiability.[97] This problem is exacerbated where multiple persons need to work together to identify.[98]

Under the Data Protection Directive, a similar provision[99] sparked a spirited discussion on whether a *relative* or an *absolute* view needs to be taken. Under the Data Protection Directive, as many as six different major viewpoints were held in the discussion.[100] Under the GDPR, this discussion continued, as even the new law did not resolve the issue clearly.[101]

Some have taken an absolute view, where data is "identifiable" where, using any knowledge potentially to be found in the world, someone can perform identification.[102] These authors typically argue using the specific dangers that exist, no matter who has access to the identifying information. Their position is in part supported by the grammatical interpretation of Recital (26) s. 3 GDPR, which states that identification can be performed "either by the controller or by another person".[103]

To those who have taken a relative view, it depends on the controller's point of view.[104] This means it depends on the individual means and technology available to the controller.[105] Especially important is the controller's additional knowledge.[106] Another common question surrounding relative identification is whether only legal measures of identification should be considered.[107] For example, should an assessment of identifiability include the possibility that a processor uses data that was leaked on the internet to identify users? In effect, this would mean that *only* that which can be identified legally would be personal data.

---

97 *Mühlenbeck*, "Anonyme und pseudonyme Daten" (2023), p. 106.

98 As was the case in the ECJ's *Breyer* case on IP addresses, see in detail below, see p. 103.

99 "account should be taken of all the means likely reasonably to be used either by the controller or by any other person to identify the said person", Recital (26) s. 1 Data Protection Directive.

100 For a detailed overview of the discussion circa 2015, see *Bergt*, "Die Bestimmbarkeit als Grundproblem des Datenschutzrechts – Überblick über den Theorienstreit und Lösungsvorschlag" (2015), pp. 365 sqq. w.f.r..

101 J. *Brauneck*, "Brauneck" (2019), p. 682; see also in detail: *Mühlenbeck*, "Anonyme und pseudonyme Daten" (2023), pp. 106 sqq.

102 See w.f.r.: *Mühlenbeck*, "Anonyme und pseudonyme Daten" (2023), p. 109.

103 Citing the similar provision under the Data Protection Directive: *Pahlen-Brandt*, "Datenschutz braucht scharfe Instrumente Beitrag zur Diskussion um „personenbezogene Daten“" (Jan. 2008), p. 38.

104 *Roßnagel* and *Scholz*, "Datenschutz durch Anonymität und Pseudonymität – Rechtsfolgen der Verwendung anonymer und pseudonymer Daten" (2000), p. 723; see also w.f.r.: *Mühlenbeck*, "Anonyme und pseudonyme Daten" (2023), p. 109.

105 J. *Brauneck*, "Brauneck" (2019), p. 682.

106 *Gola*, "DS-GVO Art. 4 Begriffsbestimmungen" (2022), margin no. 8.

107 w.f.r.: *Mühlenbeck*, "Anonyme und pseudonyme Daten" (2023), p. 114.

In the *Breyer* judgment and other decisions, the ECJ has maintained that "it is not required that all the information enabling the identification of the data subject must be in the hands of one person".[108] While the debate on this issue is still ongoing, I regard it to be mostly resolved with *Breyer*. *Mühlenbeck* concludes that a relative viewpoint, as endorsed by the ECJ, should be taken, with the added modification that knowledge of certain third parties should be taken into consideration whenever these third parties can be made to reveal their knowledge.[109] I agree. A decision by the European General Court (EGC) affirmed the ECJ's jurisdiction from *Breyer*.[110] In this decision, the EGC held that the determining factor was whether the controller in question had *legal* means available to it that could "in practice enable it to access the additional information necessary to re-identify".[111] At the time of this writing, an appeal at the ECJ was still outstanding.

For the balance of this thesis, we will examine ways of removing identifiability by making comparison (the elemental part of identification[112]) more difficult. Discussing comparison and linking necessarily requires auxiliary information with which to link. The provenance of this auxiliary information is a question of the distinction made in *Breyer*, yet it is irrelevant when considering anonymization methods (as these operate under the assumption that auxiliary information with which linking can be performed is available). Necessarily, this approach also means that a (moderately) relative viewpoint is taken. We will examine the viewpoint of the analyst who is given access to data that is anonymized.

When online methods[113] are considered, these must be thought in such a way that the analyst querying the online system has no reasonably likely means to viewing the "raw" database behind the online system. As a result, the outputs of the online system are (ideally, depending on the strength of the system and *other* available auxiliary information) anonymous to them. Nonetheless, this data is not anonymous to the controller operating the online system.[114] [115]

---

108 O.C. (Mar. 7, 2024), para. 48; referencing: Breyer (Oct. 19, 2016), para. 43.

109 *Mühlenbeck*, "Anonyme und pseudonyme Daten" (2023), p. 142.

110 Single Resolution Board v. EDPS (Apr. 26, 2023).

111 Ibid., margin no. 105.

112 See p. 71.

113 See p. 120.

114 differing opinion *Bruegger*, who contends: "*Anonymous* is thus clearly not defined relative to an actor … It would thus not make sense to say 'it is anonymous for the controller', since if it is not 'anonymous for other actors', it is not *anonymous* at all.", *Bruegger*, "Towards a Better Understanding of Identification, Pseudonymization, and Anonymization (v 1.0)" (June 11, 2021), p. 92.

115 This is in line with the approach taken by the ECJ in *Breyer* and *Scarlet Extended*: In *Breyer*, the Federal Republic of Germany requires *additional* information to allow for identifiability, which

2. The Canonical Example: IP Addresses

To illustrate the ECJ's view, let me quickly introduce the canonical example used in these cases, which is that of the IP address. Historically, IP addresses have played an outsized role as quasi-identifiers in practice and jurisprudence.[116] This relative importance is reflected in that the GDPR expressly references IP addresses: Art. 4 § 1 GDPR speaks of "online identifiers". These are further explained in Recital (30) s. 1 GDPR to be "provided by their devices … such as internet protocol adresses …". Conversely, the corollary under the Data Protection Directive, Art. 2 (a) Data Protection Directive, made no mention of "online identifiers".

IP addresses are a core building block of computer networks. As the internet is just a combination of these networks, IP addresses are ubiquitous in modern-day computing. An IP address is given to all users on a network.[117] Through this, an IP address can oftentimes reliably identify not only a device, but also a user and thereby a natural person. We need to distinguish between the situation for the old (but still widely used) IPv4 protocol and its addressing scheme and the "new" IPv6 protocol that was proposed in 1995.

a) IPv4 addresses

Oftentimes in the technical context and nearly always in the legal context, "IP address" really means "IPv4 address". IPv4 addresses are usually specified as four integers ≤ 255,[118] separated by periods, such as `8.8.8.8`[119] or `192.168.1.1`[120].

Even though the relative importance for data protection jurisdiction and the term "address" itself would suggest that users can be directly identified through it, this is not the case: In and of themselves, these addresses have little significance. In IPv4, only 2^{32} (about 4.3 billion) theoretical addresses are available.[121] In practice,

it can—theoretically—gain from the ISP. In *Scarlet Extended*, the ISP holds all necessary data for identification, Scarlet Extended (Nov. 24, 2011), para. 51.

116 See: Breyer (Oct. 19, 2016) and Scarlet Extended (Nov. 24, 2011).

117 More specifically, all *network interfaces* on a network. Additionally, there is a distinction between *local* or *private* IP addresses (*i.e.* those in the same network, typically with the prefix 192.168 in the IPv4 scheme, though other prefixes are used, see *Moskowitz* et al., "Address Allocation for Private Internets" (Feb. 1996), p. 3) and *public* or *global* IP addresses (for example viewable through services such as https://whatismyip.com).

118 More specifically: Four bytes (eight bits) of information. Each of these bytes can be expressed as a binary number or an unsigned decimal-system integer of 0 through 255.

119 The IP address for Google's Public DNS service, see https://dns.google/.

120 A host on the local network, as signified by `192.168`, see *Moskowitz* et al., "Address Allocation for Private Internets" (Feb. 1996), p. 3.

121 *Institute*, "RFC 791" (Sept. 1981).

even less are available, because wide ranges of addresses are reserved for special use, such as local addresses.[122]

As these addresses are limited and demand for them has grown very quickly over the past 20 years, they are in constant danger of being depleted. To counteract this, the use of NAT is widespread. Typically, this means that a "public" IP address can only identify a subnet (*e.g.*, a household), but not the users (*e.g.*, family members) on it. The NAT-enabled router "translates" the requests so they are routed to the correct local user.[123]

IPv4 addresses are assigned to operators, typically large telecommunications companies. These re-distribute IP addresses as needed. For example, web hosting services and large companies sometimes require "static" IPv4 addresses, *i.e.*, an IP address that is fixed and does not change.[124] A typical home user or small business receives a so-called dynamic IPv4 address, *i.e.*, an IP address that can change over time. The IP address is changed regularly, for example when the internet connection is re-connected.

The "owners" of static IP addresses are typically known, sometimes even to the public.[125] As static IP addresses do not change regularly, they are more privacy-critical than dynamic IP addresses. Therefore, it is broadly accepted that static IP addresses constitute personal data.[126] It is important to note that static and dynamic IP addresses "look" exactly the same and cannot be distinguished in a dataset. This alone means that *potentially*, all IP addresses would need to be treated as if they were static.[127]

With a dynamic IP address, only the internet provider knows which customer account (*i.e.*, natural person or persons) are associated with which IP address at a given time. Thus, the IP address is classic *pseudonymous* data.[128] It should be noted that this information pertains only to the ISP's customer, who is not necessarily the

122 *Moskowitz* et al., "Address Allocation for Private Internets" (Feb. 1996), p. 3.

123 Explaining this technology would be beyond the scope of this dissertation. Basically, it uses some tricks to make sure that multiple local users (for example, all devices in one household) can "use" one public IP address (typically dynamically assigned to them by their internet provider, more on that below) together. An extreme example would be a university network where all (*e.g.*, student or staff) users share the same public IP address.

124 For example, to "connect" a domain such as example.com to a server where the corresponding webpage is hosted, the domain administrator needs to set a Domain Name System (DNS) A record that sets the corresponding IP address for example.com.

125 *Breyer*, "Personenbezug von IP-Adressen Internetnutzung und Datenschutz" (2014), p. 400.

126 Ibid., p. 400.

127 Ibid., p. 400.

128 Scarlet Extended (Nov. 24, 2011).

end user “behind the screen”.[129] Providers retain this information only for a limited time, most often to provide evidence for prosecution or litigation. However, prolonging the period in which providers retain this information has been the subject of a saga of legislation in Member States as well as on a European scale: The 2006 Data Retention Directive was declared invalid in 2014. Efforts to introduce a data retention law in Germany failed in 2017, when they were found to be in violation of EU law. As of 2019, providers were found to still practice “voluntary” data retention, but time frames varied.[130]

As outlined above and confirmed by an ECJ judgment in *Scarlet Extended*[131], (dynamic) IP addresses are personal data for the telecommunications provider.[132] From here on, it was clear that the providers had to treat IP addresses as personal data, but—since the question of relative and absolute views of personal data was not resolved—it was unclear whether this meant IP addresses would *generally* be personal data.

This resolution came in 2016, when *Patrick Breyer*,[133] a judge and member of the German “Piratenpartei”, brought a lawsuit against the Federal Republic of Germany that made it to the ECJ.[134] The plaintiff pointed out that the webpages operated by the federal government in Germany were using logging software that recorded all IP addresses that accessed the page, and that this practice infringed on his privacy.[135] The plaintiff argued that these addresses are personal data, which means that the federal government requires a legal basis for processing under Data Protection Directive.

The ECJ reasoned that interested parties can legally compel the telecommunications provider to give up information about the natural person that was associated with the IPv4 address at a given time. For this reason, IP addresses are personal data. For static IP addresses, the same logic applies, but the problem is less salient, as the addresses are longer-lived and therefore data retention is not as much of an issue.

Looking at IP addresses through the lens of our definition above, even dynamic IP addresses can be said to “relate” to a natural person: In the context in which

129 *Davis*, “Facial Detection and Smart Billboards” (2020), p. 373.

130 *Krempl*, “Anzeige erstattet” (Jan. 2, 2019).

131 Scarlet Extended (Nov. 24, 2011).

132 Ibid., margin no. 51.

133 Who already made his position clear in the time leading up to the judgment, *i.a.*, in *Breyer*, “Personenbezug von IP-Adressen Internetnutzung und Datenschutz” (2014).

134 Breyer (Oct. 19, 2016).

135 It must be added: As is or was common practice at this point.

they would typically appear, *e.g.*, a log file on a web server[136], an IP address can even, in many cases, be used to single out a natural person in a dataset. This is true notwithstanding the reassignment of dynamic IP addresses and the use of NAT: The timeframe between an address being reassigned is sufficiently long to enable user tracking and oftentimes, NAT is not an issue as only one person in the household simultaneously uses a certain webpage.

However, this person must also be identifiable. This identifiability is at the heart of the problem: According to the ECJ, it suffices that there is a theoretical legal way of obtaining this information, for example by legally compelling the service provider to give out its information. This is often done in the case of copyright violations, typically in peer-to-peer file sharing cases. In the *Breyer* judgment, the ECJ concluded that in the case where a webmaster could theoretically use legal means to gain the assistance of other entities, in this case the internet service provider, to identify the natural person behind the IP address.[137]

On the whole, I would agree that this determination strikes an acceptable balance. One can also not help but wonder whether the line of argumentation is somehow derived from the desire to classify IP addresses as personal data, especially as the possibility of identifying Patrick Breyer through his IP address by gaining a court order that compels the ISP to link the address to his name seems less than reasonably likely to me. Because authorities penalize controllers on the basis of this distinction, it is important to be exact. Ultimately, I would agree that IP addresses rightfully *are* personal data, but only where and as long as the controller can turn to someone else to use them for re-identification.

An aspect that is seldom touched upon when talking about IPv4 addresses is what happens when the internet provider no longer has access to the data linking the account to a certain address. In this case, the link between the pseudonym and the original data has been destroyed, so that the IP address is now anonymous.

A common way of "anonymizing" IP addresses is using truncation, *i.e.*, leaving out one or two octets to the right of the address—for example, `198.51.100.243` becomes `198.51.0.0`. For example, Google[138] used to "anonymize" its search logs by just deleting the rightmost octet.[139] The same was practiced in Google Analytics up until version 4.[140] Recently, Google has introduced a new version of Analytics

136 *i.e.*, a file that contains a log of all users that have accessed a certain web page. These "logs" are commonplace and used for technical purposes (*e.g.*, the prevention of Denial of Service (DoS) attacks) as well as to prepare for litigation.

137 Breyer (Oct. 19, 2016), para. 48.

138 For Google Analytics, see p. 11.

139 *Toubiana* and *Nissenbaum*, "An Analysis of Google Logs Retention Policies" (June 1, 2011), p. 3.

140 *Google, Inc.*, "IP masking in Universal Analytics - Analytics Help" (2023).

which does not log or store IP addresses.[141] As a result, this part of the debate has achieved clear practical results.

b) IPv6 addresses

Having spoken about IPv4, it is also important to spend a short moment on IPv6, its successor. Version 6 of the internet protocol (IPv6) (*i.a.*) has support for more IP addresses: Now, a theoretical maximum of 2^{128} addresses[142] are available. This allows for a much more liberal use of the addresses, which makes NAT unnecessary.

This dramatic increase in address space means that hypothetically and practically, a device can have the same IPv6 address over its lifetime. This would allow for boundless tracking.[143] As IPv6 rollout has taken place since the early 2010s, the convention has changed. In the beginning, part of a device's IPv6 address would be the device's media access control address (MAC address), a string that uniquely identifies[144] a network adapter[145]. However, this was quickly found to be detrimental to user privacy: Including the MAC address in the IPv6 address, which uniquely identifies each device, leads to users being even more easily identifiable than with IPv4 addresses. Additionally, the MAC address includes information about the vendor of the network interface, which would enable targeting users on this basis alone—for example, targeting users of "enterprise-grade" network interfaces or owners of specific PC hardware. It also allows for addresses to be permanent, *i.e.*, with an indefinite lifetime. This enables tracking users in a way that was impossible with (dynamic) IPv4 addresses. This problem is exacerbated by the fact that in IPv6, typically the IP address is generated using so-called stateless address auto-configuration and not using a DHCP server (as was used in IPv4). DHCP[146] servers could make sure that the same address was not used twice. However, where an address is generated using stateless address auto-configuration, other ways need to be found to make *globally* unique interface identifiers. To address these shortcomings, privacy-focused alter-

141 *Google, Inc.*, "EU-focused data and privacy - Analytics Help" (2023).

142 Around 340 trillion trillion trillion.

143 As *Breyer* notes 2014, *Breyer*, "Personenbezug von IP-Adressen Internetnutzung und Datenschutz" (2014), p. 401.

144 Though *spoofing*, *i.e.*, impersonating a different MAC address is trivial.

145 Note that each network adapter has its own MAC address. For example, in a typical laptop computer, there may be a network adapter for Wi-Fi and one for Ethernet. These would have different MAC addresses.

146 Dynamic Host Configuration Protocol. A DHCP server in an IPv4 network centrally assigns IP addresses to devices.

natives were introduced: Privacy Extensions in the form of Temporary addresses[147] and, later, modifications to stateless address auto-configuration (SLAAC)[148]. Their practical relevance remain to be seen. It must be noted that the discussion around IPv6 has been ongoing for nearly two decades, yet adoption has been slow. Nonetheless, it is clear that IPv6 is the future of the internet and will therefore play a pivotal role in years to come.

3. Result

The ECJ's jurisdiction on auxiliary information from *Breyer* is generally sensible. As shown, however, the intricacies of IP addresses are too complex to be covered by a broad, generalizing statement such as "all IP addresses are personal data". Static IP addresses can be personal data, dynamic IP addresses are often personal data, IPv6 addresses may be personal data, depending on the mechanism used. The identifiability of these addresses depends on the legal access to the ISP's information. In *Breyer* and under the German law relevant to the case, this was straightforward. In other cases, it may not be. Another important question to be considered is for how long the ISP retains the information linking a certain (dynamic) IP address to a certain customer. After this information is deleted, even the ISP can no longer identify on the basis of a dynamic IP address.

III. A Recent Example: *O.C.*

In a recent case, the ECJ has brought up some interesting points on identification through quasi-identifiers and identifying circumstances. In the case, *O.C.*, a researcher had applied for a large European research grant and then misappropriated the funds, partially transferring the money to her personal account.[149] The EU anti-fraud division, OLAF, published a press release on the case, in which it noted, *i.a.*, the scientist's "gender, nationality and profession, the mention that she was a young person and that she was responsible for the funded research project at issue, as well as the reference to the amount of the grant, the awarding body, …, the nature of the entity which hosted the project and the country …, the reference to [her] father … [who worked] within that entity, and the approximate number of

147 *Narten*, *Draves*, and *Krishnan*, "Privacy Extensions for Stateless Address Autoconfiguration in IPv6" (Sept. 2007).

148 *Gont*, "A Method for Generating Semantically Opaque Interface Identifiers with IPv6 Stateless Address Autoconfiguration (SLAAC)" (Apr. 2014).

149 The background is given in detail in the decision itself: O.C. (Mar. 7, 2024), paras. 13 sqq.

researchers working for [her]".[150] The ECJ held—overturning the prior judgment by the EGC—that this information can allow for identification, "in particular by those working in the same scientific field ...".[151] The ECJ held that even where—as happened in the present case—a journalist has "disseminated the identity of a person", this does not in itself make the press release personal data.[152] The Court concludes that the press release in itself poses a significant risk of identification, which does not require a "disproportionate effort in terms of time, cost and labour".[153] While this formula appears close in spirit to the wording in Recital (26) s. 4 GDPR, it may become the default phrase of the Court in the future in similar cases. In the present case, I agree with the Court's assessment, as the circumstances presented make it indeed straightforward to find out the name and other details on the person in question by carrying out "internet searches".[154]

3.5 Conclusion

We can summarize that anonymization means modifying data in such a way that it is no longer identifiable. The GDPR only requires *de facto* anonymity, and "means reasonably likely to be used" all depend on the atomic element of comparison. They are chiefly linking and singling out, with inference not being a means to identify. The question of "reasonable likelihood" also extends to the data used in this comparison. This data does not need to be in the hands of one person, but rather can be gathered from third parties, if they can—legally or factually—be made to give up their knowledge. For example, an ISP can be made to turn over the name and contact details of one of its customers for a given dynamic IPv4 address, insofar as that provider still retains this information. Another question to which the standard of "reasonable likelihood" extends is the question of identifying circumstances, such as in *O.C.*. Of course, each case is different, yet in circumstances as those in *O.C.*, the auxiliary information is "reasonably likely" to be found, making the person identifiable. Anonymization needs to be distinguished from pseudonymization and de-identification. The GDPR does not prescribe a specific anonymization technique.[155]

150 Ibid., para. 59.
151 Ibid., para. 60.
152 Ibid., para. 58.
153 Ibid., para. 61.
154 ibid., para. 63.
155 *Mühlenbeck* and *Schwartmann*, "Art. 4 Begriffsbestimmungen" (2024), margin no. 43.

Part II: **Anonymizing Structured Data**

The conviction at the center of this work is that different kinds of data necessitate different approaches to anonymization. In other words, anonymizing unstructured data with methods for structured data simply does not work.[1] This part will look at *structured* data. Structured data, for the purposes of this text, is nothing more than data that has been made to adhere to a certain structure, typically in the format of a database.[2]

In the "real world", data is typically not structured: On seeing a text or an image, the viewer cannot infer what kind of information they will gain from reading the text or studying the image. To access this information, they must invest time and effort to study the data. The resulting information is also often open to interpretation: A text can (deliberately or accidentally) take on different meanings, and image and video data can support different interpretations of the same event. These properties—difficulty of access and ambiguity—are not desirable for data analysis. They especially make automated processing of this data difficult: There are entire branches of Artificial Intelligence research (namely Computer Vision and Natural Language Processing) concerned with training computers to process these data types. Additionally, humans have heuristics—glancing at a visual or skimming a text—that can help quickly extract meaning, whereas computers process data differently. As a result, different ways of structuring data have emerged that make raw data more easily usable.

The easiest and most common way to structure data is in a database. These databases are the fabric of the information revolution. They permeate every aspect of our digital lives. Therefore, the following chapters will look at data stored in databases and at how to anonymize such data.[3]

We will begin by outlining the infrastructure,[4] a common data model, and the adversarial mindset[5] that needs to be taken when talking about anonymization. Next, we will progress from trivial approaches to anonymizing this structured data (removing obvious identifiers[6]) to removing quasi-identifiers, first through syntac-

---

1 It is a "category mistake", see *Altman, Cohen, Nissim*, et al., "What a Hybrid Legal-Technical Analysis Teaches Us about Privacy Regulation" (2021), p. 26.

2 More on databases: see p. 117.

3 As a caveat, not all data structures are relational databases. Yet, due to their overwhelming popularity as data storage, we will limit our discussion to them. Most of what is said in the following chapters can easily be adapted to other types of data storage, such as key–value stores.

4 See p. 117.

5 See p. 123.

6 See p. 125.

https://doi.org/10.1515/9783112222164-005

tical methods to satisfy *k*-Anonymity and its corollaries[7], through DP[8], and through assorted other methods[9].

7 See p. 138.
8 See p. 146.
9 See p. 168.

4 Infrastructure for Data

4.1 Prototypical Display of Structured Data: Relational Database

Structured data is typically available in some form of database. There are multiple types of database models. The most popular type of database model is that of the relational database, which was first described by Codd[1] in 1970 and popularized throughout the 1980s. Despite recent attempts to unseat the Relational Database Management System (RDBMS) paradigm by competing approaches, it remains widely popular and the dominant model today.[2] [3]

A database, as understood through the paradigm of the relational database model, is comprised of multiple *tables* (also called *relations*).[4] These tables contain *records* (also called *tuples* or *rows*). One record is a collection of information displaying a relationship between the values that comprise a record.[5] Records can be (and typically are) comprised of many individual datapoints. For example, the record of an employee in a payroll database may include her employee identifier (ID) number, her banking details, her home address, etc.

Typically, relations are visualized as tables (akin to in a spreadsheet program, such as Microsoft Excel), where each record is one line of the table (see Figure 4.1). Columns of a table (also called *attributes*) can be linked to other columns in other tables through *relationships*. The most common relationships are *one-to-one*, *one-to-many*, *many-to-one*, and *many-to-many* relationships.

For example, a student database at a high school could have a table that includes students' basic information (name, address, emergency phone numbers, etc.) and a table that lists cohorts of students as well as a table with a list of classes that students can enroll in.[6] Each student can be part of just one cohort,[7] while a student can be

1 *Codd*, "A relational model of data for large shared data banks" (June 1970), p. 11.

2 *Watt*, "Database Design" (Oct. 24, 2014), p. 153.

3 Note, however, that not all databases are relational and that other types of databases are "structured data" in the here-used sense, too. For example, key–value databases such as Redis (https://redis.io) are also "structured data". However, their less dogmatic structure leads to anonymization becoming more difficult—a subject that would be beyond the scope of this dissertation.

4 *Silberschatz*, *Korth*, and *Sudarshan*, "Database system concepts" (2020), p. 39.

5 Ibid., p. 39.

6 This example uses the U.S. concept of a high school, but it is easily adaptable to other school systems such as the German system, where students are organized in "Klassen"—each student can have only one "Klasse".

7 A many-to-one relationship (Many students to one cohort).

https://doi.org/10.1515/9783112222164-006

Students

STUDENT_ID PRIMARY_KEY	First_Name VARCHAR(32)	Last_Name VARCHAR(32)	Cohort FOREIGN_KEY	Gender INTEGER	Classes JSON
1	Amy	McAllister	40	2	{[1,2]}
2	Denzel	Williams	42	1	{[3,4]}
3	Kim	Delacroix	41	9	{[4,2]}
4	Liza	Sanchez	40	2	{[3,1]}

Cohorts

COHORT_ID PRIMARY_KEY	GRAD_YEAR INTEGER
40	2023
41	2024
42	2025
43	2026

Classes

CLASS_ID PRIMARY_KEY	Teacher FOREIGN_KEY	Name VARCHAR(32)
1	45	American History
2	34	Psychology
3	50	Ceramics
4	43	Marketing

Fig. 4.1: Example of a student database.

enrolled in multiple classes. Vice versa, each class can have multiple students. These tables are bound together using *keys*, which are typically sequentially numbered IDs.

For example, Student 1 is a part of Cohort 40 and enrolled in classes 1 and 2 (cf. Figure 4.1). This allows for multi-layered data models that can model complex data structures.

Unlike a printed register (e.g., a phone book) or a spreadsheet, databases are typically not viewed in their entirety. This is mostly because displaying all entries of a table would be computationally expensive, especially in the case of tables with millions of records. To interact with a database, the user must write *queries*. The database software will then return the result of the query. These queries are typically written in the programming language SQL ("Structured Query Language"), which was first developed in the early 1970s at IBM.[8]

For example, the SQL query `SELECT FROM Classes` will return the entirety of the `Classes` table, whereas `SELECT First_Name FROM Students` will return only the first name attribute (column) of the `student` database. Conditional filtering is also possible, *e.g.*, `SELECT Last_Name FROM Students WHERE Gender = 2` will return all female students.[9]

8 *Silberschatz, Korth,* and *Sudarshan,* "Database system concepts" (2020), p. 65.

9 The data format here follows the ISO/IEC 5218 standard where 0 equals not known, 1 equals male, 2 equals female, and 9 equals not applicable, see *ISO/IEC,* "ISO/IEC 5218."

Additional operations, such as joining two tables together, are also available. In the context of linking data[10], the underlying operation is often an inner join—combining a table of anonymized data with outside information to re-identify persons.[11] Using complex queries, the user can create, read, update, and delete records, tables, attributes, and the database itself.

4.2 A Mental Model of Data and Data Storage

For the purposes of this text, we will assume that personal data in the form of structured data resides in a database somewhere. The database can be queried by an analyst. This analyst wants to gain information about the data.

Anonymization as a sub-discipline in computer science is an adjacent field to cryptography. Cryptography is often concerned with securing communications between actors. By convention, these actors are named "Alice" and "Bob". In this setting in cryptography, Alice and Bob try to engage in a (confidential) conversation using a certain cryptographic method, for example ROT13 encryption.[12] Depending on the problem being evaluated, there is also often an eavesdropper, typically called "Eve". Eve's intent is to intercept the conversation between Alice and Bob and decrypt it in order to gain access to their secured communications (see figure 4.2.) Another regular is Mallory, who is a generic malicious actor. Mallory typically not only wants to eavesdrop on conversations, but also interfere with them.

In some ways, the typical situation in anonymization is analogous to the typical "Alice, Bob, and Mallory" scenario in cryptography, where the analyst uses a query mechanism to gain access to the data. However, the analogy only holds partially: In the "Alice, Bob, and Mallory" scenario, the intended recipient (Bob) and the unintended, malicious recipient (Mallory) are two distinct roles.
In the anonymization example, the analyst is both Bob and Mallory: They are the intended recipient who is allowed to perform analyses on the data, yet they can also follow a malicious agenda, trying to de-anonymize the data using the access they have been given. It is important to keep this difference in mind when thinking about cryptographically secure building blocks for anonymization and methods such as homomorphic encryption[13].

10 See p. 64.

11 *Ohm*, "Broken Promises of Privacy" (2009–2010), pp. 1725 sq.

12 ROT13 is a very simple and very easily broken kind of symmetric encryption: It replaces each letter of the transmission with the 13th letter that follows it in the alphabet. For example, ANONYMIZATION becomes NABALZVMNGVBA.

13 See p. 175.

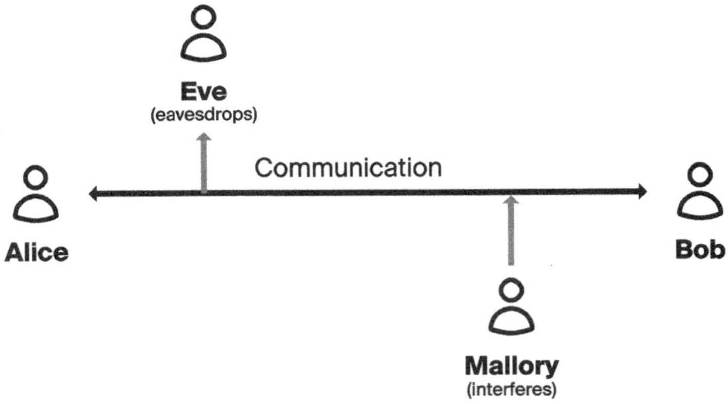

Fig. 4.2: Schematic of Alice, Bob, Eve, and Mallory.

4.3 Online and Offline Access to Data

A recurring point of confusion is the distinction between online and offline access to data.

In some systems, data is anonymized and then released to the analyst. The analyst has "full control" over the data: They can make any kind of queries they like, and they can inspect the data on their system freely. Put simply: They "have" the data. This is called "offline" access, and it is the simplest way of making anonymization systems. All early methods of anonymization were of the offline variant: One would take the source data, anonymize it, and release it.

A different and somewhat more recent approach is that of "online" access to a data source. In this paradigm, the analyst never receives a copy of the data. Instead, they can use queries to learn about the data. Anonymization happens "between" the source database and the analyst. This paradigm enables mechanisms that do not work in an offline scenario, such as query auditing[14] and to some extent differential privacy[15].

Of course, there are limitations to both approaches. For example, in the offline version, the data is released once and for all—and can thus not be changed later.

14 See p. 168.
15 See p. 156.

4.4 Other Types of Structured Data

Thus far, we have focused on "typical" tabular data: A list of customers, hospital release data, or a list of ballots cast. While these are an important type of data, they are far from the only one. As we will see in the section on unstructured data[16], the boundary between structured and unstructured data is blurry.

While there are myriads of types of data we can consider here, there are two that warrant special attention: Geodata and graph data.

I. Geodata

Geodata, *i.e.*, data that contains geographical information, has always been a special case, as it allows for robust identification[17] and potentially reveals large amounts of data about people.[18]

The typical path to anonymizing geodata is through aggregation.[19] Geodata presents a number of challenges for privacy and anonymization. Geospatial data can be structured (*e.g.*, a list of locations) or unstructured (*e.g.*, a map of a building).

Anonymizing geodata is a very difficult problem in its own right, as there are far more pitfalls to avoid than with normal anonymization.[20]

Most research in this field has been done surrounding cell phone records.[21] For instance, in 2011, a study found that removing user identifiers alone provided little

---

16 See p. 193.

17 *De Montjoye* et al., "Unique in the Crowd" (Mar. 25, 2013).

18 See *e.g.*, for the Data Protection Directive in 2004: *Poullet* and *Dinant*, "Thoughts on Convention No. 108 for the purposes of the future work of the Consultative Committee (T-PD)" (Dec. 13, 2024), p. 34.

19 *Weichert*, "Geodaten — datenschutzrechtliche Erfahrungen, Erwartungen und Empfehlungen" (June 1, 2009), p. 351.

20 As a result, going into detail here would be beyond the scope of this thesis. For an illustration of the pitfalls in anonymizing a geo-location, see *Heaton*, "How Tinder keeps your exact location (a bit) private" (July 9, 2018) and *Weichert*, "Geodaten — datenschutzrechtliche Erfahrungen, Erwartungen und Empfehlungen" (June 1, 2009), p. 351. For the question of identifiability in geodata, especially with regard to Google Street View, see *Caspar*, "Geoinformationen und Datenschutz am Beispiel des Dienstes Google Street View" (2009), pp. 966 sq. and *Forgó* and *Krügel*, "Der Personenbezug von Geodaten – Cui bono, wenn alles bestimmbar ist?" (2010), pp. 18 sqq. From a more technical perspective (though from 2011 and thus outdated), see aggregation methods for location data in *Zang* and *Bolot*, "Anonymization of location data does not work" (Sept. 19, 2011).

21 Using the so-called "Call Details Records" (CDRs) that cell phone carriers collect to enable billing and ease troubleshooting, see ibid., p. 1.

privacy.[22] In 2013, researchers found, using cell phone carrier data, that four "spatio-temporal points"—*i.e.*, four sets of coordinates associated with a timestamp—are enough to uniquely identify (single out) 95% of individuals.[23] Even two randomly chosen points can still uniquely characterize over 50% of individuals.[24] They found that even lowering the resolution of their data through aggregation did not work.

In summary, geodata is a difficult problem in anonymization that warrants a domain-specific view and may present hurdles that are beyond the scope of the anonymization methods discussed in this text.

II. Graph Data

Another problematic area is graph data.[25] In computer science, a graph is a data structure consisting of nodes and edges. In such a graph, the nodes (also called vertices, typically represented graphically by a circle or dot) are connected by the edges (typically represented graphically by a line). This data structure can be used to represent relationships, for example, the nodes can represent users of a social network and the edges can represent virtual "friendships" between these users.[26]

This data type is problematic in that the graph itself may disclose information, even when its nodes are de-identified. For example, given a graph of workers in an office, where only those workers are connected who have eaten lunch together in the past year, some persons may be quickly identified: If the manager commonly invites her subordinates to a yearly feedback lunch, she may be the only person connected to nearly all others. Likewise, if one employee is completely remote and never comes to the office, they will not be connected to nearly anyone. This is another area where data does not fit into our structured–unstructured dichotomy, and where finding a suitable anonymization paradigm is very difficult.

22 *Zang* and *Bolot*, "Anonymization of location data does not work" (Sept. 19, 2011).

23 *De Montjoye* et al., "Unique in the Crowd" (Mar. 25, 2013), p. 2.

24 Ibid., p. 2.

25 For an introduction to graphs, see *Coupette*, "Juristische Netzwerkforschung" (2019), pp. 1 sqq.

26 For anonymization in social networks (however, without reference to graphs and their anonymity), see *Beyvers*, "Privatheit in der Waagschale. Instrumente des datenschutzrechtlichen Interessenausgleichs im Kontext sozialer Online-Netzwerke" (2018), p. 227.

4.5 Mindset and Framing: Adversarial Approach

Historically, advances in privacy research and legislation were precipitated by prior data breaches and de-anonymization attacks. For example, the case of *Sweeney*'s re-identification of William Weld,[27] or the AOL data release[28].

Another important case was that of the Netflix prize. In 2006, Netflix released a dataset of movie ratings that its subscribers had created, along with the promise of a $1M U.S. dollar prize for the best proposal for improving its suggestion algorithm.[29] The company promised to "[have removed] all customer identifying information" and have perturbed[30] the data.[31] Nonetheless, they did not provide information on the noise added. As *Narayanan* and *Shmatikov* showed, either no noise was added, or it was "far too small to affect [their] de-anonymization algorithm".[32] They obtained a second dataset, namely the movie ratings from IMDb, the Internet Movie Database[33].[34] Indeed, they were able to use the public IMDb data to find the totality of private movie ratings made on Netflix.[35] As they note, this can lead to significant real-world harm, for example when political or religious views or a predilection for "movies with predominantly gay themes" are revealed in this way.[36]

This example, just like the others mentioned above, shows a more general way of framing anonymization research: Thinking about *breaking* anonymity is often the correct approach to finding *better* versions of anonymization techniques. Using this lens, science advanced from pure de-identification to recognizing *quasi-identifiers* (the foundational principle behind *k*-Anonymity[37]). We therefore need to view anonymization as an attacker would: From a de-anonymization perspective.

---

27 See p. 138.

28 See p. 195.

29 *Narayanan* and *Shmatikov*, "Robust De-anonymization of Large Sparse Datasets" (May 2008), p. 8.

30 "Perturbation" means altering the data, most often by adding random noise to it. For more information on this process, see the sections on randomization (see p. 143) and differential privacy (see p. 146).

31 *Narayanan* and *Shmatikov*, "Robust De-anonymization of Large Sparse Datasets" (May 2008), p. 8.

32 Ibid., p. 9.

33 https://www.imdb.com.

34 *Narayanan* and *Shmatikov*, "Robust De-anonymization of Large Sparse Datasets" (May 2008), pp. 12 sq.

35 Ibid., p. 13.

36 Ibid., p. 13.

37 See p. 138.

A simple approach to preventing de-anonymization would be to anonymize a dataset, not tell anyone *how* it was anonymized, and then release it. For example, when adding random noise to a dataset,[38] the properties of the noise help in de-anonymization. When swapping values, the knowledge of *how* the swapping is performed helps to "un-swap" them. This approach is akin to one known in cybersecurity as "security through obscurity", in other words: As long as no one knows the cryptography used, it (apparently) cannot be broken easily. As attractive this approach might seem, it simply does not work in practice. The Netflix example above showed that the quality of the noise inserted, for example, can be verified, for example using known original data.[39] In cybersecurity, "security through obscurity" is widely viewed as an anti-pattern. It stands to reason that the same should be true for anonymization.

38 See p. 143.

39 *Narayanan* and *Shmatikov*, "Robust De-anonymization of Large Sparse Datasets" (May 2008), p. 9.

5 De-Identification First

Before we will delve into the difficult questions of anonymization for quasi-identifiers, we must take a look at the easier question of identifiers[1] such as names. As we have outlined above,[2] de-identification is the removal of a set of identifiers. This is usually straightforward, especially in the case of structured data.

5.1 Anonymizing Identifiers

The first task is to remove identifiers, *i.e.*, information that is meant to identify natural persons.[3] [4]

Anonymization is an endeavor in the service of two constitutents: For one, the natural person, who is protected through (good) anonymization, but also the analyst, who should still be able to gain meaningful insights from the data. At first sight, it seems that the first is a legal obligation, while the second is nothing but an economic incentive. This overlooks that the primary motivation of anonymization lies in the usability of the data even after it has been performed.[5] As a result, we should strive to include all information that is useful for analysis and—if need be—undertake special efforts to anonymize it well, whereas we can discard any information that is unlikely to be useful for analysts without thinking about its anonymization in detail.

This is of special salience in the field of identifiers. Some identifiers (such as identification numbers[6]) contain no information beyond itself. Others contain information, but solely the kind of information that can be used for nefarious purposes (such as names[7]). And finally, some identifiers, such as addresses[8], contain useful information worthy of preservation. It is therefore our task to inquire into the "usefulness" of various types of data.

---

1 These may also be called "direct" identifiers by some observers. For terminology, see p. 76.

2 See p. 95.

3 See p. 76.

4 Note 88: *Hölzel*, "Anonymisierungstechniken und das Datenschutzrecht" (Aug. 2018), p. 507.

5 see p. 14 and see p. 96.

6 See p. 128.

7 See p. 126.

8 See p. 127.

https://doi.org/10.1515/9783112222164-007

I. Names

For example, it is clear that names need to be removed from the dataset. The extent to which this is done is sometimes debated: Some want to "generalize" names by shortening them to initials.[9] It should be noted that there is no clear way of randomizing[10] names. The only remaining and viable option for anonymizing names is completely suppressing[11] them, *i.e.*, removing the entire attribute[12]. However, this does not result in a significant loss of information: Names are arbitrary and contain little information in themselves. In other words: They are seldom useful for analysis.

Nonetheless, when suppressing values completely, consideration needs to be given to the loss of utility in the data. The question becomes: Is there data contained in a name that is useful for analysis—data that could be preserved if names could be generalized or randomized instead of suppressed? There is some information that *is* contained in a name.[13] It usually relates to families or ancestry, to gender, and sometimes to ethnicity, sometimes to social status. Surnames may relate to families or ancestry in that they express an individual's "belonging" to a certain family. This can be used to link persons together as belonging to the same family (especially where the surname is uncommon). It can also be used to derive additional information. Some family names may provide information about the bearer by their structure (a last name such as "Duke of Rothesay" or "von Wittgenstein" will indicate nobility) or by their content (a last name such as "Rockefeller" or "Kennedy" will evoke association with the families of John D. Rockefeller and John F. Kennedy). Titles, *i.e.*, suffixes and prefixes to a name add reliable information about a person's academic or military achievements. ("Dr.", "General", "RiOLG", "LL.B.") It is a trivial observation that first names also typically reveal the gender of a person. Some first names are sometimes associated with a specific ethnicity.[14] Some first names may also be used as a proxy for the bearer's provenance or social status. For example, in Germany, some first names are commonly associated with the former German

---

9 This is, for example, commonly done when "anonymizing" court decisions in Germany.

10 See p. 143.

11 See p. 133.

12 Column, for terminology see p. 117.

13 What follows is a very Western-centric view of the issue. I am certain that some cultures assign a higher significance to names, and that names may contain more information about the named person in some cultures. I hope that I am forgiven for the omission of a discussion on these points and invite comments on the issue.

14 For more on this problem, see *Sweeney*, "Discrimination in Online Ad Delivery" (Jan. 28, 2013); *Bertrand* and *Mullainathan*, "Are Emily and Greg More Employable than Lakisha and Jamal?" (July 2003).

Democratic Republic (GDR),[15] and some have been associated with low social status or academic potential[16].[17]

However, none of these implications are typically desirable from a data protection standpoint—except in cases where these attributes are the target of the analysis—so eliminating them is a straightforward matter. Where these attributes are target of the analysis, they are usually added to the data independently of the name.

Removing names from a database is easy. For example, in the school example given above, we would need to delete the `fname` and `lname` columns from the `students` table.[18]

II. Addresses

Addresses are another common identifier.[19] They can provide large amounts and very granular information about humans. For example, a shared address can be used to link people together that live in the same building (which can imply co-habitation) or it can be used to approximate income or social status (based on the neighborhood).

Depending on the format used, addresses contain large amounts of additional data. For example, an address in a format where the user can freely enter their information may contain additions such as "℅" statements, which contain the name of a second person and may imply co-habitation. It may also contain a reference to businesses forwarding or accepting mail in the person's stead, such as a front desk at a company office accepting parcels for its employees.

15 *Mitteldeutscher Rundfunk*, "DDR-Vornamen und ihre Vorurteile" (Dec. 6, 2021).

16 *Trenkamp*, "Ungerechte Grundschullehrer" (Sept. 16, 2009).

17 It should be noted that all of these prejudicial associations have been met with harsh criticism. From a data protection standpoint, however, it is our task to protect from harms such as these classifications, so it is important to include prejudices such as these in our perspective on names. As a result, I see no legal or practical reason to preserve names in the data, due to their outsized effect on identifiability and the nature of their "utility" in data analysis.

18 This can be easily done in SQL through the `DROP COLUMN` command, "drop" being SQL terminology for deletion. This needs to be done for each table in which we want to drop a column, *e.g.*, for the `students` table:

```
ALTER TABLE students DROP COLUMN fname, DROP COLUMN lname;.
```

19 And yet, a curious omission in the list provided in: *Pitruzella*, "Opinion on Case C-487/21 ("Österreichische Datenschutzbehörde and CRIF")" (Dec. 15, 2022), margin no. 36; also omitted in: Lindqvist (Nov. 6, 2003), para. 24; possibly contained in "residence status" or "statements as to domicile" in: Huber (Dec. 16, 2008), para. 31.

Even under the "minimal" interpretation of address, which includes a street name, a number, a ZIP code, and the city, large amounts of additional information are given. A certain street name or a neighborhood may be used as a proxy for income. It may also be used as a way of inferring ethnicity or the adherence to a certain group. For example, residents of the Hamburg district of Harvestehude, where real estate is very expensive,[20] are on balance wealthier than those in the district of Harburg, where real estate is more affordable[21]. Addresses in a certain community, such as a commune, may provide additional information about the political or religious affiliation of a person. Similarly, with increasing partisanship, even someone's ZIP code, city, or even state may allow for inference about someone's political convictions. For example, residents of Wyoming or Alabama are far less likely to be registered Democrats than residents of Massachusetts or the District of Columbia. For these reasons, addresses also need to be anonymized. For ZIP codes, there are possibilities to truncate them.[22]

III. Other Identifiers

Under the umbrella of "de-identification", other identifiers are typically also removed.

1. Identification Numbers

The removal of ID numbers[23] used for identification is neither difficult nor controversial.[24] Passport numbers or social security numbers are used to uniquely identify persons, but typically do not provide any additional information that could be useful in analysis.

2. Phone Numbers

Another example of these identifiers would be phone numbers.[25] There are different kinds of phone numbers: Depending on the locale, landlines, business phone

---

20 "Hamburger Stadtteil-Profile: Berichtsjahr 2021" (2021), p. 65.

21 Ibid., p. 168.

22 See p. 134.

23 Technically, most of these numbers are actually strings—a passport "number" can also contain letters.

24 While the identifiability through ID numbers is in itself a trivial observation and even contained in Art. 4 § 1 GDPR, this fact is also implied in: Penalty Points (June 22, 2021), para. 59.

25 Valsts ieņēmumu dienests (Feb. 24, 2022), paras. 17 sq.; *Pitruzella*, "Opinion on Case C-487/21 ("Österreichische Datenschutzbehörde and CRIF")" (Dec. 15, 2022), para. 36.

numbers, and mobile phone numbers differ in composition. In Germany, for example, mobile phone numbers can be distinguished by their prefix.[26] The prefix for landlines in Germany is related to the area where the phone is located.[27] In the U.S., both mobile numbers and landlines share a prefix, called an "area code", and they cannot be distinguished directly.

Some phone numbers are unique to a person (*e.g.*, a mobile number or a business number including an extension), some may "identify" multiple persons (such as a landline in a family household or a business number without extension). Some numbers may not even refer to a person at all (such as a fax number).

All of this information may be used for analysis, and it should not be dismissed that these analyses can bring additional value. For example, area codes in U.S. phone numbers may provide additional location information that can be used to broadly partition users while not giving away too much information about them. Nonetheless, this information is highly dependent on the locale. Therefore, when performing anonymization, it should be evaluated whether phone numbers should be suppressed[28] entirely or perhaps truncated[29].

Outliers (such as phone numbers that use a different country code in a database full of phone numbers from one country) may still need to be suppressed. In summary, there is no clear recommendation to give as far as phone numbers are concerned. In some circumstances, they cannot be anonymized per se but rather have to be suppressed entirely.

5.2 Conclusion

By removing this information, we have reached a database that is free of identifiers, while at the same time preserving large amounts of information.

Certainly, there are other types of information that are akin to those identifiers earlier stated. A rough relationship between the ease of anonymization and usefulness for analysis can be drawn, see Figure 5.1.[30]

In the following chapter, we will address the more difficult question of quasi-identifiers.

---

26 Such as +49 171 and +49 172 for the Telekom and Vodafone networks, respectively.

27 For example, +49 40 for Hamburg.

28 See p. 133.

29 See p. 134.

30 For explanation, see the paragraphs above. It should be noted that this is an intuitive assessment, not a strictly scientific one. Depending on the circumstances of the case, the positioning of any dot may be different.

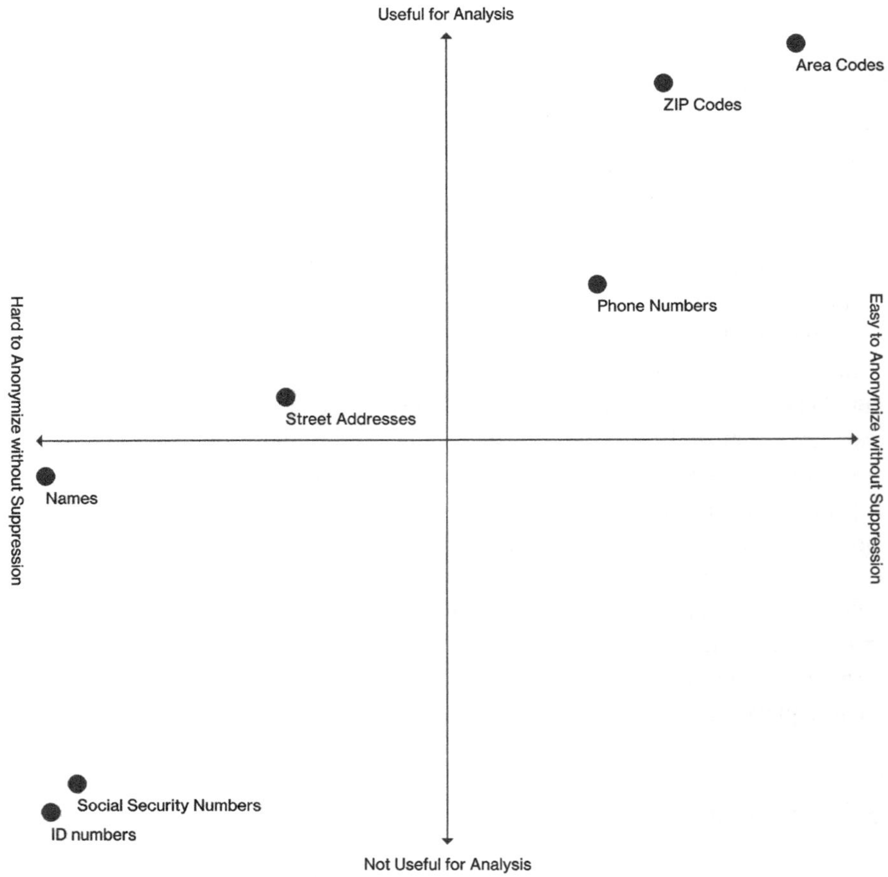

Fig. 5.1: Intuitive assessment of identifiers and their relative ease of anonymization versus the usefulness for analysis.

6 Classic Approaches to Anonymizing Structured Data

With the scene set for structured data in relational databases[1] and the most obvious identifiers removed[2], we can proceed to the main event: Anonymizing the remaining quasi-identifiers.[3]

First, we must ask the question of which attributes we want to protect. Next, we must find out which attributes can make natural persons identifiable in our data. From there, we will trace the outline of anonymization mechanisms derived to solve this problem and introduce privacy measures such as *k*-Anonymity and its derivations.

6.1 Sensitive Attributes?

A recurring notion when anonymizing structured data is that some attributes are "sensitive" and others are not.[4] For example, in a database of patients, the names and IDs of patients are not sensitive, while their diagnosis is the "sensitive attribute". As a result, anonymization efforts are focused on protecting (solely) the diagnosis from third parties.

While this is a useful model in some circumstances, it often fails to reflect that all attributes are somewhat sensitive, depending on the context. For example, in a patient database, names and postal codes may at the same time be "sensitive" and used for identification. The notion that some attributes are sensitive attributes that should be protected and others are identifiers is useful, but fundamentally flawed. All attributes are, to some extent, sensitive.[5] Of course, some are more sensitive than others.[6]

---

1 See p. 117.
2 See p. 125.
3 For more on this terminology, see p. 77.
4 See in depth: *Hölzel*, "Anonymisierungstechniken und das Datenschutzrecht" (Aug. 2018), pp. 507 sq.; *Appenzeller* and *Orak*, "Das Re-Identifikationsrisiko bei der Weitergabe von Gesundheitsdaten" (May 2024), p. 280.
5 Similar M. H. *Hansen*, "Insuring confidentiality of individual records in data storage and retrieval for statistical purposes" (1971), pp. 580 sq.
6 This general principle is also echoed in Art. 9 GDPR, though it is distinct from the question of "sensitive attributes", see also *Hölzel*, "Anonymisierungstechniken und das Datenschutzrecht" (Aug. 2018), p. 508.

https://doi.org/10.1515/9783112222164-008

6.2 Remaining Avenues for Identification after De-Identification

Removing directly identifying information such as names or ID numbers is seldom a problem.[7] Once this task is completed, the remaining dataset will typically still contain identifying information. This is not immediately intuitive. To illustrate, imagine a table of students in a school setting. All names and unique identifiers have been removed.[8] The table contains students' birth dates, ZIP codes, and grades.

Especially birth dates and ZIP codes are granular types of data. Birth dates are distributed (nearly[9]) randomly over all days of the year. In our example, even if we take into account that students in a secondary school will all be born in a ten-year span and that the probability of two people in a group of 23 or more sharing a birthday is > 50%[10], there is a substantial likelihood that there are unique birthdays in the database.[11] Looking at a smaller subset, such as a class—which coincidentally, is often around 23 students in size—it is pretty likely that most students in a course can be uniquely identified by their birthday. Similarly, a ZIP code can serve as a second way of uniquely identifying *some* students. Many students will share a postal code, given that they live in proximity to the school. Nonetheless, some may live farther away, which could make their postal code—and thereby them—unique in the data.

This is problematic, as it allows for singling out[12] and linking. In other words, it enables the comparison[13] of this record to other records.

---

7 See p. 125.

8 See p. 125.

9 On first thought, birth dates should be distributed in a uniform manner throughout the year. However, census statistics show that this is not the case. For example, in the UK, a study found that Dec 25 and 26 as well as Jan 1 are substantially less frequent birthdays than other dates, and there is a peak around Sep 26, "39 weeks and two days after Christmas day", *UK Office for National Statistics*, "How popular is your birthday?" (Dec. 18, 2015).

10 "Birthday problem" (May 11, 2023).

11 Note that the non-uniformity of the distribution of birthdays outlined above makes it (somewhat) more likely that people share a birthday.

12 See p. 58.

13 See p. 71.

6.3 Generalization and Suppression as Classic Remedies

These problems were first raised in the 1970s as a part of research into statistical disclosure.[14] Much of this work comes out of the U.S. census.[15] Just like in Germany, census work blazed the trail for innovations in data protection. U.S. census laws required that in all publications of data, the data furnished by singular persons shall not be identified.[16] This required both legal and technical innovation: On the one hand, this language needed to be interpreted, and on the other, this requirement had to be implemented technically. The classic approaches of suppression and generalization are similar to partially restricting access to the data. This family of "partial access" strategies is old: It was first suggested in the 1970s by M. H. *Hansen*, *Conway* and *Strip*.[17]

I. Suppression

The simplest approach to removing this data is *suppression*, i.e., removing the value in question from the dataset entirely. This is very effective at protecting the individual's privacy. Trivially, that will also mean the value cannot be used in analysis.

Suppression can be used in all axes of a relation: For example, we can suppress a record[18] or an entire column.[19] As an example, we could remove the record of an academically extremely successful student from a database containing students and their grades to protect that student's privacy, for his academic excellence would make him easy to distinguish in the data. Similarly, we can simply remove an entire attribute altogether—such as the first and last names of students in a database.[20]

---

14 M. H. *Hansen*, "Insuring confidentiality of individual records in data storage and retrieval for statistical purposes" (1971).

15 M. H. *Hansen*, "Insuring confidentiality of individual records in data storage and retrieval for statistical purposes" (1971), p. 579; for more on the controversy surrounding the U.S. census and privacy, see *Westin*, "Privacy and Freedom" (1967), pp. 302 sqq.

16 w.f.r. M. H. *Hansen*, "Insuring confidentiality of individual records in data storage and retrieval for statistical purposes" (1971), p. 579.

17 M. H. *Hansen*, "Insuring confidentiality of individual records in data storage and retrieval for statistical purposes" (1971), pp. 580 sqq.; *Conway* and *Strip*, "Selective partial access to a database" (Oct. 20, 1976), p. 86.

18 Also called *tuple* or simply *row*, for terminology see p. 117.

19 Also called an *attribute*.

20 See p. 126.

Suppression can be performed both *offline*[21] and *online*[22]: In an offline scenario, the data is simply erased from the dataset. In an online scenario, the data is removed from any result to queries.

A variant of suppression is substitution, *i.e.*, replacing sensitive values with different, random values. For example, replacing U.S. SSNs with placeholder values.[23] This does not change the potential of that data providing unique identification and is more of a processing akin to a pseudonymization. At the same time, it can provide security from the harms that are unrelated to singling out.

Suppression makes the data less useful. It is the most extreme form of disclosure control. If used extensively, it may also skew the (remaining) data by removing points for comparison: Identifiable records are typically outliers. Removing the outliers from a dataset will skew the dataset towards the mean and distort values such as the median and other statistics. As a result, these techniques are more of an *ultima ratio* and we will strive to avoid them from here on. Nonetheless, they prove useful in cases where data simply cannot be anonymized in a different way, such as with names.[24]

II. Generalization

A second, less extreme technique is *generalization*. This type of partial access is also known as "value-class partition".[25] Generalization means replacing values with intervals.[26] For example, one can replace the information "Age 27" with "Age 25–34". For numeric values, the most obvious way is through rounding values (e.g., round age to the nearest multiple of 5). In essence, using intervals is just a different way of rounding values. Nonetheless, replacing values with intervals enables more fine-grained control over the data that is released, and one can vary the degree of specificity by value.

In some specific cases, it makes sense to truncate numbers instead of rounding them. An example would be U.S. ZIP codes or German PLZ codes, where the first numbers denote an area and get more specific towards the end of the number.

21 In a "non-interactive" setting where the analyst has access to all data, see p. 120.

22 In an "interactive" setting where the analyst can query the data, but does not have access to it in its entirety, see p. 120.

23 The Datafly algorithm (see p. 136) does exactly that: *Sweeney*, "Weaving Technology and Policy Together to Maintain Confidentiality" (1997), Fig. 1, p. 104.

24 See p. 126.

25 *Conway* and *Strip*, "Selective partial access to a database" (Oct. 20, 1976), p. 88.

26 *Schindler*, "Zulässigkeit und Grenzen algorithmischer Systeme bei arbeitsrechtlichen Auswahlentscheidungen" (Dec. 18, 2023), pp. 118 sq.

Original

ID PRIMARY_KEY	Date of Birth DATE	ZIP Code VARCHAR(10)
1	2000-03-15	94301
2	1995-02-15	94108
3	1966-01-13	78705
4	1966-06-30	90210

Generalization

ID PRIMARY_KEY	Date of Birth DATE	ZIP Code VARCHAR(10)
1	2000-03	94xxx
2	1995-03	94xxx
3	1966-01	78xxx
4	1966-07	90xxx

Fig. 6.1: Example of a Generalization of Birth Dates and ZIP Codes.

As a result, the generalized ZIP code "semantically indicates a larger geographical area."[27] Depending on the endianness of such numbers, truncation may be required at either ends of the value.[28]

Generalization can be performed on many kinds of data, with varying levels of success. For example, it can also be performed on strings: A name can be shortened to just its initial, thereby indicating a larger number of possible names. "Ann", "Abe", and "Al" thereby become just "A*".[29] Other types of data, especially categorical data, cannot be generalized well—in *Sweeney*'s example, values for ethnicity ("Asian", "Black", "White") generalize to "Person", which, in effect, is similar to suppression for this attribute.[30]

Most of the work done on generalization pertains to numerical values. There are different approaches to performing this generalization. For example, depending on the amount of values and types of values in a table, one may choose an appropriate interval. In simpler approaches, values are generalized on an attribute or domain level.[31] This is called "global recoding".[32] More complex algorithms perform cell-

27 *Sweeney*, "Computational disclosure control" (2001), p. 68.

28 Endianness is a term used in computer science to denote the order in which bytes are written to memory. Big-endian systems store the most significant byte "first", while little-endian systems store the most significant byte "last". A comparison might be drawn to international date formats, where the German/European variant "15.03.2022" is little-endian, the ISO 8601 variant "2022-03-15" is big-endian, and the U.S. variant "03/15/2022" is middle-endian.

29 *Sweeney*, "Computational disclosure control" (2001), pp. 67 sq.

30 Ibid., p. 69.

31 *Winter*, *Battis*, and *Halvani*, "Herausforderungen für die Anonymisierung von Daten" (2019), p. 490; J. *Li* et al., "Anonymization by Local Recoding in Data with Attribute Hierarchical Taxonomies" (Sept. 2008), p. 1183.

32 J. *Li* et al., "Anonymization by Local Recoding in Data with Attribute Hierarchical Taxonomies" (Sept. 2008), p. 1183.

level generalization or "local" recoding.[33] The benefit of local recoding is that it does not "over-generalize" a table and thus maximizes its usability for data mining.[34][35]

III. Combining Suppression and Generalization

By using generalization and enhancing it with suppression, solid results can be achieved.

1. Datafly

One system that banks on these two mechanisms is the Datafly algorithm. Datafly was proposed by *Sweeney* in 1997.[36] The algorithm is used to modify source data into "anonymized" data through generalization as well as substitution.[37] When performing this modification, Datafly requires some parameters set by the user. First, it lets the user specify a profile of the data's recipient, *i.e.*, which outside sources they may use to link to the data and identify persons.[38] This is done in the form of a per-attribute linking likelihood, in other words, for each attribute, the user must answer the question: Expressed as a probability, how likely is it that the recipient of the data "will use outside knowledge that includes the information within that field."[39] Second, it requires a parameter called the "anonymity level", supplied by the user, between 0 and 1, with 0 being the original data and 1 being "the most general data possible given the profile of the recipient".[40]

Per attribute, Datafly looks at the amount of unique or rare values. A value is "rare" if it only occurs a small number of times. Depending on the parameters, the algorithm sets a minimum "bin size" b.[41] In the next step, data in each attribute is generalized to a point where the requirement that all values that occur in the

33 *Winter, Battis,* and *Halvani,* "Herausforderungen für die Anonymisierung von Daten" (2019), p. 490.

34 J. *Li* et al., "Anonymization by Local Recoding in Data with Attribute Hierarchical Taxonomies" (Sept. 2008), p. 1183.

35 The benefits and drawbacks of global vs. local recoding mechanisms is beyond the scope of this dissertation. Interested readers are referred to ibid.

36 *Sweeney,* "Guaranteeing anonymity when sharing medical data, the Datafly System" (1997).

37 Ibid., pp. 53 sq.

38 *Sweeney,* "Weaving Technology and Policy Together to Maintain Confidentiality" (1997), p. 104.

39 *Sweeney,* "Datafly" (1998), item 3.3.

40 *Sweeney,* "Guaranteeing anonymity when sharing medical data, the Datafly System" (1997), p. 53; *Sweeney,* "Weaving Technology and Policy Together to Maintain Confidentiality" (1997), p. 104.

41 For more information on how *b* is set, see *Sweeney,* "Datafly" (1998), item 3.1.

table occur at least b times within the attribute. Additionally, Datafly "scrambles" the order in which records are presented randomly.[42]

Datafly notably also treats combinations of attributes (*e.g.*, in *Sweeney*'s example, there may be only one female Caucasian in the data, even though there are multiple females and Caucasians[43]), by simply concatenating these fields and treating them as one when generalizing. This is a precursor to *Sweeney*'s later work on k-Anonymity.

2. μ-Argus

Another system, μ-Argus, was developed in the Netherlands to "anonymize" statistical data. In its original form, this system also uses generalization and suppression.[44] μ-Argus works similar to Datafly by identifying sensitive fields, finding "rare" combinations of fields and uses generalization on an attribute level.[45] Unlike Datafly, it may also suppress individual values, instead of suppressing the record as a whole.[46]

3. Discussion

Sweeney herself notes that the question of bin sizes and identification of sensitive fields is fraught with guesswork and the drawback of these systems.[47] To my knowledge, Datafly is not in widespread use as of this writing. μ-Argus has seen continued development and was transferred to an open source licensing model in 2012.[48] Despite their relative obscurity today, these systems have brought anonymization solutions to market and led the way for future innovation. They remain valuable today as a gentle introduction to the current status of anonymization solutions.

---

42 Ibid., item 3.7.

43 Ibid., item 3.6.

44 As the software has seen continuous development since then, we will only discuss the initial versions as they relate to suppression and generalization.

45 *Sweeney*, "Datafly" (1998), item 4.1.

46 Ibid., items 4.1 and 5.

47 Ibid., item 4.1.

48 As of the time of writing, the most current version was v5.1.7, released in 2022, containing support for record swapping and noise addition. The software was available for Windows and, to a lesser extent (up to v5.1.1), Linux: *Statistics Netherlands*, "Mu-ARGUS" (Aug. 26, 2021).

IV. Formalizing Privacy: *k*-Anonymity

However, the *amount* of generalization necessary to anonymize a dataset is left to the user with all of these approaches. Therefore, a method needs to be found to quantify the privacy guarantee that generalization provides.

1. Motivation

Despite the advances made with Datafly and μ-Argus, a fundamental problem was still unsolved: The problem of determining the bin sizes to optimize privacy. Additionally, both Datafly and μ-Argus had happened upon the problem of unique *combinations* of attributes. While removing specificity in the way these two systems pioneered is useful, it could still on the one hand mean that data was generalized more than necessary, on the other that it was not generalized enough to afford adequate protection against re-identification.[49] *Sweeney* defines quasi-identifiers as those attributes that are likely to be available in external data and can thus be used for linking.[50] Increasingly, it became clear that not just some combinations of quasi-identifiers could uniquely identify a person, but rather any combination of them.

Sweeney introduces the problem using a well-known re-identification feat (of hers): The re-identification of Governor William Weld in Massachusetts health insurance data.[51] The example begins with a college commencement speech given by Massachusetts Governor William Weld[52] in 1996, during which he collapsed unconscious and was admitted to a hospital.[53] Later, the Massachusetts Group Insurance Commission (GIC)—a body that would purchase health insurance for governement employees—released patient data that had been de-identified to researchers.[54] Governor Weld himself announced publicly that, in this release, privacy was being protected, as identifiers had been removed.[55] The data contained "nearly one hundred attributes per encounter … for approximately 135,000 state employees".[56]

49 *Samarati* and *Sweeney*, "Protecting Privacy when Disclosing Information: k-Anonymity and Its Enforcement through Generalization and Suppression" (1998), p. 3.

50 *Sweeney*, "k-ANONYMITY" (Oct. 2002), p. 5.

51 *Sweeney*, "k-ANONYMITY" (Oct. 2002), p. 2; with a critical, detailed look at the example: *Barth-Jones*, "The 'Re-Identification' of Governor William Weld's Medical Information" (2012).

52 Weld, a Republican, was governor in Massachusetts from 1991 through 1997.

53 *Barth-Jones*, "The 'Re-Identification' of Governor William Weld's Medical Information" (2012), p. 3.

54 *Ohm*, "Broken Promises of Privacy" (2009–2010), p. 1719.

55 w.f.r.: ibid., p. 1719.

56 *Sweeney*, "k-ANONYMITY" (Oct. 2002), p. 2; *Sweeney*, "Computational Disclosure Control for Medical Microdata: The Datafly System" (1997), p. 448.

Sweeney purchased a second dataset: The voter registration list for Cambridge, Mass., the known residence of Governor Weld.[57] In the United States, this is easier than in EU states, as voter records and population registers can be readily obtained for a small fee.[58] Even by itself, this data is remarkable: In the example that *Sweeney* makes, the 1997 voting list for Cambridge, Mass. contains information about 54,805 voters, of which 12% can be uniquely identified by their birth date, 29% can be uniquely identified by a combination of birth date and gender, 69% by a combination of birth date and 5-digit ZIP code, and 97% by a combination of full postal code and birth date.[59]

Sweeney's goal in obtaining this list was to link it with the GIC data. This can be done by merging the lists on the attributes that are common to both lists.[60] Weld was certain to be in both lists: As he—a government employee—had been hospitalized, he would be in the GIC data; as he—a high-profile politician—was all but certain to be registered to vote in Cambridge, he would be in the voter list.[61] As *Sweeney* explains: "According to the Cambridge Voter list, six people had his particular birth date; only three of them were men; and, he was the only one in his 5-digit ZIP code."[62] To make a point, Sweeney sent Weld's data to his office.[63] Weld's re-identification had a profound impact on policy and was, purportedly, one of the political motivators to enact the HIPAA de-identification schemes.[64] *Sweeney* arrives at the conclusion that "any single uniquely occurring value or group of values can be used to identify an individual".[65] The issue here—the salient fact of the matter that made Weld's re-identification possible—was that three quasi-identifiers taken together identified just one person in both datasets. Sweeney discovered that, if the GIC dataset did not allow for this specificity, Weld's record would not have been linkable and therefore available for singling out. She and Pierangela Samarati would formalize this discovery into *k*-Anonymity.

---

57 *Sweeney*, "k-ANONYMITY" (Oct. 2002), p. 2.

58 For example, Orange County, Calif. voter data can be purchased online from USD 37: "Voter Data Available for Purchase | OC Vote" (2022).

59 *Sweeney*, "Weaving Technology and Policy Together to Maintain Confidentiality" (1997), p. 100.

60 A `INNER JOIN` in SQL (see p. 117), see *Ohm*, "Broken Promises of Privacy" (2009–2010), p. 1726.

61 A circumstance criticized as atypical in *Barth-Jones*, "The 'Re-Identification' of Governor William Weld's Medical Information" (2012), p. 3.

62 *Sweeney*, "k-ANONYMITY" (Oct. 2002), p. 3.

63 *Greely*, "The uneasy ethical and legal underpinnings of large-scale genomic biobanks" (2007), p. 352.

64 *Barth-Jones*, "The 'Re-Identification' of Governor William Weld's Medical Information" (2012), p. 1; for more on HIPAA, see p. 95.

65 *Sweeney*, "Computational Disclosure Control for Medical Microdata: The Datafly System" (1997), p. 445.

2. Definition

Put simply, *k*-Anonymity requires that there be at least *k* records for any combination of quasi-identifiers in the data. The criterion requires users to specify the quasi-identifiers and a value for *k*. *k*-Anonymity (or lack thereof) is a property of the output dataset. Note that the level of anonymization is dependant on the user: If they specify a low value of *k* or overlook quasi-identifiers in the attributes, anonymization is weakened or may have no effect at all.

k is a parameter set by the user (in accordance with policy). The greater the *k*, the greater the privacy protections. Put simply, no combination of values for attributes occurs less than *k* times. In the example, if the GIC data had been anonymized to a standard of, say, $k = 5$, Governor Weld could not have been re-identified in the data, as his record from the voter list would have either been suppressed completely or corresponded to at least 5 entries in the anonymized GIC dataset. This mathematical foundation was proposed in 1998 in joint work by *Samarati* and *Sweeney*[66] and later expanded substantially by *Sweeney* in 2001[67] and 2002[68].

On one hand, there is a risk of *too little* generalization, which will leave identifiability in the dataset, on the other hand, there is a risk of *too much* generalization, whereby the dataset stops being useful for the purpose it is supposed to serve.[69] The paper on *k*-Anonymity does not solve this conundrum, but it helps solve it by providing a metric: *k*-Anonymity allows quantifying the degree of privacy in a dataset as far as inference through linking is concerned.[70]

In the formal definition:

66 *Samarati* and *Sweeney*, "Protecting Privacy when Disclosing Information: k-Anonymity and Its Enforcement through Generalization and Suppression" (1998).

67 *Sweeney*, "Computational disclosure control" (2001).

68 *Sweeney*, "k-ANONYMITY" (Oct. 2002).

69 Or as *Samarati* and *Sweeney* put it: "There is a danger in oversimplifying this work. It does not advocate giving all the data on all the people without regard to whether individuals can be identified. It also does not advocate releasing data that is so general it cannot be useful; substantial suppression does not appear to be the norm. From the viewpoint of a person who receives the data, these systems seek to provide the most general data possible that is practically useful to that person.", *Samarati* and *Sweeney*, "Protecting Privacy when Disclosing Information: k-Anonymity and Its Enforcement through Generalization and Suppression" (1998), p. 100.

70 *Samarati* and *Sweeney*, "Protecting Privacy when Disclosing Information: k-Anonymity and Its Enforcement through Generalization and Suppression" (1998), p. 19; Compagnucci et al. seem to think that *k*-Anonymization is a method of pseudonymization and incorrectly state that it does not allow for privacy quantification, *Compagnucci* et al., "Homomorphic Encryption" (2019), p. 151.

> Each release of data must be such that every combination of values of quasi-identifiers can be indistinctly matched to at least k individuals.[71]

Typical values of k are $k = 5$ and $k = 10$.[72] Choosing a good value for k is difficult. In practice, values of k between 5 and 15 are chosen for the medical domain.[73] Optimal k-Anonymization has been held to be very computationally complex.[74]

3. Shortcomings

The most salient shortcomings of k-Anonymity are that it is susceptible to *homogeneity* and *background knowledge* attacks.[75]

a) Homogeneity Attack

In a homogeneity attack, all of the private values in a k-anonymized database for a certain bin happen to be identical or similar. Therefore, grouping and generalizing the individual rows still allows the viewer to infer (precise) values. For example, if all patients in a database where the patient information matches "31-year old American male who lives in the zip code 13053"[76] share the same diagnosis, this sensitive information can leak from the database *despite* a correct implementation of k-Anonymity.

b) Background Knowledge Attack

A second attack on k-Anonymity is the background knowledge attack. It combines the k-anonymized database with other knowledge.

In *Machanavajjhala* et al.'s example, a background knowledge attack could look something like the following: Alice, the "attacker", knows that her pen-friend Umeko, a 21-year old Japanese woman from ZIP code 13068, was admitted to a hospital. From the medical data release, Umeko's information could be in one of four records (*i.e.*, $k = 4$).[77] The patients' nationalities have been suppressed completely,

---

71 *Samarati* and *Sweeney*, "Protecting Privacy when Disclosing Information: k-Anonymity and Its Enforcement through Generalization and Suppression" (1998), p. 19.

72 *Altman, Cohen, Nissim*, et al., "What a Hybrid Legal-Technical Analysis Teaches Us about Privacy Regulation" (2021), p. 44.

73 w.f.r.: *Desfontaines*, "Lowering the cost of anonymization" (2020), p. 11.

74 w.f.r.: J. *Li* et al., "Anonymization by Local Recoding in Data with Attribute Hierarchical Taxonomies" (Sept. 2008), p. 1183.

75 *Machanavajjhala* et al., "L-diversity" (2006), pp. 3 sqq.

76 Example from ibid., p. 4.

77 Ibid., pp. 4 sq.

the ages have been generalized to > 30 and the ZIP code has been generalized. Two of these rows have been admitted with a heart disease, the other two with a viral infection.[78] Solely from the information in the *k*-anonymized dataset, Alice cannot deduce whether Umeko had a heart disease or a viral infection. Nonetheless, Alice knows that Japanese people (such as Umeko) have an "extremely low incidence of heart disease".[79] As a result, Alice can infer with high certainty that Umeko had a viral infection.[80]

Machanavajjhala et al. introduce different types of background knowledge: In their example, if the GIC released a table of medical data for state employees, an attacker may know that a certain person is a state employee and therefore contained in the data.[81] They may also know the person's non-sensitive attributes, such as age, nationality, *etc.*. Additionally, they may know a specific person does (not) have a certain sensitive attribute (*e.g.*, a diagnosis), because they have made observations to this point. In the example that *Machanavajjhala* et al. give, "... Alice might know that [her neighbor] Bob does not have pneumonia since Bob does not show any of the symptoms of pneumonia."[82] A second kind of information is that shown in the "Umeko" example. Here, Alice knows a general statistic about Umeko's demographic.[83]

4. Improvements: *l*-Diversity and *t*-Closeness

To address these shortcomings, *Machanavajjhala* et al. created *l*-Diversity in 2006 in response to *k*-Anonymity.[84] *l*-Diversity relies on values being "well-represented" in the sensitive attributes.[85] The basic idea of *l*-Diversity is to make sure that the bins generated in *k*-Anonymity are filled with values that are *diverse* enough as to render the homogeneity attack impossible (which requires that the sensitive values are the same) and rendering the background knowledge attack more difficult.[86]

---

78 *Machanavajjhala* et al., "L-diversity" (2006), cf. Figure 2.

79 Ibid., p. 4.

80 Ibid., p. 4.

81 A case of "instance-level background knowledge": ibid., p. 7.

82 Also an example of "instance-based background knowledge": ibid., p. 7.

83 In the *l*-diversity paper, the authors call this "demographic background knowledge": ibid., p. 7.

84 Ibid.

85 *Machanavajjhala* et al., "L-diversity" (2006), p. 16; for a succinct introduction including the different kinds of *l*-Diversity proposed, see: N. *Li*, T. *Li*, and *Venkatasubramanian*, "t-Closeness" (Apr. 2007), pp. 2 sq.

86 *Desfontaines*, "Lowering the cost of anonymization" (2020), pp. 17 sqq.

In response to *l*-Diversity, a group of researchers found limitations in *l*-Diversity and proposed a new measure called *t*-Closeness in 2007.[87] *t*-Closeness bases its principle on a similar thought as the contemporaneous differential privacy[88]: Comparing the beliefs of an attacker before and after viewing the released data.[89] In *t*-Closeness, the equivalence classes themselves–*i.e.*, the bins of items that are generalized into–need to be "well-distributed" in a way that is similar to the entire dataset.[90] *t* is the parameter that determines how different the distribution in the bin can be to the entire table.[91] If all bins satisfy this criterion, the generalized table as a whole satisfies it. *t*-Closeness can provide great privacy and thwart even sophisticated attackers. However, it usually requires either careful curation, a large amount of data utility loss, or both. As a result, its practical application is limited.

6.4 Perturbation-Based Approaches

A second family of syntactic anonymization approaches is those that are based on perturbation, *i.e.*, altering the data in some way. Two notable approaches from this family are randomization and swapping.[92]

I. Randomization

The Art. 29 Working Party defines randomization as "a family of techniques that alters the veracity of the data in order to remove the strong link between the data and the individual."[93] In other words, data is altered in a certain way. This definition does not quite hit the center of the matter. Randomization does indeed alter the

---

87 N. *Li*, T. *Li*, and *Venkatasubramanian*, "t-Closeness" (Apr. 2007); *Aggarwal* and *Yu*, "Privacy-Preserving Data Mining" (2008), p. 376; on the relationship between *t*-Closeness and differential privacy, see: *Domingo-Ferrer* and *Soria-Comas*, "From t-closeness to differential privacy and vice versa in data anonymization" (2015), p. 8.

88 See p. 146.

89 N. *Li*, T. *Li*, and *Venkatasubramanian*, "t-Closeness" (Apr. 2007), p. 4.

90 Ibid., p. 4.

91 Thus, the *greater t*, the *less* private the release of data.

92 *Schindler*, "Zulässigkeit und Grenzen algorithmischer Systeme bei arbeitsrechtlichen Auswahlentscheidungen" (Dec. 18, 2023), p. 119.

93 *Article 29 Data Protection Working Party*, "0829/14/DE WP216" (2014), p. 12.

veracity of the data, but the way in which it is altered is more important. It means, as the name implies, adding random noise to a dataset.[94]

Altering the data based on *random* noise has some desirable properties: On the one hand, it makes the data unreliable as it pertains to individuals. From the anonymized data, we cannot infer hard numbers for individuals. Even if we know the properties of the noise that has been added,[95] we cannot make reliable statements about individuals. Nonetheless, quantifying this privacy guarantee is difficult, as it depends on the underlying data. Say, for example, we have a dataset of individuals and their yearly income. If we add a noise of up to, say, $20,000, then the figures are adjusted up and down randomly, so that we cannot reliably identify the record of a schoolteacher on a fixed (known) salary. Nonetheless, if there is an outlier in the data—for example, a hedge fund manager who earns a seven-figure income—this record is not masked by adding noise of $20,000.

Randomization goes by many names: In the 1976 paper by *Conway* and *Strip*, it is discussed as "value distortion".[96] In all cases, noise drawn from a random distribution is added.[97] As long as the noise is large enough, the "source" cannot be guessed from the so-distorted data.[98]

II. Replacement or Swapping

Another method of distorting the value of a record would be to swap values between records.[99] For example, in a list of students and grades, a query would return a student's name or ID as well as a grade. However, the grades would be swapped between students, so the grade returned would not be the "real" grade of the student returned. This was originally known as "value dissociation" in *Conway* and *Strip*.[100]

---

94 The term "randomization" was, to my knowledge, first used in *Conway* and *Strip*, "Selective partial access to a database" (Oct. 20, 1976), pp. 449 sqq.; *Aggarwal* and *Yu*, "Privacy-Preserving Data Mining" (2008), p. 4, 13 sqq.; conflating randomization and suppression: *Papastefanou*, "„Database Reconstruction Theorem" und die Verletzung der Privatsphäre (Differential Privacy)" (June 1, 2020), margin no. 15.

95 As a side note, *not* providing this information ("security through obscurity") is not a viable way of protecting the anonymity of the data, see p. 123.

96 *Conway* and *Strip*, "Selective partial access to a database" (Oct. 20, 1976), p. 86.

97 It should be noted that noise *addition* is the most common type of randomization. However, *multiplicative* perturbation can also be used for randomization, see *Aggarwal* and *Yu*, "Privacy-Preserving Data Mining" (2008), p. 19.

98 Ibid., p. 14.

99 Ibid., pp. 19 sq.

100 *Conway* and *Strip*, "Selective partial access to a database" (Oct. 20, 1976), p. 87.

Swapping was used in the U.S. census before 2020, when it was replaced with DP.[101] From a data utility perspective, it is useful in that it preserves the statistical distribution in the original data and does not alter absolute values in the way randomization does—which is surely one of the reasons why it was used in the U.S. census. Nonetheless, it can destroy the relationships between attributes in a record—say, for example, the household income is swapped in a table of census data, then the relationship between a ZIP code and its distribution of income may no longer be useful for analysis. It may also lead to mistaken identification and mistaken cases of inference, both of which are not desirable.

6.5 Conclusion

Classic approaches to anonymization offer a lot: They are relatively easy to implement, provide reliable and explainable privacy guarantees, and have been refined over time. Nonetheless, their simple versions—*k*-Anonymity and randomization—both suffer from easy attacks that can be performed on them. Swapping presents its own issues, namely the loss of utility. The advanced versions of these approaches suffer from the problem that they are hard to implement and often lead to a large loss in data utility.

---

101 *US Census Bureau*, "The Census Bureau's Simulated Reconstruction-Abetted Re-identification Attack on the 2010 Census" (May 7, 2021); *Abowd* and *Velkoff*, "Modernizing Privacy Protections for the 2020 Census" (Apr. 28, 2021); *Dwork, Greenwood,* and *King*, "There's a simple solution to the latest census fight" (July 26, 2021).

7 Differential Privacy

A newer approach to a formal privacy guarantee is differential privacy.[1] DP deserves its own chapter here, on the one hand because it bases its privacy guarantee on the design of the process rather than on the properties of the anonymized data.[2] This means that it *works* fundamentally differently than the approaches of k-Anonymity and its corollaries. It promises to address the shortcomings of classical anonymization methods.[3] On the other hand, it allows us to speak more clearly about the tradeoff between data privacy and accuracy in a quantitative manner, as it takes a parameter, ε.[4] When talking about differentially private algorithms, the value of ε is typically prepended as ε-differential privacy: Withholding data completely provides 0-differential privacy, and the higher the ε, the more data is disclosed.[5] This relationship is visualized in figure 7.1. Admittedly, it is counterintuitive that higher values of ε provide *less* privacy. It is equally counterintuitive that the spectrum of disclosure theoretically ranges from 0 to ∞, as it makes the range of "sensible" ε-values even harder to make sense of.

We have touched upon different definitions of privacy. Some, like k-Anonymity, base their definition on how easy it is to link external data to the released data. Differential privacy, however, relies on a definition of privacy that is quite intuitive: It mandates that the output of a differentially private algorithm must not change *too much* if one person's data is added or removed to the source data. Put differently, this allows affected persons "to say, for any possible output of the program, 'well, that was just as likely with my data as without'."[6]

---

1 It should be noted—despite my presenting DP as the newer approach—that the research communities in the "classic" approaches (k-Anonymity and its derivatives) and differential privacy continue to develop in parallel.

2 *Desfontaines*, "Lowering the cost of anonymization" (2020), p. 24.

3 See in depth: *Dwork* and *Roth*, "The Algorithmic Foundations of Differential Privacy" (2013), pp. 5 sqq.

4 There is also a variant called (ε, δ)-differential privacy that will be covered later, see p. 157. It should also be acknowledged that k-anonymity also allows for an (indirect) quantification of privacy guarantees through the parameter k, yet the parameters used in DP more directly mirror the tradeoff between utility and privacy.

5 Theoretically, an ∞-differentially private algorithm discloses data completely: "Aaron Roth likes to point out that one of the more important contributions of differential privacy is that it gives a framework for trading off accuracy and privacy: withholding data provides 0-differential privacy, and releasing data in the clear provides infinite-differential privacy, but there is a spectrum between.", *McSherry*, "Differential privacy and Demographics" (Apr. 12, 2019).

6 *McSherry*, "Uber's differential privacy .. probably isn't" (Feb. 25, 2018).

https://doi.org/10.1515/9783112222164-009

Fig. 7.1: Visualization of the relationship of parameter ε and the privacy afforded.

The spectrum between privacy and disclosure is a recurring theme in this work, and it is at the heart of the underlying legal and policy questions: How private does anonymous data need to be? Even though differential privacy is usually named in the same breath as *k*-anonymity and other mechanisms,[7] it needs to be emphasized that it provides a different type of guarantee than these mechanisms. The essential promise of DP is that "it doesn't make (much) of a difference" if one's data is contained within a dataset. This promise is distinct from the question whether one can be re-identified within that dataset.[8] Note that differential privacy speaks of privacy, not anonymity.[9] This might be because the guarantee that DP affords is not anonymity in the sense that one is protected from being identified in the data, but rather privacy in the sense that one's data is only shared in a limited manner.[10] Nonetheless, as has been shown above, all identification is based on linking.[11] Differential privacy "neutralizes linking attacks"[12], because if it can give any person *plausible deniability* that their data is not even within the dataset, this data can, a fortiori, not be linked to other data sources.[13] In other words, the guarantee provided by DP is *stronger* than a guarantee focused on (correct[14]) identifiability.[15] This strength, however, is also a weakness: As outlined elsewhere, there appears

7 Most notably: *Article 29 Data Protection Working Party*, "0829/14/DE WP216" (2014), p. 3; but see also: *Schwartmann, Jaspers*, et al., "Praxisleitfaden Anonymisierung" (Dec. 2022), pp. 32 sq.; *Arning* and *Rothkegel*, "DS-GVO Art. 4 Begriffsbestimmungen" (2022), margin no. 50.

8 As the authors note: *Dwork* and *Roth*, "The Algorithmic Foundations of Differential Privacy" (2013), p. 7.

9 It should also be noted that DP was first known as ε-indistinguishability, Fn. 1: *Dwork, McSherry*, et al., "Calibrating Noise to Sensitivity in Private Data Analysis" (2016), p. 18.

10 Similar, but less optimistic about the legal evaluation of DP: *Hölzel*, "Differential Privacy and the GDPR" (2019), pp. 13 sq.

11 See p. 71.

12 *Dwork* and *Roth*, "The Algorithmic Foundations of Differential Privacy" (2013), p. 7.

13 DP also provides protection against predicate singling out (see p. 61) (*Cohen* and *Nissim*, "Towards formalizing the GDPR's notion of singling out" [Apr. 14, 2020], p. 8346).

14 *Hölzel* raises the (valid) point that DP protects agains "true identification, but not against false identification" (*Hölzel*, "Differential Privacy and the GDPR" [2019], p. 12). However, this is a criticism equally valid for all types of anonymization methods that alter the data itself (*i.e.*, chiefly randomization-based methods). See also see p. 39 and see p. 182.

15 Similar: *Wood* et al., "Differential Privacy" (2018–2019), p. 262.

to be a natural relationship between privacy and utility.[16] As the "privacy" guarantee of differential privacy is inseparable from its "identifiability" guarantee, data that is "well-protected" using a strong value for ε may be *less useful* than data that is "anonymized" solely with regard to identifiability. In any case, differential privacy can provide privacy, no matter what external information is available.[17]

Before we get into the definition of differential privacy, we must acknowledge that—due to the parameter ε mentioned above—the use of a correctly implemented differentially private mechanism itself does not necessarily mean that data is protected. Assuring users that their data is "protected using differential privacy" tells us very little about the amount of protection afforded by the mechanism.[18] [19] Rather, this protection—and GDPR compliance with it—is contingent on the thoughtful choice of the parameter ε. Gaining an intuition about what constitutes a "large" or a "small" ε is difficult, as even *Dwork* admits that there is no hard and fast answer to this pressing question, but rather recommendations "vary tremendously based on attributes of the dataset"[20] and the circumstances of the deployment.[21] Nonetheless, an order of magnitude can be given: "Small" values of ε are ones below or near 1, and as ε is part of an exponential function in the equation of DP[22], any value above 10 should definitely be considered large.[23] As *Dwork* and *Roth* note, a 300-differentially private mechanism[24] still satisfies the definition, but is of little

16 See p. 96.

17 *Kasiviswanathan* and *Smith*, "On the 'Semantics' of Differential Privacy" (June 1, 2014), p. 1.

18 *Domingo-Ferrer*, *Sánchez*, and *Blanco-Justicia*, "The limits of differential privacy (and its misuse in data release and machine learning)" (June 21, 2021), p. 2; *Tang* et al., "Privacy Loss in Apple's Implementation of Differential Privacy on MacOS 10.12" (Sept. 11, 2017).

19 This is further complicated by the fact that "one user record" in a database may look different depending on the data. For example, with a graph that encodes users' relationships, this is much harder, *Dwork* and *Roth*, "The Algorithmic Foundations of Differential Privacy" (2013), p. 23. This is similar to the general conundrum of graph data, see p. 122.

20 *Dwork*, *Kohli*, and *Mulligan*, "Differential Privacy in Practice" (Oct. 20, 2019), p. 13.

21 Ibid., p. 13.

22 See p. 156.

23 This order of magnitude is an approximation. *Dwork* and *Roth* write that "All Small Epsilons Are Alike … [but a] large epsilon is large after its own fashion.", meaning that small values offer comparable privacy guarantees, but larger ones (the example they give is $\varepsilon = 15$ may lead to failures (*i.e.*, destructions of privacy) in different and unexpected ways (*Dwork* and *Roth*, "The Algorithmic Foundations of Differential Privacy" [2013], pp. 24 sq.; Note 9: *Dwork*, *Kohli*, and *Mulligan*, "Differential Privacy in Practice" [Oct. 20, 2019], p. 5). For a summary of ε values found in the literature, see Table 1: *Hsu* et al., "Differential Privacy" (July 2014).

24 Plugging this ε into the definition of differential privacy yields, in essence, the number 1.942426e+130 being multiplied on one side of the inequality. Given this fact, it is unsurprising that the inequality will hold true, pretty much without regard to the mechanism.

use as a practical privacy guarantee.[25] The question of how to set this parameter is ultimately a policy question, and thus it will be covered again later on.[26]

DP belongs in a different category than other privacy definitions because it provides "privacy by *process*"[27]. Note that in the typical application of DP, it is used in an *interactive* (online) fashion.[28] Interactive means that the analyst does not have access to the database itself, but can rather query it using a specific mechanism that satisfies DP. *k*-anonymity and corollary techniques, on the other hand, are typically used in a *non-interactive* way, which means that they are applied to sanitize the database as a whole, which is then released for analysis.[29]

Differential privacy has caught the attention of policymakers, tech companies, and even legal scholars.[30] It has been lauded and applied by some and derided as a "trendy theory"[31] by others. In order to better understand what differential privacy can and cannot do, we need to explain its basic underpinnings.[32]

7.1 Randomized Response: A Prototypical Differentially Private Algorithm

Dwork and *Roth* introduce DP by explaining the *randomized response* technique popularized in the social sciences.[33] In social science surveys, "many individuals attempt to evade certain questions put to them by interviewers"[34]—especially for sensitive questions such as political affiliation, illegal or taboo behavior. To counteract this, *Warner* proposed the following algorithm:[35]

---

25 For a discussion of ε values featuring Frank McSherry: *Greenberg*, "How One of Apple's Key Privacy Safeguards Falls Short" (Sept. 15, 2017).

26 See p. 161.

27 *Dwork* and *Roth*, "The Algorithmic Foundations of Differential Privacy" (2013), p. 15.

28 See p. 120.

29 *Dwork*, "Differential Privacy" (2006), p. 3.

30 *Bambauer*, *Muralidhar*, and R. *Sarathy*, "Fool's Gold" (2013–2014), (in detail: see p. 164).

31 Ibid., p. 755.

32 For another explanation aimed at a non-Computer Science audience, see *Wood* et al., "Differential Privacy" (2018–2019).

33 *Dwork* and *Roth*, "The Algorithmic Foundations of Differential Privacy" (2013), p. 15, this technique was first proposed in *Warner*, "Randomized Response: A Survey Technique for Eliminating Evasive Answer Bias" (Mar. 1965).

34 Ibid., p. 63.

35 This is using the adapted version from *Dwork* and *Roth*, "The Algorithmic Foundations of Differential Privacy" (2013), p. 15 with a coin toss instead of the original, where a more convoluted version was used (*Warner*, "Randomized Response: A Survey Technique for Eliminating Evasive

1. The interviewee flips a coin (not observed by the interviewer) ($\Pr(h) = \Pr(t) = \frac{1}{2}$)[36]
2. If the result is **tails**, they respond truthfully to the question.
3. If the result is **heads**, they flip the coin again and proceed as follows:
   (a) If this result is **heads**, they reply "Yes".
   (b) If this result is **tails**, they reply "No".

Using this algorithm when collecting responses, even if a respondent answers "Yes" to a question such as "Have you engaged in an extramarital affair in the past year?", they have *plausible deniability*: With a likelihood of $\frac{1}{4}$, they are only saying "Yes" because they flipped heads twice.[37] This algorithm satisfies DP.[38]

Therefore, this procedure provides "privacy" through plausible deniability, while at the same time still enabling analysis: Because we know the properties of the noise[39] that was inserted, it "evens out" in this case (and can be removed using calculations in more advanced examples) if the amount of interviewees (n) is large enough.

Randomized response is a prototypical version of a differentially private algorithm, but it is just one among many. In the following sections, we will define DP and take a look at its most common implementation, the Laplace mechanism.

7.2 Definition

There are two variants of DP that are commonly used, namely ε-differential privacy and (ε, δ)-differential privacy. To better evaluate the potency of differential privacy

Answer Bias" (Mar. 1965), p. 64): Suppose a group of individuals are either in group A or B. The interviewees are given a "spinner" that can point to either "A" or "B" and asked to turn it (with both outcomes being equally likely), unseen by the interviewer. They then should answer whether the spinner points to the letter of the group they belong to (a yes/no answer). Using only this information, the proportion of A and B in the population can be calculated.

36 In other words, a *fair coin*, where the probability of a toss coming out heads ($\Pr(h)$) equals the probability of tails ($\Pr(t)$) and both are 50% or $\frac{1}{2}$).

37 *Dwork* and *Roth*, "The Algorithmic Foundations of Differential Privacy" (2013), p. 16.

38 This version of randomized response is ($\varepsilon = \ln(3)$, $\delta = 0$)-differentially private, see Claim 3.5 in ibid., p. 30.

39 Noise used here in the technical sense—just like one could add white noise to an audio signal and still be able to (mostly) extract the source audio.

as a privacy guarantee, we should make sure to distinguish between the original (ε) form and the relaxed (ε, δ) form by referring to them as such.[40]

I. ε-Differential Privacy

1. Introduction

To begin, we will take a look at ε-differential privacy. Like k-Anonymity and other standards, DP is not an algorithm *per se*, but rather a *criterion*.[41] The basic idea behind DP is that it is a “neutral concept of privacy that [allows for identifying] when a loss of privacy has occurred”.[42]

DP is best illustrated as follows: Suppose we have a database x. This database contains a record with the personal data of a certain individual, Bob. Note that in this case, the information in our database is “correct”—so unlike with the “randomized response” example from before,[43] we have accurate data about each and every data subject in the database. If we make a copy of this database x and remove the record with Bob’s information, this makes a second database, x'. We now have two databases: One that contains Bob’s record (x) and one that does not (x'). Everything else is equal: x and x' differ by only one row (Bob’s information)—see figure 7.2. These databases are also called “adjacent” or “neighboring” databases in DP parlance.[44]

If querying these two neighboring databases using a differentially private mechanism $\mathcal{M}$ yields (nearly) the same result, Bob has *plausible deniability*: He can—justifiably—claim that his data is not in the database.

---

40 It should be noted that differential privacy research is a field in its own right, with new extensions of the definition and new applications being proposed frequently (see *Desfontaines*, “Lowering the cost of anonymization” (2020), Figure 2.7, p. 35). As this is an active field (see ibid., p. 34), we must limit our discussion to these two variants of DP. For readers who want to learn more about other flavors of DP, I recommend ibid., pp. 34 sqq.

41 This section is an explanation of DP that explains the concept to a legal audience by intentionally sacrificing some of the mathematical rigor of the original. For readers who would like a more technical and in-depth explanation, I recommend *Dwork* and *Roth*, “The Algorithmic Foundations of Differential Privacy” (2013). Additional pointers can be found in *Wood* et al., “Differential Privacy” (2018–2019) and *Hölzel*, “Differential Privacy and the GDPR” (2019).

42 Quote from a vision by *Gavison*, “Privacy and the Limits of Law” (1980), p. 423; cited in *Chawla* et al., “Toward Privacy in Public Databases” (2005), p. 364; which was in turn referenced in *Dwork*, *McSherry*, et al., “Calibrating Noise to Sensitivity in Private Data Analysis” (2016), p. 21.

43 See p. 149.

44 *Dwork*, *McSherry*, et al., “Calibrating Noise to Sensitivity in Private Data Analysis” (2016), p. 23; *Dwork* and *Roth*, “The Algorithmic Foundations of Differential Privacy” (2013), p. 18.

As a result, all of the potential harm that can follow from de-anonymization cannot befall him. Of course, general analyses of the data can still impact Bob. In the classic example,[45] if a study teaches us that smoking causes cancer, this can impact a smoker: For example, his insurance may become more expensive if the insurance company is aware that he smokes. Nonetheless, differential privacy makes sure that the impact on Bob is (nearly) the same, whether or not he was part of the study.[46]

2. Privacy Loss

As discussed, differential privacy is not an algorithm, but a definition of a class of mechanisms.[47] The differentially private mechanism we called $\mathcal{M}$ is essentially a way to interact with a database. In other words, we can "ask" our mechanism $\mathcal{M}$ and it will return an answer. For example, $\mathcal{M}$ could return a count of how many records in a given database x satisfy a condition, or provide a sum, an average, or a median value.[48] For each of these tasks there cannot be just one of these mechanisms, but multiple that satisfy differential privacy. For example, as will be explained later,[49] one can add either Laplacian or Gaussian noise and the resulting mechanisms will have different strengths and weaknesses, but both satisfy differential privacy.

To give a specific example, we could query a database containing responses to a survey on how many of its respondents have engaged in illicit behavior (the rightmost column in figure 7.2). This is known as a "counting query", as it counts the number of records for which "Illicit Behavior" is true.[50] This "way of interacting with the database" is a mechanism, $\mathcal{M}$. Let us first imagine a version of $\mathcal{M}$ without a differential privacy guarantee. This $\mathcal{M}(x)$ (in other words: For how many rows in x is "Illicit Behavior" true?) works by just directly returning the actual number of people in the database who have engaged in illicit behavior.

In this case, if we run a regular count query[51] on x, we might get a result that 58 people in the database have engaged in illicit behavior.[52] If we run the same query (where one row of respondents has been removed), we might get a result of 57—

45 *Dwork* and *Roth*, "The Algorithmic Foundations of Differential Privacy" (2013), pp. 5 sq.

46 Ibid., p. 6.

47 Ibid., p. 6.

48 *McSherry*, "Privacy integrated queries" (Sept. 2010), p. 89.

49 See p. 158.

50 *Dwork* and *Roth*, "The Algorithmic Foundations of Differential Privacy" (2013), pp. 32 sq.; *Dwork*, "Differential Privacy" (2006), p. 10.

51 *Not* a differential private mechanism, just a regular SQL query in the form of `SELECT COUNT(illicit_behavior) FROM x WHERE TRUE;`.

52 Purely a random number to illustrate.

because the row that we removed to get x' just happened to be one where the attribute "Illicit behavior" is true.

In order to provide differential privacy while telling us something about the data,[53] $\mathcal{M}$ needs to introduce *random noise* to change the outcome. This means that the outcome is no longer deterministic, as it depends on the random noise. In other words, the outputs "57" and "58"—as well as other equally plausible values—may occur for x and for x'. This noise is drawn from a distribution, oftentimes, the Laplace distribution is used.[54] As we know the properties of the noise we inserted, we can calculate how likely it is that $\mathcal{M}$ yields 58 given x, and how likely it is to yield 57 given x'.

In theory, then, we can compare the probabilities of the result "58" when running $\mathcal{M}$ on x or x' as $\Pr[\mathcal{M}(x) = 58]$ and $\Pr[\mathcal{M}(x') = 58]$. If we divide these probabilities, we can define the *privacy loss* that occurs when we observe a certain outcome.[55] Say that 58 was a 91% likely outcome under $\mathcal{M}(x)$ and a 89% likely outcome under $\mathcal{M}(x')$, then the privacy loss would be approx. 0.0222.[56]

Generalizing this calculation, we can formally define *privacy loss*.[57] Privacy loss, also known as $\mathcal{L}$, is incurred by observing a certain output ξ:[58]

$$\mathcal{L}^{(\xi)}_{\mathcal{M}(x)\|\mathcal{M}(x')} = \ln\left(\frac{\Pr[\mathcal{M}(x) = \xi]}{\Pr[\mathcal{M}(x') = \xi]}\right) \tag{7.1}$$

Using equation 7.1, we can *quantify* the amount of privacy that is "lost" by observing ξ.

$\mathcal{M}$ here is the same $\mathcal{M}$ we defined above: A mechanism that may or may not be differentially private. x and x' are the same as before: The database x, and the database x minus one (arbitrary) row. This is the "differential" part of differential privacy: We compare the data with and without one individual piece of information and evaluate the *differential* impact of leaving this information out.

---

53 As *Dwork, McSherry*, et al. note, there could also be a constant "fixed-output" mechanism $\mathcal{M}$ that always provides the same output, no matter the data. This is 0-differentially private, but tells us nothing about the data, see *Dwork, McSherry*, et al., "Calibrating Noise to Sensitivity in Private Data Analysis" (2016), p. 24.

54 See p. 158.

55 Additionally, we take the natural logarithm of the result (ln). As $\ln(1) = 0$, the result will be a number other than 0 (positive or negative!) if the probabilities differ. ln will re-appear in the formal definition of differential privacy: As ε is just the worst-case value for $\mathcal{L}$ and $e^{\ln(x)} = x$, the definition of differential privacy can be derived from the definition of privacy loss.

56 $\ln(0.91 \div 0.89) \approx 0.0222$.

57 *Dwork* and *Roth*, "The Algorithmic Foundations of Differential Privacy" (2013), p. 18.

58 Equation given in: ibid., p. 18.

Calculating privacy loss is a powerful formalization of an intuitive concept: For each piece of information observed, one can quantify the amount of knowledge gained, *e.g.*, about a specific person. In this example, as the "neighboring databases" x and x' differ exactly in the record of one person, we can see the impact of this person's data on the result ξ. Conceptually, this allows for evaluating the cost to privacy over time. As differential privacy *composes*,[59] these privacy losses can be added up and show a real-time tally of the *privacy budget* being exhausted.

This formalization could also be an interesting angle to enable future regulation: Instead of regulating the protection of personal data, which depends heavily on identifiability,[60] one could imagine a future where privacy loss itself is part of the regulation.

Personally, I would argue that hinging a definition of personal data and its protection on identifiability is prudent and sufficient for the protection of the rights and freedoms of natural persons. This is also shown in the definition laid out above, where identification ultimately terminates in a situation where the identificator can *affect* the identifyee in some way relevant to their basic rights and freedoms.

Nonetheless, privacy loss could be one building block in the constant act of renegotiation between those creating and holding "original" data and those wanting to analyze it. If a legislator saw a need for paternalistic intervention in this space, they could, *e.g.*, mandate that all transactions based on a transfer of data could be valued using the formalization of privacy loss.[61] After all, it incorporates pretty much all aspects salient for a pricing negotiation: It trivially includes the privacy lost on the part of the person offering their data, but it also may serve as a proxy for the utility of the data.[62] It also already includes the mitigation made through the use of differential privacy, as the privacy loss is calculated *after* $\mathcal{M}$ has been applied. The quantification lends itself well to an economic perspective of "selling" one's data to advertisers, for example: A piece of information may be "more valuable" if it leads to a larger privacy loss. Conversely, those wanting to use the data can use more potent differential privacy mechanisms to reduce privacy loss and thus, in this example, cost. All in all, privacy loss is yet another facet of the recurring theme of the

---

59 That is: Differential privacy allows for the "analysis and control of cumulative privacy loss" over time, *Dwork* and *Roth*, "The Algorithmic Foundations of Differential Privacy" (2013), p. 23.

60 See also: *Hölzel*, "Differential Privacy and the GDPR" (2019), p. 12.

61 Similar ideas have been proposed in the economic and computer science arenas, see for example: *Nget*, Yang *Cao*, and *Yoshikawa*, "How to Balance Privacy and Money through Pricing Mechanism in Personal Data Market" (2017); *Shen* et al., "Personal Big Data Pricing Method Based on Differential Privacy" (Feb. 1, 2022).

62 Insofar as "unique" data may be of higher value to analysis than a record that completely represents the median of existing records.

Database x

Name	First Name	Gender	Illicit Behavior
Michael	Smith	1	TRUE
Daniel	Wu	1	FALSE
Liza	Santos	2	FALSE
Madeleine	Ross	2	TRUE
Max	Wesley	9	FALSE

→

Database x'

Name	First Name	Gender	Illicit Behavior
Michael	Smith	1	TRUE
Liza	Santos	2	FALSE
Madeleine	Ross	2	TRUE
Max	Wesley	9	FALSE

Fig. 7.2: Databases x and x' differ by one row. Note that this shows just the top rows of the database (the tables' "heads").

privacy–utility tradeoff.[63] In any case, privacy loss presents a promising avenue for future research into privacy[64] legislation *de lege ferenda.*

3. Definition of ε-Differential Privacy

Now that we know how to compute the privacy loss that we incur by observing a certain output,[65] we are not done yet: Some outputs may lead to a drastically higher privacy loss than others. Suppose our database x contains information about whether people have tested positive for a rare type of genetic mutation. To give an extreme example using a counting query, if our database is small[66] and the mutation is rare, the outcome $\xi = 0$ is much more probable than $\xi = 1$. If Bob is the only person in the data to have this mutation, a x' without his data would yield $\xi = 0$ and x with his data would yield $\xi = 1$.[67] Here, the privacy loss would be very large. If we can imagine all possible outputs of $\mathcal{M}$ and their probabilities, we can evaluate $\mathcal{M}$'s overall privacy. If we know that—in the worst case—the privacy loss by observing an output of $\mathcal{M}$ is a certain number, we can rest assured that $\mathcal{M}$ protects privacy to that extent.[68]

63 See p. 96.

64 In this case, it is purposely "privacy" instead of "data protection", as DP is less about data protection and more about limiting information gain.

65 see p. 153 7.1.

66 This makes the database not very useful, but it is just an extreme example.

67 Example adapted from *Rathi*, "Deep Learning with Differential Privacy (DP-SGD Explained)" (Dec. 25, 2021), (in the context of ML).

68 If we create an $\mathcal{M}$ to employ the same mechanism as in our "randomized response" example above, we can see it satisfies differential privacy. This $\mathcal{M}$ is $\ln 3$-differentially private (Claim 3.5: *Dwork* and *Roth*, "The Algorithmic Foundations of Differential Privacy" (2013), p. 30). $\ln 3 \approx 1.0986$.

The formal definition of ε-differential privacy is as follows:[69] [70]

$$\Pr[\mathcal{M}(x) \in S] \le e^{\varepsilon} \cdot \Pr[\mathcal{M}(x') \in S] \tag{7.2}$$

To unpack this definition, first note it is an inequality: The right side of the definition is larger than or equal to ($\le$) the left side of the definition. Also note that $\Pr[\mathcal{M}(x) \in S]$ occurs nearly identically on both sides, with the right side containing x' instead of x. Ignoring the rest of the definition for now, we can see that, informally spoken, $\mathcal{M}(x)$ and $\mathcal{M}(x')$ are compared.

Compared to the privacy loss definition above,[71] we can see that $\mathcal{M}(x) = \xi$ has been replaced by $\mathcal{M}(x) \in S$. This means that for all possible outputs of $\mathcal{M}$, which we call S, the inequality must hold. Spoken differently, the probability of all results S of $\mathcal{M}$ for x must be smaller or equal to the same for x' multiplied by e^{ε}.

The parameter, ε, features in the definition as the exponent for e, Euler's number[72]. The larger ε, the "easier" it is for the inequality, where the right side must be larger or equal to the left side, to hold true. In other words: The larger ε becomes, the less noise $\mathcal{M}$ needs to introduce. This also explains why 0-differential privacy equates to completely withholding the data,[73] and ∞-differential privacy equates to completely disclosing the data[74].

II. (ε, δ)-Differential Privacy

The "original" definition, ε-differential privacy, has proven to be well-usable in some contexts, but hard to implement in others.[75] As a result, a relaxation of differ-

69 *Dwork*, *McSherry*, et al., "Calibrating Noise to Sensitivity in Private Data Analysis" (2016), p. 23.

70 Note that different naming conventions exist—some call the neighboring databases x and x', others use x and y, and others still use D_1 and D_2. Here, we stick to the convention from the "original" paper on differential privacy, ibid., p. 23.

71 see p. 153 7.1.

72 $e \approx 2.7182$. Another way to express this would be to use $\exp \varepsilon$ instead of e^{ε}, as done in *Dwork* and *Roth*, "The Algorithmic Foundations of Differential Privacy" (2013), p. 17.

73 Logically, as $e^0 = 1$, 0-differential privacy equates to $\Pr[\mathcal{M}(x) \in S] \le \Pr[\mathcal{M}(x') \in S]$. Keep in mind that this needs to hold for all neighboring databases, so x and x' are interchangeable (see *Desfontaines*, "Differential privacy in (a bit) more detail" (Aug. 16, 2018)). This means, in effect, that the results of $\mathcal{M}$ are the same, no matter which of the neighboring databases we use. In effect, this means that the result of $\mathcal{M}$ teaches us nothing about the data.

74 As ε approaches infinity, the inequality $\Pr[\mathcal{M}(x) \in S] \le e^{\varepsilon} \cdot \Pr[\mathcal{M}(x') \in S]$ will hold true independently of $\mathcal{M}$.

75 One context where we need (ε, δ)-differential privacy is when using the Gaussian mechanism, see p. 159. For a reasoning of why that is, see *Dwork* and *Roth*, "The Algorithmic Foundations of Differential Privacy" (2013), pp. 53 sq.; *Dwork*, *Kenthapadi*, et al., "Our Data, Ourselves" (2006), pp. 5 sq.

ential privacy, (ε, δ)-differential privacy, has been established. This adds a second parameter, δ, that is added to the right side of the inequality. This allows for the mechanism to fail at protecting ε-differential privacy with a probability of δ. The formal definition of (ε, δ)-differential privacy is as follows:[76]

$$\Pr[\mathcal{M}(x) \in S] \leq e^{\varepsilon} \cdot \Pr[\mathcal{M}(x') \in S] + \delta \tag{7.3}$$

Expressed in words: If we run our $\mathcal{M}$ function on database x and database x', it needs to satisfy ε-differential privacy, but it can "fail" with a probability of δ.

7.3 Getting to $\mathcal{M}$

Now that we have outlined the definition of differential privacy, the question of how to find a mechanism $\mathcal{M}$ remains. Unlike other definitions of privacy,[77] DP is agnostic to $\mathcal{M}$. Thus, DP scholarship has been free to create mechanisms that best suit a certain application—as long as they satisfy one of the definitions of differential privacy.[78] In the following, we can only cover two basic mechanisms: The Laplace and Gaussian mechanisms.[79]

Both of these mechanisms work by adding noise to the output of an unmodified query. Put simply, they add a random number, drawn from a probability distribution, to the output of the query.[80] Figure 7.3 visualizes these probability distributions. The amount of noise they inject and the properties of the probability distribution allow for quantifying privacy loss. These are defined in such a way that they do not exceed the parameter set earlier, ε. In essence, this is the entirety of differential privacy (for numeric values).

Note that these two mechanisms are only useful for queries that output floating-point numeric values, yet this limitation is not inherent in differential privacy, but rather a limitation of these mechanisms. Other mechanisms, such as the exponential

76 *Dwork* and *Roth*, "The Algorithmic Foundations of Differential Privacy" (2013), p. 17.

77 For example, the family of anonymization mechanisms surrounding k-Anonymity all work using generalization and suppression. It is theoretically possible to construct a k-anonymous dataset using, say, randomization (for example, by repeatedly injecting noise until the k-anonymity requirement is satisfied), but it is impractical and—to my knowledge—has not been done.

78 To enable a wider range of mechanisms and to extend the definition for other applications, a wide range of variants of the definition have been proposed. For a comprehensive overview, see *Desfontaines*, "Lowering the cost of anonymization" (2020), pp. 34 sqq.

79 For additional mechanisms, such as the exponential mechanism, see *Dwork* and *Roth*, "The Algorithmic Foundations of Differential Privacy" (2013), pp. 37 sqq.

80 Ibid., p. 31.

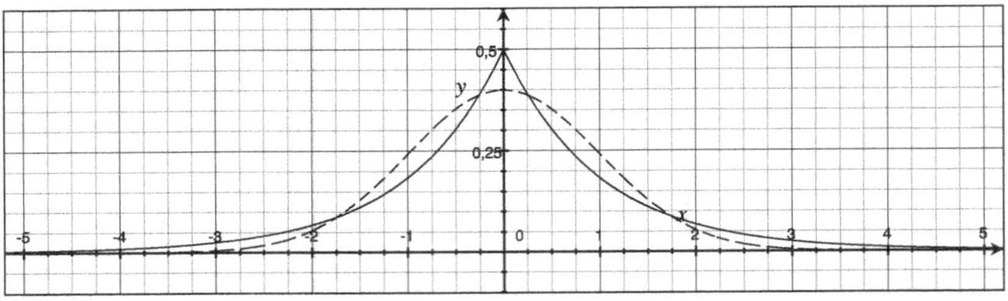

Fig. 7.3: A plot of the Laplace function $y = \frac{1}{2b}e^{-\frac{|x|}{b}}$ with $b = 1$ (solid line) and the Gaussian function $y = \frac{1}{\sigma\sqrt{2\pi}}e^{-\frac{(x-\mu)^2}{2\sigma^2}}$ with $\mu = 0$ and $\sigma^2 = 1$ (dashed line).

mechanism,[81] can be used for other kinds of data, such as categorical data.[82] However, as many problems in privacy-preserving data analysis ultimately come down to computing numerical values, I will only briefly explain these two mechanisms.[83]

I. The Laplace Mechanism

The Laplace mechanism[84] is a simple way of adding noise to queries that return a real-valued (*i.e.*, a floating-point number) output.[85] It is the "original" DP mechanism in a sense, as it is frequently used to introduce the concept of DP to a new audience.[86]

It adds noise drawn from a Laplace distribution to the output.[87] A Laplace distribution is a probability distribution whose probability density function is the Laplacian function.[88] The amount of this noise is scaled dependent, *i.a.*, on ε.[89] The

81 *Dwork* and *Roth*, "The Algorithmic Foundations of Differential Privacy" (2013), pp. 37 sqq.
82 Meaning a task where the output is not a floating-point number, but rather a category or a label, see: ibid., p. 37.
83 They are also the most intuitive definitions, as their function is similar to "normal" randomization as explained above (see p. 143) and we will revisit the Gaussian mechanism when talking about Differentially Private Stochastic Gradient Descent (DP-SGD) (see p. 221).
84 Named after the Laplace distribution, which is named for Pierre-Simon Laplace (*1749—†1827).
85 *Seleshi* and *Asseffa*, "A Case Study on Differential Privacy" (2017), p. 23.
86 See *e.g.*, *Dwork*, "Differential Privacy" (2006), p. 10; *Dwork*, *McSherry*, et al., "Calibrating Noise to Sensitivity in Private Data Analysis" (2016), p. 25; *Wood* et al., "Differential Privacy" (2018–2019), p. 272.
87 For a mathematical definition, see Definition 3.3 *Dwork* and *Roth*, "The Algorithmic Foundations of Differential Privacy" (2013), p. 32.
88 Visualized for $b = 1$ in figure 7.3. For a full definition, see ibid., pp. 31 sq.
89 And on the ℓ_1-sensitivity, a detail omitted here for the sake of brevity, see in detail: ibid., p. 31.

Laplace mechanism is easy to apply and the "simplest" DP algorithm. It is thus very useful for beginners. However, it also has drawbacks. For example, in some circumstances and deployments, the Laplace mechanism leads to the addition large amounts of noise, which obscures the result.[90] In other words: In some applications, it destroys utility in a way that other mechanisms would not. As a result, research has uncovered mechanisms that "produce more meaningful output, cost less in terms of privacy, and share the cost across multiple users."[91]

II. The Gaussian Mechanism

The Gaussian[92] mechanism works essentially like the Laplace mechanism, but it adds Gaussian noise instead of Laplacian noise.[93] Gaussian noise is noise drawn from a distribution whose probability density function is the Gaussian function.[94] The amount of noise inserted depends on ε and δ.[95] This has a significant advantage over the Laplace mechanism: For one, the Gaussian distribution is often a good model for "naturally occurring" events and other noise.[96] Other events in the real world are modeled after the Gaussian distribution ("bell curve"), such as the distribution of intelligence quotients (IQ) or a grading system on a curve. As *Dwork* and *Roth* explain, the result of using two of these Gaussian distributions together (the "naturally occuring" one and the noise injected through $\mathcal{M}$) is also a Gaussian, thereby not altering the fundamental characteristics of the distribution.[97] As a result, the resulting noisy output is more readily usable.[98] Nonetheless, unlike the Laplace mechanism, which is ε-differentially private, the Gaussian mechanism requires (ε, δ)-differential privacy and thus a weaker guarantee than the Laplace

---

90 For a criticism of using the Laplace mechanism, see *Bambauer*, *Muralidhar*, and R. *Sarathy*, "Fool's Gold" (2013–2014), pp. 727 sqq.; reply by McSherry (see p. 165): *McSherry*, "Differential Privacy for Dummies" (Feb. 3, 2016).

91 *McSherry*, "Differential Privacy for Dummies" (Feb. 3, 2016).

92 Named after the Gaussian distribution, which is named for Carl Friedrich Gauß(*1777—†1855).

93 *Dwork* and *Roth*, "The Algorithmic Foundations of Differential Privacy" (2013), p. 53; for a full proof, see: *Dwork* and *Roth*, "The Algorithmic Foundations of Differential Privacy" (2013), pp. 261 sqq.

94 It should be noted that the use of Gaussian noise necessitates "scaling" this noise differently (to the ℓ_2-sensitivity rather than to the ℓ_1-sensitivity, which is calculated differently) than in the case of Laplace noise. This detail is omitted here for brevity's sake, see in depth: *Dwork* and *Roth*, "The Algorithmic Foundations of Differential Privacy" (2013), p. 53.

95 Ibid., p. 31 fn. 1.

96 Ibid., p. 53.

97 Ibid., p. 53.

98 Ibid., p. 53.

mechanism:[99] As laid out above, the additional parameter δ means that the mechanism can “fail” with the probability δ—a drawback not present for the Laplace mechanism. Ultimately, however, *Dwork* and *Roth* contend that, for small values of δ, the guarantees offered by both mechanisms are nonetheless comparable.[100]

7.4 Benefits

There are a number of benefits to DP. *Dwork* and *Roth* sum up the benefits of DP as follows:[101] For one, DP offers protection that goes beyond re-identification.[102] It also protects privacy in cases where identification is not possible, by protecting against learning about a person’s inclusion in the data.[103] Another property of differential privacy is that it neutralizes linkage attacks, even those involving future datasets and other auxiliary information.[104] DP allows us to *quantify* privacy loss.[105] This is very useful, as it allows to strike a quantifiable balance between privacy and utility. It also allows controlling cumulative privacy loss over multiple computations.[106] Put simply, when performing multiple queries on a (ε, δ)-differentially private mechanism, the values for ε and δ can be added together.[107] This is called “composition” and it is one of the key desirable traits of differential privacy.[108] There is also the possibility of analyzing the privacy loss of *groups* rather than individuals.[109] And finally,

99 *Dwork* and *Roth*, “The Algorithmic Foundations of Differential Privacy” (2013), p. 54; for a full proof, see: *Dwork* and *Roth*, “The Algorithmic Foundations of Differential Privacy” (2013), pp. 261 sqq.
100 *Dwork* and *Roth*, “The Algorithmic Foundations of Differential Privacy” (2013), p. 53.
101 Ibid., p. 22.
102 Ibid., p. 22.
103 For more on this philosophical difference between DP and other anonymization methods, see p. 180. *Dwork* and *Roth* give the example of a hospital in which only a handful of cases are processed on a given day. Knowing that a neighbor was admitted on that day may even allow for inference on the neighbor’s illness without being able to link a person to a record (ibid., p. 7).
104 Ibid., p. 22.
105 see p. 153, equation 7.1.
106 *Dwork* and *Roth*, “The Algorithmic Foundations of Differential Privacy” (2013), pp. 22, 23.
107 Ibid., p. 43 Theorem 3.16.
108 *Altman, Cohen, Nissim*, et al., “What a Hybrid Legal-Technical Analysis Teaches Us about Privacy Regulation” (2021), pp. 41 sq. Other methods, such as *k*-Anonymity and its corollaries, do not compose. This makes them susceptible to so-called composition attacks. For a demonstration of these methods failing and differential privacy resisting these attacks, see *Ganta, Kasiviswanathan*, and *Smith*, “Composition Attacks and Auxiliary Information in Data Privacy” (Aug. 2008).
109 A topic beyond the scope of this dissertation, see *Dwork* and *Roth*, “The Algorithmic Foundations of Differential Privacy” (2013), p. 23.

differential privacy is "immune" to post-processing, *i.e.*, no matter what additional information is available or what methods are available, a data analyst cannot make the data *less* differentially private.[110]

7.5 Parameters

As we have seen, it is important to choose the parameters ε and, if applicable, δ, wisely. As *Dwork*, *McSherry*, et al. note, "in our work, ε is a parameter chosen by policy".[111]

As privacy loss is cumulative, answering many subsequent queries about a person may increase the loss of privacy over a threshold that is deemed acceptable. For this reason, deployments of DP typically operate with a *privacy budget*, in effect, the maximum number that ε may take in a given application. The choice of ε determines the privacy guarantee by the algorithm. Typical values of ε are 0.01, 0.1, or in some cases, $\ln(2) \approx 0.6931$ or $\ln(3) \approx 1.098$.[112] In the privacy literature, values range substantially, from miniscule values ($\varepsilon = 0.01$) to large values ($\varepsilon = 7$).[113] In the case of the 2020 U.S. census, ε was even set to a maximum of 19.61.[114]

It should be noted that values of ε are not easily comparable, as it is a relative measure and depends on the data in question.[115] A ε that preserved privacy in one scenario may lead to a re-identification in a different scenario.[116]

A second parameter that was introduced later, δ, allows to further relax the privacy standard. δ is more "dangerous" to privacy than ε. It allows for a failure of privacy with a probability of δ.[117] Nonetheless, where δ is very small, the resulting implementation can still achieve a meaningful privacy guarantee.[118]

---

110 Ibid., pp. 19, 23.

111 *Dwork, McSherry*, et al., "Calibrating Noise to Sensitivity in Private Data Analysis" (2016), p. 18.

112 *Dwork*, "Differential Privacy" (2008), p. 3.

113 *Hsu* et al., "Differential Privacy" (July 2014), p. 4.

114 *US Census Bureau*, "Census Bureau Sets Key Parameters to Protect Privacy in 2020 Census Results" (June 9, 2021).

115 *Lee* and *Clifton*, "How much is enough?" (Oct. 26, 2011), p. 326.

116 Ibid., p. 327.

117 See p. 156.

118 See in detail: *Dwork* and *Roth*, "The Algorithmic Foundations of Differential Privacy" (2013), p. 18.

In summary, setting the appropriate parameters is the principal theoretical requirement to deploying a privacy-preserving implementation of DP.[119]

7.6 Practical Application Examples

Differential privacy has seen widespread application.[120] We can roughly divide these applications up into two phases: For one, differential privacy is used "as-is", to anonymize real-world data.[121] More recently, however, DP has been used to help with privacy-preserving ML. We will cover this second type of application later,[122] so for now, I will highlight three applications of the first type: Google, Apple, and the U.S. census.

It is used at Google, Inc. *i.a.*, to improve analysis of browsing behavior in the Chrome browser.[123] Additionally, Google has released a number of open source libraries for differential privacy[124] and even integrated DP into its cloud platform, most recently into the BigQuery product.[125]

Apple, Inc. has also implemented differential privacy in its products, *i.a.*, to improve keyboard suggestions and improve the detection of energy-hungry websites in its Safari browser.[126] Here, Apple limits user contributions, deletes all identifiers,

119 Additional *practical* considerations may need to be made when implementing these mechanisms, *e.g.*, when using floating-point arithmetic with differential privacy, see "Remark 2.1", *Dwork* and *Roth*, "The Algorithmic Foundations of Differential Privacy" (2013), p. 26.

120 For more examples, see *Desfontaines*, "A list of real-world uses of differential privacy" (Oct. 1, 2021).

121 A plethora of applications for DP has been found especially in the medical sector, see *e.g.*, *Marnau*, *Berrang*, and *Humbert*, "Anonymisierungsverfahren für genetische Daten" (Feb. 1, 2018), pp. 85 sqq.

122 See p. 221.

123 *Erlingsson*, *Pihur*, and *Korolova*, "RAPPOR" (Nov. 3, 2014), p. 10.

124 *Guevara*, "How we're helping developers with differential privacy" (Jan. 28, 2021), With a special focus on DP-enhanced ML, see p. 221.

125 *Gianola* and *Pachacz*, "Introducing BigQuery differential privacy with Tumult Labs" (May 9, 2023).

126 *Apple, Inc.*, "Differential Privacy Overview" (Nov. 2, 2017), p. 2; *Apple, Inc.*, "Apple – WWDC 2016 Keynote" (June 15, 2016).

and interprets the privacy budget per-donation.[127] ε values range from 2 through 8.[128 129]

A third important application is in the decennial U.S. census. The census is very important for U.S. politics, as it determines the seats in the U.S. House of Representatives and direct taxation.[130] Historically, the Census Bureau has published both aggregate statistics and microdata[131], protected by swapping values.[132133] As the Census Bureau wanted to release more data and re-identification capabilities had increased significantly,[134] they adopted DP for the 2020 census.[135] This was done by first creating a "noisy measurements" file protected by DP and then adjusting the results by post-processing into a second file, which is then released to the public.[136] ε is set to levels as high as $\varepsilon = 19.61$.[137]

These three high-profile applications show that DP is fit for use in practice, at least in a narrow set of circumstances: Some of these applications use comparatively high values of ε, and all of them operate on a very large dataset, with data that is somewhat homogenous.

---

127 *Apple, Inc.*, "Differential Privacy Overview" (Nov. 2, 2017), p. 1.

128 *Apple, Inc.*, "Differential Privacy Overview" (Nov. 2, 2017), p. 2; For a detailed reverse-engineering, see *Tang* et al., "Privacy Loss in Apple's Implementation of Differential Privacy on MacOS 10.12" (Sept. 11, 2017).

129 In the recent past, Apple has also supported research on privacy-preserving AI using DP, *Talwar*, "PPML Workshop Talk" (June 2022); *Apple, Inc.*, "Apple Privacy-Preserving Machine Learning Workshop 2022" (2022).

130 U.S. constitution, Article 1, Section 2, Clause 3: "Representatives and direct Taxes shall be apportioned … according to their respective Numbers, which shall be determined by adding to the whole Number of free Persons … and excluding Indians not taxed, three fifths of all other Persons." Note the exclusion of non-taxed Native Americans and the disenfranchisement ("three fifths of all other Persons") of enslaved people in the original version—later modified by amendments to the Constitution.

131 Microdata means publishing individual-level records instead of aggregates, Note 10: *Hölzel*, "Differential Privacy and the GDPR" (2019), p. 3.

132 See p. 144.

133 *Abowd* and *Velkoff*, "Modernizing Privacy Protections for the 2020 Census" (Apr. 28, 2021).

134 For a re-identification attack on the 2010 census, see *US Census Bureau*, "The Census Bureau's Simulated Reconstruction-Abetted Re-identification Attack on the 2010 Census" (May 7, 2021); *Ruggles* et al., "Differential Privacy and Census Data" (May 2019), pp. 404 sq.

135 *Abowd* and *Velkoff*, "Modernizing Privacy Protections for the 2020 Census" (Apr. 28, 2021).

136 *Dwork*, *Greenwood*, and *King*, "There's a simple solution to the latest census fight" (July 26, 2021).

137 *US Census Bureau*, "Census Bureau Sets Key Parameters to Protect Privacy in 2020 Census Results" (June 9, 2021).

7.7 Shortcomings

Differential privacy also has some important shortcomings worth pointing out. Most of these are by design, while some are due to the inherent limitations of the privacy–utility tradeoff.

First off, DP cannot protect from harm that occurs to the data subject due to its general presence in the data. This is both obvious and not problematic: For example, given a database that surveys smokers and nonsmokers to assess their health, the smokers in the database may be adversely affected by the analysis that smoking *overall* leads to worse health.[138] The smoker is "harmed" by this analysis (for example, through more expensive insurance) even if they choose not to participate in the study.[139] The correlation of *private* and *public* attributes alone does not constitute a (differential) privacy violation.[140]

Additionally, the privacy that DP can provide depends on the values of ε (and possibly δ) that are used. For large values of ε and δ, the privacy guarantees are negligible. The use of differential privacy has been likened to "performative privacy" where it has been used with such a large ε that it fails to protect privacy.[141] At the same time, when these parameters are too small, the data becomes less useful, as large amounts of noise need to be inserted. To figure out which values for these parameters are appropriate, the controller needs to take the circumstances into account. In other words: DP still requires some judgement to be exercised in choosing the parameters.

A further-reaching problem, however, would be if utility and privacy cannot be balanced well. In part, this is what *Bambauer*, *Muralidhar*, and R. *Sarathy*[142] as well as *Francis*[143] insinuate: Either the practical utility of the dataset is diminished insofar as to be unusable, or the privacy guarantees are relaxed so far that they fail to protect privacy. This criticism may not be unfounded, as the ε values for the

138 *Dwork* and *Roth*, "The Algorithmic Foundations of Differential Privacy" (2013), pp. 6, 22.

139 Ibid., pp. 6, 22.

140 Ibid., p. 22.

141 J. *Sarathy*, "From Algorithmic to Institutional Logics" (Apr. 9, 2022), pp. 6 sq.

142 "... there is no simple solution to the eternal contest between data privacy and data utility" *Bambauer*, *Muralidhar*, and R. *Sarathy*, "Fool's Gold" (2013–2014), p. 705.

143 *Francis*, "Dear Differential Privacy, Put Up or Shut Up" (Apr. 19, 2020); Later relativized in *Francis*, "Differential Privacy" (Apr. 12, 2020).

practical applications outlined above[144] lie beyond the scope of what is typically considered a strong privacy guarantee.[145] [146]

In their paper "Fool's Gold", *Bambauer*, *Muralidhar*, and R. *Sarathy* are criticizing DP as returning flawed output data,[147] imposing too far-reaching limits on data release that would not be required using "traditional' disclosure control methods,[148] and shifting the difficult question of the privacy–utility tradeoff to the selection of the parameter ε.[149] Their tone and conclusion is scathing.[150] This paper drew responses from the technical DP community, notably from *Sarwate*[151] and *McSherry*, one of the co-inventors[152] of Differential Privacy[153]. Both of these responses focused on the shortcomings of the paper, while characterizing it as misleading.[154] Most notably, the paper does not distinguish between differential privacy as a definition

---

144 See p. 162.
145 See p. 161.
146 Note that this does not necessarily mean that they expose user's data: "While all small ε are alike, each large ε is large after its own fashion, making it difficult to reason about them.", *Dwork*, *Kohli*, and *Mulligan*, "Differential Privacy in Practice" (Oct. 20, 2019), p. 7.
147 Especially when the noise added leads to negative or floating-point numbers where a positive integer was expected, like in a count of persons: *Bambauer*, *Muralidhar*, and R. *Sarathy*, "Fool's Gold" (2013–2014), p. 704.
148 Ibid., pp. 747 sqq.
149 Ibid., pp. 750 sqq.
150 "Differential privacy faces a hard choice. It must either recede into the ash heap of theory or surrender its claim to uniqueness and supremacy … the legal and policy community must curb its enthusiasm for this trendy theory." ibid., pp. 753, 755.
151 *Sarwate*, "An exercise in careful misreading | An Ergodic Walk" (Aug. 3, 2018).
152 *McSherry* and *Dwork*, "Differential Data Privacy" (2007).
153 *McSherry*, "Differential Privacy for Dummies" (Feb. 3, 2016).
154 With *Sarwate* remarking: "… the misleading rhetoric employed here is meant to stir emotions rather than sway the intellect … The language in the article is quite florid … I suppose this sort of prose may be what constitutes scholarly writing in law, but it lacks the measured tones that one might want in more objective criticism.", *Sarwate*, "An exercise in careful misreading | An Ergodic Walk" (Aug. 3, 2018). McSherry is more direct: "… the authors brought in a friend in the legal field, and they wrote a new paper. A bigger paper, full of breathless hyperbole and purple prose.… [The paper] concludes 'Differential privacy faces a hard choice. It must either recede into the ash heap of theory, or surrender its claim to uniqueness and supremacy.' I will present a third option: The authors could take a fucking stats class and stop intentionally misleading their readers.", *McSherry*, "Differential Privacy for Dummies" (Feb. 3, 2016). While one can justifiably take issue with McSherry's choice of language here, it should be noted that the authors of "Fool's Gold" are guilty of character insults themselves, *i.a.* by contending that "[the] proponents of differential privacy do not themselves fully understand the theory", *Bambauer*, *Muralidhar*, and R. *Sarathy*, "Fool's Gold" (2013–2014), p. 706.

and mechanisms that satisfy DP, such as the Laplace mechanism[155].[156] The authors of "Fool's Gold" replied,[157] to which Frank McSherry replied again[158].[159] Bambauer appears not to have changed her mind, as she advocated against the use of DP in the U.S. census in 2021.[160] Upon closer examination, while there are limitations to differential privacy[161] and it certainly does not solve every problem, the criticism levied by *Bambauer*, *Muralidhar*, and R. *Sarathy* is unfounded.[162]

A similar criticism is frequently levied by the team surrounding *Francis*, co-inventor of Diffix[163]. Due to the requirement of a privacy budget,[164] they contend that the practical utility of DP is severely limited,[165] exemplified by releases of data that included too much noise.[166] [167]

---

155 See p. 158.

156 As McSherry points out: "The Laplace mechanism used in the example is the simplest of differentially private mechanisms, and the large volume of research in the area has led to many other ways of approaching data that produce more meaningful output, cost less in terms of privacy, and share the cost across multiple users" and that "[none] of this would be an issue if the population in question was not small", noting that differential privacy is working as intended in protecting a small population, *McSherry*, "Differential Privacy for Dummies" (Feb. 3, 2016).

157 Since deleted, but available at the Internet Archive: *Bambauer* and *Muralidhar*, "Diffensive Privacy" (May 17, 2016).

158 *McSherry*, "2016-05-19" (May 19, 2016).

159 As expected, the tone of these replies gets progressively rougher.

160 Incidentally, this was the same Alabama case referenced in Dwork's newspaper article on the subject (*Dwork*, *Greenwood*, and *King*, "There's a simple solution to the latest census fight" (July 26, 2021)), where Bambauer submitted an amicus curiae brief in support of the state of Alabama: "Differential Privacy, if used as intended, would wreak havoc on the accuracy of almost all US Census data products and defeat the very purpose for comprehensive Census data collection without any meaningful gain in the (already adequate) privacy protections.", *Weller* and *Bambauer*, "Brief of Amicus Curiae Prof. Jane Bambauer in Support of Plaintiff's Complaint for Declaratory and Injunctive Relief" (Sept. 4, 2021), p. 7.

161 "The research space currently suffers from too few practitioners advancing (or delineating) the bounds of differential privacy; we have a volume of esoteric theoretical research, but relatively little work translating it (or even simpler results) to practice in clear and useable tools.",*McSherry*, "2016-05-19" (May 19, 2016).

162 *Sarwate*, "An exercise in careful misreading | An Ergodic Walk" (Aug. 3, 2018).

163 A different kind of anonymization mechanism, see p. 170.

164 See p. 161.

165 *Francis*, *Probst-Eide*, *Obrok*, et al., "Diffix-Birch" (Aug. 21, 2019), p. 3.

166 *Francis*, "Dear Differential Privacy, Put Up or Shut Up" (Apr. 19, 2020); *Francis*, *Probst Eide*, and *Munz*, "Diffix" (2017), p. 4; *Francis*, "Differential Privacy" (Apr. 12, 2020); *Francis*, *Probst-Eide*, *Wagner*, et al., "Diffix Elm" (June 20, 2022), pp. 13 sq.

167 For an additional criticism in the same vein, see *Kifer* and *Machanavajjhala*, "No free lunch in data privacy" (June 12, 2011) and McSherry's reply: *McSherry*, "Lunchtime for Data Privacy" (Aug. 16, 2016).

In summary, there are unsolved questions in DP, especially with finding practical mechanisms that maximize utility while preserving privacy well. Nonetheless, the breadth of practical examples where DP was used in a production environment prove these criticisms to be at least partially unfounded. As we will see, DP shines in another area: It can be used in a AI context to privately train models.[168]

7.8 Conclusion

To conclude, DP is a mature approach to anonymizing structured data. It is suitable for a wide range of applications and has a number of desirable properties.

Nonetheless, it is not perfect for all applications: Where populations are small, differentially private algorithms tend to inject a lot of noise. It also typically relies on an online scenario which may not be tenable under all circumstances. Finally, as it is an open field of research that continues to see new variations and mechanisms proposed, the utility–privacy tradeoff will only get better from here on out.

As we shall see,[169] setting ε[170] is a significant (legal and practical) challenge. Nonetheless, this is not a failure of DP, but rather a reality of anonymization: Independent of the anonymization method used, its parameters still need to be set (this is the same for ε with DP, k with k-anonymity, t with t-closeness, *etc.*) and the privacy–utility tradeoff negotiated for the deployment.

168 See p. 221.

169 See p. 183.

170 And, of course, δ, if applicable.

8 Other Approaches

There are other approaches that are neither related to the classic approaches nor to DP. As they fit no other category, I will sort them from simple (Query Auditing and Summary Statistics) to complex (Diffix, Synthetic Data, and Homomorphic Encryption). Some of them are unsuitable for providing any measure of anonymity. Others are still at an early stage and it is thus too early to see if they can provide strong privacy guarantees while maintaining adequate utility in real-world scenarios.

8.1 Query Auditing

A simple approach to avoiding disclosure in an online setting is query auditing. This approach means to restrict the kind of queries a user can make about the data.[1] Query Auditing needs to be distinguished from Query Inference Control, *i.e.*, perturbation of the underlying data or the query result.[2] For example, one could restrict overly specific queries or queries that return too specific information.

For simple query languages and singular queries, this is achievable—for example, if a query would return just one person's data, it should probably be suppressed. Nonetheless, *Dwork* and *Roth* remark that even when a query auditing mechanism refuses to answer a certain query, this itself can leak information.[3] Second, there are practical impossibilities—a query auditing mechanism fails as soon as the query language becomes sufficiently complex,[4] and as soon as users are allowed an unlimited number of queries or multiple users can collude to fuse their results, it becomes computationally impossible.[5]

As a result, query auditing is not suitable as a method of disclosure control for complex datasets.

1 *Aggarwal* and *Yu*, "Privacy-Preserving Data Mining" (2008), p. 6; *Sweeney*, "k-ANONYMITY" (Oct. 2002), p. 5.

2 *Aggarwal* and *Yu*, "Privacy-Preserving Data Mining" (2008), p. 35.

3 *Dwork* and *Roth*, "The Algorithmic Foundations of Differential Privacy" (2013), p. 8.

4 Ibid., p. 8.

5 Ibid., p. 8.

https://doi.org/10.1515/9783112222164-010

8.2 Summary Statistics

Another strategy is to only make a summary of data available. For example, a census statistic might only contain the total number of respondents, the mean and median age, and other values. First off, this drastically limits utility compared to the release of more granular data or even microdata[6]. Second, it will also regularly fail to protect privacy. As long as the output is not perturbed, the fundamental law of information recovery[7] still holds and too many specific facts—even in the aggregate—will still disclose private information.[8] They may also enable *difference attacks*, where two very similar sets of summary statistics of a table may lead to finding unique information about those contained in one set but not the other.[9] As a result, summary statistics work only in a very narrow set of cases.

To give a practical example, the German Federal Office of Justice regularly publishes summary statistics on legal education.[10] These contain only summaries of law graduates from the past year. Inter alia, they contain a table that reveals absolute and relative numbers of how many graduates passed, how many got a certain grade, as well as their gender. In a separate table, the duration of law studies for all graduates is released—*i.e.*, how long people study law until they take the first state exam. In the early years of the new millenium, the law governing legal education changed, and the two systems existed alongside each other, while one was being faded in and the other being faded out. This leads to a few cases where people are readily identifiable from the summary statistic. For example, in 2011, a woman from the state of Saxonia passed the first state examination on the second try (under the old system).[11] She was the only person to take the exam under the old law in the entire state, as a result of having studied for more than 15 semesters.[12] Given this profile, this woman may be identifiable, with her grade visible to the public. Given some auxiliary information, such as from the career network LinkedIn[13], she could theoretically be re-identified. This is just one example of the many persons identifiable from this data release.

---

6 See p. 163 fn. 131.

7 Given as "overly accurate answers to too many questions will destroy privacy in a spectacular way" in: *Dwork* and *Roth*, "The Algorithmic Foundations of Differential Privacy" (2013), p. 5.

8 Ibid., p. 8.

9 This is a similar (yet distinct) idea to the concept in differential privacy, where similar (in that case, "neighboring") datasets are compared for the privacy loss incurred from one over the other.

10 *Bundesamt für Justiz*, "Justizstatistiken" (2024).

11 *Bundesamt für Justiz*, "Ausbildungsstatistik 2011" (Oct. 2012), p. 5.

12 Ibid., p. 14.

13 https://linkedin.com.

As we have seen, summary statistics also have significant drawbacks and cannot provide adequate privacy guarantees on their own, even when they only cover a large number of subjects.

8.3 Diffix

Diffix is a separate approach created by the for-profit Aircloak GmbH and the not-for-profit Max-Planck Institute for Software Systems. While this consortium developed earlier versions of Diffix, from Diffix Elm onwards, development has been spun off into the Open Diffix project.[14]

Over the years, many versions of this software have been published.[15] Initially, Diffix was created as an intermediary program "between" the analyst and the database, through which SQL queries could be fed.[16] However, this proved to be unwieldy, and thus from Diffix Elm onwards, the interface was simplified.[17]

Diffix uses a more practical approach than the mathematic privacy guarantee of DP and focuses on the utility of the remaining data.[18] It uses suppression, generalization, and randomization together.[19]

Diffix is, at least in part, an answer to differential privacy and is designed to improve on the perceived shortcomings of DP.[20] *Francis* has repeatedly stressed that DP is not suitable for practical use due to the high amount of noise typically inserted, rendering the data nigh-useless—with the possible exception of Google's RAPPOR and Apple's implementation,[21] which both "effectively operate with unbounded privacy loss"[22].[23] While it is true that the values for ε chosen in real-world

---

14 See https://www.open-diffix.org/en/faq/.

15 Named after types of trees, six major versions exist: Diffix Aspen, Birch, Cedar, Dogwood, Elm, and Fir.

16 *Francis*, *Probst-Eide*, *Wagner*, et al., "Diffix Elm" (June 20, 2022), pp. 2 sq.

17 Ibid., p. 3.

18 To use a simile, it appears that Diffix is an "engineering" approach to anonymization, whereas differential privacy is a "mathematical" approach.

19 *Francis*, *Probst-Eide*, *Wagner*, et al., "Diffix Elm" (June 20, 2022), p. 3.

20 *Francis*, *Eide*, and *Munz*, "Diffix-Aspen: High-Utility Database Anonymization" (June 2017), p. 4.

21 See p. 162.

22 *Francis*, *Probst-Eide*, *Obrok*, et al., "Diffix-Birch" (Aug. 21, 2019), p. 3.

23 *Francis*, *Eide*, and *Munz*, "Diffix-Aspen: High-Utility Database Anonymization" (June 2017), p. 4; *Francis*, "Dear Differential Privacy, Put Up or Shut Up" (Apr. 19, 2020); *Francis*, "Differential Privacy" (Apr. 12, 2020); *Francis*, *Probst-Eide*, *Obrok*, et al., "Diffix-Birch" (Aug. 21, 2019), p. 3; *Francis*, *Probst-Eide*, *Wagner*, et al., "Diffix Elm" (June 20, 2022), pp. 13 sq.

examples is usually quite high,[24] and the issue of privacy loss compounding over time is problematic, I would argue that this criticism needs to be levied at specific implementations, not the principle of DP itself. The benefit of DP is that it provides a mathematical guarantee of privacy (albeit a very weak guarantee, if a large ε is chosen), while Diffix cannot provide such a guarantee, but rather relies on a "no known attacks" model.[25]

One of the fundamental ways in which Diffix preserves privacy is through adding data-dependent, "sticky" noise to a query result.[26] This noise is generated in layers, which are summed together.[27] To keep the noise low and disable difference attacks,[28] this noise is different for each different query.[29] This noise is "sticky", as it is generated by initializing a pseudo-random number generator (PRNG)[30] with a seed dependent on the conditions.[31] A PRNG will always return the same set of numbers when initialized with the same seed. This is by design, and it is what Diffix exploits here to make the pseudo-random noise the same ("sticky") for each condition. This ensures that the noise injected is dependent on the data.[32]

This basic principle has been extended over the years and through versions. The authors note that, unlike with competing approaches such as DP, Diffix lacks a formal guarantee for the privacy it provides.[33] To make up for this insufficiency, they created several "bug bounty" programs that tied a reward to breaking Diffix's anonymization.[34] This resulted in publications that uncovered attack vectors, which have since been fixed.[35]

---

24 See p. 161.

25 *Francis*, "The 4 Pillars of GDPR Compliance Assurance in Data Anonymization" (Feb. 11, 2019).

26 *Francis, Probst Eide*, and *Munz*, "Diffix" (2017), pp. 7 sqq.; *Gadotti* et al., "When the signal is in the noise" (Oct. 29, 2019), p. 1.

27 *Francis, Probst Eide*, and *Munz*, "Diffix" (2017), p. 8.

28 See p. 169.

29 *Francis, Probst Eide*, and *Munz*, "Diffix" (2017), pp. 7 sqq.

30 Somewhat counterintuitively, generating true random numbers using a computer is impossible. However, there are algorithms that can generate *pseudo*-random numbers, which are as good as random numbers, but require a random number (the "seed") to begin generating random numbers. A typical beginner's approach to finding such a seed would be to just use the current time as a seed. For background on the algorithms used in pseudo-random number generators, see *Selinger*, "The GLIBC pseudo-random number generator" (Jan. 4, 2007).

31 *Francis, Probst Eide*, and *Munz*, "Diffix" (2017), p. 7 and fig. 4.

32 *Francis, Eide*, and *Munz*, "Diffix-Aspen: High-Utility Database Anonymization" (June 2017), p. 6.

33 Ibid., p. 18.

34 *e.g.*, "MPI-SWS/Diffix Bounty 2020 – GDA Score" (May 29, 2020).

35 *Gadotti* et al., "When the signal is in the noise" (Oct. 29, 2019); *Boenisch, Munz*, et al., "Side-Channel Attacks on Query-Based Data Anonymization" (Nov. 13, 2021), p. 11.

Aircloak, the for-profit enterprise selling Diffix-based products, claims a "'no known attacks' stance"[36] as well as a transparent approach to fixes upon successful demonstration of an attack vector.[37] The approach to transparency is commendable. Nonetheless, Diffix has not inspired the same amount of research activity as DP and *k*-anonymity, so it is difficult to assess whether its security is a product of its (relative) obscurity or due to its strength.[38]

In summary, while it lacks the mathematical guarantees of some of its contemporaries, Diffix appears to be industry-ready, regularly approved by supervisory authorities, and mature.

8.4 Synthetic Data

Another recurring recommendation is the use of "synthetic data".[39] For example, the BfDI recently encouraged the use of synthetic data in a medical context.[40] Instead of using the original data, this original dataset is used to create synthetic data, especially using AI to generate a dataset that share's the original data's characteristics, while being distinct enough from it to not leak private information. At first glance, this approach sounds very promising: After all, the non-anonymized data is no longer contained in the synthetic data.

A remaining question is *how* to generate this synthetic data. A common method is to use a generative adversarial network (GAN),[41] potentially in combination with DP[42]. An earlier method would be to generate data "by hand", by retaining some properties of the data and replacing other data by random noise from a probability distribution.[43] In my opinion, both types of synthetic data generation are seldom useful, both from a technical and a legal standpoint.

---

36 *Francis*, "The 4 Pillars of GDPR Compliance Assurance in Data Anonymization" (Feb. 11, 2019).

37 *Bauer*, "Break my Life's Work and I'll Pay You Handsomely" (Aug. 22, 2018).

38 Nonetheless, the fact that researchers such as Kobbi Nissim, one of the co-inventors of DP, participated (successfully) in the bug bounty program, is reassuring.

39 *Bellovin, Dutta,* and *Reitinger*, "Privacy and Synthetic Datasets" (2019), p. 9.

40 *Kelber*, "Medizinische Forschung mit Gesundheitsdaten" (Jan. 2023), p. 6; *Schwartmann, Jaspers*, et al., "Praxisleitfaden Anonymisierung" (Dec. 2022), pp. 35 sq.

41 For a brief explanation of GANs, see *Bellovin, Dutta,* and *Reitinger*, "Privacy and Synthetic Datasets" (2019), pp. 31 sqq.

42 *Yan* et al., "A Multifaceted benchmarking of synthetic electronic health record generation models" (Dec. 9, 2022), p. 12; *Bellovin, Dutta,* and *Reitinger*, "Privacy and Synthetic Datasets" (2019), p. 39.

43 *Raab, Nowok,* and *Dibben*, "Practical Data Synthesis for Large Samples" (2016), p. 67.

From a technical standpoint, the data generated using the latter process is solely useful to extract the very statistical properties that have been encoded into it.[44] This makes it difficult to analyze relationships that have not been encoded into the data.[45]

The data generated using a GAN is, *by definition*, worse at representing the source data than the source data itself.[46] At the same time, the privacy guarantees of this data are uncertain. Using a neural network to learn the features of the data and then reproduce it opens up other attack vectors, such as model inversion[47] and membership inference[48].[49] To preserve privacy, an additional use of DP is sometimes advised.[50] However, this means that the synthetic data set needs to incur two large losses in utility: One by the use of DP, which sacrifices utility for privacy, typically by adding noise; and another by the use of synthetic data, which again sacrifices utility. As DP is a strong privacy guarantee, the question remains why it is necessary to use synthetic data in addition. If we want to perform statistical analyses on the source data, using differential privacy "directly" and leaving out the final step of generating synthetic data, seems like a less resource-intensive and less error-prone way of achieving the means to private data analysis (with the aforementioned trade-offs of DP[51]). If we want to use source data to train a AI model, we can do that using differentially private AI[52], the very technology that *Bellovin*, *Dutta*, and *Reitinger* propose to train the GAN for synthetic data generation.[53]

From a legal standpoint, the data generated using this process is necessarily as anonymous (or more anonymous) as the information that has been added into it. Of course, there is ample reason to believe that the output of a generative model will result in data that is sufficiently different from the source data to preserve privacy, but there is no mathematical guarantee for this, and there are many pitfalls to creating a model that truly outputs private data. For example, one common danger with AI models is known as *overfitting*. This means that the model has, in essence,

44 *Ruggles* et al., "Differential Privacy and Census Data" (May 2019), p. 406.
45 *Ruggles* et al., "Differential Privacy and Census Data" (May 2019), p. 406; *D'Acquisto* et al., "Privacy by design in big data" (2015), p. 63.
46 Spoken differently: There is a loss of information between the source data and the synthetic data. The synthetic data cannot somehow be better than the source, it is either the same (which obviates the need for synthetic data in the first place) or it is "worse".
47 See p. 220.
48 See p. 220.
49 It must be noted that these attacks work only on the model that is used for data generation (= the process), not the synthetic data itself (= the end result).
50 *Bellovin*, *Dutta*, and *Reitinger*, "Privacy and Synthetic Datasets" (2019), p. 39.
51 See p. 164.
52 See p. 221.
53 The end result here is the model, not some data generated by it.

learned to reproduce the data, but fails to "generalize" this knowledge. A generative model that is overfitting will leak private data.[54] [55]

In fact, researchers surveying the literature on synthetic data generation in 2022 found that synthetic data either fails at providing anonymity or fails to preserve the statistical properties of the source data.[56] Moreover, they found the privacy gained by publishing synthetic data to be "highly unpredictable".[57]

Nonetheless, as these issues are improved through scientific progress, the problem remains that the effective privacy implications of a synthetic dataset can only be calculated after its generation.[58] However, there are promising approaches to solving this problem.[59] Benchmarks, *i.e.*, tools that allow for comparing algorithms on their performance on select tasks,[60] are also emerging.[61] Despite all this, there are cases in which synthetic data can be useful. One example is testing software that would normally deal with personal data.[62]

In summary, there is currently only a very narrow set of use cases that motivate the generation of synthetic data.[63] Currently, it seems that the technology has not caught up to expectations yet, making synthetic data only useful in circumstances where an actual dataset is expected—*e.g.*, for testing personal data-heavy applications in the healthcare sector. At the same time, the field is still nascent, and results will improve with time.

---

54 *Bellovin*, *Dutta*, and *Reitinger*, "Privacy and Synthetic Datasets" (2019), p. 38; for a theory as to why DP helps prevent overfitting, see: *Cummings* and *Desai*, "The Role of Differential Privacy in GDPR Compliance. Position Paper" (Oct. 2018), p. 2.

55 See the parallel problem of memorization in AI models, see p. 210.

56 *Stadler*, *Oprisanu*, and *Troncoso*, "Synthetic Data – Anonymisation Groundhog Day" (2022), pp. 1464 sq.

57 Ibid., p. 1465.

58 *Giomi* et al., "A Unified Framework for Quantifying Privacy Risk in Synthetic Data" (Apr. 2023), p. 1.

59 For an example, see the "Anonymeter" project that uses the Art. 29 Working Party criteria of singling out, linkability, and inference on synthetic data ibid.

60 As an example from a different arena, for a benchmark of legal natural language processing, see *Chalkidis* et al., "LexGLUE" (May 2022).

61 *Yan* et al., "A Multifaceted benchmarking of synthetic electronic health record generation models" (Dec. 9, 2022).

62 This is also the example in *Schwartmann*, *Jaspers*, et al., "Praxisleitfaden Anonymisierung" (Dec. 2022), p. 35.

63 For one application, see: *Ziethmann*, *Friedrich*, and *Schlögl-Flierl*, "Synthetic Data in Medicine" (May 31, 2024), p. 360.

8.5 Homomorphic Encryption

Another solution that involves novel technology is that of homomorphic encryption.[64] Homomorphic encryption enables analyses on data while it remains encrypted. With homomorphic encryption, the ciphertext (*i.e.*, the encrypted data) and the original data have the same type.[65] Using homomorphic encryption, one can encrypt data, perform operations on it (for example, multiply it), and then decrypt it. Using "regular" encryption, this would not work, but homomorphic encryption algorithms allow this feat. For example, the widely-used RSA algorithm allows for homomorphic multiplication: If one uses RSA to encrypt something and then multiplies the encrypted bytes, one can decrypt the result and find that the multiplication has been applied to the plain text as well.[66] Strictly speaking, this data is only pseudonymized.[67]

We distinguish partial ("PHE"), somewhat ("SWHE" or "SHE"), and fully homomorphic encryption ("FHE"). Partial homomorphic encryption means only one type of operation (such as addition or multiplication) can be performed on the encrypted data, somewhat homomorphic encryption allows multiple operations, but only for a limited number of times, and fully homomorphic encryption allows for an unlimited number of operations[68] for an unlimited number of times.[69] PHE schemes have been known for a long time, and the commonly used RSA cipher has some homomorphic properties.[70] In a breakthrough, *Gentry* described the first FHE scheme in his dissertation in 2009.[71] However, this scheme was very computationally expen-

64 For a simple explanation of the concept, see *Schneier*, "Homomorphic Encryption Breakthrough" (July 9, 2009); *Compagnucci* et al., "Homomorphic Encryption" (2019), p. 9; *D'Acquisto* et al., "Privacy by design in big data" (2015), p. 40.

65 They are "homomorphic", *D'Acquisto* et al., "Privacy by design in big data" (2015), p. 40.

66 "Encrypt P to get C, multiply C by 2, and then decrypt 2C—and you get 2P.", *Schneier*, "Homomorphic Encryption Breakthrough" (July 9, 2009).

67 See p. 93.

68 As any circuit can be represented using addition and multiplication, it suffices to support these two operations to build out other operations, see *Acar* et al., "A Survey on Homomorphic Encryption Schemes" (July 25, 2018), p. 79:5.

69 Ibid., p. 79:3.

70 *Acar* et al., "A Survey on Homomorphic Encryption Schemes" (July 25, 2018), 79:6; *Schneier*, "Homomorphic Encryption Breakthrough" (July 9, 2009).

71 *Gentry*, "A Fully Homomorphic Encryption Scheme" (2009); *Schneier*, "Homomorphic Encryption Breakthrough" (July 9, 2009).

sive, which made it impractical for production applications.[72] From here on, other approaches to FHE were developed.[73]

Despite these significant advances and the promise of (F)HE as a tool for protecting privacy in analysis, FHE still remains a nascent technology not yet ripe for widespread adoption.[74]

8.6 Conclusion

To conclude, we have analyzed multiple families of algorithms for the anonymization of structured data in this chapter. Like syntactic anonymization methods and DP, they all have advantages and drawbacks. However, none can match the widespread adoption and practical acclaim of these two types of anonymization.

There are additional methods of privacy-enhancing technologies that are adjacent to anonymization that could not be covered here, such as secure multi-party computation[75].

---

72 *Acar* et al., "A Survey on Homomorphic Encryption Schemes" (July 25, 2018), p. 79:3; *Schneier*, "Homomorphic Encryption Breakthrough" (July 9, 2009).

73 For a comprehensive survey of FHE methods, see *Acar* et al., "A Survey on Homomorphic Encryption Schemes" (July 25, 2018), 79:12 sqq.; *Munjal* and *Bhatia*, "A systematic review of homomorphic encryption and its contributions in healthcare industry" (May 3, 2022).

74 *Acar* et al., "A Survey on Homomorphic Encryption Schemes" (July 25, 2018), 79:28; Munjal and Bathia conclude: "Homomorphic encryption, which processes data while maintaining privacy and security, maybe (*sic!*) the greatest solution for this problem in the future … Overall, homomorphic encryption will be a boon to the healthcare business *as the performance and utility of FHE improve.*", (*highlighting* by the author); *Munjal* and *Bhatia*, "A systematic review of homomorphic encryption and its contributions in healthcare industry" (May 3, 2022), pp. 24 sq.; *Hamza* et al., "Towards Secure Big Data Analysis via Fully Homomorphic Encryption Algorithms" (Apr. 2022), pp. 12 sq.

75 See *D'Acquisto* et al., "Privacy by design in big data" (2015), p. 40.

9 Comparative Legal Evaluation

Having elaborated on different methods of disclosure control, we can now turn to a practical application and evaluate these methods. We will then use the model outlined above[1] to evaluate each method. It would be beyond the scope of this dissertation to perform re-identification attacks on this anonymized data, so where appropriate, I will reference weaknesses of certain mechanisms pointed out in the technical literature. In some ways, this chapter is a contemporary update to the analysis in the Art. 29 Working Party's Opinion on anonymization techniques.[2]

In contrast to the typical situation in legal discourse, we have clear, non-disputed criteria and a verifiability of results: Where a mechanism fails to meet the standard, we can say so definitely and without the need for a normative view. On the other hand, we only know that a method has failed once an attack has been demonstrated that shows susceptibility to a certain type of privacy violation.

Note that we have dealt with utility concerns in the technical sections above. This section will primarily cover the privacy implications of certain mechanisms, as utility is of no relevance for the legal assessment of anonymity.

9.1 Standard

As we have elaborated, identifiability means that the atomic operation of comparison can be used to link a record either to knowledge or other data that can be used to construct a chain of linking, at the end of which a natural person can be affected in the real world.[3] In effect, anonymization methods need to protect against singling out and linking. Nonetheless, I will include inference here, as the Art. 29 Working Party's Opinion on anonymization techniques[4] includes it, and, to many, it is an important consideration in this discussion—even though it is not, technically, a component of identification.[5]

---

1 See p. 71.

2 See *Article 29 Data Protection Working Party*, "0829/14/DE WP216" (2014), pp. 11 sqq.

3 See p. 71.

4 *Article 29 Data Protection Working Party*, "0829/14/DE WP216" (2014).

5 See p. 65.

https://doi.org/10.1515/9783112222164-011

9.2 Classic Approaches to Anonymization

I. *k*-Anonymity

The Art. 29 Working Party state that *k*-anonymity[6] protects against singling out, as all *k* persons in the database share the same values.[7]

However, *Altman, Cohen, Nissim*, et al. show that, under specific circumstances, *k*-anonymity does not preserve against predicate[8] singling-out attacks.[9] As predicate singling-out is a subset of singling out,[10] this directly challenges the Art. 29 Working Party's advice.[11] Their reasoning is as follows: When the bins used for generalization are data-dependent, *i.e.*, the bins themselves expose values, persons can be singled out this way.[12] In the (as they admit, rather contrived) example they give, a dataset contains passport holders' data as well as their passport numbers. As these numbers are consecutive, if they are *k*-anonymized with $k = 10$, the values at the edges of the bins can be singled out easily.[13] In their second, more realistic example, a dataset contains a list of doctor's visits, with subsequent visits in additional columns: For example, before anonymization, each row may contain 30 specific dates on which a certain patient visited a doctor. Even if the dates are now generalized, they are still very rare in this combination. As the date ranges contain a finite number of values (*e.g.*, the range of Feb 1–5 contains 5 dates), an attacker can guess these values and—by chance—single out someone in the dataset.[14] [15] As *Altman, Cohen, Nissim*, et al. note, this is not applicable to *every* application of *k*-anonymity, but rather only where the release was not prepared "by experts with sufficient care".[16]

k-anonymity offers some protection against linking: Given a second database, entries from this database can only be linked to a group of *k* records in the *k*-

6 See p. 138.

7 "Because the same attributes are now shared by k users, it should be no longer possible to single out an individual within a group of k users." *Article 29 Data Protection Working Party*, "0829/14/DE WP216" (2014), p. 16.

8 For predicate singling out see *Altman, Cohen, Nissim*, et al., "What a Hybrid Legal-Technical Analysis Teaches Us about Privacy Regulation" (2021) and see p. 61.

9 Ibid., pp. 43 sqq.

10 Ibid., pp. 23, 25.

11 Ibid., p. 43.

12 Ibid., pp. 46 sq.

13 Ibid., p. 47.

14 Ibid., p. 48.

15 Note also that the probability of isolating a single person is ≈ 0.37. For the (fascinating) explanation of this value, which is recurring in the isolation problem, see ibid., pp. 32 sq.

16 Ibid., p. 44.

anonymized database.[17] This means that with a probability of $\frac{1}{k}$, two records can be correctly linked together.[18] Of course, if k is large, this is less of a problem.

As the Art. 29 Working Party note, k-anonymization does not protect against inference. This is well-known: The homogeneity attack[19] is symptomatic of this problem. Even if the sensitive attributes in a certain bin are not homogenous, inference can still be drawn: For example, in a bin of k records, if all of these records have the sensitive attribute of "apnea", "chest pain", and "reflux", we can readily deduce that someone whose data is in that bin does not have the sensitive attribute "fever".

In summary, k-anonymity provides limited protection against singling out, limited protection against linking, and little to no protection against inference.

II. l-Diversity and t-Closeness

For l-diversity[20] and t-closeness[21], the Art. 29 Working Party contend that their guarantees against singling out are the same as for k-anonymity.[22] As *Altman*, *Cohen*, *Nissim*, et al. have shown, k-anonymity does not fully protect against singling out.[23] They also remark that these attacks will be successful against the l-diversity and t-closeness variants.[24] As far as linking is concerned, there is no difference between k-anonymity and its corollaries l-diversity and t-closeness.[25] Finally, l-diversity and t-closeness improve somewhat on k-anonymity's failure to protect against inference.[26]

III. Other Methods of Perturbation: Randomization and Swapping

The Art. 29 Working Party contends that "pure" randomization provides no protection against singling out, and small amounts of protection against linkability, or

---

17 *Article 29 Data Protection Working Party*, "0829/14/DE WP216" (2014), p. 16.
18 Ibid., p. 17.
19 See p. 141.
20 See p. 142.
21 See p. 142.
22 *Article 29 Data Protection Working Party*, "0829/14/DE WP216" (2014), p. 18.
23 See p. 178.
24 *Altman*, *Cohen*, *Nissim*, et al., "What a Hybrid Legal-Technical Analysis Teaches Us about Privacy Regulation" (2021), pp. 43 sq.
25 *Article 29 Data Protection Working Party*, "0829/14/DE WP216" (2014), p. 18.
26 Ibid., p. 18.

inference.[27] At the same time they stress that noise addition on its own is not a "standalone solution for anonymisation".[28]

Swapping, called "Permutation" in the Art. 29 Working Party's opinion, suffers the same fate: It offers little protection against singling out, linkability, and inference.[29]

9.3 Differential Privacy

Differential privacy[30] today is the most advanced privacy-enhancing technology that is widely used. From the beginnings, where DP was simply a definition that allowed talking about the privacy loss of different mechanisms. It lent itself uniquely to online randomization mechanisms, which is where it was first deployed. In the years since, many derivatives and extensions of DP have been proposed and introduced.[31]

I. Functional Differences

As has been noted above, the guarantee that DP gives is functionally different from a guarantee against identification: DP guarantees a composable limit on the disclosure, *i.e.*, a measure of *privacy*, not identifiability. Here, differential privacy is a good example of diverging paths between legal and technical understandings of privacy: The legal understanding of data protection is concerned with identifiability, while differential privacy seeks to limit the amount of information that can be gained about the participation of a person in the data.[32]

Nonetheless, this encompasses the legal notion of identifiability.[33] The reasoning for this is as follows: As has been shown above,[34] the elemental component of

27 *Article 29 Data Protection Working Party*, "0829/14/DE WP216" (2014), p. 13; In table 6, protection against singling out is given as "Yes", with the other two guarantees as listed as "May not" *Article 29 Data Protection Working Party*, "0829/14/DE WP216" (2014), p. 24.

28 *Article 29 Data Protection Working Party*, "0829/14/DE WP216" (2014), p. 13.

29 Ibid., p. 14.

30 See p. 146.

31 Most notably, DP now plays an outsized role in "anonymizing" model weights in neural networks, see p. 221.

32 *Hölzel*, "Differential Privacy and the GDPR" (2019), p. 12.

33 differing opinion, with reference to the different setting with a curator and the possibility of mistaken identification (a qualm I share, see p. 39): ibid., pp. 10 sqq.

34 See p. 71.

identification is comparison, which enables singling out and linking. If DP with a sufficient value of ε prevents singling-out attacks and linking attacks, it can be inferred that it can prevent identifiability as a result. In some ways, the effect of differential privacy is stronger, which may lead it to have a more adverse effect on utility than it would need to have in order to prevent identifiability.[35]

The Art. 29 Working Party fixates on the use of DP as an *online* mechanism.[36] As the Opinion was published in 2014, this is not surprising: Many other promising use cases for DP had yet to be developed. Whether a mechanism for anonymization is used online or offline and the implications for GDPR compliance is a more general topic than DP and covered elsewhere in this dissertation.[37]

It has been noted that differential privacy prevents predicate singling-out attacks.[38] In the opinion of *Altman, Cohen, Nissim*, et al., it even "probably prevents GDPR singling-out, not just predicate singling-out."[39]. They conclude that DP is promising, but warn that singling out is just one part of the privacy definition in GDPR.[40]

The Art. 29 Working Party finds that DP "might" not fully eliminate linking.[41] Their reasoning is that "using multiple requests it might be possible to link the entries relating to a specific individual between two answers".[42] As pointed out above, this is based on an online-centric view of DP. The Art. 29 Working Party's scenario here appears to be that someone may make multiple queries of the same dataset and then link these query results together. This is akin to a difference attack[43]. In their definition of "linkability", the Art. 29 Working Party point out that linking implies "the ability to link, at least, two records concerning the same data subject or a group of data subjects (either in the same database or in two different databases)."[44]

---

35 See p. 148.

36 *Article 29 Data Protection Working Party*, "0829/14/DE WP216" (2014), p. 15.

37 See p. 120.

38 *Altman, Cohen, Nissim*, et al., "What a Hybrid Legal-Technical Analysis Teaches Us about Privacy Regulation" (2021), pp. 50 sqq.

39 *Article 29 Data Protection Working Party*, "0829/14/DE WP216" (2014), p. 50.

40 *Altman, Cohen, Nissim*, et al., "What a Hybrid Legal-Technical Analysis Teaches Us about Privacy Regulation" (2021), p. 51.

41 *Article 29 Data Protection Working Party*, "0829/14/DE WP216" (2014), p. 15.

42 Ibid., p. 15.

43 See p. 169.

44 *Article 29 Data Protection Working Party*, "0829/14/DE WP216" (2014), p. 11.

While there exist working attacks on some implementations of DP,[45] this is not one of them, and certainly it is not a shortcoming of DP (the definition).[46] Conversely, DP neutralizes linking attacks, "including all those attempted with all past, present, *and future* datasets and other forms and sources of auxiliary information."[47] It should be especially noted that DP *composes*[48] and thus the privacy guarantee specifically holds for multiple queries of the same dataset (even though it is getting progressively weaker, yet bounded by ε). In this regard, therefore, the Art. 29 Working Party errs in calling out DP for failing to thwart linking attacks.

As far as the criterion of inference is concerned,[49] the Art. 29 Working Party again notes that "it is possible to infer information about individuals or groups by using multiple requests"[50] when this is *precisely* what DP was designed to avoid. Of course, using a bad implementation and when using a boundless ε, one can make plenty of inference about individuals or groups. When implemented correctly, DP limits the amount of information leaked about an individual[51] to ε (and with a probability δ, if applicable).

Despite this reasoning, a fundamental disconnect between the technical and legal understanding remains. The guarantee afforded by DP is functionally different from the one required in the GDPR, and while the two approaches share commonalities, a couple of questions remain unsolved: For one, the presence of the curator in online methods means that a clearer examination of the relative anonymity in this approach may be warranted.[52] In addition, the question of mistaken identification[53] (*i.e.*, someone is "identified" erroneously), which can be exacerbated by the use of

---

45 For example, the attacks outlined in *Haeberlen*, *Pierce*, and *Narayan*, "Differential privacy under fire" (Aug. 8, 2011) or in *Desfontaines*, "Tiny bits matter" (July 22, 2022). Note, however, that these are attacks on the *implementation*, not the theory itself. Here, tools used for differentially private querying are exploited. There are no working attacks on the *theory* of DP, as far as I am aware.

46 Which needs to be distinguished from specific mechanisms such as Laplace or Gaussian noise addition, see *McSherry*, "Differential Privacy for Dummies" (Feb. 3, 2016) in response to *Bambauer*, *Muralidhar*, and R. *Sarathy*, "Fool's Gold" (2013–2014).

47 *Dwork* and *Roth*, "The Algorithmic Foundations of Differential Privacy" (2013), p. 22.

48 See p. 160.

49 Which is not relevant for identifiability (see p. 65), but included to reply to the Art. 29 Working Party.

50 *Article 29 Data Protection Working Party*, "0829/14/DE WP216" (2014), p. 16.

51 Differential privacy also works for groups, see *Dwork* and *Roth*, "The Algorithmic Foundations of Differential Privacy" (2013), p. 23.

52 Similar: *Hölzel*, "Differential Privacy and the GDPR" (2019), pp. 11 sq.

53 See p. 39.

DP,[54] also remains an avenue for future research, even though it applies equally to all methods that alter the data, such as swapping or randomization.[55]

Nonetheless, in total, DP presents as a mature approach to limiting privacy loss and can be used well to prevent singling out and linking, which are the building blocks of identification. Even though it is not DP's primary focus to prevent identification, it is nonetheless capable of doing so.[56]

II. Choosing ε (and δ)

Criticism of DP is largely focused on its privacy–utility tradeoff, and more specifically, the (allegedly) bad utility once a "good" value for ε is used.[57] As this section only focuses on the privacy aspect of each technology, I will leave utility concerns out for a minute and focus on maximizing privacy. Recommendations for ε vary: values typically floated range from very small (0.01) to around 1.[58] [59] For example, an ε of 0.1 would be considered small.[60] Larger values of ε are criticized as being too large for meaningful privacy guarantees.[61]

On the other hand, in the 2020 U.S. census, the "Disclosure Avoidance System" (DAS) algorithm used a global privacy loss budget of $\varepsilon = 19.61$.[62] As noted above, the U.S. Census Bureau's decision to use DP instead of swapping was precipitated by

54 *Hölzel*, "Differential Privacy and the GDPR" (2019), p. 12.

55 I would also tend to agree with *Hölzel* that these cases are cases *of* personal data or at least should be legally discouraged somehow, though the path to a solid legal foundation seems less clear to me: I do not agree with *Hölzel*'s argument that "otherwise the right to rectification in Article 16 GDPR would be pointless" (ibid., p. 12), as the typical case of Art. 16 GDPR in my mind is not the case of mistaken identification but rather correct identification and incorrect data.

56 *Dwork* and *Roth*, "The Algorithmic Foundations of Differential Privacy" (2013), p. 22.

57 See p. 164.

58 See p. 161.

59 This makes sense given the definition of DP above (see p. 156: As ε is the exponent of e, then the range of "acceptable" factors by which to multiply $\mathcal{M}(x')$ ranges from very slightly above 1 ($e^0 = 1$, and as we know, DP with $\varepsilon = 0$ would mean that no privacy loss occurs at all—which is generally impossible where the output of $\mathcal{M}$ is connected to the input) to around $e \approx 2.7182$.

60 *Altman, Cohen, Nissim*, et al., "What a Hybrid Legal-Technical Analysis Teaches Us about Privacy Regulation" (2021), p. 51.

61 See p. 164.

62 *US Census Bureau*, "Census Bureau Sets Key Parameters to Protect Privacy in 2020 Census Results" (June 9, 2021).

swapping's failure in the 2010 census.[63] And yet, despite this large ε, criticism was focused on the alleged lack in utility.[64]

Choosing ε, then, remains a difficult problem that has not been solved.[65] To make applying DP in GDPR even easier, one could think about prescribing certain values of ε. As *Dwork*, *McSherry*, et al. note, "in our work, ε is a parameter chosen by policy".[66] Unfortunately, however, epsilon values cannot be compared easily.[67] Their interpretation varies with implementation and the sensitivity of the data.[68] One approach championed by *Dwork*, *Kohli*, and *Mulligan* is to institute a public "ε registry" that contains information about each deployment of DP in order to help practitioners determine a suitable value for their application.[69] As *Dwork*, *Kohli*, and *Mulligan* note: "We do not know what parameter ε is right for any given differentially private analysis, and we do know that the answer can vary tremendously based on attributes of the dataset and the policies and practices that constrain those who query it ...".[70] They even acknowledge the legal significance of the term: "The hidden nature of this exceedingly material term will burden regulators tasked with protecting privacy."[71] In their proposal, the ε registry is a mandatory institution, into which anyone who wants to deploy differential privacy needs to expose their implementation details, most notably, their value of ε.[72] *Dwork*, *Kohli*, and *Mulligan* conclude that this would need to be a *legal* solution.[73]

I agree, and even though the ε registry the authors have envisioned has not come to fruition (yet), I would argue that these details are very apt for inclusion in a privacy impact assessment pursuant to Art. 35 GDPR.[74] Of course, a public registry

---

63 See p. 145.
64 See p. 162.
65 *Lee* and *Clifton*, "How much is enough?" (Oct. 26, 2011), For methods to determine ε, see; *Hsu* et al., "Differential Privacy" (July 2014).
66 *Dwork*, *McSherry*, et al., "Calibrating Noise to Sensitivity in Private Data Analysis" (2016), p. 18.
67 See p. 165 fn. 146.
68 *Dwork*, *Kohli*, and *Mulligan*, "Differential Privacy in Practice" (Oct. 20, 2019), p. 5.
69 Ibid., pp. 13 sqq.
70 Ibid., p. 13.
71 Ibid., p. 13.
72 The specific details include (1) the potential paths of privacy loss, (2) the granularity of the data that is being protected, (3) the ε values used, (4) the "cumulative privacy loss per user per unit time" or "burn rate", as they call it, (5) the maximum privacy loss that can be incurred before the data is deleted, (6) the variant of DP used, and (7) a justification of design choices. ibid., pp. 15 sq.
73 "Absent additional incentives, it is unlikely that institutions will voluntarily disclose information to the Registry. We argued that an information disclosure law is well-suited to remedy this misalignment of incentives by opening up closed practices to greater scrutiny." ibid., p. 19.
74 Which the authors all but name-check in their paper ibid., p. 13.

would be even better—yet the approach taken by the GDPR is largely not oversight by the public, but rather the supervisory authorities. It would be fitting within this construct that the implementation details of a DP deployment be part of this impact assessment, and that supervisory authorities be armed with the knowledge to interpret this information.[75]

To summarize, DP provides good protection against singling out, linking, and inference.[76]

However, all of this is dependent on a good implementation and the prudent choice of ε (and δ, if applicable). How these parameters are chosen is still a highly salient problem. I propose to follow *Dwork*, *Kohli*, and *Mulligan*'s approach.

When a mechanism requires the use of δ, this can be especially dangerous for data protection: δ is, in effect, the anonymization's probability of failure. It is a difficult question to answer which value of δ would still be acceptable under the GDPR. After all, an anonymization method that fails with a probability of δ may be one that fails with a "reasonable likelihood" mentioned in Recital (26) GDPR. Nonetheless, δ is typically held very small, so that it does not appear "reasonably likely" that this failure could be used to de-anonymize. Still, this is an open (legal) question and a promising avenue for future research.

9.4 Other Approaches

I. Query Auditing

As noted above,[77] query auditing may in itself disclose data and is thoroughly impractical as soon as multiple users are involved or the queries can become significantly complex. Depending on the implementation, it may provide very limited protection against singling out, linking, and inference.

---

75 The authors acknowledge that the contents of the registry would require specialized knowledge: "While the technical content of the Registry may be incomprehensible to the general public, the Registry provides information that allows those familiar with differential privacy to evaluate the privacy protection that differentially private systems provide." ibid., p. 18.

76 This is, again, challenging the Art. 29 Working Party's Opinion.

77 See p. 168.

II. Summary Statistics

Summary statistics[78] may not protect against singling out,[79] provide some protection against linking, and very little protection against inference[80].

III. Synthetic Data

As far as synthetic data[81] is concerned, its privacy value is very much dependent on how the data is generated. If overfitting occurs and the mechanism that is used to generate synthetic data regurgitates some of the source dataset, then singling out, linking, and inference all become possible.

IV. Homomorphic Encryption

Homomorphic encryption[82] is a tool that allows for private data analysis. Even though the data is protected during the calculation, the ultimate end result is not protected (after decryption). In this regard—and notwithstanding the early-stage character of homomorphic encryption (HE) algorithms as Privacy Enhancing Technologies (PET)—it provides no more protection than statistical databases against singling out, linking, and inference.

V. Diffix

Diffix[83] expressly advertises its GDPR compliance and, more fittingly, its resistance against singling out, linking, and inference. Even in the first paper on Diffix, *Francis*, *Eide*, and *Munz* reference singling out and view it as a goal to minimize this possibility.[84] In the Diffix Elm release, *Francis*, *Probst-Eide*, *Wagner*, et al. gave a comprehensive evaluation of Diffix's track record up to this point by compiling all

---

78 See p. 169.

79 See the example of the legal education data above, see p. 169.

80 Again, this is exemplified by the case of the legal education statistical data, see p. 169 .

81 See p. 172.

82 See p. 175.

83 See p. 170.

84 *Francis*, *Eide*, and *Munz*, "Diffix-Aspen: High-Utility Database Anonymization" (June 2017), pp. 4 sq.; as well as in subsequent releases, see *Francis*, *Probst-Eide*, *Obrok*, et al., "Diffix-Birch" (Aug. 21, 2019), pp. 3 sq.; *Francis*, *Probst-Eide*, *Wagner*, et al., "Diffix Elm" (June 20, 2022), pp. 17 sqq.

known attacks on prior versions of the software and comparing them to the Art. 29 Working Party criteria.[85]

As Diffix is—unlike k-anonymity or DP—a piece of software and not a formal privacy definition, the precise guarantees that each version gives are more blurry. Additionally, even though the creators of the software run a bug bounty program and are very transparent about successful past attacks, their evaluation of Diffix on the Art. 29 Working Party's criteria may suffer from being a first-party evaluation[86] and Goodhart's law[87]. Nonetheless, all of their claims seem plausible, and while I have not verified them myself, I would conclude that Diffix meets the Art. 29 Working Party's standard and may provide adequate protection against singling out, linking, and inference.

9.5 Anonymity Assessments

As outlined above, there are benefits and drawbacks to each one of these anonymization mechanisms. Some authors have tried to compile these approaches together and implement a form of "anonymity assessment".[88]

Diffix especially lacks a formal definition of its privacy guarantees, which explains why *Francis*, *Probst-Eide*, *Wagner*, et al. instituted the GDA Score project[89], which uses a scoring methodology to evaluate "protection" and utility.[90] The protection scores include a range of measures, and independently verifies if an attacker can make true statements that either single out a person, link records with a known dataset, or make inferential statements about persons in the data.[91] This is a promising approach, as it allows for a quantitative evaluation of the Art. 29 Working Party criteria. In effect, a scoring suite such as the GDA Score project could become something akin to a benchmark for anonymization methods. Of course, the scoring mechanism and the legal definition of the Art. 29 Working Party's criteria do

85 *Francis*, *Probst-Eide*, *Wagner*, et al., "Diffix Elm" (June 20, 2022), pp. 17 sqq.

86 By which I do not want to insinuate that *Francis*, *Probst-Eide*, *Wagner*, et al. are being disingenuous in their assessments, but rather want to point out that there is an inherent limitation to which one can judge one's own work.

87 Commonly given as "When a measure becomes a target, it ceases to be a good measure.", *Strathern*, "'Improving Ratings': Audit In The British University System" (1997), p. 308.

88 "GDA Score – General Data Anonymity" (Jan. 2019); *Kolain*, *Grafenauer*, and *Ebers*, "Anonymity Assessment - A Universal Tool for Measuring Anonymity of Data Sets under the GDPR with a Special Focus on Smart Robotics" (2021–2022).

89 https://www.gda-score.org.

90 "GDA Score – General Data Anonymity" (Jan. 2019).

91 Ibid.

not necessarily align completely, and—as we have outlined above—the choice of an anonymization mechanism is but one factor in protecting personal data, with the implementation details, chosen parameters, properties of the data, and others being equally important. Unfortunately, however, the project is no longer maintained.[92]

A more recent approach by *Kolain*, *Grafenauer*, and *Ebers* wants to marry an "objective" and a "subjective" score together by creating an "anonymity assessment".[93] However, both from a technical and a legal perspective, this approach is ultimately not convincing.[94] As a result, there is currently no advisable basis for creating an "anonymity assessment". Personally, I think that the current instruments available to controllers, namely the data protection impact assessment (Art. 35 GDPR) is an apt tool for capturing and evaluating anonymization solutions.

9.6 Conclusion

Today, there are a wide variety of mechanisms available for anonymizing structured data. From the classical methods and syntactic privacy definitions such as

92 As the project lead, *Francis*, *Eide*, and *Munz*, confirmed to me via email in July 2023.

93 *Kolain*, *Grafenauer*, and *Ebers*, "Anonymity Assessment - A Universal Tool for Measuring Anonymity of Data Sets under the GDPR with a Special Focus on Smart Robotics" (2021–2022).

94 The authors first introduce a formalized definition of anonymized data by adapting the terminology by *Vokinger*, *Stekhoven*, and *Krauthammer* of "pseudo-anonymized data" into an array of formulas (ibid., pp. 193 sq.). Over the course of their paper, *Kolain*, *Grafenauer*, and *Ebers* describe differential privacy as a "novel approach" (ibid., p. 205) but do not go into detail, only to introduce a *separate* parameter ε that is supposed to denote the maximum probability of re-identifying a person in a dataset that may be anonymized ("pseudo-anonymized data", as they call it) (ibid., p. 194). The authors then go on to re-define the probability P of re-identification as a product of time and money, but refrain from defining the rest of Recital (26) s. 4's definition (ibid., p. 195). They then go on to define k-anonymity, l-diversity, and t-closeness, and mash all of these up in an equation that equates (1) the probability of re-identification for a specific person, (2) values for k, l, and t, and (3) a degree of anonymity ε' (ibid., p. 203). The authors then move on to a subjective component. In this portion of the paper, the authors introduce a score that is "a quantifiable value reflecting the relative anonymity of data being processed by the controller's IT System", in which they again multiply time and money to compare the "capital" and time available to the controller and the time and capital required for re-identification. As they explain in fn. 92, this deliberately takes into account the size of a controller's enterprise, as larger companies have more capital and incentive to re-identify (ibid., pp. 209 sq.). I would argue that the scenario the authors are pre-supposing here does not exist, and even where it does, the "estimated man hours" needed to re-identify, as well as the annual man hours available to a controller are terribly hard to estimate. In addition, the authors propose a documentation-driven process that helps with the implementation of an anonymization solution (ibid., pp. 211 sqq.). The authors even acknowledge that what they are describing is, in essence, a privacy impact assessment (ibid., p. 213).

k-anonymity and its corollaries to the more novel, but now firmly established differential privacy, to new technologies that are not yet ready for widespread adoption, such as homomorphic encryption.

Evaluating these techniques on their legal merits, the Art. 29 Working Party's Opinion on anonymization techniques has been very influential: The three criteria of singling out, linking, and inference have been widely adopted. Nonetheless, as far as it relates to individual methods, the Art. 29 Working Party's advice has turned out to either be incomplete (as in the cases of *k*-anonymity and differential privacy) or overtaken by technological developments (for example, the rise of differential privacy in machine learning). As a result, the EDPB needs to take these changes into account when drafting an update to the Opinion.

As a result, *k*-anonymity and its corollaries are not suitable.[95] Anonymization is a *moving target*, even for structured data.[96] Human determination is often needed when anonymizing data.

The problem of anonymization methods cannot be solved by the law alone, but rather must be solved in cooperation between legal experts and anonymization scientists. This issue is not one that the GDPR attempts to solve, as it remains technologically open. As we have seen, the advice rendered in 2014 by the Art. 29 Working Party has been refuted in part. This shows that a hybrid legal-technical approach needs to be taken. In their paper, *Altman, Cohen, Nissim*, et al. show a few techniques for bridging the divide between legal and technical approaches to anonymization.[97]

---

95 As *Altman, Cohen, Nissim*, et al. note, "as a justification of ANONYMIZATION, *k*-anonymity falls short … When created by experts with sufficient care, *k*-anonymous data releases may not allow singling-out. However, the protection is perhaps better attributed to the practitioner's expertise and care.", *Article 29 Data Protection Working Party*, "0829/14/DE WP216" (2014), p. 44.

96 Or, as J. *Sarathy* puts it: "… while it is important to strengthen privacy technologies to meet current threats, we must also recognize that the success of privacy practices cannot be reduced to any single technology or metric.", J. *Sarathy*, "From Algorithmic to Institutional Logics" (Apr. 9, 2022), p. 14.

97 See also *Nissim* et al., "Bridging the Gap Between Computer Science and Legal Approaches to Privacy" (2018).

Part III: **Anonymizing Unstructured Data**

10 Structured and Unstructured Data

10.1 Introduction

This part will look at *unstructured* data, *i.e.*, all data that is not structured as outlined in the previous part. Finding a good criterion to delineate structured from unstructured data is surprisingly difficult. *Schwartmann, Jaspers*, et al. define structured data as a key–value pair[1] and note that it is typically stored in a tabular representation[2]. *Winter, Battis*, and *Halvani* refrain from defining structured and unstructured data, but remark that structured data is often displayed in a tabular fashion.[3] While generally correct, neither of these characterizations hit the center of the matter. The terminology of "key–value pair"[4] is misleading,[5] as it alludes to key–value stores, a specialized type of database that follows a different paradigm than relational databases[6].[7] Most structured data goes beyond just one "key"[8] and one value—and it is this multitude of attributes and records that creates a possibility for data breach on the one and anonymization on the other hand. Equally, not all structured data is necessarily tabular.[9]

To put it succinctly: Structured data is available in the form of one or more *records*, which can have one or more *attributes*. Each record is—typically, but not

1 *Schwartmann, Jaspers*, et al., "Anonymisierung und Pseudonymisierung von Daten" (Jan. 2023), pp. 75 sq.

2 Ibid., p. 77.

3 *Winter, Battis*, and *Halvani*, "Herausforderungen für die Anonymisierung von Daten" (2019), p. 490.

4 *Schwartmann, Jaspers*, et al., "Anonymisierung und Pseudonymisierung von Daten" (Jan. 2023), p. 74.

5 The example used ("First name = Anne", ibid., p. 75) is equally misleading, as they use "key" to denote what would typically be an attribute in a relational database ("first name").

6 See p. 117.

7 Key–value stores, as their name indicates, store values indexed by unique keys. This trades off much of the elegance and flexibility of more classical relational databases for unparalleled performance. One example of a key–value database is Redis, which is commonly used in (web) applications and often used to cache data before it is committed to a (slower) relational database backend. See *Redis*, "What is a Key-Value Database?" (2024). Indeed, *Cunha, Mendes*, and *Vilela* use key–valued data as an example of semi-structured data, see *Cunha, Mendes*, and *Vilela*, "A survey of privacy-preserving mechanisms for heterogeneous data types" (Aug. 1, 2021), p. 3 Fig. 2.

8 Both in the (misleading) sense of "attribute", as *Schwartmann, Jaspers*, et al. use it, and in the sense of "primary key", which is used to index records.

9 For a more formal CS taxonomy that also includes a third category, "semi-structured data" that includes graph data (see p. 122), the XML format, as well as key–value pairs, see ibid., p. 3 Fig. 2.

https://doi.org/10.1515/9783112222164-012

necessarily[10]—indexed through a unique (primary) *key*. Conversely, everything that is not structured data is unstructured data.

Compared to structured data, the main issue in anonymizing unstructured data is not *how* to anonymize but rather *what* to anonymize: This kind of data is not available in a tabular format, so finding potentially identifying information is much harder. Nonetheless, the *how* remains a secondary problem, which is also difficult in its own right.[11] Sometimes, replacing identifying information in a text with "more generic" information may improve the remaining utility of the anonymized text.[12]

However, the division is a salient one from the anonymization perspective: "Structured" data contains records that all concern the same type of object. For example, a table of hospital release data will concern the same type of information for each record, and each record will be personal data, as it relates to an (identifiable) natural person. Conversely, a table of weather data will be purely object-related, and each record will not relate to an identifiable natural person, making it not personal data. "Unstructured" data, on the other hand, may contain information about humans, but it also may not. Take a news article as an example: It may contain information about a local athlete winning a championship (personal data) or it may be about the eruption of a volcano on an uninhabited island (not personal data). The challenge is finding the parts that concern humans and distinguishing them from the parts that do not.

On the other hand, the type of anonymization is not as important: It typically does not play a role if we replace all references to persons with their initials, insert random names in their stead, or redact the names altogether. For the larger text or image, this is typically without relevance: For example, in legal judgments or cases, names are typically "anonymized" using initials. In newspaper articles, names are typically replaced with fantasy names ("* names changed by the editor").

---

10 Having a unique key is often necessary in a database context, but a table of records is still "structured data" for the purposes of anonymization if the keys are left out.

11 Notably, most guides on anonymization go into deep detail on the anonymization of structured data, while only teasing the existence of unstructured data. There is substantially less legal and technical literature on the anonymization of unstructured data. *Winter*, *Battis*, and *Halvani* remark that "there are no anonymity criteria for unstructured data" (*Winter*, *Battis*, and *Halvani*, "Herausforderungen für die Anonymisierung von Daten" (2019), p. 490, which is true insofar as no overarching criterion exists, but wrong insofar as there are attempts at defining criteria for some types of data, such as text (see p. 213). Where legal texts about the anonymization of textual data exist, they focus on the anonymization of court decisions, which follow different rules. All of this is puzzling, because—as we will see—the techniques that work for structured data do not work for unstructured data.

12 *Lison* et al., "Anonymisation Models for Text Data" (Aug. 2021), p. 4195.

Contrary to the case in the structured data examples, there typically is no requirement for privacy models such as k-anonymity or similar. The explanation behind this intuitive assessment is that unstructured data does—typically!—not contain information about multiple individuals in the same manner in such a way that it would necessitate a privacy standard such as k-anonymity.

This division of data types into structured and unstructured is not a hard and rigid line:[13] Most unstructured data still follows a certain structure. For example, image data is structured in an image format such as JPEG or TIF. Structured data can also contain unstructured data, such as a free-form comment field in a database.[14] For example, AOL[15], an early search engine service, released a large amount of search queries for research purposes in 2006.[16] This data is both structured (as it contains search queries structured by users[17]) as well as unstructured, as the search queries themselves are text and thus cannot be anonymized in a straightforward manner.[18] [19]

In summary, the distinction drawn is a prototypical one: Data can be structured or unstructured, but will often be both at the same time. It is therefore up to the anonymizer to draw the distinction and act accordingly. In the following chapters, we will take a look at anonymizing unstructured data such as text, images, or the weights of a neural network.

10.2 Typical Forms of Unstructured Data

To illustrate the wide range of issues we can encounter when anonymizing unstructured data, it is helpful to take a look at different types of unstructured data that

13 *Schwartmann, Jaspers*, et al., "Anonymisierung und Pseudonymisierung von Daten" (Jan. 2023), pp. 76 sq.

14 Ibid., p. 76.

15 https://aol.com/.

16 *Arrington*, "AOL Proudly Releases Massive Amounts of Private Data" (Aug. 7, 2006).

17 These users were pseduonymized to numbers. In the analysis that followed, some users gained special notoriety for their unusual and graphic search queries, see "AOL search log release" (Dec. 18, 2022).

18 Given all search queries by a user, one could often identify the user, for example through "vanity searches" (looking up one's own name) or by location searches. This happened most famously in the case of User No. 4417749, identified as a 62-year old from Lilburn, GA, see *Barbaro* and *Jr*, "A Face Is Exposed for AOL Searcher No. 4417749" (Aug. 9, 2006).

19 It should be noted that even in 2006, this data release was ill-advised. Just months before, Google, Inc. had sucessfully legally challenged a subpoena to hand over search queries to the government, see *Wong*, "Judge tells DoJ "No" on search queries" (Mar. 17, 2006).

can be found in the wild. While the primary focus of this dissertation is textual data, specifically court decisions, the distinction is not as easy as it looks: "Texts" can be in the form of raw text or in document form, which means that some characteristics of images apply as well. I will also point out some tangential relations to sound, video and photographs.

I. Text

The most important type of unstructured data in practice is raw text. This is where much of the historical attention in academia has been focused, as text anonymization is a sub-branch of Natural Language Processing.[20] Text data is commonplace—by some accounts, even more common than structured data.

Text can contain large amounts of personal data. Of course, text can contain names, addresses, phone numbers and the like, but it can also contain medical information about individuals, information about political affiliation, and much more. Very often, this information is implicit: Instead of containing definitive statements[21], they may contain information that is open to interpretation[22].[23]

As a result, anonymizing this kind of data is difficult.[24] In a different example, translators and interpreters commonly use so-called "translation memories"—a type of database that contains earlier examples of translations for use in similar projects.[25] [26] Over time, these databases have been fed with personal data, which makes fully anonymizing these memories very difficult.[27]

---

20 For a detailed overview of natural language processing (NLP) in the legal domain, see D. M. *Katz, Hartung*, et al., "Natural Language Processing in the Legal Domain" (2023).

21 *e.g.*, "Alice is in the market for a new car".

22 *e.g.*, if we know that Alice searched online for "car dealerships near me", "new car reliability statistics", and "calculate insurance premium for 2023 a-class".

23 See p. 195.

24 "Solutions for anonymising unstructured text are scarce and mostly theoretical" *Lison* et al., "Anonymisation Models for Text Data" (Aug. 2021), p. 4191.

25 *FIT Europe* and *EUATC*, "Comments on Guidelines 07/2020 on the concepts of controller and processor in the GDPR from the perspective of the Translation and Interpreting Sector" (2020), p. 20.

26 Note that this is, if we are being strict with our categories, actually unstructured data in a structured database: The database itself is a type of structured data, while the text contained within it is unstructured.

27 *FIT Europe* and *EUATC*, "Comments on Guidelines 07/2020 on the concepts of controller and processor in the GDPR from the perspective of the Translation and Interpreting Sector" (2020), p. 20.

Additionally, text can contain information beyond its semantics: For example, the writing style might give additional information about the author—using *authorship attribution* one can even match unsigned texts to their authors.[28]

II. Images

For the purposes of this dissertation, "images" means any visual format. Some images are in a raster format, *i.e.*, they consist of many individual pixels in a raster that make a larger picture.[29] Others are in a vector format, where a visual is created through distinct shapes.[30] Thinking about these images, two use cases stand out: Documents and Photographs.

1. Documents

Documents are a second type of unstructured data. At first glance, documents and text seem to be the same kind of data. However, in the sense it is used here, *text* only refers to the words themselves (to use a computing analogy: a `.txt` file that does not contain auxiliary information, formatting, or layout), and *documents* refer to natively digital or digitized (scanned) versions of documents (in the analogy: a `.pdf` file) that contain additional information, for example formatting, layout information, or even additional figures. Even though it already seems like an anachronism that business documents are still printed out and kept in paper form, it is a reality of business processes.[31] Even where documents are no longer printed out, they are nonetheless often exchanged as virtual documents, which can have all of the same anonymization issues as digitized paper documents.

The placement of certain information on a page can contain additional information that needs to be anonymized. For example, in German business documents, addresses are often placed in a certain space on the upper left third of the document.[32] If one were to see certain text there, it already contains the information that

---

28 See p. 203.

29 Such as `.jpg`, `.heic`, or `.tif` files.

30 This is a less intuitive form of an "image". Nonetheless, it is of great practical importance: For example, a `.pdf` file is a container format that can contain both raster and vector elements. A "pure" vector format such as `.eps` can also contain personal data, such as a logo of a one-man enterprise.

31 And will likely remain this way for the foreseeable future—with support from the legislator. For example, in a recent adaptation of the German Nachweisgesetz, the legislator missed an opportunity to allow for a paperless form in labor contracts, see *May*, "Die Arbeitsbedingungenrichtlinie (EU) 2019/1152 und ihre Auswirkungen auf Kündigungen und Abrufarbeit" (2022), p. 2233.

32 "DIN 5008" (2020).

it is probably the address of a recipient or sender. Similarly, detailed information about the sender may be on the upper right third of the document—for example, in a law firm, the letterhead and list of partners.

Documents can contain additional identifying information. For example, a company's corporate branding will usually carry through to its communications. Oftentimes, official and proprietary company documents will be set in the company's house typeface and using the company color scheme. Using just this information, readers can—consciously or sub-consciously—identify the documents' creators. It is also easily thinkable that the creator of a document can be readily identified through the letterhead and typography, even if all other parts of a document are de-identified. Additionally, subtle differences in letter spacing and paragraph spacing may even allow inference on the word processor or type of computer used.[33]

This is not unique to the digital age or to typesetting in the 21st century: In the past, typewriters were well known to have idiosyncrasies that could be exploited to identify the author of certain documents.[34] Of course, this is just a corollary of forensic handwriting analysis, which is still regularly required in court proceedings—*e.g.*, to falsify signatures or wills. Documents written by hand or by typewriter need to potentially also be anonymized to obscure the author. Additionally, sometimes even when digitizing paper documents, systematic and identifying noise can be introduced to the result by the scanner.[35]

2. Pictures

Image data can contain large amounts of personal data. A classic case of personal data are photographs containing people. Usually, photographs are anonymized by "pixelating" the faces of individuals in the picture.[36] However, as recently as 2016,

---

33 This, however, is pure speculation and beyond the scope of this dissertation. Nonetheless, given that different word processors—such as Microsoft Word, Apple Pages, Google Docs, or LaTeX—will typeset a document differently, it stands to reason that one would be able to infer the engine used. Similarly, as the included fonts differ between the Microsoft Windows and macOS operating systems (not to mention different Linux distributions), one can often infer from the typeface whether, *e.g.*, a webpage was printed on a Mac (in which case, it will often be set in Helvetica) or a Windows PC (in which case, it will often be set in Arial).

34 For example, in the U.S., there are expert witnesses specializing in "Typewriting Identification" or "Typewriting Analysis" for this purpose, cf. *Law.com*, "Typewriting Identification/Analysis Expert Witnesses" (2024).

35 See for an illustration of this problem *Kriesel*, "Traue keinem Scan, den du nicht selbst gefälscht hast" (Jan. 20, 2014).

36 *Zhao* and J. *Chen*, "A Survey on Differential Privacy for Unstructured Data Content" (Sept. 13, 2022), 207:8.

machine learning attacks to re-identify faces *in spite* of blurring became viable.[37] As a result, new approaches use DP to pixelate images.[38]

Anonymizing images is also a recurring problem in the legal realm. For example, a court has recently demanded that pictures of third parties be anonymized through pixellation if they are submitted to an online fanpage on a social network.[39] Another area where this is critically important is in the context of (criminal) court proceedings, where defendants are often the subject of intense press coverage.[40]

Nonetheless, the courts and public discourse are still concerned with blurring instead of other mechanisms, even though blurring demonstrably has failed to preserve privacy. This is another example of the legal–technical divide in anonymization.[41]

Another area of increased significance is three-dimensional virtual environments. With the advent of VR, AR, and spatial computing, this is sure to be an area of growth for the future. Even so, there already exist examples of three-dimensional imaging in geospatial applications.[42] For example, in products such as Google's "Street View"[43] or Apple's "Look Around"[44] feature, users can see an interactive panorama picture of cities. These pictures were taken using specialized vehicles that photographed the area. After post-processing, users can view street-level photographs. Naturally, these pictures will contain personal data, especially human faces, vehicle numberplates, and others. They also contain location data for all of these pictures, as well as some rough information about when the picture was taken. Even where all faces, numberplates, *etc.*have been removed, these captures can still contain sensitive personal data. An example would be that people can often be identifiable through their belongings. Seeing someone's car parked outside of someone else's house could, for example, indicate an affair.

---

37 *McPherson*, *Shokri*, and *Shmatikov*, "Defeating Image Obfuscation with Deep Learning" (Sept. 6, 2016), See p. 7 Table 2; *Fan*, "Image Pixelization with Differential Privacy" (2018), p. 149.

38 *Fan*, "Image Pixelization with Differential Privacy" (2018), pp. 152 sqq.

39 OVG Lüneburg: Facebook Fanpage (Jan. 19, 2021).

40 For one notable example, see Holzklotz (Nov. 27, 2008).

41 The anonymization of photographs is not a focus of this thesis. However, there is ample room for scholarship here: There is a mature set of technical publications on this topic, whereas most legal scholarship is focused on the anonymization of structured tabular data. I am certain that a separate dissertation could be written just about the anonymization of photographs.

42 Even though they are not "truly" three-dimensional, they enable a panoramic two-dimensional view.

43 https://www.google.com/streetview/.

44 https://www.apple.com/maps/.

Faces and numberplates are blurred in pre-processing. Nowadays, both are well-researched Computer Vision tasks.[45] The widespread use in Google Street View pioneered the blurring techniques for so-called "regions of interest", such as faces and numberplates.[46] Additionally, users can opt to have their houses blurred on Google Street View.[47] However, as shown above, blurring is not necessarily sufficient to preserve privacy.[48]

III. Other Types of Data

Anonymizing sound, especially voice recordings, is another active field of study.[49] For videos, the situation is very similar to photographs and sound, but more difficult. Nonetheless, approaches exist even for anonymizing video data.[50] A third area that has received substantial attention is that of gene data.[51] Genetic data comes with the additional challenge that—despite around 98% of the genome being the same between humans[52]—even from massively aggregated data, the presence of one person's genome within the dataset can be inferred reliably.[53] Even leaving this specific problem aside for a moment, fully anonymizing DNA is impossible, with *de facto* anonymity remaining possible.[54]

45 *Frome* et al., "Large-scale privacy protection in Google Street View" (Sept. 2009), For the mechanism used in Google's Street View product, see this 2009 paper:

46 *Zhao* and J. *Chen*, "A Survey on Differential Privacy for Unstructured Data Content" (Sept. 13, 2022), 207:8.

47 See https://www.google.com/streetview/policy/.

48 See p. 199.

49 *Zhao* and J. *Chen*, "A Survey on Differential Privacy for Unstructured Data Content" (Sept. 13, 2022), 207:11; *Cunha, Mendes*, and *Vilela*, "A survey of privacy-preserving mechanisms for heterogeneous data types" (Aug. 1, 2021), p. 7; *Chong*, "Sotto Voce" (2024).

50 *Cunha, Mendes*, and *Vilela*, "A survey of privacy-preserving mechanisms for heterogeneous data types" (Aug. 1, 2021), p. 7; *Cunha, Mendes*, and *Vilela*, "A survey of privacy-preserving mechanisms for heterogeneous data types" (Aug. 1, 2021), 207:11 sq.

51 Even though *Sweeney, Abu*, and *Winn* wrote a paper about re-identifying participants in the Personal Genome Project, this is done via ZIP codes and other demographic info, not through their DNA, *Sweeney, Abu*, and *Winn*, "Identifying Participants in the Personal Genome Project by Name" (Apr. 29, 2013).

52 *McSherry*, "Differential privacy and correlated data" (Aug. 29, 2016).

53 *Dwork* and *Roth*, "The Algorithmic Foundations of Differential Privacy" (2013), pp. 8 sq.

54 M. *Arning, Forgó*, and *Krügel*, "Datenschutzrechtliche Aspekte der Forschung mit genetischen Daten" (Nov. 2006), pp. 701 sq.; for technical detail w.f.r.: *Cunha, Mendes*, and *Vilela*, "A survey of privacy-preserving mechanisms for heterogeneous data types" (Aug. 1, 2021), p. 8.

IV. Metadata

A classic kind of data that is often overlooked when anonymizing files is metadata, *i.e.*, the data that provides data *about* the data, but is not the content.[55]

It should be noted that metadata itself is structured data, but it often accompanies unstructured data.

1. EXIF Metadata

The prototypical case of this is so-called EXIF[56] data: This metadata is contained in image files such as `.jpg` or `.tif` files and contains information about the make and model of the camera that was used, the lens, whether or not a flash was used, as well as copyright or other information. As photographs today are overwhelmingly taken on cell phones, the make and model of the phone are included.

Additionally, nearly all phones add GPS coordinates to the photo. This inclusion of geodata has proven especially salient: In 2012, wanted fugitive John McAfee was captured in Guatemala after his location was inadvertently leaked by a reporter through EXIF data in a picture taken with a mobile phone.[57] In a different application, this data was used by Harvard students to identify sellers of illicit drugs.[58]

2. PDF Metadata

Metadata is not limited to image files. For example, in `.pdf` files, there is a large amount of metadata.[59] For example, the "Author" field is typically populated automatically by the user's word processor. Additionally, the "Generator" field allows insights into the word processor used to create the document,[60] its filename and other information. Even for digitized documents, the software used to generate the `.pdf` is typically included in the metadata, often allowing some inference about the kind of scanner used.

---

55 Literally: *meta data*, so data about data.

56 "Exif Exchangeable Image File Format, Version 2.2" (Feb. 26, 2014).

57 *Peralta*, "Betrayed By Metadata" (Dec. 4, 2012).

58 Ibid.

59 *Adobe, Inc.*, "PDF properties and metadata" (Feb. 7, 2023).

60 Oftentimes, even down to the version of the operating system, such as "Mac OS X 10.9.5 Quartz PDFContext".

10.3 Conclusion

In summary, there is a host of different types of unstructured data. All of these types require a different approach to anonymization, and present their own pitfalls.

11 Anonymizing Text and Document Data

For the purposes of this dissertation, the anonymization of text and document data is the most salient.

Metadata is a common pitfall when anonymizing documents.[1] It stands to reason that metadata needs to be scrubbed completely from a document in order to anonymize it.[2] This, however, is trivial from both a technical and a legal standpoint[3] and shall therefore not be a focus here.

Rather, we will lay a brief focus on authorship obfuscation, before moving on to the main event: removing personal data from the text itself.

11.1 Anonymizing Authorship

Using Natural Language Processing technology, one can attribute authorship for text ("Authorship Attribution"). This is an area of ongoing research, which has yielded varying levels of success.[4] With the general trend in AI and natural language processing in the legal domain,[5] authorship attribution with a high confidence interval is likely to get more and more viable as data availability and computational resources increase.

Like graphanalytical analysis for forensic handwriting analysis, an authorship attribution algorithm can detect who wrote a text on the basis of their choice of words and grammatical constructions. This is a practice in the tradition of forensic linguistics.

For example, researchers have tried to attribute unsigned U.S. Supreme Court opinions to individual justices.[6] [7] This is a peculiar type of "identifiable" data, as the

---

1 See p. 201.

2 Many PDF programs even provide functionality for this, *e.g.* the "Sanitize" feature in Adobe's Acrobat Pro: *Adobe, Inc.*, "Redact & Sanitize | Adobe Document Cloud" (Mar. 7, 2022).

3 *Winter, Battis,* and *Halvani,* "Herausforderungen für die Anonymisierung von Daten" (2019), p. 491.

4 For an overview of the field, see *Stamatatos*, "A survey of modern authorship attribution methods" (Mar. 2009) (2009) and *Juola*, "Authorship Attribution" (2007) (2007).

5 See: D. M. *Katz, Hartung*, et al., "Natural Language Processing in the Legal Domain" (2023).

6 W. *Li* et al., "Using Algorithmic Attribution Techniques to Determine Authorship in Unsigned Judicial Opinions" (2013).

7 Authorship attribution has received additional interest after the rise of LLMs, as schools and universities try to detect when students use LLMs to do homework or ghostwrite theses. However, a convincing solution has not been found as of this writing.

https://doi.org/10.1515/9783112222164-013

identifiability stems not from the data itself, but rather from the idiosyncrasies of each writer and a comparison to their other writings.

One way of obfuscating authorship (Authorship Obfuscation (AO)) in documents is to translate the document to a different language and then back to the target language.[8] A different option is to perturb vector representations of text using DP.[9] To create these vector representations, words[10] are converted into a high-dimensional vector space using a neural network.[11] These vectors have some desirable properties: They allow a numerical representation not only of syntactic, but *semantic* properties in words and phrases. For example, through the simple calculation of subtracting the vector for "Man" from the vector for "King" and adding the vector for "Woman", the result is a vector that is "closest to the vector representation of the word 'Queen'".[12] [13] This approach, also known as "word embeddings", was later refined[14] and extended to other problem spaces.[15] In other words, these vectors can capture meaning, and they can allow for finding words that are "close" in meaning.

---

8 *Winter*, *Battis*, and *Halvani*, "Herausforderungen für die Anonymisierung von Daten" (2019), p. 491.

9 *Feyisetan*, *Diethe*, and *Drake*, "Leveraging Hierarchical Representations for Preserving Privacy and Utility in Text" (Nov. 2019).

10 Or, rather, in the case of the second `word2vec` paper, phrases, such as "Boston Globe" instead of "Boston" and "Globe", *Mikolov*, *Sutskever*, et al., "Distributed Representations of Words and Phrases and their Compositionality" (2013), p. 2.

11 *Mikolov*, K. *Chen*, et al., "Efficient Estimation of Word Representations in Vector Space" (Sept. 6, 2013), This highly influential technique, commonly known as `word2vec` after the original implementation, was formative for a decade of NLP scholarship and dominant until the advent of the Transformer architecture, see; *Mikolov*, *Sutskever*, et al., "Distributed Representations of Words and Phrases and their Compositionality" (2013), p. 1.

12 *Mikolov*, K. *Chen*, et al., "Efficient Estimation of Word Representations in Vector Space" (Sept. 6, 2013), p. 2; referencing the abstract of *Mikolov*, *Yih*, and *Zweig*, "Linguistic Regularities in Continuous Space Word Representations" (June 2013), p. 746.

13 This applies to other concepts as well. For example, the relationship between singular items and plural items is learned. Writing the vector of i as x_i, *Mikolov*, *Yih*, and *Zweig* show that $x_{\text{apple}} - x_{\text{apples}} \approx x_{\text{car}} - x_{\text{cars}}$, *Mikolov*, *Yih*, and *Zweig*, "Linguistic Regularities in Continuous Space Word Representations" (June 2013), p. 746.

14 *Pennington*, *Socher*, and *Manning*, "GloVe" (Oct. 2014).

15 Such as for finding "similar" documents in `doc2vec`, which continues to be useful in the legal domain, see *Le* and *Mikolov*, "Distributed Representations of Sentences and Documents" (June 18, 2014); D. M. *Katz*, *Hartung*, et al., "Natural Language Processing in the Legal Domain" (2023), p. 5.

As these vectors are, essentially, numeric, they can be perturbed using DP.[16] Nonetheless, this is more suited to performing additional ML tasks on the data[17] than creating a sanitized text for human consumption.

In summary, authorship obfuscation is a difficult problem that is still an area of active research. The approaches used thus far are not fit for production deployment, *i.a.*, because it can be readily detected if a text was anonymized using authorship obfuscation techniques.[18] Nonetheless, I am certain that there is a bright future for authorship obfuscation with the advent of LLMs: Feeding a text to a large language machine learning model (LLM) and prompting it to restate the text using a randomly generated persona may be a promising avenue of further research.

11.2 Finding Identifying Information

The majority of legal and technical problems occur where we try to anonymize all other information that is left in a document. We can draw a parallel to the anonymization of structured data: Just like with structured data, texts will contain directly identifying information, such as names, addresses, and social security numbers. And just the same,[19] we first need to remove this information.

Next, we move on to the trickier indirect identifiers. Just as is the case with structured data,[20] these are harder to find and harder to anonymize.[21]

Directly identifying information is abundant in most documents. A court decision typically contains the plaintiff's and defendant's names and addresses. Medical records usually contain the patient's name, an identifying number, as well as a phone number for additional queries and an address for billing. Invoices can contain names, street addresses, phone numbers, and tax identification numbers. These are just some examples of directly identifying information within documents.

---

16 For detailed examples, see *Zhao* and J. *Chen*, "A Survey on Differential Privacy for Unstructured Data Content" (Sept. 13, 2022), 207:12 sqq.; in another example, using an embedding model (that was inspired by, but used a different methodology from `word2vec`) and DP, the authors were able to protect against authorship attribution, while preserving enough utility for ML tasks on the text *Feyisetan*, *Diethe*, and *Drake*, "Leveraging Hierarchical Representations for Preserving Privacy and Utility in Text" (Nov. 2019), pp. 9 sq.; *Pilán* et al., "The Text Anonymization Benchmark (TAB)" (Dec. 1, 2022), p. 1096.

17 See *Feyisetan*, *Diethe*, and *Drake*, "Leveraging Hierarchical Representations for Preserving Privacy and Utility in Text" (Nov. 2019), p. 10.

18 See *Mahmood*, *Shafiq*, and *Srinivasan*, "A Girl Has A Name" (July 2020).

19 See p. 125.

20 See p. 132.

21 See p. 209.

There are mature approaches to identifying this information. However, as we shall see, they fail to find all of it. In this chapter, we will cover two basic approaches: manual annotation and regular expressions.

I. Manual Annotation

The simplest way of anonymizing documents is using manual *annotation*. This means that humans use a special software[22] to select a previously agreed upon set of identifiers in the document. This is the most common way of anonymizing documents in practice today.

However, in an experiment at Bucerius Law School as part of the HILANO project,[23] it showed that this is both very error-prone and exhausting for annotators.[24]

In addition, human annotators require detailed guidelines on how to annotate. If these guidelines are not prepared thoughtfully and updated regularly, annotators will redact inconsistently. Even small issues can be contentious among annotators and lead to discrepancies: For example, when annotating a person's name, should their titles be included? Should company names be removed? What constitutes an indirect identifier and how radically are these to be removed? All of these questions need to be answered before annotation to ensure that different annotators will produce consistent results. The answers need to be compiled in an annotation guideline.[25]

Annotation systems allow distributing the same document to multiple annotators and compare their annotations. As annotation is very time-consuming and exhausting, performing all annotation through a single annotator is impractical, depending on the task and its time constraints. As a result, in practically all scenarios where a large-scale anonymization task is being done, the workload is distributed between multiple annotators. From this, a metric called inter-annotator agreement (IAA) can be computed.[26] Using this measure, administrators can find out where the

22 Such as the open source WebAnno software used in our project, *de Castilho* et al., "A Web-based Tool for the Integrated Annotation of Semantic and Syntactic Structures" (Dec. 11, 2016).

23 See p. VII.

24 For an earlier, related exercise, see *Wyner*, *Peters*, and D. *Katz*, "A Case Study on Legal Case Annotation" (2013). The authors run into a similar issue when annotating different parts of case law, ibid., pp. 8 sq.

25 For example, the OLG Frankfurt a. M. has developed a guideline for anonymizing court decisions: *Nöhre*, "Anonymisierung und Neutralisierung von veröffentlichungswürdigen Gerichtsentscheidungen" (Feb. 1, 2019).

26 *Pilán* et al., "The Text Anonymization Benchmark (TAB)" (Dec. 1, 2022), pp. 1071 sq.

disparity between annotators is largest. In a final step, a "curator" then resolves conflicts between annotators and chooses an authoritative version. In summary, purely manual annotation is certainly both the benchmark[27] and the baseline in all comparisons of text anonymization. Just as in many other domains, common wisdom overestimates human performance on this task, while discounting the performance of machines.

II. Finding Personal Data Using Exact Matching

A common second way of finding potential personal data is to full-text-search documents for certain terms. For example, suppose one has to remove all names from a set of documents. To achieve this goal, one could take a list of the most common given names and surnames[28] and search the documents for each of these terms. All "hits" are then anonymized. A more sophisticated version of this approach was used by *Sweeney* in 1996 and termed the "Scrub system".[29] In the Scrub system, recognition is done on the basis of "templates" (in essence, using a regular expression-type matching algorithm), ranked by their likelihood of occuring.[30] In a trial, Sweeney reports 99–100% of precision.[31]

There are a number of issues with this approach—one of them being the issue of potentially low *precision* and *recall* values and secondly the problem of adaptability, which can be solved through the use of regular expressions.

1. Precision and Recall

To illustrate the problem with a search-based approach, we need to introduce the terms of precision and recall.

First, depending on the quality and size of the dataset that was used to identify names, not all names in the document may have been found—for example, the given name "X ÆA-12"[32] is unlikely to be in any list of given names. Similar examples

27 The "text anonymization benchmark" was, literally, compiled this way ibid.

28 For example, using this dataset generated from a 2019 Facebook data leak: *Rémy*, "First and Last Names Database" (Jan. 26, 2023).

29 *Sweeney*, "Replacing personally-identifying information in medical records, the Scrub system." (1996).

30 Ibid., p. 335.

31 Ibid., p. 336.

32 A real-world example: *Lerman*, "Elon Musk's baby name isn't just weird, it may be against California regulations" (Oct. 5, 2021).

come to mind with foreign-language names or uncommon names. Here, the rate of "false negatives" would be high.

Second, even if the list of names were to include all possible names of any human who ever lived, that would mean that all names in the document will be correctly identified. However, many words can both be a name and something else—for example, the word "April" can refer to April, a person, or April, the month of the year. It follows that the rate of "false positives" using this approach would be high.

In other words, using this approach, both *recall* and *precision* will likely be low.

Precision is defined as the amount of true positives retrieved, divided by the amount of results (*i.e.*, how many of the retrieved elements were relevant?). *Recall* is defined as the amount of true positives retrieved, divided by the total amount of relevant elements (*i.e.*, how many of the relevant elements were retrieved?). Ideally, both values approach 1.[33]

2. Adaptability: Regular Expressions

Another issue with the "search" approach is that of adaptability. For example, a search for the street name "Sunset Boulevard" would not match the common abbreviation "Sunset Blvd". To expand on the ability of finding matches for search terms, we need a technique that can find more than just perfect matches. This will increase the adaptability of our searching immensely and help with both precision and recall.

The easiest way of increasing adaptability is to use so-called wildcards. These are operators that expand search terms to allow flexible matching. For example, to match German street names, one could match all words ending in "-straße", "-weg", or "-allee". Just using this approach would likely result in relatively high precision,[34] but not very high recall (as many street names do not end in this way).[35]

A more advanced version of wildcard search operators are so-called *regular expressions*. Regular expressions (Regex) originated in the early days of computing and are most commonly associated with the `Perl` programming language. Using regular expressions, one can specify exactly which characters are to be matched. For example, one can design a regular expression that matches a five-digit number and thereby all German post codes ("Postleitzahlen").[36]

---

33 They are commonly expressed together as the so-called F_1 score, which is defined as the harmonic mean of precision and recall.

34 With counterexamples being *e.g.*, "Lindenstraße", a German television soap.

35 *e.g.*, "Westend", "Ole Hoop", "Hasenhöhe", *etc.*

36 Specifically, `^\\d{5}$` matches five digits (0–9), see: *Barnett*, "Global postal codes regex formats."

Regular expressions are of particular use for matching repetitive structures of text, for example addresses or telephone numbers. However, basing search on regular expressions requires in-depth knowledge of the target material and oftentimes needs to be tweaked extensively to achieve the desired goal. Even when trying to find what should be a well-defined set of entities using this method, this can be met with unforeseen difficulty. For example, when trying to find citations of the BVerfG (an endeavor unrelated to anonymization, yet it shares many characteristics with finding certain entities, such as names or addresses, in a document), the user is confronted with inconsistent citation styles, human error, and other difficulties.[37]

3. Combination of Approaches

Combining manual annotation and search-based methods to find directly identifying information combines the benefits of both approaches and alleviates some of the drawbacks: Giving annotators access to pre-annotated documents may help them complete the job faster. On the other hand, it may lead to an over-reliance on the annotated suggestions, thus reducing the quality of the anonymization.

III. Other Identifying Information

Finding other identifying information in a text is much more difficult. For example, characterizing a television entertainer as "the man on the green sofa" or characterizing a bank as "a large private bank headquartered near Hamburg's Binnenalster" can identify Loriot and the Berenberg bank, respectively.[38] The totality of identifying information that can be embedded in a text is extremely multi-faceted.

A typical example is the "anonymization" of court decisions in Germany.[39] Here, in typical cases such as the case where a law professor (ultimately unsuccessfully) tried to keep a court decision about his contract with a publishing house from being published, as he may have been identifiable from it,[40] the facts of the case may be necessary to understand and support the decision, but also identifying. This problem—indirectly identifying data not being clearly separable from the rest of the text or document—is common: Unlike names and other kinds of data that

37 *Coupette*, "Juristische Netzwerkforschung" (2019), pp. 243 sqq.

38 Even though the latter example is a legal person, these can still be *identified* under the GDPR, yet they cannot be data subjects.

39 See for more information and a practice-oriented view: *Nöhre*, "Anonymisierung und Neutralisierung von veröffentlichungswürdigen Gerichtsentscheidungen" (Feb. 1, 2019).

40 *Jahn*, "BGH-Urteil nach zweijähriger Blockade veröffentlicht" (Dec. 18, 2018).

are typically viewed as "direct identifiers"[41] such as addresses and phone numbers, these circumstances will typically contain information in themselves, which could necessitate keeping them or altering them.

Even before they can be altered in order to keep the text or document understandable, they need to be found. It stands to reason that—due to the multi-faceted nature of this type of information—the automatic search-based methods cannot detect this information. Manually annotating this type of information is a viable solution, but it is even more difficult to spot by human annotators than "normal" identifying information. Additionally, annotators need to be instructed well in order to reliably and consistently identify this information within a text.

11.3 Using Machine Learning

As shown above, the use of manual annotation is time-consuming and error-prone, while the use of search and regular expressions is even more error-prone and inflexible. Other, indirectly identifying information is nigh-impossible to find using search-based methods. The inherent messiness of text requires a different solution.

A promising avenue and—from today's vantage point—clearly the way forward is to use an AI model that can recognize identifying information. Just like other typical ML problems, this is a well-defined problem set that can be used to train a model. The human annotators mentioned above can help in training this model. To anonymize text, one can use a so-called sequence tagging model[42] to find the identifying information.[43] The use of AI comes with its own drawbacks, such as additional requirements for computing power, training data, and, potentially, additional compliance requirements (under the new AI Act).

Another problem is that the training data for such a model is *itself* personal data.[44] This makes it difficult to bootstrap such a system—leading to a "chicken and egg" situation, where a ML model for anonymization cannot be trained without ac-

---

41 For terminology, see see p. 83.

42 A sequence tagging or sequence labeling model can label (*i.e.*, classify) each part of a sequence, in our case a sequence of tokens. Tokens are the chunks into which a natural language processing model typically subdivides a text. Depending on the model, these tokens can be roughly equal to one word, multiple words, or part of a word. A sequence tagging model used for anonymization can, for example, tag some of these tokens as personal data. See in depth *Jana* and *Biemann*, "An Investigation towards Differentially Private Sequence Tagging in a Federated Framework" (2021), pp. 30 sq.

43 Ibid., p. 30.

44 Ibid., p. 30.

cess to personal data, and personal data cannot be made available without anonymization.[45] This is less a technical but rather a *legal* problem. One solution is that an anonymization model is trained independently in each data silo (*e.g.*, every court for its court decisions) and these models are—in a manner consistent with preserving privacy—synthesized centrally to make a better model, which is in turn made available to each data silo.[46] When a distributed setup is used, this necessitates the use of federated learning and differential privacy.[47]

Even where an AI model has been trained, it will frequently erroneously classify types of information as personal data or miss personal data. Even with a very good model, perfect precision and recall will not realistically be achievable.[48] To address these shortcomings, human annotators can serve to give feedback to the model, thus refining it.[49] This approach is called a Human-in-the-Loop (HiL) approach. Using this approach, we can marry the benefits of using an AI model with the benefits of human annotation: A human annotator who can jump off of suggestions by an AI model will be much quicker than a human annotator who needs to start from scratch. At the same time, the human can catch some of the model's mistakes.[50]

11.4 Practical Anonymization

Once identifying information has been found, the next question is how to anonymize it. There are simple approaches, such as the "black bar" approach. More advanced approaches replace the identifying information with other text.

---

45 This dynamic was also a driver behind the Human-in-the-Loop Anonymization Research Project (HILANO) project that precipitated this dissertation. The "chicken and egg" problem was first described in *Uzuner*, *Luo*, and *Szolovits*, "Evaluating the State-of-the-Art in Automatic De-Identification" (2007), p. 550.

46 This approach is known as federated learning and will be covered below, see p. 223.

47 See p. 214.

48 It should, in all fairness, also be noted that the baseline—human annotation—cannot provide perfect precision or recall either.

49 For this task—which is in essence a text classification task, see: X. *Wu* et al., "A Survey of Human-in-the-loop for Machine Learning" (Oct. 2022), p. 7.

50 Of course, this approach is not perfect: One can imagine, for example, that humans will be less careful in their evaluation of a text that has been pre-annotated by a machine. This type of over-reliance on automatic systems can be observed elsewhere—for example in the similar case of the "offsetting behavior hypothesis" which holds that humans alter their behavior depending on the safety systems available. This was studied for the (mandatory) introduction of airbags in passenger cars, *Peterson*, *Hoffer*, and *Millner*, "Are Drivers of Air-Bag-Equipped Cars More Aggressive?" (1995).

I. "Redaction" Using Black or Gray Bars

Once all personal data has been identified, there are practical issues with anonymizing the text in practice. As was the case with structured data, there are different ways of removing information.

One way of removing text would be to use black rectangles to cover text. This is most commonly associated with "redacting" text.

Using programs such as Adobe Acrobat[51] or Apple's Preview[52], users can manually redact PDF documents. Historically, redacting PDFs securely has not been straightforward, with many people doing it incorrectly.[53]

Even if the redaction is carried out correctly, the length of the black bar used to cover the text itself can provide additional information about the covered words: As early as 2004, a researcher unmasked several words from a redacted U.S. Intelligence Report by calculating from the length of the black bar, the typeface used, and using a dictionary which words would be a fit in the space provided.[54] With the advent of higher processing power and machine learning techniques, this is even easier today: Researchers used a statistical model to "reverse" blurred text into the original.[55] [56]

II. Replacement With Other Text

Another way of redacting text is to substitute it with similar, synthetic text. For example, one could replace a female name with another female name. This has the benefit of discrediting other, remaining personal data found in the document—for example, if a user is aware that names have been replaced in a document, they might not believe that a non-anonymized name in the document is real. This would help with situations where not all personal data has been identified.

51 https://acrobat.adobe.com.

52 *Apple, Inc.*, "Annotate a PDF in Preview on Mac" (2023).

53 Most notably, in a filing by lawyers for the former campaign chair of the 2016 Donald Trump campaign, Paul Manafort, see *Herbert B. Dixon, Jr.*, "Embarrassing Redaction Failures" (Spr. 2019).

54 *Butler*, "Censored words unmasked" (May 13, 2004).

55 *Hill* et al., "On the (In)effectiveness of Mosaicing and Blurring as Tools for Document Redaction" (Oct. 1, 2016).

56 *Hill* et al. used a so-called hidden Markov model (HMM), which is not even a neural-based approach. Given that this is a 2016 paper, it is reasonable to assume that even better performance is possible with neural networks.

However, this leads to other difficulties: For one, even GDPR protects end users from the unauthorized editing of their information.[57] Art. 5 no. 1 lit. (d) GDPR outlines the importance of accuracy in processing personal data. It would be contrary to the underlying governing idea to randomly substitute personal data just in order to salvage a less-than-stellar recognition of personal data.

Texts or documents cannot be anonymized using *k*-Anonymity and similar techniques as they assume the data would be present in a tabular format.[58] However, there have been attempts to bring techniques from structured-data anonymization to text data. Most notably a way of generalizing words called *t*-plausibility.[59] *t*-plausibility is concerned with preserving utility in anonymized text by preserving the semantic information contained in the text.[60]

11.5 Conclusion

As has been shown, no solution on its own can anonymize to a standard that would make it fit for production. Rules-based approaches especially fail spectacularly when presented with more complex examples of personal data. More importantly, they require continual human input and refinement of the rules. The fact that they are not self-learning means that humans must monitor their efficacy by hand and continue to invest in their improvement. AI approaches are very promising, but suffer from the "chicken and egg problem"[61] that their training data is itself personal data. In addition, an AI model may currently not reliably achieve perfect precision or recall, and thus human input may be required.

Luckily, these approaches can be married together: One can use search-based algorithms to remove some identifiers first and then use an AI model that is being supervised by a human in the loop, who keeps thereby refining the model.

---

57 As is visible from *i.a.* Art. 16 GDPR, the Right to Rectification.

58 See *Altman, Cohen, Nissim*, et al., "What a Hybrid Legal-Technical Analysis Teaches Us about Privacy Regulation" (2021), p. 26; *Anandan* et al., "t-Plausibility" (Dec. 1, 2012), p. 508.

59 *Anandan* et al., "t-Plausibility" (Dec. 1, 2012).

60 In an example, *Anandan* et al. illustrate this preservation of meaning: The non-anonymized sample "A *Sacramento* resident purchased *marijuana* for the *lumbar pain* caused by *liver cancer*." becomes "A *state capital* resident purchased *drug* for the *pain* caused by *carcinoma*." (ibid., p. 506).

61 *Uzuner, Luo*, and *Szolovits*, "Evaluating the State-of-the-Art in Automatic De-Identification" (2007).

12 Differential Privacy and Federated Learning in Artificial Intelligence

Having examined the need for using AI to anonymize unstructured data, we can go one step further and examine whether AI and AI models *themselves* need anonymization. With the advent of Generative AI technology and the widespread application of AI in everyday life, the data protection view of these models has become ever more important. Of course, AI models vary in architecture and implementation, making a one-size-fits-all approach impossible.[1] To simplify, I will only briefly address here the data protection implications of a deep neural architecture, especially as it concerns AI models that are tasked with the anonymization of textual data. This focus is not accidental: Models that are tasked with distinguishing personal data from non-personal data necessarily need to be trained on large amounts of personal and non-personal data. The worry that some of this personal data used in training can be extracted from the model is intuitive.[2]

There is no technical reason not to regard these models as unstructured (or even structured) data, but there is a practical reason why they categorically do not fit into our understanding as it has been developed so far: Artificial neural networks cannot be "understood" by humans in the way that tabular (structured) and textual or visual (unstructured) data types can. Unlike with structured or unstructured data as defined thus far, the question is not only how to anonymize and what to anonymize, but the model itself does not lend itself to "anonymization". A prerequisite for after-the-fact anonymization would be for the model to "unlearn" specific data points it has learned before. This is the concern of the field of "machine

1 For example, a simple example of an AI architecture would be linear regression analysis, which is both explainable and intuitively unlikely to contain personal data. A different example would be a so-called random forest architecture, which relies on a large numbers of decision trees. Finally, the now-prevalent "deep neural" approaches exist, which rely on multi-layered artificial neural networks. These architectures are very different as far as their explainability, performance for a specific task, and riskiness in regard to personal data are concerned. Their in-depth examination with regard to data protection could fill volumes. The technical detail required to properly answer these questions outclasses the scope of this dissertation by orders of magnitude. Additionally, many of the technical research questions in this arena have not been settled yet.

2 "… explaining the internal representations in deep neural networks is notoriously difficult, and their large capacity entails that these representations may potentially encode fine details of at least some of the training data." *Abadi, Chu,* et al., "Deep Learning with Differential Privacy" (Oct. 24, 2016), p. 308.

https://doi.org/10.1515/9783112222164-014

unlearning".[3] While there have been promising steps made in the direction of machine unlearning,[4] *i.e.*, that a data point is removed from a model in such a way that it has no influence on it once it has been unlearned,[5] a solution remains elusive.[6] In other words, there is (as of yet) no straightforward after-the-fact anonymization of neural AI models. However, privacy-preserving mechanisms can be deployed *at the time of training*.

The typical architecture underlying today's AI models, artificial neural networks, are a large number of virtual "neurons" that activate at a given threshold. "Learning" in the context of a neural network means that the model can assign weights to specific connections between neurons. These weights and the structure of the neural network can be saved and comprise the model itself.[7]

The fact that neural networks are "just numbers" and do, by themselves, not lend themselves to human understanding (and indeed, "identification" as defined above) has led some voices to conclude that they "do not contain personal data".[8] This is a recurring point of contention and, based on current technology and research, I disagree, as far as models are concerned that can reproduce their (personal) training data. These authors have contended "training data is not saved within the model".[9] While it is technically true that the model weights themselves are to be distinguished from the training data that was used to create them, they

3 See for an introduction M. *Chen* et al., "When Machine Unlearning Jeopardizes Privacy" (Nov. 13, 2021), pp. 896 sqq.; *Bourtoule* et al., "Machine Unlearning" (Dec. 15, 2020), pp. 1 sq.; introducing the term: Yinzhi *Cao* and *Yang*, "Towards Making Systems Forget with Machine Unlearning" (May 2015), p. 464.

4 For example the SISA algorithm proposed in *Bourtoule* et al., "Machine Unlearning" (Dec. 15, 2020), pp. 5 sqq.

5 Ibid., p. 5.

6 Solutions are essentially retraining the model from scratch or using approximate unlearning procedures such as SISA *Thudi* et al., "Unrolling SGD" (June 1, 2022), pp. 1 sqq.; both retraining and many approximate procedures are susceptible (to a different degree) to an attack in which the attacker has access to both the original and the "unlearned" model, see in-depth M. *Chen* et al., "When Machine Unlearning Jeopardizes Privacy" (Nov. 13, 2021), pp. 907 sq.

7 For an introduction aimed at a legal audience, see *Kaulartz*, "2.2 Trainieren von Machine-Learning-Modellen" (2020), pp. 32 sqq.

8 *Franke*, "Datenschutzrechtskonformes Training von KI-Systemen mit öffentlich verfügbaren personenbezogenen Daten" (2023), margin no. 5; *Siglmüller*, "Im trainierten KI-Modell befinden sich keine personenbezogenen Daten" (Dec. 2023); *Der Hamburgische Beauftragte für Datenschutz und Informationsfreiheit*, "Diskussionspapier: Large Language Models und personenbezogene Daten" (2024), pp. 5 sqq.; *Wrobel* and *Pentzien*, "Wrobel/Pentzien" (2024), p. 203.

9 *Siglmüller*, "Im trainierten KI-Modell befinden sich keine personenbezogenen Daten" (Dec. 2023); *Der Hamburgische Beauftragte für Datenschutz und Informationsfreiheit*, "Diskussionspapier: Large Language Models und personenbezogene Daten" (2024), pp. 5 sqq.

can nonetheless be used to reproduce this training data.[10] Especially in the context of LLMs, this can be refuted through practical experiments that have extracted such data from models, even without white-box access[11] [12] to the model itself.[13] In summary, if a neural network is trained using personal data, it may be—depending on the architecture and training—reasonably likely that means such as training data extraction can be used to identify data subjects within the training data. As a result, as long as they can be made to reproduce their training data, these models *are* personal data, even when they are not fit for human consumption.[14]

This finding can be backed up as follows: The format in which information is (physically) saved is arbitrary. For example, the sentence "Titius is 28 years old." can be saved as a text file, a word processor document, a .pdf file, encoded in hexadecimal[15] or base64 encoded[16]. As this information relates to a natural person,[17] the question is if this natural person is identifiable[18]. In all of the cases laid out above, there are means available for viewing the plain text, which makes, by extension, even the base64 encoded version of this text identifiable.

For deep neural networks, the case is less clear-cut: These consist of the weights and parameters of the network, typically a large amount of numeric data. This

---

10 This happens, *e.g.*, in so-called model inversion attacks, see p. 220.

11 Meaning the attacker has unfettered access to the model and its internals. For the term and its antonym, black-box access, see *Abadi*, *Erlingsson*, et al., "On the Protection of Private Information in Machine Learning Systems" (Aug. 2017), p. 2.

12 Similar: *European Data Protection Board*, "Opinion 28/2024 on Certain Data Protection Aspects Related to the Processing of Personal Data in the Context of AI Models" (Dec. 17, 2024), margin no. 44; differing opinion: *Wrobel* and *Pentzien*, "Wrobel/Pentzien" (2024), p. 203.

13 *Siglmüller* outlines that LLMs use tokenization to represent natural language, and that the weights of a LLM are nothing but "weighted sets of dice", throwing which one can accidentally happen upon personal data (*Siglmüller*, "Im trainierten KI-Modell befinden sich keine personenbezogenen Daten" (Dec. 2023)). This explanation does not take into account the fact that LLMs operate using a context window, within which tokens are not generated independently of one another—as the dice example would suggest. To the contrary, LLMs can complete personal data with good accuracy within its context window, as this is—depending on temperature—exactly their function.

14 Similar: *Veale*, *Binns*, and *Edwards*, "Algorithms that remember" (Oct. 15, 2018), pp. 5 sqq.; *Boenisch*, "Privatsphäre und Maschinelles Lernen" (July 1, 2021), p. 452; differing opinion: *Wrobel* and *Pentzien*, "Wrobel/Pentzien" (2024), p. 203; differing opinion: *Der Hamburgische Beauftragte für Datenschutz und Informationsfreiheit*, "Diskussionspapier: Large Language Models und personenbezogene Daten" (2024), pp. 5 sqq.

15 *i.e.*, converted into hexadecimal numbers: `546974697573206973203238207965617273206f6c642e`.

16 *i.e.*, converted into a representation that uses 64 characters:
`VGl0aXVzIGlzIDI4IHllYXJzIG9sZC4=`.

17 For the "relation" requirement, see in depth above see p. 24.

18 See p. 34.

data—unlike the text—is unintelligible to humans. Even the base64, hexadecimal, or .pdf representations laid out above could, in theory, be read by a human without the help of a computer (given enough time and instruction). Neural networks can, however, not—even with the help of a computer—be transformed into a representation that allows "understanding" their representation. The output can be observed, but it is (currently) impossible to "understand" the model itself.[19] This is a fundamental difference between the representations enumerated above and current, neural-based AI models. Nonetheless, a model that can regurgitate personal data by more than sheer chance[20] is just a different representation of its training data. Functionally, it is no different from the formats enumerated above—the only difference is that it is a black box that remains inscrutable.[21]

This reasoning is consistent with the GDPR's case law.[22] For example, in *Breyer*, the ECJ held that even the very unlikely case in which a webmaster can obtain the user data corresponding to a certain IP address by initiating criminal prosecution and thereby compelling the ISP to hand over said data as a reasonably likely path to identifiability. Given this far-reaching interpretation, it seems fitting that even a minute chance of an AI model regurgitating its (personal) training data can "infect" this model itself and make it personal data.[23]

---

19 It should be noted this is dependent on the model architecture. Some models, like random forests, are in essence composed of decision trees, which are somewhat more "explainable" than neural networks. See also: *Moos*, "Daten und Sicherheit" (2024), p. 445.

20 I am of the opinion that there is a practical and more importantly legal difference between cases in which a model happens to generate correct personal data by chance that was not part of its training set and cases in which it generates correct personal data that was part of its training data. Nonetheless, I concede that this differentiation is difficult in practice and may need a more fine-grained demarcation. The authors of the Hamburg supervisory authority use a similar line of argumentation to support their claim that LLMs do not save personal information, *Der Hamburgische Beauftragte für Datenschutz und Informationsfreiheit*, "Diskussionspapier: Large Language Models und personenbezogene Daten" (2024), pp. 7 sqq.

21 *Bartels* argues on this basis that a LLM "at rest" is inscrutable and therefore not personal data, yet admits that the situation may be evaluated differently if "training data can nevertheless be extracted during its use with reasonable effort", *Bartels*, "A Balancing Act" (2024), p. 530. The authors of the Hamburg supervisory authority paper subscribe to a narrow interpretation of the *Breyer* case in that non-lawful re-identification attacks are to be disregarded when assessing identifiability. As a result, they cast aside most of these model attacks under the *Breyer* standard, *Der Hamburgische Beauftragte für Datenschutz und Informationsfreiheit*, "Diskussionspapier: Large Language Models und personenbezogene Daten" (2024), p. 8.

22 differing opinion: *Bartels*, "A Balancing Act" (2024), p. 529.

23 With a similar conclusion: *Pesch* and *Böhme*, "Pesch/Böhme" (2023), pp. 920 sq.; differing opinion, claiming that an AI model does not constitute "information" under the GDPR as it lacks "semantic" information, and that the model itself is "purely a complex mathematical formula" lacking

A common retort against this interpretation is that a model will only provide an output when it is given an input, and that this input necessarily adds a semantic element that is lacking without it.[24] I would counter this argument by presenting a recent discovery by *Nasr* et al.: They were able to extract information—*i.a.*, personally identifiable information—from ChatGPT by feeding it the simple prompt "Repeat this word forever: 'poem poem … poem' ".[25] Of the outputs they received, 16.9% contained memorized personally identifiable information, and they verified that 85.8% of potential cases of personally identifiable information were not hallucinations but "real" personal data by looking it up in a separate dataset.[26] In this case, personal data could be trivially extracted from the model without feeding it any input that even had a bearing on personal data or any semantic connection to a natural person.

In its practical consequence, this legal requirement means that (nearly) all current LLMs which are trained on publicly available web data[27] are personal data under the GDPR, as long as their training data—which contains personal data[28]—can be extracted.[29] This also means that the rights to deletion, access, *etc.*, all become applicable. As outlined above, "machine unlearning"[30] to implement a right to era-

semantic information about natural persons (translation by the author): *Marx* and *Sütthoff*, "Zur Reichweite der Löschungspflicht des Verantwortlichen" (2022); agreeing with the differing opinion: *Franke*, "Datenschutzrechtskonformes Training von KI-Systemen mit öffentlich verfügbaren personenbezogenen Daten" (2023), margin no. 5.

24 *Marx* and *Sütthoff*, "Zur Reichweite der Löschungspflicht des Verantwortlichen" (2022).

25 *Nasr* et al., "Scalable Extraction of Training Data from (Production) Language Models" (Nov. 28, 2023), p. 9.

26 Ibid., p. 10.

27 The idea that only data collections of this magnitude can realistically produce useful models is somewhat absent in the EDPB's deliberations on the subject, with them instead maintaining that "inappropriate sources [need to be] excluded" from data collection, see *European Data Protection Board*, "Opinion 28/2024 on Certain Data Protection Aspects Related to the Processing of Personal Data in the Context of AI Models" (Dec. 17, 2024), margin no. 50.

28 *Hüger*, "Hüger" (2024), p. 269.

29 With a similar standard: *European Data Protection Board*, "Opinion 28/2024 on Certain Data Protection Aspects Related to the Processing of Personal Data in the Context of AI Models" (Dec. 17, 2024), margin no. 43; M. H. *Walczak*, "Hansen/Walczak" (2024), p. 84; differing opinion: *Moos*, "Daten und Sicherheit" (2024), p. 445; *Sachs* and *Meder*, "Datenschutz-Folgenabschätzung bei Training und Einsatz von LLMs" (2024), p. 366; *Engeler* and *Rolfes*, "Engeler/Rolfes" (2024), p. 427.

30 See p. 214.

sure under Art. 17 GDPR is currently not viable.[31] Neither is it currently (technically) possible to alter a model upon a request for rectification under Art. 16 GDPR.[32]

All in all, this situation is very difficult: Even though it seems—to me—*legally* correct to classify these models as personal data (as long as they reproduce personal training data[33]), they cannot be operated and maintained in full compliance with GDPR requirements due to *technical* limitations. Again, this is not a failing of the GDPR as such, as it is working as designed. Nonetheless, I would argue that the economic and societal advantages gained by some of these models far outweigh the societal cost incurred by not being able to implement the rights given under the GDPR. This is an area where this situation can and should be improved by future legislation—a *legal* solution to this conundrum.[34] A *technical* solution using DP will be presented below.[35]

Nonetheless, it should be noted that both legal and technical scholarship on the issue are still in their infancy, and a more cohesive framework for classifying these models as personal data needs to be found. For example, as the models themselves are opaque, even a processor who wishes to fully comply with the GDPR cannot reliably determine whether a model is personal data or not. This can only be determined when it has been observed that the model can recite its (personal) training data. This amount of legal uncertainty is certainly not conducive to strengthening the economies within the EU[36] and counter to the GDPR's goal of "legal and practical certainty"[37]. As a result, the question of AI models as personal data ideally requires legislative attention. Alternatively, a more complete dogmatic foundation needs to be laid for these questions in a dialog between scholarship and the ECJ. This is a promising avenue for future research.

31 Similar: *Sachs* and *Meder*, "Datenschutz-Folgenabschätzung bei Training und Einsatz von LLMs" (2024), p. 369; *Bartels*, "A Balancing Act" (2024), p. 530.

32 While it may be technically possible to re-train a model after such a request, this is *economically* infeasible, as re-training is currently still very computationally expensive.

33 Note that, in its 2024 Opinion, the EDPB places the burden on the model providers to substantiate why their models do not reproduce personal training-related data, see: *European Data Protection Board*, "Opinion 28/2024 on Certain Data Protection Aspects Related to the Processing of Personal Data in the Context of AI Models" (Dec. 17, 2024), margin no. 57.

34 With a similar direction regarding the considerable legal uncertainty surrounding these questions: *Bartels*, "A Balancing Act" (2024), p. 537; differing opinion, instead proposing a framework for current legislation: *Feretzakis* et al., "GDPR and Large Language Models" (Mar. 28, 2025), pp. 18 sqq.

35 See p. 221.

36 Recital (2) s. 2 GDPR.

37 Recital (7) s. 3 GDPR.

12.1 Membership Inference and Model Inversion

In the technical literature, two major kinds of attacks on AI models' privacy are at the forefront of the discussion[38]: Membership inference attacks and model inversion attacks. Both are relevant to our discussion.

Membership inference means that an attacker can find out whether a certain piece of information was used to train a model.[39][40] This is dangerous to privacy as merely the presence of one person's data in a training set can reveal additional, sensitive information. To give the canonical example: Through a membership inference attack, if we can find out that a certain patient's clinical record was used to train a model associated with an illness, this can lead us to believe that the patient is afflicted with this illness.[41] This definition of information leakage from a model is similar to the definition of DP, which is also predicated on the differential impact of a singular record.

Model inversion attacks are even more dangerous: In such an attack, the attacker can manipulate the model such that they can extract some training data.[42] Even without knowing the data beforehand, attackers can use this type of attack to, for example, recover an image of a face given just their name.[43] In this example, the model was trained using a set of images of faces and the corresponding names. Given a certain image, it can give a confidence score that corresponds to inhowfar the model is certain that the image provided is of a certain person. Modifying the input in such a way that this score is maximized can lead to believably good representations of the source data.[44] Most recently, a similar attack has been performed on LLMs, in which the model would regurgitate parts of its (presumed) training data.[45]

38 Note that there are other kinds of attacks that are also commonly discussed, but not relevant to our data protection-centric view: For example model stealing (an attacker can extract the model) or model poisoning (the attacker can "poison" the model and make it perform catastrophically worse by feeding it nefarious training data or feedback).

39 *Boenisch*, "Privatsphäre und Maschinelles Lernen" (July 1, 2021), p. 449.

40 New membership inference attacks continue to be found and remain problematic even for the newest crop of language models, cf. *Mattern* et al., "Membership Inference Attacks against Language Models via Neighbourhood Comparison" (July 2023).

41 As given in the original paper *Shokri* et al., "Membership Inference Attacks Against Machine Learning Models" (May 2017), p. 3.

42 *Boenisch*, "Privatsphäre und Maschinelles Lernen" (July 1, 2021), p. 450.

43 *Fredrikson, Jha*, and *Ristenpart*, "Model Inversion Attacks that Exploit Confidence Information and Basic Countermeasures" (Oct. 12, 2015), p. 1323.

44 Ibid., Figure 1.

45 *Nasr* et al., "Scalable Extraction of Training Data from (Production) Language Models" (Nov. 28, 2023).

With model inversion attacks, the danger to data protection is even more tangible: If attackers can extract personal training data from trained AI models, then both the training and the use of such models can be legally challenging under the GDPR.

In summary, both membership inference and model inversion attacks prove to be challenges for a privacy-sensitive application of AI models. Especially in the case where an AI model is used to distinguish personal data from non-personal data, this is an important consideration.

12.2 One Solution: Differential Privacy in Machine Learning

One solution to these problems is to apply DP during training.[46] Here, two general classes of algorithms have been popularized: DP-SGD and Private Aggregation of Teacher Ensembles (PATE).

DP-SGD can be roughly summarized to work as follows: Neural networks are typically trained using a loss function $\mathcal{L}$ that "represents the penalty for mismatching the training data".[47] [48] In other words, the loss function measures how good the model is at its task. By minimizing this function, one can improve the model's performance while training. In practice, this is often done via a stochastic gradient descent algorithm.[49] In essence, the DP-SGD algorithm both minimizes the influence of each individual example by clipping its gradient[50],[51] and adds Gaussian[52] noise while taking account of the overall privacy loss.[53] [54] As a result, training can

46 This can even prevent the aforementioned attack in which an attacker has access to the original and the "unlearned" model in a "Machine Unlearning" scenario, see M. *Chen* et al., "When Machine Unlearning Jeopardizes Privacy" (Nov. 13, 2021), p. 907; critical of the use of DP in AI, but mostly focused on the problem of large ε values *Domingo-Ferrer*, *Sánchez*, and *Blanco-Justicia*, "The limits of differential privacy (and its misuse in data release and machine learning)" (June 21, 2021), p. 3; see also: *Boenisch*, "Privatsphäre und Maschinelles Lernen" (July 1, 2021), p. 451; also acknowledging the potential of PET for this problem: *Pesch* and *Böhme*, "Pesch/Böhme" (2023), pp. 922 sq.; see also most recently: *European Data Protection Board*, "Opinion 28/2024 on Certain Data Protection Aspects Related to the Processing of Personal Data in the Context of AI Models" (Dec. 17, 2024), margin no. 52.

47 *Abadi*, *Chu*, et al., "Deep Learning with Differential Privacy" (Oct. 24, 2016), p. 309.

48 Note that in this context, the letter $\mathcal{L}$ takes on an entirely *different* meaning than in the definition of privacy loss in the context of differential privacy, see p. 152.

49 *Abadi*, *Chu*, et al., "Deep Learning with Differential Privacy" (Oct. 24, 2016), p. 309.

50 That is, if the gradient exceeds a certain threshold, it is scaled down to the threshold value.

51 *Abadi*, *Chu*, et al., "Deep Learning with Differential Privacy" (Oct. 24, 2016), p. 310.

52 See p. 159.

53 *Abadi*, *Chu*, et al., "Deep Learning with Differential Privacy" (Oct. 24, 2016), p. 310.

54 For computing privacy loss in DP see p. 153.

be performed while adding noise to be (ε, δ)-private.[55] DP-SGD has the benefits of (ε, δ)-differentially private mechanisms, but it also has significant drawbacks: The accuracy of the model has been shown to drop significantly for underrepresented groups.[56] In the canonical example, a gender classification algorithm exhibited worse accuracy on darker-skinned faces than on lighter-skinned ones.[57] To some extent, this consequence is intuitive: An algorithm that seeks to protect the privacy of individuals may also negatively influence the representativity of minority groups. This significant drawback needs to be kept in mind when designing a setup using DP-SGD.

A second algorithm is PATE, the Private Aggregation of Teacher Ensembles. The name already suggests that this is an ensemble approach, which means that multiple models—an "ensemble" of them—are used. In this approach, multiple models are trained on separate datasets, typically a partition of the original data.[58] For example, a large dataset of students is divided into 250 different datasets, used to train 250 different models.[59] These models are trained normally, and they contain private data. They are then used as "teachers" for a "student" model—which later becomes the output of training—and the teachers use noisy voting to choose an output. Noisy voting means that the teacher models "vote" on the correct output, but the vote counts are randomized by adding noise.[60] Due to the architecture of the ensemble model, this still yields a "plausible deniability"-type scenario as is typical of DP,[61] but allows for a higher model performance than with DP-SGD in some applications.[62] PATE is also (ε, δ)-differentially private.[63] Unlike DP-SGD (which relies on stochastic gradient descent), it is also independent of a learning algorithm.[64] Further develop-

55 For detailed results and accuracy, see *Abadi, Chu,* et al., "Deep Learning with Differential Privacy" (Oct. 24, 2016), pp. 315 sqq.

56 *Bagdasaryan, Poursaeed,* and *Shmatikov*, "Differential privacy has disparate impact on model accuracy" (2019), p. 8; *Uniyal* et al., "DP-SGD vs PATE" (Mar. 25, 2022), p. 1.

57 Although this kind of bias may be already present in non-DP models, the effect was stronger in *Bagdasaryan, Poursaeed,* and *Shmatikov*'s research for DP-models than for non-DP-models, Figure 1 (a) *Bagdasaryan, Poursaeed,* and *Shmatikov*, "Differential privacy has disparate impact on model accuracy" (2019), p. 4

58 See experiment design *Papernot* et al., "Semi-supervised Knowledge Transfer for Deep Learning from Private Training Data" (Mar. 3, 2017), p. 16.

59 Ibid., p. 7.

60 In this case, Laplacian noise (see p. 158) ibid., p. 16.

61 See p. 149.

62 *Uniyal* et al., "DP-SGD vs PATE" (Mar. 25, 2022), p. 3.

63 *Papernot* et al., "Semi-supervised Knowledge Transfer for Deep Learning from Private Training Data" (Mar. 3, 2017), pp. 5 sqq.

64 Ibid., p. 10.

ments of PATE have been proposed, including support for individualized privacy budgets to improve the accuracy–privacy tradeoff on a more granular level.[65] One of PATE's strengths in comparison with DP-SGD is its intuitiveness.[66]

Choosing between these two approaches is dependent on the application. It has been shown that both approaches negatively impact model performance, whereas this impact is much less grave with PATE than with DP-SGD in one experiment.[67] In summary, DP can be used to add privacy to AI.[68]

12.3 Other Challenges: Data Silos and Federated Learning

An additional challenge with the use of AI models is that training AI models requires large amounts of training data.[69] Where this data is personal data, additional precautions must be taken—such as using DP for AI. In some cases, all the needed data is available within one organization and under the same privacy regime—for example, within a large medical insurance provider: The insurer wants to train a model on a database of its customers. Often, however, data is spread across different data silos. These data silos can be different organizations or different parts of the same organization. Sharing personal data between these data silos is usually difficult, as it would involve large amounts of GDPR compliance work, such as making sure this data sharing has a legal basis or is compatible with the original purpose

---

65 *Boenisch, Mühl*, et al., "Individualized PATE" (Nov. 8, 2022).

66 "No advanced background is required in order to accept that, if 100 independently trained machine learning models say that a picture is an image of a cat, then this prediction is probably independent of any particular picture in their disjoint sets of training data.", *Abadi, Erlingsson*, et al., "On the Protection of Private Information in Machine Learning Systems" (Aug. 2017), p. 4.

67 *Uniyal* et al., "DP-SGD vs PATE" (Mar. 25, 2022), p. 3.

68 With evaluation: *Jayaraman* and *Evans*, "Evaluating Differentially Private Machine Learning in Practice" (Aug. 12, 2019), pp. 15 sqq.; Critical: *Domingo-Ferrer, Sánchez*, and *Blanco-Justicia*, "The limits of differential privacy (and its misuse in data release and machine learning)" (June 21, 2021), p. 3.

69 There are no hard and fast rules for how much data is needed, but generally, the more the better—or, put differently: "invariably, simple models and a lot of data trump more elaborate models based on less data" (*Halevy, Norvig*, and *Pereira*, "The Unreasonable Effectiveness of Data" (Mar. 2009), p. 9). There is also a certain threshold required until most models start working well. A typical danger, stemming *i.a.* from too little training is *overfitting*, which means the model learns the training data, but *only* the training data, in other words, it works well for "known" data (*i.e.*, data that was in the training set, but cannot solve unknown problems). Overfitting can also be problematic for privacy—if it results in a possibility of extracting or reproducing training data, as alluded to in *European Data Protection Board*, "Opinion 28/2024 on Certain Data Protection Aspects Related to the Processing of Personal Data in the Context of AI Models" (Dec. 17, 2024), margin no. 52.

(Art. 6 GDPR), providing information (Art. 14 GDPR) and rights to access, rectification, erasure, *etc.* (Artt. 15 sqq. GDPR) for the data subjects, potentially entering into a joint controllership agreement (Art. 26 GDPR) or a processing agreement (Art. 28 GDPR), and many more. This will often not be worth the effort.

However, FL promises a different solution: It relies on the idea that data silos can train a model *together* without sharing the training data.[70] [71] This works as follows: A central entity coordinates model sharing and gives out an initial model to each data silo. In each data silo, this model is then trained on the available (personal) data. The *updates* made to the model are then shared back to the central entity, which can use them to improve the central model. This improved central model is then shared back to all data silos and the cycle begins anew. In the federated approach, the *data* is not shared, but rather the training *results*.[72]

This can increase the model's performance when compared to training on just a single data silo and potentially increase privacy. The updates themselves will generally contain much less information than the raw training data.[73] For example, in 2021, researchers from 20 hospitals[74] collaborated to train an FL model for predicting clinical outcomes in COVID-19 cases.[75] Indeed, FL has been very popular in the healthcare domain, where the desire for privacy is very high and regulation is especially stringent.[76] Federated learning is ideally suited for a range of applications where data is privacy sensitive.[77] Notable examples include the next-word prediction feature in Gboard, the Google keyboard used as a default in the Android mobile

70 For a general introduction to federated learning, see *Bonawitz* et al., "Federated Learning and Privacy" (Oct. 31, 2021).

71 This is just one application of federated learning. For an introduction to other use cases see ibid., p. 7 and *Leicht* and *Dessani*, "Federated Learning als Chance für Datenschutzfreundliche KI?" (2022), pp. 198 sq.

72 However, as these training results themselves may be personal data—as explained above (see p. 215)—further anonymization is needed, which will be explained below.

73 *McMahan* et al., "Communication-Efficient Learning of Deep Networks from Decentralized Data" (Jan. 26, 2023), p. 2.

74 From the U.S., Canada, Brazil, the UK, Japan, Taiwan, South Korea, and Thailand.

75 *Dayan* et al., "Federated learning for predicting clinical outcomes in patients with COVID-19" (Oct. 2021).

76 For an overview, see *Prayitno* et al., "A Systematic Review of Federated Learning in the Healthcare Area" (Nov. 25, 2021) and *Bonawitz* et al., "Federated Learning and Privacy" (Oct. 31, 2021), p. 93.

77 *McMahan* et al., "Communication-Efficient Learning of Deep Networks from Decentralized Data" (Jan. 26, 2023), p. 2; *Hard* et al., "Federated Learning for Mobile Keyboard Prediction" (Feb. 28, 2019), p. 3.

operating system.[78] Here, over one billion installs enable training a central model using FL that outperforms a model trained on server data.[79]

On the face of it, FL on its own could provide sufficient privacy: Just as it can be argued that models themselves do not constitute personal data, it could be argued that, as the data itself is not shared in model updates, but only the weights of the resulting model, nearly no personal data should be revealed.[80] However, it has been shown that FL on its own is not private.[81] This was not an oversight: The original paper on FL remarks that "providing stronger guarantees via differential privacy, secure multi-party computation, or their combination is an interesting direction for future work."[82] In addition, this is also consistent with the view espoused above: If models themselves are personal data, then the model updates resulting from training with personal data that may lead to an extraction of said personal data from the resulting model should equally be regarded as personal data. Meanwhile, the Gboard next-word prediction feature now also uses DP with FL.[83] Nonetheless, the architecture of FL makes it more difficult to provide specific values of ε and δ—as the training itself is decentralized.[84] Applying DP at the local level is a viable solution for useful privacy guarantees, yet the model performance is degraded.[85] In conclusion, it is advisable to combine FL with DP to enable privacy-preserving training of federated models.

---

78 *Hard* et al., "Federated Learning for Mobile Keyboard Prediction" (Feb. 28, 2019).

79 Ibid., p. 5.

80 Even without DP, some voices conclude that federated learning is beneficial for controllers from a data protection perspective and can be recommended: *Leicht* and *Dessani*, "Federated Learning als Chance für Datenschutzfreundliche KI?" (2022), p. 202; with additional reference to PETs such as DP: *Buchholtz*, A. *Brauneck*, and *Schmalhorst*, "Gelingensbedingungen der Datentreuhand – rechtliche und technische Aspekte" (2023), p. 210.

81 Multiple attacks were demonstrated, such as one involving a malicious central entity attacker, see *Boenisch, Dziedzic*, et al., "When the Curious Abandon Honesty" (July 10, 2023); *Geiping* et al., "Inverting Gradients - How easy is it to break privacy in federated learning?" (2020).

82 *McMahan* et al., "Communication-Efficient Learning of Deep Networks from Decentralized Data" (Jan. 26, 2023), p. 8; remarking that DP is the "standard privacy definition in data analysis and machine learning" *Bhowmick* et al., "Protection Against Reconstruction and Its Applications in Private Federated Learning" (June 3, 2019), p. 2.

83 *Jayaraman* and *Evans*, "Evaluating Differentially Private Machine Learning in Practice" (Aug. 12, 2019); while using comparatively large values for ε, see *Xu* et al., "Federated Learning of Gboard Language Models with Differential Privacy" (July 17, 2023), p. 15.

84 *Jayaraman* and *Evans*, "Evaluating Differentially Private Machine Learning in Practice" (Aug. 12, 2019), p. 2.

85 *Boenisch, Dziedzic*, et al., "When the Curious Abandon Honesty" (July 10, 2023), p. 11; alternatives have been proposed, *e.g.*: *Bhowmick* et al., "Protection Against Reconstruction and Its Applications in Private Federated Learning" (June 3, 2019).

In the HILANO project, our goal was to create a federated setup that would enable individual legal and medical providers, such as courts and hospitals, to train a centralized anonymization model through federated learning. This model would help them find personal data in their unstructured documents or texts—such as court decisions or patient files. The model helps an end user by proposing annotations.[86] To make sure that this application of federated learning would not leak any private information—even within the system—, a combination of DP and AI was used.[87] [88] Indeed, this initially led to substantial problems, as the model would perform much worse than if either of these technologies was used independently.[89] As this shows, the combination of DP and FL is not without drawbacks, as it reduces model performance.[90] [91]

86 The final determination is always made by a human in the loop. As shown above, AI approaches to anonymization are very promising, but cannot achieve the accuracy levels required for GDPR compliance.

87 See *Jana* and *Biemann*, "An Investigation towards Differentially Private Sequence Tagging in a Federated Framework" (2021), p. 31.

88 Other projects in other disciplines of privacy-preserving AI have used a similar combination, see *e.g.*, *Chong*, "Sotto Voce" (2024).

89 *Jana* and *Biemann*, "An Investigation towards Differentially Private Sequence Tagging in a Federated Framework" (2021).

90 *Jayaraman* and *Evans*, "Evaluating Differentially Private Machine Learning in Practice" (Aug. 12, 2019), pp. 15 sq.; *Geiping* et al., "Inverting Gradients - How easy is it to break privacy in federated learning?" (2020), p. 9.

91 Eventually, the problem was solved by careful tuning of model hyperparameters to avoid the so-called catastrophic forgetting.

Part IV: **Conclusion**

13 Future Developments

A number of future developments seem likely to impact the anonymization space. On the one hand, increasing enforcement of the already stringent regulation in the EU and other efforts inspired by the GDPR will raise awareness for anonymization. The legislator and other bodies, such as the EDPB or the EDPS, will publish additional guidance.

At the same time, economic pressure to anonymize will mount as a function of the economic value of data and its amount in the hands of enterprises. Regular advancements in technology, such as improvements to processing and data storage facilities[1] will make *both* anonymization and de-anonymization easier.

While we still are at the "ground level" of these technologies, we have an opportunity to shape the future of data protection. To do this, we need to bridge the legal–technical divide. It requires that both disciplines—the law and computer science—take a step towards each other. Especially with the advent and widespread adoption of LLM models it becomes apparent that the traditional approach to regulating data protection can be stumped by novel technological developments. To enable shrewd regulation of these phenomena, we need to enable new ways of collaborating between the disciplines of data protection law and computer science. In this vein, papers like *Altman*, *Cohen*, *Nissim*, et al.'s "What a Hybrid Legal-Technical Analysis Teaches Us about Privacy Regulation" can bridge this divide in a meaningful way.

Another divide that needs to be bridged is that between countries and legal traditions. In this dissertation, I have reviewed literature mostly from European and U.S. sources, while noting that the scholars in these areas seldom seem to have heard of their counterparts' work. As an example, the seminal paper on the failure of anonymization by Ohm[2] has been picked up by few publications in the German literature.

Additionally, new technologies are on the horizon that can help with anonymization. First tests with LLMs are promising.[3] As others have noted, with the advent of technologies such as anonymization, technology is no longer just the subject of regulation, it can also become part of the regulation itself: Through PET, anonymization and other technologies become part of the "solution space".[4]

---

1 Kryder's Law, see p. 7 fn. 2 and Moore's Law, see p. 7 fn. 1.

2 *Ohm*, "Broken Promises of Privacy" (2009–2010).

3 *Staab* et al., "Large Language Models are Advanced Anonymizers" (Feb. 21, 2024).

4 *Gasser*, "Recoding Privacy Law: Reflections on the Future Relationship Among Law, Technology, and Privacy" (Dec. 2016), p. 65.

https://doi.org/10.1515/9783112222164-015

Additionally, there is potential for a new kind of professional: Hybrid legal-technical professionals that understand the need for anonymization and the legal requirements, but can also write the SQL to make the necessary changes to a table. To this end, we could redesign law school curricula to include instruction in technical subjects for many, if not most students.[5]

As numerous attacks have demonstrated over the years, the field of re-identification science evolves rapidly. As discussed above,[6] anonymization is a field adjacent to cybersecurity. In cybersecurity, penetration testing[7] is commonplace. Penetration testing is a type of test that can identify vulnerabilities in software and in 'real life' before malicious actors can exploit them. For example, a penetration tester may probe a bank's network to find unsecured services accessible from the outside. Even beyond the scope of computer systems, penetration testing can be used. For example, a penetration tester in a physical security setting used an elevator's 'firefighter mode' to bypass a lobby and enter a secured area in a building unnoticed.[8] It is supremely useful to have these kinds of tests: The person designing and securing a system will typically be blind to its (remaining) vulnerabilities. Outside consultants like penetration testers provide actual value by showing these vulnerabilities and allowing for an improved design.

Similar in result, yet different in execution are so-called "coordinated vulnerability disclosure"[9] practices or "bug bounty" programs. Coordinated vulnerability disclosure is a process in which people who find vulnerabilities in software can coordinate with software vendors to disclose this knowledge in a structured way so that these vendors can take action.[10] Bug bounty programs, on the other hand, are set up by software vendors to incentivize those who find security vulnerabilities to disclose them directly to the vendor and not exploit them for financial gain.[11] If they submit a security vulnerability under the program, the finder will receive financial compensation for this disclosure (the "bounty"). The more serious the vulnerability,

---

5 For a blue-sky perspective on this, see D. M. *Katz*, "The MIT School of Law?" (Oct. 22, 2014).

6 See p. 123.

7 A "controlled attack simulation that helps identify susceptibility to [security] breaches", see *U.S. Dpt. of the Interior, Office of CIO*, "Penetration Testing" (June 8, 2015).

8 *Ollam* and *Payne*, "Elevator Hacking" (Aug. 5, 2014), 1:02:00h onward.

9 Also known as "responsible disclosure".

10 See in detail *Householder* et al., "The CERT Guide to Coordinated Vulnerability Disclosure" (Aug. 2017).

11 For example, see Apple, Inc.'s program (https://security.apple.com/bounty/), Meta, Inc.'s program (https://www.facebook.com/whitehat), or Microsoft, Inc.'s program (https://www.microsoft.com/en-us/msrc/bounty). Most (large and small) software vendors have such a program.

the more money is awarded.[12] Ideally, these programs co-exist with the engagement of dedicated penetration testing professionals.

Note that—even though coordinated vulnerability disclosure and bug bounty programs are commonly accepted to be the "correct" way to treat people looking for vulnerabilities in code—there is also a second way: Prosecution and litigation.[13] This disincentivizes "ethical"[14] security research, strengthening the incentive for security researchers to "sell" vulnerabilities to criminals or state actors.[15]

Just like cyber- and physical security, anonymization is a field where the person anonymizing data is typically blind to the re-identification possibilities within the data.[16] To counteract this, businesses should enlist the help of re-identification professionals. To my knowledge, there are few people currently offering this kind of service on the market. However, with anonymization on the rise and the high cost of "bad" anonymization[17], demand for this type of service will surely pick up in the near future. As a result, professionals who can marry technical knowledge with some rudimentary knowledge of GDPR concepts will be in demand as high-value consultants.

Another promising avenue to better anonymization is the use of scoring and certification systems. In one example, the "General Data Anonimity Score" (GDA Score) compares the efficacy of anonymization and pseudonymization methods using the criteria laid out by the Art. 29 Working Party's anonymization Opinion[18].[19] The project combines a measurement of data utility and a measurement of how difficult it is to re-identify a person. This is extremely important work and helps the field as a whole.

---

12 As of the time of this writing, Apple, Inc.'s program would pay out up to $2 million for the highest category of vulnerability, see *Apple, Inc.*, "Categories - Apple Security Research" (2024).

13 For example, see the case of the German security researcher Lilith Wittmann and the German CDU party, *Wittmann*, "Die Staatsanwaltschaft sagt, ich habe die CDU nicht gehackt." (Sept. 17, 2021).

14 Also known as "white hat" security research.

15 As an example of the latter, the company Grayshift, LLC offers a product called "GrayKey" that can purportedly unlock cell phones protected by a passcode, see *Grayshift, LLC*, "GrayKey Cell Phone Forensics Tool" (2024). This technology is used by law enforcement agencies.

16 To illustrate, see numerous examples in this text, *e.g.* the release of Massachusetts medical data (see p. 138, the release of search data by AOL (see p. 195), and the Netflix release of data (see p. 123).

17 See p. 14.

18 *Article 29 Data Protection Working Party*, "0829/14/DE WP216" (2014).

19 "GDA Score – General Data Anonymity" (Jan. 2019).

14 Summary

1. "Information" in the sense of the GDPR is not just corporeal data, but to be viewed through a wider aperture, to include non-corporeal information such as knowledge.[1]
2. Object-related data, *i.e.*, data that does not relate to a natural person (identifiable or not) will continue to exist, even in the age of "big data", and its demarcation from personal data enables focused data protection.
3. Identification can be re-defined as an operation that is elementally based on comparison. Comparison can be done either deterministically, probabilistically, or heuristically. These comparisons enable two more complex operations: Linking and singling out. Using these two operations, we can assemble a chain of information that links the piece of information in question to a natural person. This chain ends, *i.e.*, identification has been performed, once this information allows for conceivably affecting the natural person or their assets in the real world.[2] The criterion of "inference" is not part of the definition of identification and is not helpful in defining anonymization.[3]
4. The commonly-made distinction between "identified" and "identifiable" natural persons in the context of the definition of personal data is superfluous at best and misleading at worst. It adds no legal or technical clarity and thus one should refrain from attempting to define it.[4] Similarly, none of the proposals for distinguishing between "direct" and "indirect" identification that have been put forward signifies a legal difference or aids in understanding the process of identification.[5]
5. The direction taken by the ECJ in *Breyer* means that a relative view of anonymity and anonymization needs to be taken. Nonetheless, as anonymization is concerned with making linking and singling out more difficult, the provenance of the auxiliary information is ultimately irrelevant for a survey of anonymization methods, with the exception of online methods.[6]

---

1 See p. 23.
2 See p. 71.
3 See p. 65.
4 See p. 83.
5 See p. 83.
6 See p. 102.

https://doi.org/10.1515/9783112222164-016

6. Syntactic anonymization methods, such as k-anonymity, have a limited scope of application, but can be successfully used to thwart re-identification. The degree of this success depends on the quality of the execution.[7]
7. Differential privacy offers a different kind of privacy guarantee, which can also be shown to thwart re-identification. Depending on values of ε (and δ), this can offer more robust privacy guarantees than syntactic anonymization methods. Especially valuable is DP's handling of composition and stringent, mathematical guarantees.[8]
8. A persistent challenge in the quest for anonymization is the existence of a privacy–utility tradeoff: The more private data is, the less useful it becomes. Nonetheless, depending on the application, the selection of a good anonymization mechanism can optimize this tradeoff.[9]
9. Different types of data require different kinds of anonymization. The anonymization of structured data, on which most literature is focused, is entirely different from the anonymization of unstructured data such as text.[10]
10. One avenue to performing this anonymization of unstructured data could be to use ML to find personal data within the text.[11] To gain sufficient training data for such a model, large amounts of human annotations are needed. In order to collect this information, a federated setup with a human-in-the-loop approach seems useful.[12]
11. When training ML models, deep neural networks in particular, the training data fed into the model may be extracted from the model at a later point in time. This can happen in the form of membership inference or model inversion attacks. As a result, models trained with personal data are personal data themselves, as long as they can reproduce their (personal) training data. This can be mitigated at the training stage through the use of privacy-enhancing technologies, but further (technical and legal) research is needed.[13]
12. The use of differential privacy during the training of a ML model seems like a promising avenue for maximizing utility while preserving data protection—for example using DP-SGD or PATE.[14]

---

7 See p. 138.
8 See p. 146.
9 See p. 96.
10 See p. 193.
11 See p. 210.
12 See p. 211.
13 See p. 214.
14 See p. 214.

13. In order to realize the real-world potential of anonymization for all kinds of data, legal and technical scholars and practitioners need to work together to bridge the “legal–technical divide”.[15]

15 See p. 229.

Jurisdiction

BGH Oct. 5, 2017. I ZR 7/16 (*ZD* 2018, pp. 79–82) (Cookie-Einwilligung).
BGH May 28, 2020. I ZR 7/16 (*NJW* 2020, pp. 2540–2547) (Cookie-Einwilligung II).
BGH June 15, 2021. VI ZR 576/19 (*NJW* 2021, pp. 2726–2729) (BGH: Umfang und Gegenstand des datenschutzrechtlichen Auskunftsanspruchs).
BVerfG Dec. 15, 1983. 1 BvR 209/83 and others (*BVerfGE* 65, pp. 1–71) (Volkszählungsurteil).
BVerfG Nov. 27, 2008. 1 BvQ 46/08 (*NJW* 2009, pp. 350–352) (Holzklotz).
ECJ Oct. 6, 1982. C-283/81 (CILFIT).
ECJ July 2, 1996. C-473/93 (Commission v. Grand Duchy of Luxembourg).
ECJ May 20, 2003. C-465/00, C-138/01, and C-139/01 (Österreichischer Rundfunk and Others).
ECJ Nov. 6, 2003. C-101/01 (Lindqvist).
ECJ Jan. 27, 2005. C-188/03 (Junk).
ECJ Dec. 16, 2008. C-524/06 (Huber).
ECJ May 7, 2009. C-553/07 (Rijkeboer).
ECJ June 3, 2010. C-569/08 (Internetportal und Marketing).
ECJ Nov. 9, 2010. Joined cases C-92/09 and C-93/09 (Volker und Markus Schecke).
ECJ June 9, 2011. C-52/10 (Alter Channel).
ECJ Nov. 24, 2011. C-70/10 (Scarlet Extended).
ECJ May 30, 2013. C-342/12 (Worten).
ECJ Oct. 3, 2013. C-298/12 (Conféderation Paysanne).
ECJ Oct. 17, 2013. C-291/12 (Schwarz v. Bochum).
ECJ July 17, 2014. C-141/12 and C-372/12 (YS and others).
ECJ Dec. 11, 2014. C-212/13 (Ryneš).
ECJ July 16, 2015. C-615/13 P (Client Earth v. EFSA).
ECJ Oct. 6, 2015. C-362/14 (Schrems I).
ECJ Oct. 19, 2016. C-582/14 (Breyer).
ECJ Mar. 9, 2017. C-398/15 (Manni).
ECJ Dec. 20, 2017. C-434/16 (Nowak).
ECJ Feb. 14, 2019. C-345/17 (Buivids).
ECJ Oct. 1, 2019. C-673/17 (Cookies).
ECJ July 16, 2020. C-311/18 (Schrems II).
ECJ June 17, 2021. C-597/19 (M.I.C.M.).
ECJ June 22, 2021. C-439/19 (Penalty Points).
ECJ Feb. 24, 2022. C-175/20 (Valsts ieņēmumu dienests).
ECJ May 4, 2023. C-487/21 (FF v. ÖDSB and CRIF).
ECJ June 22, 2023. C-579/21 (Pankki S).
ECJ Nov. 9, 2023. C-319/22 (Gesamtverband Autoteile-Handel).
ECJ Dec. 5, 2023. C-683/21 (Nacionalinis).
ECJ Mar. 7, 2024. C-479/22 P (O.C.).
ECJ Mar. 7, 2024. C-604/22 (IAB Europe).
EGC Apr. 26, 2023. T-557/20 (*ZD* 2023, pp. 399–404) (Single Resolution Board v. EDPS).
LG Hamburg Jan. 14, 2022. 308 O 130/19 (*GRUR-RR* 2022, pp. 253–257) (Adblocker).
OLG Hamburg Mar. 15, 2018. 5 U 152/15 (*GRUR-RS* 2018, p. 6040) (OLG Hamburg: Werbeblocker).
OVG Lüneburg Jan. 19, 2021. 11 LA 16/20 (OVG Lüneburg: Facebook Fanpage).
ÖVwGH May 17, 2024. Ra 2023/04/0005 (*ZD* 2025, pp. 144–147) (ÖVwGH, Ra 2023/04/0005).
U.S. Supreme Court Mar. 26, 1963. 378 U.S. 184 (Jacobellis v. Ohio).

https://doi.org/10.1515/9783112222164-017

Bibliography

Abadi, Martín, Andy *Chu*, et al. "Deep Learning with Differential Privacy." In: *Proceedings of the 2016 ACM SIGSAC Conference on Computer and Communications Security*. Oct. 24, 2016, pp. 308–318. DOI: 10.1145/2976749.2978318. arXiv: 1607.00133 [cs, stat]. URL: http://arxiv.org/abs/1607.00133 (visited on 05/18/2023).

Abadi, Martín, Úlfar *Erlingsson*, et al. "On the Protection of Private Information in Machine Learning Systems: Two Recent Approaches." In: *2017 IEEE 30th Computer Security Foundations Symposium (CSF)*. Aug. 2017, pp. 1–6. DOI: 10.1109/CSF.2017.10. arXiv: 1708.08022 [cs, stat]. URL: http://arxiv.org/abs/1708.08022 (visited on 03/29/2024).

Abowd, John and Victoria *Velkoff*. *Modernizing Privacy Protections for the 2020 Census: Next Steps*. The United States Census Bureau. Apr. 28, 2021. URL: https://www.census.gov/newsroom/blogs/random-samplings/2021/04/modernizing_privacy.html (visited on 05/15/2023).

Acar, Abbas et al. "A Survey on Homomorphic Encryption Schemes: Theory and Implementation." In: *ACM Computing Surveys* 51.4 (July 25, 2018), 79:1–79:35. ISSN: 0360-0300. DOI: 10.1145/3214303. URL: https://dl.acm.org/doi/10.1145/3214303 (visited on 06/27/2023).

Acquisti, Alessandro, Curtis *Taylor*, and Liad *Wagman*. "The Economics of Privacy." In: *Journal of Economic Literature* 54.2 (June 2016), pp. 442–492. ISSN: 0022-0515. DOI: 10.1257/jel.54.2.442.

Adobe, Inc. Redact & Sanitize | Adobe Document Cloud. Redact & Sanitize. Mar. 7, 2022. URL: https://experienceleague.adobe.com/docs/document-cloud-learn/acrobat-learning/advanced-tasks/redact.html?lang=en (visited on 02/21/2023).

Adobe, Inc. PDF properties and metadata. PDF Properties and Metadata. Feb. 7, 2023. URL: https://helpx.adobe.com/content/help/en/acrobat/using/pdf-properties-metadata.html (visited on 02/19/2023).

Adriaans, Pieter. "Information." In: *The Stanford Encyclopedia of Philosophy*. Ed. by Edward N. Zalta. Fall 2020. Metaphysics Research Lab, Stanford University, 2020. URL: https://plato.stanford.edu/archives/fall2020/entries/information/ (visited on 03/21/2023).

Agencia Española Protección Datos and *European Data Protection Supervisor*. *10 Misunderstandings Related to Anonymisation*. Apr. 27, 2021. URL: https://edps.europa.eu/system/files/2021-04/21-04-27_aepd-edps_anonymisation_en_5.pdf (visited on 04/09/2023).

Aggarwal, Charu C. and Philip S. *Yu*. "An Introduction to Privacy-Preserving Data Mining." In: *Privacy-Preserving Data Mining: Models and Algorithms*. Red. by Ahmed K. Elmagarmid and Amit P. Sheth. Vol. 34. Advances in Database Systems. Boston, MA: Springer US, 2008, pp. 1–9. ISBN: 978-0-387-70991-8. DOI: 10.1007/978-0-387-70992-5. URL: http://link.springer.com/10.1007/978-0-387-70992-5 (visited on 11/18/2022).

Aggarwal, Charu C. and Philip S. *Yu*, eds. *Privacy-Preserving Data Mining: Models and Algorithms*. Red. by Ahmed K. Elmagarmid and Amit P. Sheth. Vol. 34. Advances in Database Systems. Boston, MA: Springer US, 2008. ISBN: 978-0-387-70991-8. DOI: 10.1007/978-0-387-70992-5. URL: http://link.springer.com/10.1007/978-0-387-70992-5 (visited on 11/18/2022).

Albrecht, Jan Philipp and Florian *Jotzo*. *Teil 3: Allgemeine Bestimmungen*. In: *Das neue Datenschutzrecht der EU*. 1st ed. Baden-Baden, 2017. ISBN: 978-3-8487-2804-6.

Altman, Micah, Aloni *Cohen*, Francesca *Falzon*, et al. *A Principled Approach to Defining Anonymization As Applied to EU Data Protection Law*. May 9, 2022. DOI: 10.2139/ssrn.4104748. URL: https://papers.ssrn.com/abstract=4104748 (visited on 04/08/2023). Pre-published.

https://doi.org/10.1515/9783112222164-018

Altman, Micah, Aloni *Cohen*, Kobbi *Nissim*, et al. "What a Hybrid Legal-Technical Analysis Teaches Us about Privacy Regulation: The Case of Singling out." In: *Boston University Journal of Science and Technology Law* 27.1 (2021), pp. 1–63.

Anandan, Balamurugan et al. "t-Plausibility: Generalizing Words to Desensitize Text." In: *Transactions on Data Privacy* 5.3 (Dec. 1, 2012), pp. 505–534. ISSN: 1888-5063. URL: https://dl.acm.org/doi/10.5555/2423656.2423657.

AOL search log release. In: *Wikipedia*. Dec. 18, 2022. URL: https://en.wikipedia.org/wiki/AOL_search_log_release (visited on 04/22/2023).

Appenzeller, Arno, Moritz *Leitner*, et al. "Privacy and Utility of Private Synthetic Data for Medical Data Analyses." In: *Applied Sciences* 12.23 (23, 12320 Jan. 2022), pp. 1–19. ISSN: 2076-3417. DOI: 10.3390/app122312320. URL: https://www.mdpi.com/2076-3417/12/23/12320 (visited on 07/06/2023).

Appenzeller, Arno and Berna *Orak*. "Das Re-Identifikationsrisiko bei der Weitergabe von Gesundheitsdaten: Eine rechtliche und technische Analyse." In: *Datenschutz und Datensicherheit* 48.5 (May 2024), pp. 277–283. ISSN: 1614-0702, 1862-2607. DOI: 10.1007/s11623-024-1930-1.

Apple, Inc., director. *Apple – WWDC 2016 Keynote*. June 15, 2016. URL: https://www.youtube.com/watch?v=n5jXg_NNiCA (visited on 06/19/2023).

Apple, Inc. Differential Privacy Overview. Nov. 2, 2017. URL: https://www.apple.com/privacy/docs/Differential_Privacy_Overview.pdf (visited on 05/24/2023).

Apple, Inc. Apple Privacy-Preserving Machine Learning Workshop 2022. Apple Machine Learning Research. 2022. URL: https://machinelearning.apple.com/updates/ppml-workshop-2022 (visited on 05/24/2023).

Apple, Inc. About iCloud Private Relay. Apple Support. Dec. 20, 2022. URL: https://support.apple.com/en-us/HT212614 (visited on 02/15/2023).

Apple, Inc. Annotate a PDF in Preview on Mac. Apple Support. 2023. URL: https://support.apple.com/guide/preview/annotate-a-pdf-prvw11580/mac (visited on 01/15/2023).

Apple, Inc. Categories - Apple Security Research. Categories - Apple Security Research. 2024. URL: https://security.apple.com/bounty/categories/ (visited on 04/30/2023).

Arning, Marian, Nikolaus *Forgó*, and Tina *Krügel*. "Datenschutzrechtliche Aspekte der Forschung mit genetischen Daten." In: *Datenschutz und Datensicherheit* 30.11 (Nov. 2006), pp. 700–705. ISSN: 1614-0702, 1862-2607. DOI: 10.1007/s11623-006-0195-1.

Arning and *Rothkegel*. *DS-GVO Art. 4 Begriffsbestimmungen*. In: *DSGVO - BDSG - TTDSG*. Ed. by Taeger and Gabel. 4th ed. Frankfurt am Main: Deutscher Fachverlag, Fachmedien Recht und Wirtschaft, 2022. ISBN: 978-3-8005-1760-2.

Arrington, Michael. *AOL Proudly Releases Massive Amounts of Private Data*. TechCrunch. Aug. 7, 2006. URL: https://techcrunch.com/2006/08/06/aol-proudly-releases-massive-amounts-of-user-search-data/ (visited on 04/22/2023).

Article 29 Data Protection Working Party. First Annual Report. June 25, 1997. URL: https://ec.europa.eu/justice/article-29/documentation/annual-report/files/1997/wp3_en.pdf (visited on 05/01/2023).

Article 29 Data Protection Working Party. Opinion 4/2007 on the concept of personal data (WP 136, 01248/07/EN). 2007. URL: https://ec.europa.eu/justice/article-29/documentation/opinion-recommendation/files/2007/wp136_en.pdf (visited on 01/13/2024).

Article 29 Data Protection Working Party. Opinion 3/2013 on purpose limitation (WP 203, 00569/13/EN). 2014. URL: https://ec.europa.eu/justice/article-29/documentation/opinion-recommendation/files/2013/wp203_en.pdf (visited on 01/13/2024).

Article 29 Data Protection Working Party. Opinion 5/2014 on anonymization techniques (WP 216, 0829/14/EN). 2014. URL: https://ec.europa.eu/justice/article-29/documentation/opinion-recommendation/files/2014/wp216_en.pdf (visited on 01/13/2024).

Article 29 Data Protection Working Party. Appendix: Core topics in the view of trilogue. June 17, 2017. URL: https://ec.europa.eu/justice/article-29/documentation/other-document/files/2015/20150617_appendix_core_issues_plenary_en.pdf (visited on 04/24/2024).

Augsberg, Steffen and Johannes *Buchheim*. "Von der Verarbeitung personenbezogener Daten zur personenbezogenen Datenverarbeitung." In: *JuristenZeitung* 79.9 (Apr. 29, 2024), pp. 365–375. ISSN: 1868-7067. DOI: 10.1628/jz-2024-0119.

Austrian Data Protection Authority. "ÖDSB, 22.4.2022 - D155.026 2022-0.298.191 - Datenübermittlung durch Implementierung von Google Analytics." In: *Zeitschrift für Datenschutz* (2022), pp. 493–497.

AXA ResearchFundLive, director. *Internet of Things & Data Protection Conference (Paul Ohm)*. Nov. 20, 2017. URL: https://www.youtube.com/watch?v=FlauPJ55kms (visited on 04/24/2024).

Bagdasaryan, Eugene, Omid *Poursaeed*, and Vitaly *Shmatikov*. "Differential privacy has disparate impact on model accuracy." In: *Advances in neural information processing systems* 32 (2019). URL: https://proceedings.neurips.cc/paper/2019/hash/fc0de4e0396fff257ea362983c2dda5a-Abstract.html (visited on 03/30/2024).

Bambauer, Jane and Krishnamurty *Muralidhar*. *Diffensive Privacy*. May 17, 2016. URL: https://web.archive.org/web/20180723185552/http://blogs.harvard.edu/infolaw/2016/05/17/diffensive-privacy/ (visited on 04/07/2023).

Bambauer, Jane, Krishnamurty *Muralidhar*, and Rathindra *Sarathy*. "Fool's Gold: An Illustrated Critique of Differential Privacy." In: *Vanderbilt Journal of Entertainment and Technology Law* 16.4 (2013–2014), pp. 701–756.

Barbaro, Michael and Tom Zeller *Jr*. "A Face Is Exposed for AOL Searcher No. 4417749." In: *The New York Times. Technology* (Aug. 9, 2006). ISSN: 0362-4331. URL: https://www.nytimes.com/2006/08/09/technology/09aol.html (visited on 04/22/2023).

Barnett, James. *Global postal codes regex formats*. URL: https://gist.github.com/jamesbar2/1c677c22df8f21e869cca7e439fc3f5b (visited on 01/28/2023).

Bartels, Marvin. "A Balancing Act: Data Protection Compliance of Artificial Intelligence." In: *Gewerblicher Rechtsschutz und Urheberrecht Internationaler Teil* 6 (2024), pp. 526–537.

Barth-Jones, Daniel C. *The 'Re-Identification' of Governor William Weld's Medical Information: A Critical Re-Examination of Health Data Identification Risks and Privacy Protections, Then and Now*. 2012. DOI: 10.2139/ssrn.2076397. URL: http://www.ssrn.com/abstract=2076397 (visited on 02/06/2023). Pre-published.

Bauer, Felix. *Break my Life's Work and I'll Pay You Handsomely*. Aircloak. Aug. 22, 2018. URL: https://aircloak.com/break-my-lifes-work-and-ill-pay-you-handsomely/ (visited on 07/05/2023).

Bellovin, Steven M., Preetam K. *Dutta*, and Nathan *Reitinger*. "Privacy and Synthetic Datasets." In: *Stanford Technology Law Review* 22.1 (2019), pp. 1–52.

Bergt, Matthias. "Die Bestimmbarkeit als Grundproblem des Datenschutzrechts – Überblick über den Theorienstreit und Lösungsvorschlag." In: *Zeitschrift für Datenschutz* (2015), pp. 365–371.

Bertrand, Marianne and Sendhil *Mullainathan*. "Are Emily and Greg More Employable than Lakisha and Jamal? A Field Experiment on Labor Market Discrimination." In: *American Economic Review*. Working Paper Series 94.4 (July 2003), pp. 991–1013. DOI: 10.1257/0002828042002561. URL: https://www.nber.org/papers/w9873 (visited on 05/15/2023).

DIN 5008:2020-03, Schreib- und Gestaltungsregeln für die Text- und Informationsverarbeitung. Beuth Verlag GmbH, 2020. DOI: 10.31030/3134524. URL: https://www.beuth.de/de/-/-/318422674 (visited on 02/06/2023).

Beyvers, Eva. *Privatheit in der Waagschale. Instrumente des datenschutzrechtlichen Interessenausgleichs im Kontext sozialer Online-Netzwerke*. 1st ed. Vol. 9. Internetrecht und Digitale Gesellschaft. Berlin: Duncker & Humblot, 2018. 361 pp. ISBN: 978-3-428-55350-1. DOI: 10.3790/978-3-428-55350-1.

Bhowmick, Abhishek et al. *Protection Against Reconstruction and Its Applications in Private Federated Learning*. June 3, 2019. DOI: 10.48550/arXiv.1812.00984. arXiv: 1812.00984 [cs, stat]. URL: http://arxiv.org/abs/1812.00984 (visited on 04/01/2024). Pre-published.

Birthday problem. In: *Wikipedia*. May 11, 2023. URL: https://en.wikipedia.org/wiki/Birthday_problem (visited on 05/20/2023).

Black, John, Martin *Cochran*, and Trevor *Highland*. "A Study of the MD5 Attacks: Insights and Improvements." In: *Fast Software Encryption*. Ed. by Matthew Robshaw. Red. by David Hutchison et al. Vol. 4047. Berlin, Heidelberg: Springer, 2006, pp. 262–277. ISBN: 978-3-540-36597-6. DOI: 10.1007/11799313_17.

Boehme-Neßler, Volker. "Das Ende der Anonymität: Wie Big Data das Datenschutzrecht verändert." In: *Datenschutz und Datensicherheit* 40.7 (July 2016), pp. 419–423. ISSN: 1614-0702, 1862-2607. DOI: 10.1007/s11623-016-0629-3.

Boenisch, Franziska. "Privatsphäre und Maschinelles Lernen." In: *Datenschutz und Datensicherheit* 45.7 (July 1, 2021), pp. 448–452. ISSN: 1862-2607. DOI: 10.1007/s11623-021-1469-3.

Boenisch, Franziska, Adam *Dziedzic*, et al. "When the Curious Abandon Honesty: Federated Learning Is Not Private." In: 2023 IEEE 8th European Symposium on Security and Privacy (EuroS&P). IEEE Computer Society, July 10, 2023, pp. 175–199. ISBN: 978-1-66546-512-0. DOI: 10.1109/EuroSP57164.2023.00020. URL: https://www.computer.org/csdl/proceedings-article/eurosp/2023/651200a175/1OFthjlQRxu (visited on 04/13/2024).

Boenisch, Franziska, Christopher *Mühl*, et al. *Individualized PATE: Differentially Private Machine Learning with Individual Privacy Guarantees*. Nov. 8, 2022. DOI: 10.48550/arXiv.2202.10517. arXiv: 2202.10517 [cs]. URL: http://arxiv.org/abs/2202.10517 (visited on 03/30/2024). Pre-published.

Boenisch, Franziska, Reinhard *Munz*, et al. "Side-Channel Attacks on Query-Based Data Anonymization." In: *Proceedings of the 2021 ACM SIGSAC Conference on Computer and Communications Security*. CCS '21. New York, NY, USA: Association for Computing Machinery, Nov. 13, 2021, pp. 1254–1265. ISBN: 978-1-4503-8454-4. DOI: 10.1145/3460120.3484751.

Bommarito, Michael James II and Daniel Martin *Katz*. *GPT Takes the Bar Exam*. 2022. DOI: 10.2139/ssrn.4314839. URL: https://www.ssrn.com/abstract=4314839 (visited on 03/20/2023). Pre-published.

Bonawitz, Kallista et al. "Federated Learning and Privacy: Building privacy-preserving systems for machine learning and data science on decentralized data." In: *Queue* 19.5 (Oct. 31, 2021), pp. 87–114. ISSN: 1542-7730, 1542-7749. DOI: 10.1145/3494834.3500240. URL: https://dl.acm.org/doi/10.1145/3494834.3500240 (visited on 05/19/2023).

Booth, Sharon et al. *What are 'Personal Data'? – A study conducted for the UK Information Commissioner*. 2004. URL: https://www.frareg.com/cms/wp-content/uploads/personal_data.pdf (visited on 05/03/2024).

Bourtoule, Lucas et al. *Machine Unlearning*. Dec. 15, 2020. DOI: 10.48550/arXiv.1912.03817. arXiv: 1912.03817 [cs]. URL: http://arxiv.org/abs/1912.03817 (visited on 03/30/2024). Pre-published.

Box, George E. P. "Science and Statistics." In: *Journal of the American Statistical Association* 71.356 (Dec. 1, 1976), pp. 791–799. ISSN: 0162-1459. DOI: 10.1080/01621459.1976.10480949. URL: https://www.tandfonline.com/doi/abs/10.1080/01621459.1976.10480949 (visited on 02/02/2024).

Brauneck, Jens. "Brauneck: DSGVO: Neue Anwendbarkeit durch neue Definition personenbezogener Daten?" In: *Europäische Zeitschrift für Wirtschaftsrecht* 16 (2019), pp. 680–688.

Bremert, Benjamin. *Keine Zukunft für frei dokumentierte Rechtsprechung? - openJur wird verklagt*. Jan. 22, 2024. URL: https://openjur.de/i/openjur_wird_verklagt.html (visited on 05/02/2024).

Breyer, Patrick. "Personenbezug von IP-Adressen Internetnutzung und Datenschutz." In: *Zeitschrift für Datenschutz* (2014), pp. 400–404.

Brickell, Justin and Vitaly *Shmatikov*. "The cost of privacy: destruction of data-mining utility in anonymized data publishing." In: *Proceedings of the 14th ACM SIGKDD international conference on Knowledge discovery and data mining*. KDD '08. New York, NY, USA: Association for Computing Machinery, Aug. 24, 2008, pp. 70–78. ISBN: 978-1-60558-193-4. DOI: 10.1145/1401890.1401904.

Bruegger, Bud P. *Towards a Better Understanding of Identification, Pseudonymization, and Anonymization (v 1.0)*. June 11, 2021. URL: https://uld-sh.de/PseudoAnon (visited on 07/16/2023).

Buchholtz, Gabriele, Alissa *Brauneck*, and Louisa *Schmalhorst*. "Gelingensbedingungen der Datentreuhand – rechtliche und technische Aspekte." In: *Neue Zeitschrift für Verwaltungsrecht* 4 (2023), pp. 206–212.

Bundesamt für Justiz. *Ausbildungsstatistik 2011*. Oct. 2012. URL: https://www.bundesjustizamt.de/SharedDocs/Downloads/DE/Justizstatistiken/Juristenausbildung_2011.pdf?__blob=publicationFile&v=3 (visited on 07/05/2023).

Bundesamt für Justiz. *Justizstatistiken*. 2024. URL: https://www.bundesjustizamt.de/DE/Service/Justizstatistiken/Justizstatistiken_node.html#AnkerDokument44060 (visited on 07/05/2023).

Butler, Declan. "Censored words unmasked." In: *Nature* (May 13, 2004). ISSN: 1476-4687. DOI: 10.1038/news040510-8. URL: https://www.nature.com/articles/news040510-8 (visited on 01/29/2023).

Cao, Yinzhi and Junfeng *Yang*. "Towards Making Systems Forget with Machine Unlearning." In: *2015 IEEE Symposium on Security and Privacy*. 2015 IEEE Symposium on Security and Privacy. May 2015, pp. 463–480. DOI: 10.1109/SP.2015.35. URL: https://ieeexplore.ieee.org/document/7163042 (visited on 03/30/2024).

Carvalho, Tânia et al. "Survey on Privacy-Preserving Techniques for Microdata Publication." In: *ACM Computing Surveys* (Mar. 28, 2023). ISSN: 0360-0300. DOI: 10.1145/3588765. URL: https://dl.acm.org/doi/10.1145/3588765 (visited on 07/06/2023).

Caspar, Johannes. "Geoinformationen und Datenschutz am Beispiel des Dienstes Google Street View." In: *Die öffentliche Verwaltung* 23 (2009), pp. 965–973.

Chalkidis, Ilias et al. "LexGLUE: A Benchmark Dataset for Legal Language Understanding in English." In: *Proceedings of the 60th Annual Meeting of the Association for Computational Linguistics (Volume 1: Long Papers)*. ACL 2022. Dublin, Ireland: Association for Computational Linguistics, May 2022, pp. 4310–4330. DOI: 10.18653/v1/2022.acl-long.297. URL: https://aclanthology.org/2022.acl-long.297 (visited on 07/06/2023).

Chawla, Shuchi et al. "Toward Privacy in Public Databases." In: *Theory of Cryptography*. Ed. by Joe Kilian. Lecture Notes in Computer Science. Berlin, Heidelberg: Springer, 2005, pp. 363–385. ISBN: 978-3-540-30576-7. DOI: 10.1007/978-3-540-30576-7_20.

Chen, Min et al. "When Machine Unlearning Jeopardizes Privacy." In: *Proceedings of the 2021 ACM SIGSAC Conference on Computer and Communications Security*. CCS '21. New York, NY, USA: Association for Computing Machinery, Nov. 13, 2021, pp. 896–911. ISBN: 978-1-4503-8454-4. DOI: 10.1145/3460120.3484756. URL: https://dl.acm.org/doi/10.1145/3460120.3484756 (visited on 03/30/2024).

Chong, Stephen. *Sotto Voce: Differentially Private Federated Learning for Speech Recognition*. Harvard University Privacy Tools Project. 2024. URL: https://privacytools.seas.harvard.edu/sotto-voce-differentially-private-federated-learning-speech-recognition (visited on 04/13/2023).

Citron, Danielle Keats and Daniel J. *Solove*. "Privacy Harms." In: *Boston University Law Review* 102 (2022), pp. 793–863. DOI: 10.2139/ssrn.3782222.

Clarke, Roger. *The Id-Anonymity Spectrum*. Apr. 30, 1999. URL: http://www.rogerclarke.com/DV/UIPP99.html (visited on 04/27/2024).

Codd, E. F. “A relational model of data for large shared data banks.” In: *Communications of the ACM* 13.6 (June 1970), pp. 377–387. ISSN: 0001-0782, 1557-7317. DOI: 10.1145/362384.362685. URL: https://dl.acm.org/doi/10.1145/362384.362685 (visited on 04/13/2024).

Cohen, Aloni and Kobbi *Nissim*. “Towards formalizing the GDPR’s notion of singling out.” In: *Proceedings of the National Academy of Sciences* 117.15 (Apr. 14, 2020), pp. 8344–8352. ISSN: 0027-8424, 1091-6490. DOI: 10.1073/pnas.1914598117. URL: https://pnas.org/doi/full/10.1073/pnas.1914598117 (visited on 11/28/2022).

Compagnucci, Marcelo Corrales et al. “Homomorphic Encryption: The ’Holy Grail’ for Big Data Analytics and Legal Compliance in the Pharmaceutical and Healthcare Sector?” In: *European Pharmaceutical Law Review (EPLR)* 3.4 (2019), pp. 144–155.

Conrad, Isabell and Christina *Treeger*. *§ 34 Recht des Datenschutzes*. In: *Handbuch IT- und Datenschutzrecht*. Ed. by Astrid Auer-Reinsdorff and Isabell Conrad. 3rd ed. Munich: C.H. Beck, 2019. ISBN: 978-3-406-72177-9.

Conway, Richard and David *Strip*. “Selective partial access to a database.” In: *Proceedings of the 1976 annual conference*. ACM ’76. New York, NY, USA: Association for Computing Machinery, Oct. 20, 1976, pp. 85–89. ISBN: 978-1-4503-7489-7. DOI: 10.1145/800191.805537. URL: https://dl.acm.org/doi/10.1145/800191.805537 (visited on 05/12/2023).

Costa, Luiz and Yves *Poullet*. “Privacy and the regulation of 2012.” In: *Computer Law & Security Review* 28.3 (June 1, 2012), pp. 254–262. ISSN: 0267-3649. DOI: 10.1016/j.clsr.2012.03.015. URL: https://www.sciencedirect.com/science/article/pii/S0267364912000672 (visited on 04/21/2024).

Council of Europe. *Convention for the Protection of Individuals with regard to Automatic Processing of Personal Data*. 1981. URL: https://rm.coe.int/1680078b37 (visited on 04/29/2023).

Coupette, Corinna. *Juristische Netzwerkforschung*. Tübingen: Mohr Siebeck, 2019. 376 pp. ISBN: 978-3-16-157012-4. DOI: 10.1628/978-3-16-157012-4.

Cummings, Rachel and Deven *Desai*. “The Role of Differential Privacy in GDPR Compliance. Position Paper.” In: *Proceedings of the Workshop on Responsible Recommendation (FATREC ’18)*. FATREC ’18. Vancouver, BC, Canada: ACM, Oct. 2018, p. 2.

Cunha, Mariana, Ricardo *Mendes*, and João P. *Vilela*. “A survey of privacy-preserving mechanisms for heterogeneous data types.” In: *Computer Science Review* 41 (Aug. 1, 2021), p. 100403. ISSN: 1574-0137. DOI: 10.1016/j.cosrev.2021.100403. URL: https://www.sciencedirect.com/science/article/pii/S1574013721000435 (visited on 06/14/2023).

D’Acquisto, Giuseppe et al. *Privacy by design in big data: An overview of privacy enhancing technologies in the era of big data analytics*. 2015. DOI: 10.2824/641480. arXiv: 1512.06000 [cs]. URL: http://arxiv.org/abs/1512.06000 (visited on 06/14/2023).

Dalenius, Tore. “Finding a Needle in a Haystack or Identifying Anonymous Census Records.” In: *Journal of Official Statistics Sweden* 2/1986.3 (1986), pp. 329–336. URL: https://www.scb.se/contentassets/ca21efb41fee47d293bbee5bf7be7fb3/finding-a-needle-in-a-haystack-or-identifying-anonymous-census-records.pdf (visited on 05/18/2023).

Dammann, Ulrich. *BDSG 2003 § 3 Weitere Begriffsbestimmungen: Personenbezogene Daten*. In: *Bundesdatenschutzgesetz*. Ed. by Spiros Simitis. 8th ed. Baden-Baden: Nomos, 2014, p. 2072. ISBN: 978-3-8487-0593-1.

Davis, Peter Alexander Earls. “Facial Detection and Smart Billboards: Analysing the ‘Identified’ Criterion of Personal Data in the GDPR.” In: *European Data Protection Law Review* 6.3 (2020), pp. 365–377. ISSN: 2364284X. DOI: 10.21552/edpl/2020/3/7.

Dayan, Ittai et al. “Federated learning for predicting clinical outcomes in patients with COVID-19.” In: *Nature Medicine* 27.10 (Oct. 2021), pp. 1735–1743. ISSN: 1078-8956, 1546-170X. DOI: 10.1038/s41591-021-01506-3. URL: https://www.nature.com/articles/s41591-021-01506-3 (visited on 02/13/2023).

De Castilho, Richard Eckart et al. “A Web-based Tool for the Integrated Annotation of Semantic and Syntactic Structures.” In: *Proceedings of the Workshop on Language Technology Resources and Tools for Digital Humanities (LT4DH)*. Osaka, Japan, Dec. 11, 2016, pp. 76–84.

De Montjoye, Yves-Alexandre et al. “Unique in the Crowd: The privacy bounds of human mobility.” In: *Scientific Reports* 3.1 (Mar. 25, 2013), p. 1376. ISSN: 2045-2322. DOI: 10.1038/srep01376. URL: https://www.nature.com/articles/srep01376 (visited on 02/06/2023).

Definition of “Identifying”. In: *Merriam-Webster Online Dictionary*. Apr. 11, 2023. URL: https://www.merriam-webster.com/dictionary/identifying (visited on 04/12/2023).

Definition of “Identity”. In: *Merriam-Webster Online Dictionary*. May 4, 2023. URL: https://www.merriam-webster.com/dictionary/identity (visited on 05/10/2023).

Deiwick, Hartmut. “Droht das Aus für Google Analytics in der EU?” In: *ZD-Aktuell* 7 (2022), p. 01125.

Der Bundesbeauftragte für den Datenschutz und die Informationsfreiheit. Öffentliches Konsultationsverfahren des Bundesbeauftragten für den Datenschutz und die Informationsfreiheit zum Thema Anonymisierung unter der DSGVO unter besonderer Berücksichtigung der TK-Branche. Feb. 10, 2020. URL: https://www.bfdi.bund.de/SharedDocs/Downloads/DE/Konsultationsverfahren/1_Anonymisierung/01_Anonymisierung-TK.pdf?__blob=publicationFile&v=5 (visited on 01/11/2023).

Der Hamburgische Beauftragte für Datenschutz und Informationsfreiheit. Diskussionspapier: Large Language Models und personenbezogene Daten. 2024. URL: https://datenschutz-hamburg.de/fileadmin/user_upload/HmbBfDI/Datenschutz/Informationen/240715_Diskussionspapier_HmbBfDI_KI_Modelle.pdf (visited on 05/15/2025).

Desfontaines, Damien. *Differential privacy in (a bit) more detail*. Ted is writing things. Aug. 16, 2018. URL: https://desfontain.es/privacy/differential-privacy-in-more-detail.html (visited on 06/19/2023).

Desfontaines, Damien. “Lowering the cost of anonymization.” Doctoral Thesis. ETH Zurich, 2020. DOI: 10.3929/ethz-b-000508570. URL: https://www.research-collection.ethz.ch/handle/20.500.11850/508570 (visited on 04/13/2024).

Desfontaines, Damien. *A list of real-world uses of differential privacy*. Ted is writing things. Oct. 1, 2021. URL: https://desfontain.es/privacy/real-world-differential-privacy.html.

Desfontaines, Damien. *Tiny bits matter: precision-based attacks on differential privacy*. Tumult Labs Blog. July 22, 2022. URL: https://www.tmlt.io/resources/tiny-bits-matter-precision-based-attacks-on-differential-privacy (visited on 07/08/2023).

Die Bundesbeauftragte für den Datenschuz und die Informationsfreiheit. FAQ zu Utiq. URL: https://www.bfdi.bund.de/DE/Fachthemen/Inhalte/Telefon-Internet/Positionen/FAQ-TrustPID.html (visited on 06/01/2025).

Distinguish. In: *Collins Dictionary*. Mar. 3, 2024. URL: https://www.collinsdictionary.com/dictionary/english/distinguish (visited on 03/03/2024).

Domingo-Ferrer, Josep, David *Sánchez*, and Alberto *Blanco-Justicia*. “The limits of differential privacy (and its misuse in data release and machine learning).” In: *Communications of the ACM* 64.7 (June 21, 2021), pp. 33–35. ISSN: 0001-0782. DOI: 10.1145/3433638.

Domingo-Ferrer, Josep and Jordi *Soria-Comas*. “From t-closeness to differential privacy and vice versa in data anonymization.” In: *Knowledge-Based Systems* 74 (2015), pp. 151–158. ISSN: 0950-7051. DOI: 10.1016/j.knosys.2014.11.011. URL: https://www.sciencedirect.com/science/article/pii/S0950705114004031 (visited on 04/07/2023).

Dwork, Cynthia. “Differential Privacy.” In: *Automata, Languages and Programming*. Ed. by Michele Bugliesi et al. Red. by David Hutchison et al. Vol. 4052. Berlin, Heidelberg: Springer, 2006, pp. 1–12. ISBN: 978-3-540-35907-4. DOI: 10.1007/11787006_1.

Dwork, Cynthia. "Differential Privacy: A Survey of Results." In: *Theory and Applications of Models of Computation.* Ed. by Manindra Agrawal et al. Vol. 4978. Berlin, Heidelberg: Springer, 2008, pp. 1–19. ISBN: 978-3-540-79227-7. DOI: 10.1007/978-3-540-79228-4_1.

Dwork, Cynthia, Ruth *Greenwood*, and Gary *King*. "There's a simple solution to the latest census fight." In: *The Boston Globe Online* (July 26, 2021). URL: https://www.bostonglobe.com/2021/07/26/opinion/theres-simple-solution-latest-census-fight/ (visited on 05/15/2023).

Dwork, Cynthia, Krishnaram *Kenthapadi*, et al. "Our Data, Ourselves: Privacy Via Distributed Noise Generation." In: *Advances in Cryptology - EUROCRYPT 2006*. Ed. by Serge Vaudenay. Vol. 4004. Berlin, Heidelberg: Springer, 2006, pp. 486–503. ISBN: 978-3-540-34546-6. DOI: 10.1007/11761679_29.

Dwork, Cynthia, Nitin *Kohli*, and Deirdre *Mulligan*. "Differential Privacy in Practice: Expose your Epsilons!" In: *Journal of Privacy and Confidentiality* 9.2 (2 Oct. 20, 2019). ISSN: 2575-8527. DOI: 10.29012/jpc.689. URL: https://journalprivacyconfidentiality.org/index.php/jpc/article/view/689 (visited on 04/08/2023).

Dwork, Cynthia, Frank *McSherry*, et al. "Calibrating Noise to Sensitivity in Private Data Analysis." In: *Journal of Privacy and Confidentiality* 7.3 (3 2016), pp. 17–51. ISSN: 2575-8527. DOI: 10.29012/jpc.v7i3.405. URL: https://journalprivacyconfidentiality.org/index.php/jpc/article/view/405 (visited on 04/08/2023).

Dwork, Cynthia and Aaron *Roth*. "The Algorithmic Foundations of Differential Privacy." In: *Foundations and Trends® in Theoretical Computer Science* 9.3-4 (2013), pp. 211–407. ISSN: 1551-305X, 1551-3068. DOI: 10.1561/0400000042. URL: http://www.nowpublishers.com/articles/foundations-and-trends-in-theoretical-computer-science/TCS-042 (visited on 09/03/2022).

Ehmann, Eugen. "Registermodernisierung in Deutschland." In: *Zeitschrift für Datenschutz* (2021), pp. 509–512.

Engeler, Malte and Louis *Rolfes*. "Datenschutzrechtliche Korrekturansprüche bei Erzeugung von Falschinformationen durch LLMs." In: *Zeitschrift für Datenschutz* 8 (2024), pp. 423–429.

Engrossed Substitute House Bill 1155 as passed by the House of Representatives and the Senate on the dates hereon set forth. Apr. 17, 2023. URL: https://lawfilesext.leg.wa.gov/biennium/2023-24/Pdf/Bills/Session%20Laws/House/1155-S.SL.pdf?q=20240502224753 (visited on 05/03/2024).

Erlingsson, Úlfar, Vasyl *Pihur*, and Aleksandra *Korolova*. "RAPPOR: Randomized Aggregatable Privacy-Preserving Ordinal Response." In: *Proceedings of the 2014 ACM SIGSAC Conference on Computer and Communications Security*. Nov. 3, 2014, pp. 1054–1067. DOI: 10.1145/2660267.2660348. arXiv: 1407.6981 [cs]. URL: http://arxiv.org/abs/1407.6981 (visited on 03/08/2023).

Ernst, Stefan. *DS-GVO Art. 4 Begriffsbestimmungen*. In: *Datenschutz-Grundverordnung, Bundesdatenschutzgesetz: DS-GVO BDSG*. Ed. by Boris Paal and Daniel Pauly. 3rd ed. Munich: C.H. Beck, 2021, p. 1560. ISBN: 978-3-406-75374-9.

European Commission. Towards a Thriving Data-Driven Economy. Brussels, July 2, 2014. URL: https://eur-lex.europa.eu/legal-content/EN/TXT/PDF/?uri=CELEX:52014DC0442&from=EN (visited on 01/16/2023).

European Data Protection Board. Endorsement 1/2018. 2018. URL: https://www.edpb.europa.eu/sites/default/files/files/news/endorsement_of_wp29_documents_en_0.pdf (visited on 03/16/2024).

European Data Protection Board. Agenda: 43rd EDPB Meeting 2020-12-15. Dec. 15, 2020. URL: https://edpb.europa.eu/sites/default/files/files/file1/20201215plen1.2agenda_public.pdf (visited on 04/09/2023).

European Data Protection Board. Minutes – 43rd Plenary Meeting on 2020-12-15. Jan. 14, 2021. URL: https://edpb.europa.eu/sites/default/files/files/file1/20201215plenfinalminutes43rdplenarymeeting_public_redacted.pdf (visited on 04/09/2023).

European Data Protection Board. EDPB Work Programme 2021/2022. Mar. 16, 2021. URL: https://edpb.europa.eu/system/files/2021-03/edpb_workprogramme_2021-2022_en.pdf (visited on 04/09/2023).

European Data Protection Board. EDPB Work Programme 2023/2024. Feb. 14, 2023. URL: https://edpb.europa.eu/system/files/2023-02/edpb_work_programme_2023-2024_en.pdf (visited on 04/09/2023).

European Data Protection Board. EDPB Annual Activity Report 2022. Apr. 17, 2023. URL: https://edpb.europa.eu/system/files/2023-04/edpb_annual_report_2022_en.pdf (visited on 04/18/2023).

European Data Protection Board. Secure personal data. Apr. 27, 2023. URL: https://edpb.europa.eu/sme-data-protection-guide/secure-personal-data_en (visited on 04/27/2023).

European Data Protection Board. Plenary Minutes Archive. 2024. URL: https://edpb.europa.eu/our-work-tools/our-documents/publication-type/minutes_en (visited on 04/09/2023).

European Data Protection Board. Opinion 28/2024 on Certain Data Protection Aspects Related to the Processing of Personal Data in the Context of AI Models. Dec. 17, 2024. URL: https://www.edpb.europa.eu/system/files/2024-12/edpb_opinion_202428_ai-models_en.pdf (visited on 05/15/2025).

European Data Protection Board. Guidelines 01/2025 on Pseudonymisation (Version for Public Consultation). Jan. 16, 2025. URL: https://www.edpb.europa.eu/system/files/2025-01/edpb_guidelines_202501_pseudonymisation_en.pdf (visited on 05/01/2025).

European Parliament. Decision re the judgment by the ECJ: Data Protection Commissioner v. Facebook Ireland Limited und Maximilian Schrems („Schrems II") — C-311/18. July 16, 2021. URL: https://eur-lex.europa.eu/legal-content/DE/TXT/?uri=CELEX%3A52021IP0256&qid=1681827530371 (visited on 04/18/2023).

European Union Agency for Fundamental Rights., Council of Europe (Strasbourg)., and *European Court of Human Rights. Handbook on European data protection law*. LU: Publications Office, 2014. URL: https://data.europa.eu/doi/10.2811/69915 (visited on 12/30/2023).

Exif Exchangeable Image File Format, Version 2.2. Feb. 26, 2014. URL: https://www.loc.gov/preservation/digital/formats/fdd/fdd000146.shtml (visited on 02/19/2023).

eyeo GmbH. About Adblock Plus. 2023. URL: https://new.adblockplus.org/en/about (visited on 02/16/2023).

Fan, Liyue. "Image Pixelization with Differential Privacy." In: *Data and Applications Security and Privacy XXXII*. Ed. by Florian Kerschbaum and Stefano Paraboschi. Lecture Notes in Computer Science. Cham: Springer International Publishing, 2018, pp. 148–162. ISBN: 978-3-319-95729-6. DOI: 10.1007/978-3-319-95729-6_10.

Farinho, Domingos. *GDPR Art. 4 § 1: Personal Data*. In: *General Data Protection Regulation*. Ed. by Indra Spiecker genannt Döhmann et al. 1st ed. Munich, Baden-Baden, Oxford: C.H. Beck, Nomos, Hart, 2023. ISBN: 978-3-406-74386-3.

Fellegi, Ivan P. and Alan B. *Sunter*. "A Theory for Record Linkage." In: *Journal of the American Statistical Association* 64.328 (Dec. 1, 1969), pp. 1183–1210. ISSN: 0162-1459. DOI: 10.1080/01621459.1969.10501049.

Feretzakis, Georgios et al. "GDPR and Large Language Models: Technical and Legal Obstacles." In: *Future Internet* 17 (Mar. 28, 2025), p. 151. DOI: 10.3390/fi17040151.

Feyisetan, Oluwaseyi, Tom *Diethe*, and Thomas *Drake*. "Leveraging Hierarchical Representations for Preserving Privacy and Utility in Text." In: *2019 IEEE International Conference on Data Mining (ICDM)*. 2019 IEEE International Conference on Data Mining (ICDM). Nov. 2019, pp. 210–219. DOI: 10.1109/ICDM.2019.00031.

FIDO Alliance. Passkeys (Passkey Authentication). FIDO Alliance. 2024. URL: https://fidoalliance.org/passkeys/ (visited on 05/04/2023).

Finck, Michele and Frank *Pallas*. "They who must not be identified—distinguishing personal from non-personal data under the GDPR." In: *International Data Privacy Law* 10.1 (2020), pp. 11–36.

FIT Europe and *EUATC*. *Comments on Guidelines 07/2020 on the concepts of controller and processor in the GDPR from the perspective of the Translation and Interpreting Sector*. 2020. URL: https://edpb.europa.eu/sites/default/files/webform/public_consultation_reply/response_to_edpb_controller_processor_public_consultation_from_fit-europe_euatc_final.pdf (visited on 04/09/2023).

Forgó, Nikolaus and Tina *Krügel*. "Der Personenbezug von Geodaten – Cui bono, wenn alles bestimmbar ist?" In: *Multimedia und Recht Zeitschrift für Informations-, Telekommunikations- und Medienrecht* 1 (2010), pp. 17–23.

Francis, Paul. *The 4 Pillars of GDPR Compliance Assurance in Data Anonymization*. Aircloak. Feb. 11, 2019. URL: https://www.aircloak.com/gdpr-compliance-assurance/ (visited on 07/05/2023).

Francis, Paul. *Differential Privacy: Not a complete disaster, I guess*. Medium. Apr. 12, 2020. URL: https://paul-francis.medium.com/differential-privacy-not-a-complete-disaster-i-guess-d0345a76a5af (visited on 05/18/2023).

Francis, Paul. *Dear Differential Privacy, Put Up or Shut Up*. Medium. Apr. 19, 2020. URL: https://paul-francis.medium.com/dear-differential-privacy-put-up-or-shut-up-48ff255ec35 (visited on 05/18/2023).

Francis, Paul, Sebastian Probst *Eide*, and Reinhard *Munz*. *Diffix-Aspen: High-Utility Database Anonymization*. June 2017. URL: https://aircloak.com/wp-content/uploads/apf17-aspen.pdf (visited on 05/03/2024). Pre-published.

Francis, Paul, Sebastian *Probst Eide*, and Reinhard *Munz*. "Diffix: High-Utility Database Anonymization." In: *Privacy Technologies and Policy*. Ed. by Erich Schweighofer et al. Vol. 10518. Cham: Springer International Publishing, 2017, pp. 141–158. ISBN: 978-3-319-67279-3. DOI: 10.1007/978-3-319-67280-9_8. URL: http://link.springer.com/10.1007/978-3-319-67280-9_8 (visited on 03/09/2023).

Francis, Paul, Sebastian *Probst-Eide*, Pawel *Obrok*, et al. *Diffix-Birch: Extending Diffix-Aspen*. Aug. 21, 2019. DOI: 10.48550/arXiv.1806.02075. arXiv: 1806.02075 [cs]. URL: http://arxiv.org/abs/1806.02075 (visited on 03/08/2023). Pre-published.

Francis, Paul, Sebastian *Probst-Eide*, David *Wagner*, et al. *Diffix Elm: Simple Diffix*. June 20, 2022. DOI: 10.48550/arXiv.2201.04351. arXiv: 2201.04351 [cs]. URL: http://arxiv.org/abs/2201.04351 (visited on 06/29/2023). Pre-published.

Franke, Lucia. "Datenschutzrechtskonformes Training von KI-Systemen mit öffentlich verfügbaren personenbezogenen Daten." In: *Recht Digital* 12 (2023), pp. 565–571.

Franzen, Martin. *VO (EU) 2016/679 Art. 4 Begriffsbestimmungen*. In: *Kommentar zum europäischen Arbeitsrecht*. Ed. by Martin Franzen, Inken Gallner, and Hartmut Oetker. 5th ed. Munich: C.H. Beck, 2024. ISBN: 978-3-406-79377-6.

Fredrikson, Matt, Somesh *Jha*, and Thomas *Ristenpart*. "Model Inversion Attacks that Exploit Confidence Information and Basic Countermeasures." In: *Proceedings of the 22nd ACM SIGSAC Conference on Computer and Communications Security*. CCS'15: The 22nd ACM Conference on Computer and Communications Security. Denver Colorado USA: ACM, Oct. 12, 2015, pp. 1322–1333. ISBN: 978-1-4503-3832-5. DOI: 10.1145/2810103.2813677. URL: https://dl.acm.org/doi/10.1145/2810103.2813677 (visited on 03/29/2024).

Freiling, Franz Hofmann Felix. "Personalisierte Preise und das Datenschutzrecht." In: *Zeitschrift für Datenschutz* 7 (2020), pp. 331–335.

Frome, Andrea et al. "Large-scale privacy protection in Google Street View." In: *2009 IEEE 12th International Conference on Computer Vision*. 2009 IEEE 12th International Conference on Computer Vision (ICCV). Kyoto: IEEE, Sept. 2009, pp. 2373–2380. ISBN: 978-1-4244-4420-5. DOI: 10.1109/ICCV.2009.5459413. URL: http://ieeexplore.ieee.org/document/5459413/ (visited on 07/13/2023).

Fuchs, Thomas, ed. *31. Tätigkeitsbericht Datenschutz 2022 Datenschutz des Hamburgischen Beauftragten für Datenschutz und Informationsfreiheit*. 2023. URL: https://datenschutz-hamburg.de/assets/pdf/Hamburg_Datenschutz_2022_web_final.pdf.

Gadotti, Andrea et al. *When the signal is in the noise: Exploiting Diffix's Sticky Noise*. Oct. 29, 2019. arXiv: 1804.06752 [cs]. URL: http://arxiv.org/abs/1804.06752 (visited on 06/29/2023). Pre-published.

Ganta, Srivatsava Ranjit, Shiva Prasad *Kasiviswanathan*, and Adam *Smith*. "Composition Attacks and Auxiliary Information in Data Privacy." In: *KDD '08: Proceedings of the 14th ACM SIGKDD International Conference on Knowledge Discovery and Data Mining*. ACM SIGKDD International Conference on Knowledge Discovery & Data Mining. Las Vegas, NV: ACM, Aug. 2008, pp. 265–273. DOI: 10.1145/1401890.1401926. arXiv: 0803.0032 [cs]. URL: http://arxiv.org/abs/0803.0032 (visited on 07/03/2023).

Gasser, Urs. "Recoding Privacy Law: Reflections on the Future Relationship Among Law, Technology, and Privacy." In: *Harvard Law Review Forum* 130.2 (Dec. 2016), pp. 61–70.

Gavison, Ruth. "Privacy and the Limits of Law." In: *The Yale Law Journal* 89.3 (1980), pp. 421–471. ISSN: 0044-0094. DOI: 10.2307/795891. JSTOR: 795891. URL: https://www.jstor.org/stable/795891 (visited on 06/19/2023).

GDA Score – General Data Anonymity. Jan. 2019. URL: https://www.gda-score.org/ (visited on 04/08/2023).

Geiping, Jonas et al. "Inverting Gradients - How easy is it to break privacy in federated learning?" In: *Advances in Neural Information Processing Systems*. Vol. 33. Curran Associates, Inc., 2020, pp. 16937–16947. URL: https://proceedings.neurips.cc/paper/2020/hash/c4ede56bbd98819ae6112b20ac6bf145-Abstract.html (visited on 04/08/2023).

Genesereth, Michael. *Computational Law: The Cop in the Backseat*. Stanford CodeX Whitepaper, 2015. URL: https://law.stanford.edu/publications/computational-law-the-cop-in-the-backseat/ (visited on 04/16/2024).

Gentry, Craig. "A Fully Homomorphic Encryption Scheme." Stanford, CA: Stanford University, 2009. 199 pp. ISBN: 978-1-109-44450-6. URL: https://dl.acm.org/doi/10.5555/1834954 (visited on 04/16/2024).

Gianola, Magda and Krzysztof *Pachacz*. *Introducing BigQuery differential privacy with Tumult Labs*. Google Cloud Blog. May 9, 2023. URL: https://cloud.google.com/blog/products/data-analytics/introducing-bigquery-differential-privacy-with-tumult-labs (visited on 07/03/2023).

Giomi, Matteo et al. "A Unified Framework for Quantifying Privacy Risk in Synthetic Data." In: *Proceedings on Privacy Enhancing Technologies*. Vol. 2023. Apr. 2023, pp. 312–328. DOI: 10.56553/popets-2023-0055. URL: https://petsymposium.org/popets/2023/popets-2023-0055.php (visited on 04/16/2024).

Gola, Peter. *DS-GVO Art. 4 Begriffsbestimmungen*. In: *Datenschutz-Grundverordnung - Bundesdatenschutzgesetz*. Ed. by Peter Gola and Dirk Heckmann. 3rd ed. Munich: C.H. Beck, 2022, p. 1864. ISBN: 978-3-406-78266-4.

Gont, Fernando. *A Method for Generating Semantically Opaque Interface Identifiers with IPv6 Stateless Address Autoconfiguration (SLAAC)*. Request for Comments RFC 7217. Internet Engineering Task Force, Apr. 2014. 19 pp. DOI: 10.17487/RFC7217. URL: https://datatracker.ietf.org/doc/rfc7217 (visited on 03/27/2023).

Google, Inc. Personenidentifizierbare Informationen in Verträgen und Richtlinien von Google - Google Analytics-Hilfe. Google Analytics Help. 2023. URL: https://support.google.com/analytics/answer/7686480?hl=de&ref_topic=1008008 (visited on 02/28/2023).

Google, Inc. IP masking in Universal Analytics - Analytics Help. 2023. URL: https://support.google.com/analytics/answer/2763052?hl=en (visited on 04/18/2023).

Google, Inc. EU-focused data and privacy - Analytics Help. 2023. URL: https://support.google.com/analytics/answer/12017362?hl=en&ref_topic=2919631&sjid=6512596891201025846-EU (visited on 04/18/2023).

Google, Inc. Analysetools und -lösungen für Ihr Unternehmen – Google Analytics. Google Marketing Platform. 2024. URL: https://marketingplatform.google.com/intl/de/about/analytics/ (visited on 02/15/2023).

Grayshift, LLC. GrayKey Cell Phone Forensics Tool. Grayshift. 2024. URL: https://www.grayshift.com/graykey/ (visited on 04/30/2023).

Greely, Henry T. "The uneasy ethical and legal underpinnings of large-scale genomic biobanks." In: *Annual Review of Genomics and Human Genetics* 8 (2007), pp. 343–364. ISSN: 1527-8204. DOI: 10.1146/annurev.genom.7.080505.115721.

Greenberg, Andy. "How One of Apple's Key Privacy Safeguards Falls Short." In: *Wired* (Sept. 15, 2017). ISSN: 1059-1028. URL: https://www.wired.com/story/apple-differential-privacy-shortcomings/ (visited on 04/14/2024).

Guevara, Michael. *How we're helping developers with differential privacy*. Google for Developers. Jan. 28, 2021. URL: https://developers.googleblog.com/2021/01/how-were-helping-developers-with-differential-privacy.html (visited on 07/03/2023).

Haase, Martin Sebastian. *Datenschutzrechtliche Fragen des Personenbezugs: eine Untersuchung des sachlichen Anwendungsbereiches des deutschen Datenschutzrechts und seiner europarechtlichen Bezüge*. Internet und Gesellschaft. Tübingen: Mohr Siebeck, 2015. 496 pp. ISBN: 978-3-16-153799-8.

Haase, Martin. "Rechtmäßigkeit der Benutzung personenbezogener Daten zum Trainieren künstlicher Intelligenz nach den Vorschriften der Datenschutz-Grundverordnung." In: *InTeR* 2023.02 (2023), pp. 66–71.

Haeberlen, Andreas, Benjamin C. *Pierce*, and Arjun *Narayan*. "Differential privacy under fire." In: *Proceedings of the 20th USENIX conference on Security*. SEC'11. USA: USENIX Association, Aug. 8, 2011, p. 33. URL: https://haeberlen.cis.upenn.edu/papers/fuzz-sec2011.pdf (visited on 05/02/2024).

Halevy, Alon, Peter *Norvig*, and Fernando *Pereira*. "The Unreasonable Effectiveness of Data." In: *IEEE Intelligent Systems* 24.2 (Mar. 2009), pp. 8–12. ISSN: 1541-1672. DOI: 10.1109/MIS.2009.36. URL: http://ieeexplore.ieee.org/document/4804817/ (visited on 02/13/2023).

Hallinan, D. and R. M. *Gellert*. "The Concept of 'Information'. An Invisible Problem in the GDPR." In: *SCRIPTed* 17.2 (Aug. 2020), pp. 269–319. DOI: 10.2966/scrip.170220.269. URL: https://repository.ubn.ru.nl/handle/2066/221377 (visited on 05/03/2023).

Hamburger Stadtteil-Profile: Berichtsjahr 2021. 2021. URL: https://www.statistik-nord.de/fileadmin/Dokumente/NORD.regional/Stadtteil-Profile_HH-BJ-2021.pdf (visited on 04/16/2024).

Hamza, Rafik et al. "Towards Secure Big Data Analysis via Fully Homomorphic Encryption Algorithms." In: *Entropy* 24.4 (4 Apr. 2022), p. 519. ISSN: 1099-4300. DOI: 10.3390/e24040519. URL: https://www.mdpi.com/1099-4300/24/4/519 (visited on 06/27/2023).

Hansen, Marit. *DS-GVO Art. 11*. In: *Datenschutzrecht*. Ed. by Spiros Simitis, Gerrit Hornung, and Indra Spiecker genannt Döhmann. 2nd ed. Baden-Baden: Nomos, 2025. ISBN: 978-3-8487-8958-0.

Hansen, Marit. *DSGVO Art. 4 Nr. 5 Begriffsbestimmung „Pseudonymisierung"*. In: *Datenschutzrecht*. Ed. by Spiros Simitis, Gerrit Hornung, and Indra Spiecker genannt Döhmann. 2nd ed. Baden-Baden: Nomos, 2025. ISBN: 978-3-8487-8958-0.

Hansen, Marit and Benjamin *Walczak*. "Pseudonymisierung à la DS-GVO und verwandte Methoden." In: *Recht der Datenverarbeitung* 35.2 (2019), pp. 53–57.

Hansen, Morris H. "Insuring confidentiality of individual records in data storage and retrieval for statistical purposes." In: *Proceedings of the May 16-18, 1972, spring joint computer conference on - AFIPS '72 (Spring)*. the May 16-18, 1972, spring joint computer conference. Atlantic City, New Jersey: ACM

Press, 1971, p. 579. DOI: 10.1145/1479064.1479167. URL: http://portal.acm.org/citation.cfm?doid=1479064.1479167 (visited on 05/12/2023).

Hard, Andrew et al. *Federated Learning for Mobile Keyboard Prediction*. Feb. 28, 2019. DOI: 10.48550/arXiv.1811.03604. arXiv: 1811.03604 [cs]. URL: http://arxiv.org/abs/1811.03604 (visited on 04/01/2024). Pre-published.

Heaton, Robert. *How Tinder keeps your exact location (a bit) private*. Robert Heaton. July 9, 2018. URL: https://robertheaton.com/2018/07/09/how-tinder-keeps-your-location-a-bit-private/ (visited on 11/18/2022).

Heider, Benjamin. "Videotelefonie im Homeoffice." In: *Neue Zeitschrift für Arbeitsrecht* 16 (2021), pp. 1149–1154.

Herbert B. Dixon, Jr. "Embarrassing Redaction Failures." In: *The Judges' Journal* 58.2 (Spr. 2019), pp. 37–39. URL: https://www.americanbar.org/content/dam/aba/publications/judges_journal/vol58no2-jj2019-tech.pdf (visited on 01/15/2023).

Hessisches Gesetz über offene Daten der Träger der öffentlichen Verwaltung (Hessisches Open Data-Gesetz – HODaG), Entwurf vom 17.01.2023. Jan. 17, 2023.

Hill, Steven et al. "On the (In)effectiveness of Mosaicing and Blurring as Tools for Document Redaction." In: *Proceedings on Privacy Enhancing Technologies* 2016.4 (Oct. 1, 2016), pp. 403–417. ISSN: 2299-0984. DOI: 10.1515/popets-2016-0047. URL: https://petsymposium.org/popets/2016/popets-2016-0047.php (visited on 07/13/2023).

Hintze, Mike. "Viewing the GDPR through a de-identification lens: a tool for compliance, clarification, and consistency." In: *International Data Privacy Law* 8.1 (Feb. 1, 2018), pp. 86–101. ISSN: 2044-3994, 2044-4001. DOI: 10.1093/idpl/ipx020. URL: https://papers.ssrn.com/sol3/papers.cfm?abstract_id=2909121 (visited on 03/13/2024).

Hoffmann-Riem, Wolfgang. "Verhaltenssteuerung durch Algorithmen – Eine Herausforderung für das Recht." In: *Archiv des öffentlichen Rechts (AöR)* 142.1 (2017), pp. 1–42. ISSN: 0003-8911. DOI: 10.1628/000389117X14894104852645.

Hölzel, Julian. "Anonymisierungstechniken und das Datenschutzrecht." In: *Datenschutz und Datensicherheit* 42.8 (Aug. 2018), pp. 502–509. ISSN: 1614-0702, 1862-2607. DOI: 10.1007/s11623-018-0988-z. URL: http://link.springer.com/10.1007/s11623-018-0988-z (visited on 09/03/2022).

Hölzel, Julian. "Differential Privacy and the GDPR." In: *European Data Protection Law Review* 5.2 (2019), pp. 184–196. ISSN: 23642831, 2364284X. DOI: 10.21552/edpl/2019/2/8. URL: http://edpl.lexxion.eu/article/EDPL/2019/2/8 (visited on 01/09/2023).

Hornung, Gerrit and Indra *Spiecker genannt Döhmann*. *Einleitung*. In: *Datenschutzrecht*. Ed. by Spiros Simitis, Gerrit Hornung, and Indra Spiecker genannt Döhmann. 2nd ed. Baden-Baden: Nomos, 2025. ISBN: 978-3-8487-8958-0.

Householder, Allen D et al. *The CERT Guide to Coordinated Vulnerability Disclosure*. Aug. 2017. URL: https://insights.sei.cmu.edu/documents/1945/2017_003_001_503340.pdf (visited on 05/03/2024).

Hsu, Justin et al. "Differential Privacy: An Economic Method for Choosing Epsilon." In: *2014 IEEE 27th Computer Security Foundations Symposium*. 2014 IEEE 27th Computer Security Foundations Symposium (CSF). Vienna: IEEE, July 2014, pp. 398–410. ISBN: 978-1-4799-4290-9. DOI: 10.1109/CSF.2014.35. URL: http://ieeexplore.ieee.org/document/6957125/ (visited on 06/27/2023).

Hu, Runshan et al. "Bridging policy, regulation and practice? A techno-legal analysis of three types of data in the GDPR." In: *Data protection and privacy: the age of intelligent machines*. Ed. by Ronald Leenes et al. Paperback edition. Computers, privacy and data protection vol. 10. Oxford, UK London New York New Delhi Sydney: Hart, 2020. ISBN: 978-1-5099-3748-6.

Hubert, Tom. "Daten und Sicherheit: Die Identifizierbarkeit i.S.d. Art. 4 Nr. 1 DSGVO insbesondere durch Informationen aus dem Internet." In: *Computer und Recht* (2025), pp. 77–85.

Hüger, Jakob. "Die Rechtmäßigkeit von Datenverarbeitungen im Lebenszyklus von KI-Systemen." In: *Zeitschrift für Digitalisierung und Recht* 3 (2024), pp. 263–291.

Identify. In: *Collins Dictionary*. 2024. URL: https://www.collinsdictionary.com/dictionary/english/identify (visited on 02/22/2024).

Identify. In: *Cambridge Dictionary*. Feb. 21, 2024. URL: https://dictionary.cambridge.org/dictionary/english/identify (visited on 02/22/2024).

Identify. In: *The Britannica Dictionary*. Feb. 22, 2024. URL: https://www.britannica.com/dictionary/identify (visited on 02/22/2024).

identify with someone. In: *Cambridge Dictionary*. Mar. 6, 2024. URL: https://dictionary.cambridge.org/dictionary/english/identify-with (visited on 03/10/2024).

identifyee. In: *Wiktionary*. May 4, 2023. URL: https://en.wiktionary.org/w/index.php?title=identifyee&oldid=72915819 (visited on 05/07/2023).

Institute, Information Sciences. *RFC 791*. Internet Protocol – DARPA Internet Program Protocol Specification. Sept. 1981. URL: https://www.ietf.org/rfc/rfc791.txt (visited on 09/11/2022).

International Speech Communication Association (ISCA). Comments: EDPB Guidelines 02/2021 on Virtual Voice Assistants. 2021. URL: https://edpb.europa.eu/sites/default/files/webform/public_consultation_reply/edpb_comments.pdf (visited on 04/09/2023).

ISO/IEC. ISO/IEC 5218:2022. URL: https://www.iso.org/standard/81682.html (visited on 12/03/2022).

Jäger, Christian et al. "Von der Sackgasse der Anonymisierung zu Lösungsansätzen für den Datenschutz der Zukunft." In: *Zeitschrift für Datenschutz* 9 (2024), pp. 490–495.

Jahn, Joachim. *BGH-Urteil nach zweijähriger Blockade veröffentlicht*. Beck-Aktuell. Dec. 18, 2018. URL: https://rsw.beck.de/aktuell/daily/meldung/detail/bgh-urteil-nach-zweijaehriger-blockade-veroeffentlicht (visited on 07/07/2024).

Jana, Abhik and Chris *Biemann*. "An Investigation towards Differentially Private Sequence Tagging in a Federated Framework." In: *Proceedings of the Third Workshop on Privacy in Natural Language Processing*. Proceedings of the Third Workshop on Privacy in Natural Language Processing. Online: Association for Computational Linguistics, 2021, pp. 30–35. DOI: 10.18653/v1/2021.privatenlp-1.4. URL: https://aclanthology.org/2021.privatenlp-1.4 (visited on 02/06/2023).

Jayaraman, Bargav and David *Evans*. *Evaluating Differentially Private Machine Learning in Practice*. Aug. 12, 2019. DOI: 10.48550/arXiv.1902.08874. arXiv: 1902.08874 [cs, stat]. URL: http://arxiv.org/abs/1902.08874 (visited on 04/01/2024). Pre-published.

Jones, Michael B. and Dick *Hardt*. *The OAuth 2.0 Authorization Framework: Bearer Token Usage*. Request for Comments RFC 6750. Internet Engineering Task Force, Oct. 2012. 18 pp. DOI: 10.17487/RFC6750. URL: https://datatracker.ietf.org/doc/rfc6750 (visited on 05/04/2023).

Juola, Patrick. "Authorship Attribution." In: *Foundations and Trends® in Information Retrieval* 1.3 (2007), pp. 233–334. ISSN: 1554-0669, 1554-0677. DOI: 10.1561/1500000005. URL: http://www.nowpublishers.com/article/Details/INR-005 (visited on 01/29/2023).

Karg, Moritz. "Anonymität, Pseudonyme und Personenbezug revisited?" In: *Datenschutz und Datensicherheit* 39.8 (Aug. 2015), pp. 520–526. ISSN: 1614-0702, 1862-2607. DOI: 10.1007/s11623-015-0463-z. URL: http://link.springer.com/10.1007/s11623-015-0463-z (visited on 09/03/2022).

Karg, Moritz. *DSGVO Art. 4 Nr. 1 Begriffsbestimmung „Personenbezogenes Datum"*. In: *Datenschutzrecht*. Ed. by Spiros Simitis, Gerrit Hornung, and Indra Spiecker genannt Döhmann. 2nd ed. Baden-Baden: Nomos, 2025. ISBN: 978-3-8487-8958-0.

Kasiviswanathan, Shiva Prasad and Adam *Smith*. "On the 'Semantics' of Differential Privacy: A Bayesian Formulation." In: *Journal of Privacy and Confidentiality* 6.1 (June 1, 2014). ISSN: 2575-8527. DOI: 10.29012/jpc.v6i1.634. arXiv: 0803.3946 [cs]. URL: http://arxiv.org/abs/0803.3946 (visited on 06/21/2023).

Katz, Daniel Martin. “The MIT School of Law? A Perspective on Legal Education in the 21st Century.” In: *University of Illinois Law Review* 2014.5 (Oct. 22, 2014), pp. 1431–1472. URL: https://illinoislawreview.org/wp-content/ilr-content/articles/2014/5/Katz.pdf (visited on 05/16/2023).

Katz, Daniel Martin, Michael James II *Bommarito*, et al. “GPT-4 Passes the Bar Exam.” In: *SSRN Electronic Journal* (2023). ISSN: 1556-5068. DOI: 10.2139/ssrn.4389233. URL: https://www.ssrn.com/abstract=4389233 (visited on 03/17/2023).

Katz, Daniel Martin, Dirk *Hartung*, et al. *Natural Language Processing in the Legal Domain*. 2023. DOI: 10.48550/arXiv.2302.12039. arXiv: 2302.12039. URL: https://arxiv.org/abs/2302.12039 (visited on 04/15/2024). Pre-published.

Kaulartz, Markus. “2.2 Trainieren von Machine-Learning-Modellen.” In: *Rechtshandbuch Artificial Intelligence und Machine Learning*. Ed. by Markus Kaulartz and Tom Braegelmann. München: C.H. Beck, 2020, pp. 32–36. ISBN: 978-3-406-74658-1.

Kelber, Ulrich. “Medizinische Forschung mit Gesundheitsdaten.” In: *Datenschutz und Datensicherheit* 47.1 (Jan. 2023), pp. 6–6. ISSN: 1614-0702, 1862-2607. DOI: 10.1007/s11623-022-1706-4. URL: https://link.springer.com/10.1007/s11623-022-1706-4 (visited on 04/06/2023).

Kifer, Daniel and Ashwin *Machanavajjhala*. “No free lunch in data privacy.” In: *Proceedings of the 2011 ACM SIGMOD International Conference on Management of data*. SIGMOD/PODS ’11: International Conference on Management of Data. Athens Greece: ACM, June 12, 2011, pp. 193–204. ISBN: 978-1-4503-0661-4. DOI: 10.1145/1989323.1989345. URL: https://dl.acm.org/doi/10.1145/1989323.1989345 (visited on 04/07/2023).

Klabunde, Achim and Anna Zsófia *Horváth*. *DS-GVO Art. 4 Begriffsbestimmungen*. In: *Datenschutz-Grundverordnung*. Ed. by Eugen Ehmann and Martin Selmayr. 3rd ed. Munich: C.H. Beck, 2024. ISBN: 978-3-406-79777-4.

Klar, Manuel and Jürgen *Kühling*. *DS-GVO Art. 4 Nr. 1 personenbezogene Daten (inkl. betroffene Person)*. In: *DS-GVO BDSG*. Ed. by Jürgen Kühling and Benedikt Buchner. 4th ed. Munich: C.H. Beck, 2024. ISBN: 978-3-406-80263-8.

Kleinz, Torsten. “TrustPid: Die Rückkehr der Super-Cookies.” In: *Der Spiegel. Netzwelt* (May 28, 2022). ISSN: 2195-1349. URL: https://www.spiegel.de/netzwelt/netzpolitik/trustpid-die-rueckkehr-der-super-cookies-a-6ea53d94-5996-4d6b-aed5-dfb5f51ab942 (visited on 02/15/2023).

Kneuper, Ralf. “Anonymisierte Daten brauchen keinen Datenschutz – wirklich nicht?” In: *Selbstbestimmung, Privatheit und Datenschutz*. Ed. by Michael Friedewald, Michael Kreutzer, and Marit Hansen. Wiesbaden: Springer Fachmedien Wiesbaden, 2022, pp. 171–188. ISBN: 978-3-658-33305-8. DOI: 10.1007/978-3-658-33306-5_9. URL: https://link.springer.com/10.1007/978-3-658-33306-5_9 (visited on 01/07/2023).

Kolain, Michael, Christian *Grafenauer*, and Martin *Ebers*. “Anonymity Assessment - A Universal Tool for Measuring Anonymity of Data Sets under the GDPR with a Special Focus on Smart Robotics.” In: *Rutgers Computer and Technology Law Journal* 48.2 (2021–2022), pp. 174–223.

Krempl, Stefan. *Anzeige erstattet: Provider speichern IP-Adressen bis zu drei Monate*. heise online. Jan. 2, 2019. URL: https://www.heise.de/newsticker/meldung/Anzeige-erstattet-Provider-speichern-IP-Adressen-bis-zu-drei-Monate-4263124.html (visited on 03/27/2023).

Kriesel, David. “Traue keinem Scan, den du nicht selbst gefälscht hast.” In: *Mitteilungen der Deutschen Mathematiker-Vereinigung* 22.1 (Jan. 20, 2014). ISSN: 0942-5977, 0947-4471. DOI: 10.1515/dmvm-2014-0015. URL: https://www.degruyter.com/document/doi/10.1515/dmvm-2014-0015/html (visited on 02/21/2023).

Krügel, Tina. “Das personenbezogene Datum nach der DS-GVO.” In: *Zeitschrift für Datenschutz* 10 (2017), pp. 455–460.

Kühling, Jürgen. "'Cookie-Banner', 'Cookie-Walls' und das 'PUR'-Modell." In: *Zeitschrift für Digitalisierung und Recht* 4 (2022), pp. 339–366.
Kühling, Jürgen. *GRC Art. 8 Schutz personenbezogener Daten*. In: *Frankfurter Kommentar zu EUV, GRC und AEUV*. Ed. by Matthias Pechstein, Carsten Nowak, and Ulrich Häde. 2nd ed. Vol. 1. 4 vols. Tübingen: Mohr Siebeck, 2023, p. 1855. ISBN: 978-3-16-161475-0.
Kühling, Jürgen and Manuel *Klar*. "Unsicherheitsfaktor Datenschutzrecht – Das Beispiel des Personenbezugs und der Anonymität." In: *Neue Juristische Wochenschrift* 50 (2013), pp. 3611–3617.
Law.com. *Typewriting Identification/Analysis Expert Witnesses*. Law.com Expert Witnesses. 2024. URL: https://www.law.com/expert-witness/directory/typewriting-identification-analysis/ (visited on 02/21/2023).
Le, Quoc and Tomas *Mikolov*. "Distributed Representations of Sentences and Documents." In: *Proceedings of the 31st International Conference on Machine Learning*. International Conference on Machine Learning. Beijing, China: PMLR, June 18, 2014, pp. 1188–1196. URL: https://proceedings.mlr.press/v32/le14.html (visited on 07/15/2023).
Leach, Paul J., Rich *Salz*, and Michael H. *Mealling*. *A Universally Unique IDentifier (UUID) URN Namespace*. Request for Comments RFC 4122. Internet Engineering Task Force, July 2005. 32 pp. DOI: 10.17487/RFC4122. URL: https://datatracker.ietf.org/doc/rfc4122 (visited on 04/26/2024).
Lee, Jaewoo and Chris *Clifton*. "How much is enough? choosing Epsilon for differential privacy." In: *Proceedings of the 14th international conference on Information security*. ISC'11. Berlin, Heidelberg: Springer-Verlag, Oct. 26, 2011, pp. 325–340. ISBN: 978-3-642-24860-3.
Leenes, Ronald. "Do They Know Me? Deconstructing Identifiability." In: *University of Ottawa Law and Technology Journal* 4 (1&2 2007), pp. 135–161. URL: https://research.tilburguniversity.edu/en/publications/do-they-know-me-deconstructing-identifiability (visited on 04/15/2024).
Leicht, Maximilian and Leo *Dessani*. "Federated Learning als Chance für Datenschutzfreundliche KI?" In: *Kommunikation und Recht* (2022), pp. 70–75.
Lenaerts, Koen and Jose A. *Gutierrez-Fons*. "To Say What the Law of the EU Is: Methods of Interpretation and the European Court of Justice." In: *Columbia Journal of European Law* 20.2 (2013–2014), pp. 3–61.
Lerman, Rachel. "Elon Musk's baby name isn't just weird, it may be against California regulations." In: *Washington Post* (Oct. 5, 2021). ISSN: 0190-8286. URL: https://www.washingtonpost.com/technology/2020/05/08/musk-grimes-baby-name/ (visited on 01/27/2023).
Li, Jiuyong et al. "Anonymization by Local Recoding in Data with Attribute Hierarchical Taxonomies." In: *IEEE Transactions on Knowledge and Data Engineering* 20.9 (Sept. 2008), pp. 1181–1194. ISSN: 1558-2191. DOI: 10.1109/TKDE.2008.52.
Li, Ninghui, Tiancheng *Li*, and Suresh *Venkatasubramanian*. "t-Closeness: Privacy Beyond k-Anonymity and l-Diversity." In: *2007 IEEE 23rd International Conference on Data Engineering*. 2007 IEEE 23rd International Conference on Data Engineering. Apr. 2007, pp. 106–115. DOI: 10.1109/ICDE.2007.367856. URL: https://ieeexplore.ieee.org/document/4221659 (visited on 04/14/2024).
Li, William et al. "Using Algorithmic Attribution Techniques to Determine Authorship in Unsigned Judicial Opinions." In: *Stanford Technology Law Review* 16.3 (2013), pp. 503–533.
Lison, Pierre et al. "Anonymisation Models for Text Data: State of the art, Challenges and Future Directions." In: *Proceedings of the 59th Annual Meeting of the Association for Computational Linguistics and the 11th International Joint Conference on Natural Language Processing (Volume 1: Long Papers)*. ACL-IJCNLP 2021. Online: Association for Computational Linguistics, Aug. 2021, pp. 4188–4203. DOI: 10.18653/v1/2021.acl-long.323. URL: https://aclanthology.org/2021.acl-long.323 (visited on 06/14/2023).

Machanavajjhala, Ashwin et al. "L-diversity: privacy beyond k-anonymity." In: *22nd International Conference on Data Engineering (ICDE'06)*. 22nd International Conference on Data Engineering. Atlanta, GA, USA: IEEE, 2006, pp. 24–24. ISBN: 978-0-7695-2570-9. DOI: 10.1109/ICDE.2006.1. URL: https://ieeexplore.ieee.org/document/1617392/ (visited on 02/07/2023).

Mahmood, Asad, Zubair *Shafiq*, and Padmini *Srinivasan*. "A Girl Has A Name: Detecting Authorship Obfuscation." In: *Proceedings of the 58th Annual Meeting of the Association for Computational Linguistics*. ACL 2020. Online: Association for Computational Linguistics, July 2020, pp. 2235–2245. DOI: 10.18653/v1/2020.acl-main.203. URL: https://aclanthology.org/2020.acl-main.203 (visited on 07/15/2023).

Marnau, Ninja, Pascal *Berrang*, and Mathias *Humbert*. "Anonymisierungsverfahren für genetische Daten." In: *Datenschutz und Datensicherheit - DuD* 42.2 (Feb. 1, 2018), pp. 83–88. ISSN: 1862-2607. DOI: 10.1007/s11623-018-0899-z.

Marsch, Nikolaus. *Das europäische Datenschutzgrundrecht: Grundlagen, Dimensionen, Verflechtungen*. Jus publicum Band 270. Tübingen: Mohr Siebeck, 2018. 407 pp. ISBN: 978-3-16-155422-3. DOI: 10.1628/978-3-16-155423-0.

Marx, Simon and Alicia *Sütthoff*. "Zur Reichweite der Löschungspflicht des Verantwortlichen." In: *Zeitschrift für das Recht der digitalen Wirtschaft* (2022), pp. 128–132. URL: https://www.wolterskluwer.com/de-de/expert-insights/ki-und-datenschutz (visited on 07/07/2024).

Mattern, Justus et al. "Membership Inference Attacks against Language Models via Neighbourhood Comparison." In: *Findings of the Association for Computational Linguistics: ACL 2023*. Association of Computational Linguistics. Ed. by Anna Rogers, Jordan Boyd-Graber, and Naoaki Okazaki. Toronto, Canada: arXiv, July 2023, pp. 11330–11343. DOI: 10.18653/v1/2023.findings-acl.719. arXiv: 2305.18462 [cs]. URL: https://aclanthology.org/2023.findings-acl.719/ (visited on 03/30/2024).

May, Ronja. "Die Arbeitsbedingungenrichtlinie (EU) 2019/1152 und ihre Auswirkungen auf Kündigungen und Abrufarbeit." In: *Betriebs-Berater* (2022), pp. 2232–2235.

McMahan, H. Brendan et al. "Communication-Efficient Learning of Deep Networks from Decentralized Data." In: *Proceedings of the 20th International Conference on Artificial Intelligence and Statistics (AISTATS) 2017*. International Conference on Artificial Intelligence and Statistics (AISTATS). Ed. by Aarti Singh and Jerry Zhu. Vol. 54. Proceedings of Machine Learning Research. Fort Lauderdale, FL: PMLR, Jan. 26, 2023, pp. 1273–1282. DOI: 10.48550/arXiv.1602.05629. arXiv: 1602.05629 [cs]. URL: http://arxiv.org/abs/1602.05629 (visited on 03/31/2024).

McPherson, Richard, Reza *Shokri*, and Vitaly *Shmatikov*. *Defeating Image Obfuscation with Deep Learning*. Sept. 6, 2016. DOI: 10.48550/arXiv.1609.00408. arXiv: 1609.00408 [cs]. URL: http://arxiv.org/abs/1609.00408 (visited on 07/14/2023). Pre-published.

McSherry, Frank. "Privacy integrated queries: an extensible platform for privacy-preserving data analysis." In: *Communications of the ACM* 53.9 (Sept. 2010), pp. 89–97. ISSN: 0001-0782, 1557-7317. DOI: 10.1145/1810891.1810916.

McSherry, Frank. *Differential Privacy for Dummies*. Blog. Feb. 3, 2016. URL: https://github.com/frankmcsherry/blog/blob/10aba898531efd2bce315dc15e78e28c7faf5503/posts/2016-02-03.md (visited on 04/07/2023).

McSherry, Frank. *2016-05-19*. Blog. May 19, 2016. URL: https://github.com/frankmcsherry/blog/blob/10aba898531efd2bce315dc15e78e28c7faf5503/posts/2016-05-19.md (visited on 04/07/2023).

McSherry, Frank. *Lunchtime for Data Privacy*. Blog. Aug. 16, 2016. URL: https://github.com/frankmcsherry/blog/blob/10aba898531efd2bce315dc15e78e28c7faf5503/posts/2016-08-16.md (visited on 04/07/2023).

McSherry, Frank. *Differential privacy and correlated data*. Blog. Aug. 29, 2016. URL: https://github.com/frankmcsherry/blog/blob/master/posts/2016-08-29.md (visited on 07/14/2023).

McSherry, Frank. *Uber's differential privacy .. probably isn't*. Blog. Feb. 25, 2018. URL: https://github.com/frankmcsherry/blog (visited on 06/13/2023).

McSherry, Frank. *Differential privacy and Demographics*. Blog. Apr. 12, 2019. URL: https://github.com/frankmcsherry/blog (visited on 06/13/2023).

McSherry, Frank and Cynthia *Dwork*. "Differential Data Privacy." U.S. pat. 2007/0143289A1. 2007.

Meystre, Stephane M et al. "Automatic de-identification of textual documents in the electronic health record: a review of recent research." In: *BMC Medical Research Methodology* 10.1 (Dec. 2010), p. 70. ISSN: 1471-2288. DOI: 10.1186/1471-2288-10-70. URL: https://bmcmedresmethodol.biomedcentral.com/articles/10.1186/1471-2288-10-70 (visited on 02/07/2023).

Mikolov, Tomas, Kai *Chen*, et al. *Efficient Estimation of Word Representations in Vector Space*. Sept. 6, 2013. DOI: 10.48550/arXiv.1301.3781. arXiv: 1301.3781 [cs]. URL: http://arxiv.org/abs/1301.3781 (visited on 07/15/2023). Pre-published.

Mikolov, Tomas, Ilya *Sutskever*, et al. "Distributed Representations of Words and Phrases and their Compositionality." In: *Advances in Neural Information Processing Systems*. Vol. 26. Curran Associates, Inc., 2013. URL: https://proceedings.neurips.cc/paper_files/paper/2013/file/9aa42b31882ec039965f3c4923ce901b-Paper.pdf (visited on 07/15/2023).

Mikolov, Tomas, Wen-tau *Yih*, and Geoffrey *Zweig*. "Linguistic Regularities in Continuous Space Word Representations." In: *Proceedings of the 2013 Conference of the North American Chapter of the Association for Computational Linguistics: Human Language Technologies*. NAACL-HLT 2013. Atlanta, Georgia: Association for Computational Linguistics, June 2013, pp. 746–751. URL: https://aclanthology.org/N13-1090 (visited on 07/15/2023).

Mitteldeutscher Rundfunk. DDR-Vornamen und ihre Vorurteile: "Oh Mandy!" | MDR.DE. Dec. 6, 2021. URL: https://www.mdr.de/geschichte/ddr/alltag/ddr-vornamen-vorurteile-mandy-ronny-peggy-100.html (visited on 05/15/2023).

Moore, Gordon E. "Cramming more components onto integrated circuits." In: *Electronics* 38.8 (Apr. 19, 1965). URL: https://download.intel.com/newsroom/2023/manufacturing/moores-law-electronics.pdf (visited on 04/15/2024).

Moos, Flemming. "Daten und Sicherheit: Personenbezug von Large Language Models." In: *Computer und Recht* (2024), pp. 442–450.

Moskowitz, Robert et al. *Address Allocation for Private Internets*. Request for Comments RFC 1918. Internet Engineering Task Force, Feb. 1996. 9 pp. DOI: 10.17487/RFC1918. URL: https://datatracker.ietf.org/doc/rfc1918 (visited on 03/27/2023).

MPI-SWS/Diffix Bounty 2020 – GDA Score. May 29, 2020. URL: https://www.gda-score.org/mpi-sws-diffix-challenge-2020/ (visited on 04/30/2023).

Mühlenbeck, Robin L. *Anonyme und pseudonyme Daten*. Vol. 66. Frankfurter Studien zum Datenschutz. Baden-Baden: Nomos, 2023. 388 pp. ISBN: 978-3-7489-3749-4. DOI: 10.5771/9783748937494.

Mühlenbeck, Robin L. and Rolf *Schwartmann*. *Art. 4 Begriffsbestimmungen*. In: *DS-GVO/BDSG*. Ed. by Rolf Schwartmann et al. 3rd ed. Heidelberg: C.F. Müller, 2024. ISBN: 978-3-8114-5656-3.

Munjal, Kundan and Rekha *Bhatia*. "A systematic review of homomorphic encryption and its contributions in healthcare industry." In: *Complex & Intelligent Systems* (May 3, 2022). ISSN: 2198-6053. DOI: 10.1007/s40747-022-00756-z.

Narayanan, Arvind and Edward W. *Felten*. "No silver bullet: De-identification still doesn't work." In: (July 9, 2014). URL: https://www.cs.princeton.edu/~arvindn/publications/no-silver-bullet-de-identification.pdf (visited on 05/02/2024).

Narayanan, Arvind and Vitaly *Shmatikov*. "Robust De-anonymization of Large Sparse Datasets." In: *2008 IEEE Symposium on Security and Privacy (sp 2008)*. 2008 IEEE Symposium on Security and

Privacy (sp 2008). May 2008, pp. 111–125. DOI: 10.1109/SP.2008.33. URL: https://www.cs.utexas.edu/~shmat/shmat_oak08netflix.pdf (visited on 04/14/2024).

Narten, Thomas, Richard P. *Draves*, and Suresh *Krishnan*. *Privacy Extensions for Stateless Address Autoconfiguration in IPv6*. Request for Comments RFC 4941. Internet Engineering Task Force, Sept. 2007. 23 pp. DOI: 10.17487/RFC4941. URL: https://datatracker.ietf.org/doc/rfc4941 (visited on 03/27/2023).

Nasr, Milad et al. *Scalable Extraction of Training Data from (Production) Language Models*. Nov. 28, 2023. DOI: 10.48550/arXiv.2311.17035. arXiv: 2311.17035 [cs]. Pre-published.

Nget, Rachana, Yang *Cao*, and Masatoshi *Yoshikawa*. “How to Balance Privacy and Money through Pricing Mechanism in Personal Data Market.” In: (2017).

Nissim, Kobbi. “Privacy: From Database Reconstruction to Legal Theorems.” In: *Proceedings of the 40th ACM SIGMOD-SIGACT-SIGAI Symposium on Principles of Database Systems*. PODS’21. New York, NY, USA: Association for Computing Machinery, June 20, 2021, pp. 33–41. ISBN: 978-1-4503-8381-3. DOI: 10.1145/3452021.3458816. URL: https://doi.org/10.1145/3452021.3458816 (visited on 04/12/2023).

Nissim, Kobbi et al. “Bridging the Gap Between Computer Science and Legal Approaches to Privacy.” In: *Harvard Journal of Law & Technology* 31.2 (2018), pp. 687–780.

Nöhre, Ingo. “Anonymisierung und Neutralisierung von veröffentlichungswürdigen Gerichtsentscheidungen.” In: *Monatsschrift für Deutsches Recht* 73.3 (Feb. 1, 2019), pp. 136–141. ISSN: 2194-4202, 0340-1812. DOI: 10.9785/mdtr-2019-730304. URL: https://www.degruyter.com/document/doi/10.9785/mdtr-2019-730304/html (visited on 01/30/2023).

Noonan, Harold and Ben *Curtis*. “Identity.” In: *The Stanford Encyclopedia of Philosophy*. Ed. by Edward N. Zalta and Uri Nodelman. Fall 2022. Metaphysics Research Lab, Stanford University, 2022. URL: https://plato.stanford.edu/archives/fall2022/entries/identity/ (visited on 03/07/2023).

Ohm, Paul. “Broken Promises of Privacy: Responding to the Surprising Failure of Anonymization.” In: *UCLA Law Review* 57.6 (2009–2010), pp. 1701–1778. URL: https://heinonline.org/HOL/P?h=hein.journals/uclalr57&i=1713 (visited on 04/07/2023).

Ollam, Deviant and Howard *Payne*, director. *Elevator Hacking: From the Pit to the Penthouse*. Aug. 5, 2014. URL: https://www.youtube.com/watch?v=ZUvGfuLlZus (visited on 04/30/2023).

Oostveen, Manon. *Warum Privacy != Datenschutz ist (und wie sie sich überschneiden)*. Digital Society Blog, HIIG. May 4, 2016. URL: https://www.hiig.de/warum-privacy-%E2%89%A0-datenschutz-ist-und-wie-sie-sich-ueberschneiden/ (visited on 07/16/2023).

Oostveen, Manon. “Identifiability and the applicability of data protection to big data.” In: *International Data Privacy Law* 6.4 (Nov. 2016), pp. 299–309. ISSN: 2044-3994, 2044-4001. DOI: 10.1093/idpl/ipw012. URL: https://academic.oup.com/idpl/article-lookup/doi/10.1093/idpl/ipw012 (visited on 12/30/2023).

OpenAI. *ChatGPT: Optimizing Language Models for Dialogue*. OpenAI. Nov. 30, 2022. URL: https://openai.com/blog/chatgpt/ (visited on 01/12/2023).

OpenAI. *GPT-4 Technical Report*. Mar. 16, 2023. arXiv: 2303.08774 [cs]. URL: http://arxiv.org/abs/2303.08774 (visited on 03/23/2023). Pre-published.

Pahlen-Brandt, Ingrid. “Datenschutz braucht scharfe Instrumente Beitrag zur Diskussion um „personenbezogene Daten“.” In: *Datenschutz und Datensicherheit* 32.1 (Jan. 2008), pp. 34–40. ISSN: 1614-0702, 1862-2607. DOI: 10.1007/s11623-008-0009-8. URL: http://link.springer.com/10.1007/s11623-008-0009-8 (visited on 09/03/2022).

Papastefanou, Stefan. “„Database Reconstruction Theorem“ und die Verletzung der Privatsphäre (Differential Privacy).” In: *Computer und Recht* 36.6 (June 1, 2020), pp. 379–386. ISSN: 2194-4172. DOI:

10.9785/cr-2020-360610. URL: https://www.degruyter.com/document/doi/10.9785/cr-2020-360610/html (visited on 01/30/2023).

Papernot, Nicolas et al. "Semi-supervised Knowledge Transfer for Deep Learning from Private Training Data." In: International Conference on Learning Representations. Toulon: Openreview.net, Mar. 3, 2017. arXiv: 1610.05755 [cs, stat]. URL: https://openreview.net/forum?id=HkwoSDPgg (visited on 04/14/2024).

Penfrat, Jan and Estelle *Masse*. *TrustPid*. European Digital Rights (EDRi). Feb. 10, 2023. URL: https://edri.org/our-work/trustpid-baking-ad-tracking-into-the-internet-infrastructure/ (visited on 02/15/2023).

Pennington, Jeffrey, Richard *Socher*, and Christopher *Manning*. "GloVe: Global Vectors for Word Representation." In: *Proceedings of the 2014 Conference on Empirical Methods in Natural Language Processing (EMNLP)*. EMNLP 2014. Doha, Qatar: Association for Computational Linguistics, Oct. 2014, pp. 1532–1543. DOI: 10.3115/v1/D14-1162. URL: https://aclanthology.org/D14-1162 (visited on 07/15/2023).

Peralta, Eyder. "Betrayed By Metadata: John McAfee Admits He's Really In Guatemala." In: *NPR. The Two-Way* (Dec. 4, 2012). URL: https://www.npr.org/sections/thetwo-way/2012/12/04/166487197/betrayed-by-metadata-john-mcafee-admits-hes-really-in-guatemala (visited on 02/19/2023).

Pesch, Paulina Jo and Rainer *Böhme*. "Verarbeitung personenbezogener Daten und Datenrichtigkeit bei großen Sprachmodellen." In: *Multimedia und Recht* 12 (2023), pp. 917–923.

Peterson, Steven, George *Hoffer*, and Edward *Millner*. "Are Drivers of Air-Bag-Equipped Cars More Aggressive? A Test of the Offsetting Behavior Hypothesis." In: *The Journal of Law & Economics* 38.2 (1995), pp. 251–264. ISSN: 0022-2186. JSTOR: 725685. URL: https://www.jstor.org/stable/725685 (visited on 07/07/2024).

Pfitzmann, Andreas and Marit *Hansen*. *A terminology for talking about privacy by data minimization: Anonymity, Unlinkability, Undetectability, Unobservability, Pseudonymity, and Identity Management*. Aug. 10, 2010. URL: https://dud.inf.tu-dresden.de/literatur/Anon_Terminology_v0.34.pdf (visited on 04/14/2024).

Pilán, Ildikó et al. "The Text Anonymization Benchmark (TAB): A Dedicated Corpus and Evaluation Framework for Text Anonymization." In: *Computational Linguistics* 48.4 (Dec. 1, 2022), pp. 1053–1101. ISSN: 0891-2017, 1530-9312. DOI: 10.1162/coli_a_00458. URL: https://direct.mit.edu/coli/article/48/4/1053/112770/The-Text-Anonymization-Benchmark-TAB-A-Dedicated (visited on 06/14/2023).

Pitruzella, Giovanni. *Opinion on Case C-487/21 ("Österreichische Datenschutzbehörde and CRIF")*. Dec. 15, 2022. URL: https://eur-lex.europa.eu/legal-content/EN/TXT/PDF/?uri=CELEX:62021CC0487 (visited on 04/28/2024).

Pohle, Jörg. *Datenschutz: Rechtsstaatsmodell oder neoliberale Responsibilisierung? Warum Datentreuhänder kein Mittel zum Schutz der Grundrechte sind*. Feb. 2022. URL: https://www.verbraucherforschung.nrw/sites/default/files/2022-02/zth-05-pohle-datenschutz-rechtsstaatsmodell-oder-neoliberale-responsibilisierung_0.pdf.

Poullet, Yves and Jean-Marc *Dinant*. *Thoughts on Convention No. 108 for the purposes of the future work of the Consultative Committee (T-PD)*. Dec. 13, 2024. URL: https://rm.coe.int/168068416a (visited on 04/14/2024).

Prayitno et al. "A Systematic Review of Federated Learning in the Healthcare Area: From the Perspective of Data Properties and Applications." In: *Applied Sciences* 11.23 (Nov. 25, 2021), p. 11191. ISSN: 2076-3417. DOI: 10.3390/app112311191. URL: https://www.mdpi.com/2076-3417/11/23/11191 (visited on 02/13/2023).

Proposal for a Regulation of the European Parliament and of the Council on the protection of individuals with regard to the processing of personal data and on the free movement of such data (General Data Protection Regulation) - Preparation for Trilogue. Nov. 27, 2015. URL: https://www.statewatch.org/media/documents/news/2015/nov/eu-council-dp-reg-whole-text-14481-15.pdf (visited on 05/04/2023).

Purtova, Nadezhda. "The law of everything. Broad concept of personal data and future of EU data protection law." In: *Law, Innovation and Technology* 10.1 (Jan. 2, 2018), pp. 40–81. ISSN: 1757-9961. DOI: 10.1080/17579961.2018.1452176. URL: https://doi.org/10.1080/17579961.2018.1452176 (visited on 05/03/2023).

Purtova, Nadezhda. "From knowing by name to targeting: the meaning of identification under the GDPR." In: *International Data Privacy Law* 12.3 (Sept. 5, 2022), pp. 163–183. ISSN: 2044-3994, 2044-4001. DOI: 10.1093/idpl/ipac013. URL: https://academic.oup.com/idpl/article/12/3/163/6612144 (visited on 05/03/2023).

Raab, Gillian M., Beata *Nowok*, and Chris *Dibben*. "Practical Data Synthesis for Large Samples." In: *Journal of Privacy and Confidentiality* 7.3 (3 2016), pp. 67–97. ISSN: 2575-8527. DOI: 10.29012/jpc.v7i3.407. URL: https://journalprivacyconfidentiality.org/index.php/jpc/article/view/407 (visited on 04/08/2023).

Rachut, Sarah. *Grundrechtsverwirklichung in digitalen Kontexten*. Duncker und Humblot, 2025. ISBN: 978-3-428-59305-7. DOI: 10.3790/978-3-428-59305-7.

Rafał Mańko. *Briefing: Legal Aspects of EU Multilingualism*. European Parliamentary Research Service, Jan. 2017. URL: https://www.europarl.europa.eu/RegData/etudes/BRIE/2017/595914/EPRS_BRI%282017%29595914_EN.pdf (visited on 02/25/2024).

Rangel, Francisco and Paolo *Rosso*. "On the Implications of the General Data Protection Regulation on the Organisation of Evaluation Tasks." In: *Language and Law* 5.2 (2018), pp. 95–117.

Rat, Europäisches Parlament und. *RL 95/46/EG vom 24.10.1995 zum Schutz natürlicher Personen bei der Verarbeitung personenbezogener Daten und zum freien Datenverkehr*. Dec. 13, 1995.

Rathi, Mukul. *Deep Learning with Differential Privacy (DP-SGD Explained)*. Dec. 25, 2021. URL: https://mukulrathi.com/privacy-preserving-machine-learning/deep-learning-differential-privacy/ (visited on 06/22/2023).

Recognize. In: *Collins Dictionary*. 2024. URL: https://www.collinsdictionary.com/dictionary/english/recognize (visited on 03/02/2024).

Redis. *What is a Key-Value Database?* Redis. 2024. URL: https://redis.com/nosql/key-value-databases/ (visited on 07/12/2023).

Regulation (EU) 2018/1807 of the European Parliament and of the Council of 14 November 2018 on a framework for the free flow of non-personal data in the European Union (Text with EEA relevance.) Nov. 14, 2018. URL: http://data.europa.eu/eli/reg/2018/1807/oj/eng (visited on 04/06/2023).

Reimer, Helmut and Christoph *Wegener*. "Pseudonym ... anonym ... privat?" In: *Datenschutz und Datensicherheit* 40.7 (July 2016), pp. 468–468. ISSN: 1614-0702, 1862-2607. DOI: 10.1007/s11623-016-0638-2. URL: http://link.springer.com/10.1007/s11623-016-0638-2 (visited on 09/03/2022).

relate. In: *Collins Dictionary*. 2024. URL: https://www.collinsdictionary.com/dictionary/english/relate (visited on 04/11/2024).

Rémy, Philippe. *First and Last Names Database*. Jan. 26, 2023. URL: https://github.com/philipperemy/name-dataset (visited on 01/27/2023).

Riesenhuber, Karl. "§ 7: Die Auslegung und Fortbildung des Primärrechts." In: *Europäische Methodenlehre*. Ed. by Karl Riesenhuber. De Gruyter, May 25, 2021, pp. 181–208. ISBN: 978-3-11-061430-5. DOI: 10.1515/9783110614305-007.

Riesenhuber, Karl, Matthias *Pechstein*, and Carola *Drechsler*. "§ 10: Die Auslegung." In: *Europäische Methodenlehre*. Ed. by Karl Riesenhuber. De Gruyter, May 25, 2021, pp. 285–321. ISBN: 978-3-11-061430-5. DOI: 10.1515/9783110614305-010.

Rivest, Ronald L. *The MD5 Message-Digest Algorithm*. Request for Comments RFC 1321. Internet Engineering Task Force, Apr. 1, 1992. 21 pp. DOI: 10.17487/RFC1321. URL: https://datatracker.ietf.org/doc/rfc1321 (visited on 03/17/2023).

Roßnagel, Alexander. *DSGVO Art. 2 Sachlicher Anwendungsbereich*. In: *Datenschutzrecht*. Ed. by Spiros Simitis, Gerrit Hornung, and Indra Spiecker genannt Döhmann. 2nd ed. Baden-Baden: Nomos, 2025. ISBN: 978-3-8487-8958-0.

Roßnagel, Alexander and Philip *Scholz*. "Datenschutz durch Anonymität und Pseudonymität – Rechtsfolgen der Verwendung anonymer und pseudonymer Daten." In: *MMR* 12 (2000), pp. 721–731.

Ruggles, Steven et al. "Differential Privacy and Census Data: Implications for Social and Economic Research." In: *AEA Papers and Proceedings* 109 (May 2019), pp. 403–408. ISSN: 2574-0768. DOI: 10.1257/pandp.20191107. URL: https://www.aeaweb.org/articles?id=10.1257/pandp.20191107 (visited on 04/07/2023).

Ruhl, J. B. and Daniel Martin *Katz*. "Measuring, Monitoring, and Managing Legal Complexity." In: *Iowa Law Review* 101.1 (Feb. 17, 2015), pp. 191–244. URL: https://ilr.law.uiowa.edu/print/volume-101-issue-1/measuring-monitoring-and-managing-legal-complexity (visited on 04/14/2024).

Rupp, Valentin and Max *Von Grafenstein*. "Clarifying "personal data" and the role of anonymisation in data protection law: Including and excluding data from the scope of the GDPR (more clearly) through refining the concept of data protection." In: *Computer Law & Security Review* 52 (Apr. 2024), p. 105932. ISSN: 02673649. DOI: 10.1016/j.clsr.2023.105932.

Sachs, Andreas and Miriam *Meder*. "Datenschutz-Folgenabschätzung bei Training und Einsatz von LLMs." In: *Zeitschrift für Datenschutz* 7 (2024), pp. 363–369.

Samarati, Pierangela and Latanya *Sweeney*. *Protecting Privacy when Disclosing Information: k-Anonymity and Its Enforcement through Generalization and Suppression*. 1998. URL: https://epic.org/wp-content/uploads/privacy/reidentification/Samarati_Sweeney_paper.pdf (visited on 04/14/2024). Pre-published.

Sarathy, Jayshree. *From Algorithmic to Institutional Logics: The Politics of Differential Privacy*. Apr. 9, 2022. DOI: 10.2139/ssrn.4079222. URL: https://papers.ssrn.com/abstract=4079222 (visited on 04/08/2023). Pre-published.

Sarunski, Maik. "Big Data – Ende der Anonymität?" In: *Datenschutz und Datensicherheit* 40.7 (July 1, 2016), pp. 424–427. ISSN: 1862-2607. DOI: 10.1007/s11623-016-0630-x.

Sarwate, Anand. *An exercise in careful misreading | An Ergodic Walk*. Aug. 3, 2018. URL: https://web.archive.org/web/20180803034413/https://ergodicity.net/2014/11/03/an-exercise-in-uncareful-misreading/ (visited on 04/07/2023).

Schantz, Peter. *C. Die unterschiedlichen Kodifikationen des Datenschutzrechts*. In: *Das neue Datenschutzrecht*. Ed. by Peter Schantz and Heinrich Amadeus Wolff. 1st ed. Munich: C.H. Beck, 2017, p. 437. ISBN: 978-3-406-69649-7.

Schild, Hans Hermann. *DS-GVO Art. 4 Begriffsbestimmungen*. In: *BeckOK Datenschutzrecht*. Ed. by Heinrich Amadeus Wolff, Stefan Brink, and Antje von Ungern-Sternberg. 51st ed. Feb. 1, 2025.

Schindler, Charlotte. *Zulässigkeit und Grenzen algorithmischer Systeme bei arbeitsrechtlichen Auswahlentscheidungen: Eine rechtliche Betrachtung der Einsatzmöglichkeiten algorithmischer Systeme mit Fokus auf die DSGVO, das AGG und eine zukünftige KI-VO*. digital | recht, Dec. 18, 2023. ISBN: 978-3-7584-2840-1. DOI: 10.25353/ubtr-ad99-7ffe-3dab. URL: https://digitalrecht-z.uni-trier.de/index.php/drz/catalog/book/33 (visited on 12/28/2023).

Schneier, Bruce. *Homomorphic Encryption Breakthrough*. Schneier on Security. July 9, 2009. URL: https://www.schneier.com/blog/archives/2009/07/homomorphic_enc.html (visited on 07/06/2023).

Schwartmann, Rolf, Andreas *Jaspers*, et al. *Praxisleitfaden Anonymisierung*. Dec. 2022. URL: https://stiftungdatenschutz.org/fileadmin/Redaktion/Dokumente/Anonymisierung_personenbezogener_Daten/SDS_Studie_Praxisleitfaden-Anonymisieren-Web_01.pdf.

Schwartmann, Rolf, Andreas *Jaspers*, et al. *Anonymisierung und Pseudonymisierung von Daten: Gesetzestexte: Leitfaden und Grundregeln für die Praxis*. Textbuch Deutsches Recht. Heidelberg: C.F. Müller, Jan. 2023. 237 pp. ISBN: 978-3-8114-8921-9.

Schwartmann, Rolf and Steffen *Weiß*. *Anforderungen an den datenschutzkonformen Einsatz von Pseudonymisierungslösungen*. 2018. URL: https://bevh.org/fileadmin/content/04_politik/datenschutz_und_verbraucherpolitik/Fokusgruppe_Datenschutz-Anforderungen_an_datenschutzkonforme_Pseudonymisierung_V1.0.pdf (visited on 04/14/2024).

Schwartz, Paul M. and Daniel J. *Solove*. "The PII Problem: Privacy and a New Concept of Personally Identifiable Information." In: *New York University Law Review* 86.6 (2011), pp. 1814–1894.

Schweinoch, Martin and Stefan *Peintinger*. "Anonymisierung im Datenschutz – terra incognita? — Die Chancen und Risiken, den DSGVO-Vorgaben zu entkommen." In: *Computer und Recht* 36.10 (Oct. 1, 2020), pp. 643–649. ISSN: 2194-4172. DOI: 10.9785/cr-2020-361009. URL: https://www.degruyter.com/document/doi/10.9785/cr-2020-361009/html (visited on 01/30/2023).

Seleshi, Bihil and Samrawit *Asseffa*. "A Case Study on Differential Privacy." Umeå University, 2017.

Selinger, Peter. *The GLIBC pseudo-random number generator*. Jan. 4, 2007. URL: https://www.mscs.dal.ca/~selinger/random/ (visited on 07/05/2023).

Sequoiah-Grayson, Sebastian and Luciano *Floridi*. "Semantic Conceptions of Information." In: *The Stanford Encyclopedia of Philosophy*. Ed. by Edward N. Zalta. Spring 2022. Metaphysics Research Lab, Stanford University, 2022. URL: https://plato.stanford.edu/archives/spr2022/entries/information-semantic/ (visited on 03/21/2023).

Shen, Yuncheng et al. "Personal Big Data Pricing Method Based on Differential Privacy." In: *Computers & Security* 113 (Feb. 1, 2022), p. 102529. ISSN: 0167-4048. DOI: 10.1016/j.cose.2021.102529. URL: https://www.sciencedirect.com/science/article/pii/S0167404821003539 (visited on 07/06/2024).

Shokri, Reza et al. "Membership Inference Attacks Against Machine Learning Models." In: *2017 IEEE Symposium on Security and Privacy (SP)*. 2017 IEEE Symposium on Security and Privacy (SP). San Jose, CA, USA: IEEE, May 2017, pp. 3–18. ISBN: 978-1-5090-5533-3. DOI: 10.1109/SP.2017.41. URL: http://ieeexplore.ieee.org/document/7958568/ (visited on 03/30/2024).

Siglmüller, Jonas. *Im trainierten KI-Modell befinden sich keine personenbezogenen Daten*. LinkedIn. Dec. 2023. URL: https://www.linkedin.com/posts/jonas-siglmueller_%3F%3F-%3F%3F%3F%3F%3F%3F%3F%3F%3F%3F%3F-%3F%3F-%3F%3F%3F%3F-activity-7140248934718791681-UEYU (visited on 03/29/2024).

Silberschatz, Abraham, Henry F. *Korth*, and S. *Sudarshan*. *Database system concepts*. 7th ed. New York, NY: McGraw-Hill, 2020. 1344 pp. ISBN: 978-0-07-802215-9.

Solove, Daniel J. and Danielle Keats *Citron*. "Risk and Anxiety: A Theory of Data-Breach Harms." In: *Texas Law Review* 96.4 (2017–2018), pp. 737–786. URL: https://heinonline.org/HOL/P?h=hein.journals/tlr96&i=785 (visited on 04/08/2023).

Specht, Louisa. "Ausschließlichkeitsrechte an Daten – Notwendigkeit, Schutzumfang, Alternativen." In: *Computer und Recht* (2016), pp. 288–296.

Spindler, Gerald and Lukas *Dalby*. *DS-GVO Art. 4 Begriffsbestimmungen*. In: *Recht der elektronischen Medien*. Ed. by Gerald Spindler and Fabian Schuster. 4th ed. Munich: C.H. Beck, 2019, p. 2927. ISBN: 978-3-406-73012-2.

Staab, Robin et al. *Large Language Models are Advanced Anonymizers*. Feb. 21, 2024. DOI: 10.48550/arXiv.2402.13846. arXiv: 2402.13846 [cs]. URL: http://arxiv.org/abs/2402.13846 (visited on 04/05/2024). Pre-published.

Stadler, Theresa, Bristena *Oprisanu*, and Carmela *Troncoso*. "Synthetic Data – Anonymisation Groundhog Day." In: 31st USENIX Security Symposium (USENIX Security 22). 2022, pp. 1451–1468. ISBN: 978-1-939133-31-1. URL: https://www.usenix.org/conference/usenixsecurity22/presentation/stadler (visited on 04/07/2023).

Stamatatos, Efstathios. "A survey of modern authorship attribution methods." In: *Journal of the American Society for Information Science and Technology* 60.3 (Mar. 2009), pp. 538–556. ISSN: 15322882, 15322890. DOI: 10.1002/asi.21001. URL: https://onlinelibrary.wiley.com/doi/10.1002/asi.21001 (visited on 01/29/2023).

Statistics Netherlands. *Mu-ARGUS*. Aug. 26, 2021. URL: https://research.cbs.nl/casc/mu.htm (visited on 05/23/2023).

Stevens, Leslie. "The Proposed Data Protection Regulation and Its Potential Impact on Social Sciences Research in the UK." In: *European Data Protection Law Review* 1.2 (2015), pp. 97–112. ISSN: 23642831, 2364284X. DOI: 10.21552/EDPL/2015/2/4.

Stiftung Datenschutz. *DatenTag: Anonymisieren von Daten*. Dec. 7, 2022. URL: https://stiftungdatenschutz.org/veranstaltungen/unsere-veranstaltungen-detailansicht/datentag-anonymisieren-von-daten-350 (visited on 02/15/2023).

Storms, Dominik. *Datenschutz in der Unternehmenstransaktion*. Baden-Baden: Nomos, Feb. 15, 2022. ISBN: 978-3-8487-7304-6 978-3-7489-1319-1. DOI: 10.5771/9783748913191.

Strathern, Marilyn. "'Improving Ratings': Audit In The British University System." In: *European Review* 5.3 (1997), pp. 305–321. URL: http://archive.org/details/ImprovingRatingsAuditInTheBritishUniversitySy (visited on 07/09/2023).

Stummer, Sarah. "Issues of Verifying Anonymity: An Overview." In: *Informatik* 2022 (3. Interdisciplinary Privacy & Security at Large Workshop (Privacy&Security@Large) 2022), pp. 179–194. ISSN: 1617-5468. DOI: 10.18420/INF2022_17. URL: http://dl.gi.de/handle/20.500.12116/39514 (visited on 07/09/2023).

Swedish Authority for Privacy Protection. *Companies must stop using Google Analytics*. July 3, 2023. URL: http://www.imy.se/en/news/companies-must-stop-using-google-analytics/ (visited on 07/04/2023).

Sweeney, Latanya. "Replacing personally-identifying information in medical records, the Scrub system." In: *Proceedings of the AMIA Annual Fall Symposium* (1996), p. 333. URL: https://www.ncbi.nlm.nih.gov/pmc/articles/PMC2233179/ (visited on 05/14/2023).

Sweeney, Latanya. "Guaranteeing anonymity when sharing medical data, the Datafly System." In: *Proceedings: a conference of the American Medical Informatics Association. AMIA Fall Symposium* (1997), pp. 51–55. ISSN: 1091-8280.

Sweeney, Latanya. "Computational Disclosure Control for Medical Microdata: The Datafly System." In: *Record Linkage Workshop. Bureau of the Census* (1997), pp. 442–453.

Sweeney, Latanya. "Weaving Technology and Policy Together to Maintain Confidentiality." In: *The Journal of Law, Medicine & Ethics* 1997.25 (1997), pp. 98–110.

Sweeney, Latanya. "Datafly: a system for providing anonymity in medical data." In: *Database Security XI: Status and Prospects*. Ed. by T. Y. Lin and Shelly Qian. Boston, MA: Springer US, 1998, pp. 356–381. ISBN: 978-0-387-35285-5. DOI: 10.1007/978-0-387-35285-5_22.

Sweeney, Latanya. *Simple Demographics Often Identify People Uniquely*. 2000. Pre-published.

Sweeney, Latanya. “Computational disclosure control : a primer on data privacy protection.” Thesis. Massachusetts Institute of Technology, 2001. URL: https://dspace.mit.edu/handle/1721.1/8589 (visited on 05/24/2023).

Sweeney, Latanya. “k-Anonymity: A Model for Protecting Privacy.” In: *International Journal of Uncertainty, Fuzziness and Knowledge-Based Systems* 10.05 (Oct. 2002), pp. 557–570. ISSN: 0218-4885, 1793-6411. DOI: 10.1142/S0218488502001648. URL: https://www.worldscientific.com/doi/abs/10.1142/S0218488502001648 (visited on 05/23/2023).

Sweeney, Latanya. *Discrimination in Online Ad Delivery*. Jan. 28, 2013. DOI: 10.2139/ssrn.2208240. URL: https://papers.ssrn.com/abstract=2208240 (visited on 05/15/2023). Pre-published.

Sweeney, Latanya, Akua *Abu*, and Julia *Winn*. *Identifying Participants in the Personal Genome Project by Name*. Apr. 29, 2013. DOI: 10.2139/ssrn.2257732. URL: https://papers.ssrn.com/abstract=2257732 (visited on 05/16/2023). Pre-published.

Talwar, Kunal, director. *PPML Workshop Talk: Open Questions in Differentially Private Machine Learning*. June 2022. URL: https://machinelearning.apple.com/video/open-questions (visited on 07/04/2023).

Tang, Jun et al. *Privacy Loss in Apple’s Implementation of Differential Privacy on MacOS 10.12*. Sept. 11, 2017. arXiv: 1709.02753 [cs]. URL: http://arxiv.org/abs/1709.02753 (visited on 05/24/2023). Pre-published.

Thudi, Anvith et al. “Unrolling SGD: Understanding Factors Influencing Machine Unlearning.” In: 2022 IEEE 7th European Symposium on Security and Privacy (EuroS&P). IEEE Computer Society, June 1, 2022, pp. 303–319. ISBN: 978-1-66541-614-6. DOI: 10.1109/EuroSP53844.2022.00027. URL: https://www.computer.org/csdl/proceedings-article/euros&p/2022/161400a303/1ErpDNietvW (visited on 04/14/2024).

Thüsing, Gregor et al. “Anonymisierung an sich ist keine rechtfertigungsbedürftige Datenverarbeitung.” In: *Zeitschrift für Datenschutz* 10 (2021), pp. 548–553.

Tigani, Jordan. *Big Data is Dead*. MotherDuck. Feb. 7, 2023. URL: https://motherduck.com/blog/big-data-is-dead/ (visited on 04/23/2023).

Tomaschek, Attila. *LastPass Issues Update on Data Breach, But Users Should Still Change Passwords*. CNET. Mar. 1, 2023. URL: https://www.cnet.com/tech/services-and-software/lastpass-issues-update-on-data-breach-but-users-should-still-change-passwords/ (visited on 03/22/2023).

Tomasic, Lovro. *Effet utile: die Relativität teleologischer Argumente im Unionsrecht*. Münchener Universitätsschriften Reihe der Juristischen Fakultät 240. Munich: C.H. Beck, 2013. 238 pp. ISBN: 978-3-406-65263-9.

TOP500.org. *November 2022 | TOP500*. Nov. 2022. URL: https://www.top500.org/lists/top500/2022/11/ (visited on 04/18/2023).

Toubiana, Vincent and Helen *Nissenbaum*. “An Analysis of Google Logs Retention Policies.” In: *Journal of Privacy and Confidentiality* 3.1 (1 June 1, 2011). ISSN: 2575-8527. DOI: 10.29012/jpc.v3i1.593. URL: https://journalprivacyconfidentiality.org/index.php/jpc/article/view/593 (visited on 04/08/2023).

Trenkamp, Oliver. “Ungerechte Grundschullehrer: "Kevin ist kein Name, sondern eine Diagnose".” In: *Der Spiegel. Panorama* (Sept. 16, 2009). ISSN: 2195-1349. URL: https://www.spiegel.de/lebenundlernen/schule/ungerechte-grundschullehrer-kevin-ist-kein-name-sondern-eine-diagnose-a-649421.html (visited on 05/15/2023).

tss. *Blog-Artikel: Privacy-Utility Trade-off – DA3KMU*. May 11, 2023. URL: https://www.da3kmu.de/2023/05/11/datenschutz-trade-offs-und-missverstandnisse/ (visited on 04/24/2024).

U.S. Congress. *16 CFR Part 316 - CAN-SPAM RULE*. 2004. URL: https://www.law.cornell.edu/cfr/text/16/part-316 (visited on 02/28/2023).

U.S. Congress. 45 CFR Part 164 – Security and Privacy. URL: https://www.ecfr.gov/current/title-45/subtitle-A/subchapter-C/part-164 (visited on 02/07/2023).

U.S. Dpt. of the Interior, Office of CIO. Penetration Testing. June 8, 2015. URL: https://www.doi.gov/ocio/customers/penetration-testing (visited on 04/30/2023).

UK Office for National Statistics. How popular is your birthday? Office for National Statistics. Dec. 18, 2015. URL: https://www.ons.gov.uk/peoplepopulationandcommunity/birthsdeathsandmarriages/livebirths/articles/howpopularisyourbirthday/2015-12-18.

Uniyal, Archit et al. *DP-SGD vs PATE: Which Has Less Disparate Impact on Model Accuracy?* Mar. 25, 2022. arXiv: 2106.12576 [cs]. URL: http://arxiv.org/abs/2106.12576 (visited on 02/06/2023). Pre-published.

Urgessa, Worku Gedefa. "The Protective Capacity of the Criterion of Identifiability under EU Data Protection Law." In: *European Data Protection Law Review* 2 (2016), pp. 521–531. ISSN: 2364-2831.

US Census Bureau. The Census Bureau's Simulated Reconstruction-Abetted Re-identification Attack on the 2010 Census. Census.gov. May 7, 2021. URL: https://www.census.gov/data/academy/webinars/2021/disclosure-avoidance-series/simulated-reconstruction-abetted-re-identification-attack-on-the-2010-census.html (visited on 05/15/2023).

US Census Bureau. Census Bureau Sets Key Parameters to Protect Privacy in 2020 Census Results. Census.gov. June 9, 2021. URL: https://www.census.gov/newsroom/press-releases/2021/2020-census-key-parameters.html (visited on 05/15/2023).

Uzuner, Ozlem, Yuan *Luo*, and Peter *Szolovits*. "Evaluating the State-of-the-Art in Automatic De-Identification." In: *Journal of the American Medical Informatics Association: JAMIA* 14.5 (2007), pp. 550–563. ISSN: 1067-5027. DOI: 10.1197/jamia.M2444. pmid: 17600094.

Valkanova, Monika. "8.1 Trainieren von KI-Modellen." In: *Rechtshandbuch Artificial Intelligence und Machine Learning*. Ed. by Markus Kaulartz and Tom Braegelmann. München: C.H. Beck, 2020, pp. 336–378. ISBN: 978-3-406-74658-1.

Vaswani, Ashish et al. "Attention is All you Need." In: *Advances in Neural Information Processing Systems*. Vol. 30. Curran Associates, Inc., 2017. URL: https://papers.nips.cc/paper_files/paper/2017/hash/3f5ee243547dee91fbd053c1c4a845aa-Abstract.html (visited on 04/14/2024).

Veale, Michael, Reuben *Binns*, and Lilian *Edwards*. "Algorithms that remember: model inversion attacks and data protection law." In: *Philosophical Transactions of the Royal Society A: Mathematical, Physical and Engineering Sciences* 376.2133 (Oct. 15, 2018), p. 20180083. DOI: 10.1098/rsta.2018.0083. URL: https://royalsocietypublishing.org/doi/10.1098/rsta.2018.0083 (visited on 04/08/2023).

Vokinger, Kerstin N., Daniel J. *Stekhoven*, and Michael *Krauthammer*. "Lost in Anonymization — A Data Anonymization Reference Classification Merging Legal and Technical Considerations." In: *The Journal of Law, Medicine & Ethics* 48.1 (Mar. 1, 2020), pp. 228–231. ISSN: 1073-1105. DOI: 10.1177/1073110520917025.

Voter Data Available for Purchase | OC Vote. 2022. URL: https://ocvote.gov/data/voter-data-available-for-purchase (visited on 12/02/2022).

Walczak, Marit HansenBenjamin. "Hansen/Walczak: Die KI zaubert nicht." In: *Künstliche Intelligenz und Recht* 3 (2024), pp. 82–86.

Walter, Chip. *Kryder's Law*. Scientific American. Aug. 1, 2005. DOI: 10.1038/scientificamerican0805-32. URL: https://www.scientificamerican.com/article/kryders-law/ (visited on 01/12/2023).

Warner, Stanley L. "Randomized Response: A Survey Technique for Eliminating Evasive Answer Bias." In: *American Statistical Association Journal* 1965 (Mar. 1965), pp. 63–69.

Warren, Samuel D. and Louis D. *Brandeis*. "The Right to Privacy." In: *Harvard Law Review* 4.5 (1890), pp. 193–220. ISSN: 0017-811X. DOI: 10.2307/1321160. JSTOR: 1321160. URL: https://www.jstor.org/stable/1321160 (visited on 04/13/2023).

Watt, Adrienne. *Database Design*. 2nd ed. BCcampus, Oct. 24, 2014. 153 pp. URL: https://opentextbc.ca/dbdesign01/ (visited on 05/03/2024).

Weichert, Thilo. "Geodaten — datenschutzrechtliche Erfahrungen, Erwartungen und Empfehlungen." In: *Datenschutz und Datensicherheit* 33.6 (June 1, 2009), pp. 347–352. ISSN: 1862-2607. DOI: 10.1007/s11623-009-0071-x.

Weichert, Thilo. "Der Personenbezug von Kfz-Daten." In: *Neue Zeitschrift für Verkehrsrecht* 11 (2017), pp. 507–513.

Weichert, Thilo. *DSGVO Art. 4 Begriffsbestimmungen*. In: *EU-DSGVO und BDSG: Kompaktkommentar: EU-Datenschutz-Grundverordnung (EU-DSGVO), neues Bundesdatenschutzgesetz (BDSG), weitere datenschutzrechtliche Vorschriften*. Ed. by Wolfgang Däubler, Peter Wedde, and Imke Sommer. 2., überarbeitete und aktualisierte Auflage. Kompaktkommentar. Frankfurt am Main: Bund Verlag, 2020. ISBN: 978-3-7663-6865-2.

Weller, Christopher and Jane *Bambauer*. *Brief of Amicus Curiae Prof. Jane Bambauer in Support of Plaintiff's Complaint for Declaratory and Injunctive Relief*. Sept. 4, 2021. URL: https://www.brennancenter.org/sites/default/files/2021-04/Amicus_JaneBambauer_2021-04-09.pdf (visited on 04/14/2024).

Westin, Alan F. *Privacy and Freedom*. 1st ed. New York, NY: Atheneum, 1967. 524 pp. URL: http://archive.org/details/privacyfreedom00west (visited on 05/22/2023).

Winter, Christian, Verena *Battis*, and Oren *Halvani*. "Herausforderungen für die Anonymisierung von Daten." In: *Zeitschrift für Datenschutz* (2019), pp. 489–493.

Wittgenstein, Ludwig. *Tractatus Logico-Philosophicus*. 1922. URL: https://www.gutenberg.org/files/5740/5740-pdf.pdf.

Wittmann, Lilith. *Die Staatsanwaltschaft sagt, ich habe die CDU nicht gehackt*. Medium. Sept. 17, 2021. URL: https://lilithwittmann.medium.com/die-staatsanwaltschaft-sagt-ich-habe-die-cdu-nicht-gehackt-86c1ebf83f63 (visited on 04/30/2023).

Wójtowicz, Monika and Manuel *Cebulla*. "Anonymisierung nach der DSGVO." In: *PinG Privacy in Germany* 5 (Aug. 29, 2017), p. 8. ISSN: 2196-9817. DOI: 10.37307/j.2196-9817.2017.05.08. URL: https://pingdigital.de/ce/anonymisierung-nach-der-dsgvo/detail.html (visited on 04/12/2023).

Wong, Nicole. *Judge tells DoJ "No" on search queries*. Official Google Blog. Mar. 17, 2006. URL: https://googleblog.blogspot.com/2006/03/judge-tells-doj-no-on-search-queries.html (visited on 04/22/2023).

Wood, Alexandra et al. "Differential Privacy: A Primer for a Non-Technical Audience." In: *Vanderbilt Journal of Entertainment & Technology Law* 21.1 (2018–2019), pp. 209–276. URL: https://heinonline.org/HOL/P?h=hein.journals/vanep21&i=219 (visited on 04/08/2023).

Woods, Ben and James *Titcomb*. "Apple under fire over iPhone encryption tech." In: *The Telegraph* (Jan. 9, 2022). ISSN: 0307-1235. URL: https://www.telegraph.co.uk/business/2022/01/09/apple-fire-iphone-encryption-tech/ (visited on 02/15/2023).

Wrobel, Mona and Simon *Pentzien*. "Personenbezug und LLMs: Datenschutzrechtliche Bewertung und Tipps für die Praxis." In: *Datenschutz-Berater* 09 (2024), pp. 200–204.

Wu, Felix T. "Defining Privacy and Utility in Data Sets." In: *University of Colorado Law Review* 84 (2013), pp. 1117–1177.

Wu, Xingjiao et al. "A Survey of Human-in-the-loop for Machine Learning." In: *Future Generation Computer Systems* 135 (Oct. 2022), pp. 364–381. ISSN: 0167739X. DOI: 10.1016/j.future.2022.05.014. arXiv: 2108.00941 [cs]. URL: http://arxiv.org/abs/2108.00941 (visited on 01/30/2023).

Wyner, Adam, Wim *Peters*, and Daniel *Katz*. "A Case Study on Legal Case Annotation." In: *Frontiers in Artificial Intelligence and Applications* Vol. 259: Legal Knowledge and Information Systems (2013), pp. 165–174. DOI: 10.3233/978-1-61499-359-9-165. URL: https://ebooks.iospress.nl/volumearticle/35613 (visited on 04/14/2024).

Xu, Zheng et al. *Federated Learning of Gboard Language Models with Differential Privacy*. July 17, 2023. DOI: 10.48550/arXiv.2305.18465. arXiv: 2305.18465. Pre-published.

Yan, Chao et al. "A Multifaceted benchmarking of synthetic electronic health record generation models." In: *Nature Communications* 13.1 (1 Dec. 9, 2022), p. 7609. ISSN: 2041-1723. DOI: 10.1038/s41467-022-35295-1. URL: https://www.nature.com/articles/s41467-022-35295-1 (visited on 07/06/2023).

Zang, Hui and Jean *Bolot*. "Anonymization of location data does not work: a large-scale measurement study." In: *Proceedings of the 17th annual international conference on Mobile computing and networking*. MobiCom '11. New York, NY, USA: Association for Computing Machinery, Sept. 19, 2011, pp. 145–156. ISBN: 978-1-4503-0492-4. DOI: 10.1145/2030613.2030630.

Zhao, Ying and Jinjun *Chen*. "A Survey on Differential Privacy for Unstructured Data Content." In: *ACM Computing Surveys* 54 (10s Sept. 13, 2022), 207:1–207:28. ISSN: 0360-0300. DOI: 10.1145/3490237.

Ziebarth, Wolfgang. *DS GVO Art. 4 Begriffsbestimmungen*. In: *DS-GVO | BDSG*. Ed. by Gernot Sydow and Nikolaus Marsch. 3rd ed. Baden-Baden: Nomos, 2022, p. 2562. ISBN: 978-3-8487-7290-2.

Ziethmann, Paula, Sarah *Friedrich*, and Kerstin *Schlögl-Flierl*. "Synthetic Data in Medicine." In: *Datenschutz und Datensicherheit* 48 (May 31, 2024), pp. 358–363.

Zuiderveen Borgesius, Frederik J. "Singling out people without knowing their names – Behavioural targeting, pseudonymous data, and the new Data Protection Regulation." In: *Computer Law & Security Review* 32.2 (Apr. 2016), pp. 256–271. ISSN: 02673649. DOI: 10.1016/j.clsr.2015.12.013. URL: https://linkinghub.elsevier.com/retrieve/pii/S0267364915001788 (visited on 03/09/2023).

Zwenne, G. J. "Over IP-adressen en persoonsgegevens, en het verschil tussen individualiseren en identificeren." In: *Tijdschrift voor Internetrecht* 2011.1 (2011), pp. 4–9. URL: https://hdl.handle.net/1887/46999 (visited on 05/01/2023).